Felix Mendelssohn Bartholdy

Felix Mendelssohn Bartholdy
A Guide to Reseach

With An Introduction to Research Concerning Fanny Hensel

John Michael Cooper

Routledge
New York and London

Published in 2001 by
Routledge
29 West 35th Street
New York, NY 10001

Published in Great Britain by
Routledge
11 New Fetter Lane
London EC4P 4EE

Routledge is an imprint of the Taylor & Francis Group.

Library of Congress Cataloging-in-Publication Data
Cooper, John Michael.
Felix Mendelssohn Bartholdy : a guide to research : with an introduction to
research concerning Fanny Hensel / John Michael Cooper
    p. cm.—(Composer resource manuals ; v. 54)
    Includes indexes.
    ISBN 0-8153-1513-9 (alk. paper)
    1. Mendelssohn-Bartholdy, Felix, 1809–1847—Bibliography. 2. Hensel, Fanny
    Mendelssohn, 1805–1847—Bibliography. I. Title. II. Series.
ML134.M53 C6 2001
016.78'092—dc21   00-045737

Printed on acid-free, 250-year-life paper.
Manufactured in the United States of America.

10 9 8 7 6 5 4 3 2 1

To Cindy,
the love of my life—
with gratitude for encouraging, supporting, watching, and waiting

Contents

Composer Resource Manuals

In response to the growing need for bibliographic guidance to the vast literature on significant composers, Routledge is publishing an extensive series of research guides. This ongoing series encompasses more than 50 composers; they represent Western musical tradition from the Renaissance to the present century.

Each research guide offers a selective, annotated list of writings, in all European languages, about one or more composers. There are also lists of works by the composers, unless these are available elsewhere. Biographical sketches and guides to library resources, organizations, and specialists are presented. As appropriate to the individual composer, there are maps, photographs, or other illustrative matter, glossaries, and indexes.

Preface

Any reader who has gone so far as to pick up this book probably already has some knowledge of the fundamental reason for its existence: Felix Mendelssohn Bartholdy, although known by name and by a few warhorse compositions to virtually everyone familiar with any classical music, remains one of the most ambivalently represented composers in the world of musical scholarship. As Mendelssohn's reception history has vacillated between excessive adulation and equally excessive dismissals, the elite canon of first-rate research sources has been almost hopelessly outnumbered by a proliferation of biographies and critical essays based on little more than the authors' prejudices and assumptions— often reflecting (but not explicitly articulating) racist agendas that most latter-day readers find untenable, irrelevant, and abhorrent. The result is a bewildering landscape in which some extraordinary fruits of scholarly research exist within a stiflingly arid wasteland of music-historical prose. This book endeavors to assist researchers in locating, assessing, and using those sources.

More directly, the book owes its existence to two of the great men of latter-day Mendelssohn scholarship. Donald Mintz, whose seminal dissertation on the manuscripts for three of the composer's major works (no. 926) broke important new ground in enabling Mendelssohn scholarship to escape the quagmire into which it had descended in the first half of the twentieth century, began collecting the data and wrote preliminary annotations for some sources. Professor Mintz was kind enough to share this material with me when I was contracted for the book, and his contributions provided the foundation for the completed project.[1] In addition, R. Larry Todd, my doctoral advisor at Duke University and by consensus one of the deans of modern Mendelssohn scholarship, contributed not only his global knowledge of sources, issues, and ideas, but also the recommendation for taking on this project.

The volume also would not have been possible without the assistance of a number of individuals and institutions. For shepherding the book through the various complexities of production I owe a special debt of gratitude to Richard Carlin (senior music editor), Rachael Shook, and Julie H. Ho at Routledge. These individuals' patience and professionalism made it possible to negotiate some difficult deadlines and thorny editorial issues that might, in less expert hands, have compromised the book. Likewise, a debt of gratitude is owed to the staffs and interlibrary loan departments at a number of libraries and universities during the preparatory stages of work: the Mary Duke Biddle Music Library at Duke University; the Warren D. Allen Music Library at The Florida State University; the Musikabteilung of the Hessische Landes und Hochschulsbiblithek in Darmstadt; the Heinrich-Heine-Institut in Düsseldorf; the Music and Strozier Libraries at Illinois Wesleyan University; the Music Division of the Library of Congress in Washington, D.C.; the Firestone Library at Princeton University; the Musikabteilung and Mendelssohn-Archiv of the Staatsbibliothek zu Berlin - Preußischer Kulturbesitz; the Musikabteilung of the Stadt- und Universitätsbibliothek Frankfurt am Main; and the Music Library of the University of Illinois at Urbana-Champaign. A debt of gratitude also goes to the two fine graduate students who assisted with the proofreading and prepared the indexes for this volume: William McGinney and Aaron West. Finally, I wish to thank the staff of Willis Library at The University of North Texas. Their extraordinary expertise, efficiency, and patience have made the completion of this book a doubly rewarding experience.

John Michael Cooper
Denton, Texas
1 December 2000

NOTE

1. For some entries Professor Mintz's information has been retained in toto or only slightly modified; these are designated by a "[DM]" or a "[DM/JMC]" at the end of the annotation.

Introduction. Problems and Potentials of Mendelssohn Scholarship

Mendelssohn scholarship has experienced prodigious growth, both in volume and in quality, since the Second World War. One might even suggest that the state of Mendelssohn research has not only regained much of the territory lost during the nadir of the second third of this century, but has opened up new horizons that probably were unforeseeable in the prewar period. Such optimistic observations seem to be corroborated by the slowly but steadily increasing presence of the names of Felix Mendelssohn and his older sister, Fanny Hensel,[1] in concert and recital programs, recordings, and general music-historical literature.

This book, like all volumes in the Composer Resource Manuals series, documents the principal achievements of Mendelssohn scholarship. In so doing, it reveals that much remains to be done before the general body of knowledge and information concerning these two important nineteenth-century composers can begin to rival the general quality of scholarship concerning many of their contemporaries. More importantly, it facilitates an overview of the enormous qualitative vacillations that have characterized scholarship concerning the musical prodigies of the Mendelssohn family—and thereby underscores the need for researchers to approach any given source with a critical understanding of how that source fits into these vacillations. The following is a brief sketch of the dynamics of this convoluted scholarly reception history.[2]

Scholarship and Reception History Concerning the Musical Mendelssohns: A Brief Review

For the eldest siblings of the Mendelssohn family,[3] fame during one's own time was both a blessing and a curse. On the one hand, Felix's international notoriety as composer and conductor and the widespread attention commanded by Fanny Hensel's presence as the organizer of Berlin's leading salon led contemporaries to approach their lives and works with an unusually high level of scholarly rigor and thoroughness. Both composers were the subject of brief and generally accurate biographical sketches in contemporary periodicals in Germany and England, and by 1847 no fewer than three catalogs of Felix's compositions had appeared in print (see chapter 4, p. 119–21). Few other composers of their generation achieved a level of virtually unanimously granted fame that justified such scholarly attention before 1847.

On the other hand, the success both siblings achieved during the *Vormärz* and the fact that both died before the wave of revolutions that swept the continent in 1848–49 resulted in a highly polarized posthumous reception history. In England, where the Mendelssohn cult had grown to virtual idolatry in the mid- and late 1840s,[4] and in many quarters within Germany and France, admirers of Felix Mendelssohn's music treated his memory with the sort of reverence generally accorded a fallen hero. As it became known in the years 1848–70 that Mendelssohn had left a sizable number of his works unpublished, his admirers' assertions that those works, like his memory, belonged to "the world"[5] led initially to the posthumous publication of a number of compositions he had suppressed (all works with opus numbers higher than 72), and then to the so-called *Gesamtausgabe* published by Breitkopf & Härtel under the general editorship of Julius Rietz in 1871–74. These posthumous publications—which presented many of the composer's youthful compositions with misleadingly high opus and serial numbers to a public that wanted to see more of his mature style—combined with the highly charged and increasingly anti-Semitic political atmosphere to produce a strong consensus that Schumann's frequent descriptions of Mendelssohn as "modern" had been wrong; that this music belonged to the past rather than the future; that while it was perhaps adequate for the (perceived) tranquility of pre-revolutionary Europe,[6] it no longer met the challenges of the present.

This transformation in reception history soon engendered one of the most notorious chapters in music history. A number of highly polemical and pseudo-scholarly essays—including Wagner's and Liszt's writings on Jews in music (nos. 394 and 386)—along with a number of similar writings that are less familiar today, but were equally widely circulated and influential at the time—asserted, in concurrence with contemporary racial and evolutionary theories, that the composer's Jewish heritage had led ineluctably to recidivist and atavistic traits after the mid-1830s.[7] In this view, Mendelssohn had devolved rather than evolved after completing his early masterpieces (including the Octet for Strings, the *Midsummer Night's Dream Overture*, and the posthumously published "Italian" Symphony). The political and personal attacks leveled by composers who had been unable to fully challenge his fame or integrity during his lifetime thus found ostensible validation in the anti-Semitic pseudo-science of the day, and the supposed scholarly authority of these writings led to the incorporation of these judgments in a number of general histories of music. (Indeed, the notion of his compositional decline remains intact—albeit without the original anti-Semitic rationalizations—in a number of scholarly and general musicological writings even today.)[8]

The descent from plausible scholarship to ludicrous lionization and polemical pseudo-research did not go unnoticed. As early as 1865 the great patron of English musical lexicography, Sir George Grove, pointed out that Mendelssohn was ill-served by the bowdlerized but widely disseminated editions of his correspondence that had appeared in print under the editorship of his brother and his nephew; Philipp Spitta and others voiced similar criticisms in the 1880s.[9]

Grove also extensively researched the available primary sources—episolary as well as musical—and published a number of insightful essays and reviews of important familiar and unknown compositions by Mendelssohn.

The culmination of these efforts was Grove's essay on Mendelssohn for the first edition of his *Dictionary of Music and Musicians*, first published in 1880 (no. 36 in this volume). Although some of the information contained in it is now dated, this essay still stands as one of the finest achievements of Mendelssohn scholarship and of musical scholarship in general: it draws extensively and accurately on a wide variety of sources; offers detailed biographical information and correlates the compositions with contemporaneous events; and provides an overview of the composer's contemporary and posthumous reception. It was revised for the second edition of the *Dictionary* and reprinted, with minor modifications, for Grove's widely disseminated book *Beethoven, Schubert, Mendelssohn* (no. 37).

The last decade of the nineteenth century and the first decade of the twentieth were in many ways a high point for Mendelssohn scholarship. In addition to Grove's numerous other contributions, these years witnessed the appearance of several more reliable collections of correspondence,[10] as well as the biography by Ernst Wolff (no. 98)—a document that, while dated in some particulars, remains largely unsurpassed in the biographical literature. Because of these and other, smaller publications, the quality of Mendelssohn scholarship at the centennial of the composer's birth was generally on a par with scholarship concerning other composers, and generally representative of musical scholarship as a whole.

It is worth noting that the late nineteenth century was also a flowering period for research concerning Fanny Hensel. Although the volume and overall quality of research devoted to Fanny never rivaled that of Felix, the last years of the century—which, after all, were precisely the years in which the concept of feminism as we now understand it emerged and gained a widespread foothold in society[11]—witnessed a proliferation of surprisingly substantive scholarly examinations and critical writings, as well as performances of her music. It is no exaggeration to state that general knowledge of Hensel and familiarity with her works in 1900 was at a level appreciably higher than in 1970, when the modern Hensel revival began.

But the period 1914–45 witnessed a precipitous decline. The heyday of Wagnerism, rampant anti-Semitism inside and outside Western Europe, and the ascendance of nationalistic musicology[12] left the German-Jewish Mendelssohns vulnerable to ceaseless tropes on the vitriolic dismissals of the New German School. Monuments and important scholarly documents[13] concerning Felix Mendelssohn were destroyed throughout Germany and elsewhere; his music was banned in Germany and his presence in the concert repertoire diminished to only a few pieces; and venerable scholars succumbed to the condescending negative generalizations of Wagner and Liszt, often in verbiage remarkably similar to their overtly anti-Semitic writings.[14] This period did produce some important documents—such as Köffler's dissertation (which has since been destroyed) and Rudolf Werner's important study of Mendelssohn's sacred works (which fortunately survives; see no. 905 in this book)—but on the whole these years represent a considerable retreat from the level of scholarship attained in the early years of the century. Historians seemed uninterested in a critical evaluation of mid- and late-nineteenth-century polemics, the concert-going public had little repertoire upon which to formulate any more substantive views, and the general trajectory of musicological inquiry discouraged serious research on "homeless Jews" *cum* cosmopolitan composers such as Felix Mendelssohn and Fanny Hensel.

After the Second World War, the growing awareness of the transgressions of the recent past gradually began to encourage a reappraisal of pre-war verdicts on Felix Mendelssohn. Initially, progress was slow—the most far-reaching scholarly achievements were two new, more critical editions of the letters from the composer's Italian sojourn of 1830–31 (nos. 328 and 329)—but the sesquicentennial of his birth generated considerable momentum. A flurry of scholarly articles on a variety of topics, together with the initiation of a new critical edition of his complete works in 1960 (see Appendix B), was supplemented by Donald Mintz's seminal dissertation in 1960 (no. 930 in this volume), as well as the first version of Eric Werner's important biography in 1963 (no. 96), the founding of the Mendelssohn-Gesellschaft in 1967, Susanna Großmann-Vendrey's important dissertation on the organ sonatas in 1965 (no. 707), and her important book and essay on Mendelssohn's relationship to the musical past in 1969 (nos. 822 and 823). In brief, these years signaled a new and committed attempt to come to grips with the nature and consequences of the scholarly abyss into which Mendelssohn scholarship had descended since 1914—and, more importantly, with Mendelssohn's life, works, and influence.

It was in the wake of this renewal of serious inquiry that Mendelssohn research, in the early 1970s, entered the ongoing phase of high-quality scholarship that continues today. In 1972 the first issue of the Berlin *Mendelssohn-Studien* (no. 9) appeared, a journal that has functioned as a clearing house for research of all aspects of the Mendelssohn family's illustrious history. Also in 1972, Carl Dahlhaus directed a symposium on the subject of *"Das Problem Mendelssohn"* in Berlin, and the papers from this conference were published two years later in Dahlhaus's important volume by the same title (no. 3). The late 1970s brought a host of small-scale but substantive inquiries, as well as two important dissertations on Felix's compositional process (nos. 931 and 934), followed in the 1980s by Karl-Heinz Köhler's Mendelssohn article in the *New Grove* (no. 46), the revised version of Werner's biography (no. 97), a flurry of studies on the life and works of Fanny Hensel, the first major published edition of Hensel's correspondence (no. 951), and a number of style-studies of specific genres within both composers' *oeuvres*. In the 1990s these trends continued, accelerating toward the sesquicentennial of both siblings' deaths in 1997; but the decade also witnessed the appearance of a number of collections of essays, many of which attempted—for the first time in the history of Mendelssohn scholarship—to address "the Mendelssohn problem" in terms of *both* Felix and Fanny. The revival of the new Gesamtausgabe of Felix's works, the first publications of a number of compositions by Fanny, and the appearance of a separate set of critical editions of Felix's complete sacred music (see Appendix B) provided further impetus for a revival of the composers' music in concert life.

Because of this ongoing *accelerando* in scholarship concerning Felix and Fanny, it is possible to report—gladly—that this book may well be dated soon after its appearance. Plans are already in the works for a number of substantial scholarly contributions that proceed from traditional lines of musicological inquiry: a complete and reliable thematic catalog with source information; a complete critical edition of his ca. 3,000 surviving outgoing letters (only about 400 of which have been published so far); a catalog of first editions and dedications; and so on. In addition to the much-needed flow of these contributions, new scholarly approaches are steadily appearing, opening up fresh avenues as the reappraisal gains momentum and Mendelssohn research gains pace with other lines of musicological scholarship of the last few decades.[15]

About this Book

This volume is organized with an eye to an optimal balance between user-friendliness and a sufficiently comprehensive coverage to convey the most important low and high points of literature concerning the Mendelssohns. To the former end, the overall organization draws upon arrangements represented in several important previous Mendelssohn bibliographies: that of the *New Grove* and its revised and updated counterpart in *The New Grove Early Romantic Masters 2*; that of Ralf Wehner's important study of the early sacred works (no. 903); and that included in the congress report based on the Berlin Mendelssohn Symposium held in 1994 (no. 12). Because many items might fit equally well into two or more of these content-units, the reader is encouraged to consult the indexes closely. Reviews are mentioned selectively in instances in which the importance or controversiality of a book warrants their inclusion, when the reviews contribute substantively to the information given in the book, or when they provide a perspective on the item that is contrary or complementary to its stated purpose.

The citations generally follow the guidelines of *The Chicago Manual of Style*, 14th Edition (Chicago: University of Chicago, 1993). For items that have appeared in multiple editions, the page-count is provided after the bibliographic information that applies to the edition most directly discussed. ISBN numbers are provided when the primary bibliographic entry is for a book to which an ISBN has been applied; as with information concerning the page-count in books, the ISBN numbers apply to the editions immediately preceding. ISSN numbers are not provided. When the main entry is for an item available in the Library of Congress, the LC call number is provided. In the interest of space, items that were not available for examination, and items whose titles are sufficiently self-explanatory, are not annotated.

The chapters are organized as follows:

Chapter 1. Life-and-Works Studies This chapter surveys three principal types of sources: (1) collections of specialized essays; (2) general surveys of Mendelssohn's life and works; and (3) studies of special aspects of Mendelssohn's biography (including Mendelssohn's relationships with specific persons, places, and contemporary topics).

Chapter 2. Memoirs, Recollections, and Editions of Letters The primary criteria for inclusion of a given source in this chapter are (1) that it is written or compiled by a first-hand acquaintance of Felix Mendelssohn; and (2) that its emphasis is on summarizing or reproducing documents and events from a first-hand perspective. By nature, of course, many of these sources are also biographical; indeed, some biographies draw heavily upon primary sources and first-hand anecdotes. In such ambivalent cases I have situated the sources according to my assessment of their primary focus.

Chapter 3. Sociological and Cultural Studies This chapter too, entails a certain ambivalence, since many biographical studies also deal extensively with related sociological and cultural issues. Nevertheless, I have included here three principal varieties of study. The first of these, studies of the Mendelssohn family, includes general overviews of the family history, as well as studies specifically devoted to the musical and/or biographical relationship between Felix and Fanny. The second group, broadly described as "studies of Jewish issues," includes inquiries that take Felix Mendelssohn's Jewish heritage as their primary point of departure. Obviously, many of these sources might equally well be classified as studies of Mendelssohn's musical style and aesthetics, while many others are also important contributions to biographical scholarship. These ambivalent sources are placed in this chapter because the composer's Jewishness is their central concern. Finally, there is a section devoted to studies of *Rezeptionsgeschichte*. Most of these sources relate to consistencies and disparities between the composer's contemporary and posthumous reception, and attempt to use these issues as vantage points for observations regarding his musical style.

Chapter 4. Documentary Studies Sources included in this chapter may be broadly described as source-inventories: they document the existence of music manuscripts and other music and papers.

Chapter 5. Studies of Individual Works and Repertoires This chapter is organized primarily along the division of secular vs. sacred works. In accordance with the organization of my philological essay and work-list for Douglass Seaton's forthcoming *Mendelssohn Companion* (no. 14), the secular works are organized according to the following categories: stage works (including incidental music), orchestral works (including symphonies, overtures, and concertos), accompanied secular choral works, concert arias, choral songs, songs and vocal duets, chamber music, music for piano alone, and organ works. The sacred works are grouped into studies of the oratorios, studies of the chorale cantatas, studies of the psalm settings, studies of other accompanied sacred choral works, and studies of other unaccompanied sacred choral works. Finally, a section is included dealing with studies of Mendelssohn's arrangements and editions of other composers' works.

Chapter 6. General Studies of the Music of Felix Mendelssohn Bartholdy Sources included in this chapter deal with a variety of issues and with groups of works from two or more genres. They deal with the composer's aesthetics, musical style, or compositional process, or with issues of performance practice as they relate to one or more of these topics.

Appendix A. This is an introduction to research concerning Fanny Hensel—a composer of considerable merit to whom no CRM or other comparable volume has yet been dedicated. Because Hensel is not the primary subject of this volume, this inventory is treated as simply that: a selective bibliographical survey of some important scholarly achievements concerning her life, music, and influence. Since annotations for these items unfortunately would exceed the limits of this book, an annotated Hensel Guide to Research must await a future undertaking.

Appendix B. This appendix is an overview of Mendelssohn's works and an inventory of their publication statuses; it identifies many of the numerous scholarly and critical editions of Felix Mendelssohn's works that have appeared since the release of the old *Gesamtausgabe*. I hope this appendix will be useful as a guide to more reliable and complete editions of Mendelssohn's works as alternatives to the conspicuously incomplete and deeply flawed editions originally included in the Breitkopf & Härtel editions of 1871–74 (especially since those editions served as the basis for many subsequent ones, and continue to be treated in many quarters as sources possessed of greater authority than they actually warrant).

For convenience, non-bibliographic references to Felix Mendelssohn are given simply as the abbreviation "FMB"; those to Fanny Hensel, as "FH." When a work appeared in more than one edition, the citations give the standard information for the first edition and any other salient information (such as modified title or orthography) for those subsequent editions that appear to be most readily available. Duplicate references have been kept to a minimum.

Finally, it should be noted that while this volume attempts to be thorough and comprehensive, it cannot be complete. Sources that are generally inaccessible or are too derivative or insignificant to warrant the term "research" are tacitly omitted; the same is true of general period-histories and general histories of music, even though such sources may include useful information, and often function as important documents of reception history. Coverage is limited to materials available in English, German, French, Italian, and Spanish.[16] Titles of Mendelssohn's works cited in book or article titles have not been regularized. Where possible and appropriate, the citations for some reviews of major book-length contributions are provided. The manuscript was submitted belatedly in order to facilitate inclusion of items released in 1999 or slated for release in 2000, but the exigencies of temporal duress and lag-time in indexing and publicizing will inevitably result in some important items from these years being overlooked. Undoubtedly, other omissions will occur as well—and for these I can only ask the reader's forgiveness.

NOTES

1. Throughout this book Fanny's name will be treated as she gave it in her own publications: Fanny Hensel. Although many different approaches to her name are represented in recent writings (including flatly misleading ones such as "Hensel-Mendelssohn" and "née Mendelssohn-Bartholdy"), Fanny's own clear wish was that she be represented by her married name. See no. 951 in this volume.

2. An excellent overview of this variety, focusing primarily on twentieth-century scholarship, has also been provided by Friedhelm Krummarcher; see no. 422 in this book.

3. It is often overlooked that Fanny (1805–47) and Felix (1809–47) had two younger siblings. Rebecca (1811–58) and Paul (1812–74) were both musically gifted (she sang and played piano, and he was an accomplished cellist), but neither achieved the musical distinction of elder siblings. There is some scholarly literature on Paul (see nos. 342, 350, and 370 in this book), but Rebecca's contributions to the Mendelssohn family's legacy remain largely unexplored.

4. For an important example of the posthumous English adulation for Mendelssohn, see Henry Chorley's memoir (no. 245), which describes the composer as "humanly speaking[,] perfect."

5. For an overview of the posthumous debate over the release of Mendelssohn's previously unpublished works, see John Michael Cooper, "Felix Mendelssohn Bartholdy and the *Italian* Symphony: Historical, Musical, and Extramusical Perspectives" (no. 570), 342–55.

6. See Donald Mintz's essay on "1848, Anti-Semitism and the Mendelssohn Reception" (no. 426 in this volume).

7. For a thorough examination of the mechanisms by which this pseudo-science acquired scholarly legitimacy and crucially informed Mendelssohn reception history, see Marian Wilson Kimber's essay on "The Composer as Other: Gender and Race in the Biography of Felix Mendelssohn" (no. 447 in this volume).

8. For examples of the how the verdict based on these arguments endures, see Charles Rosen, "Mendelssohn and the Invention of Religious Kitsch" (no. 788) and Greg Vitercik, *The Early Works of Felix Mendelssohn: A Study in the Romantic Sonata Style* (no. 801 in this book).

9. See J. Rigbie Turner, "Mendelssohn's Letters to Eduard Devrient: Filling in Some Gaps" (no. 334 in this book), 200–03.

10. Especially important in this regard are the collections edited by Julius

Schubring (no. 267 in this book), Eduard Hanslick (no. 295 in this volume), Ernst Wolff (no. 338 in this book), Karl Klingemann, Jr., (no. 303 in this volume), and L. Dahlgren (no. 275 in this book).

11. For most of the century, the prevalent variety of feminism was what Karen Offen has called "relational feminism," but the last years of the century witnessed a pronounced cultivation of the individualist variety most commonly associated with the term today. For an overview of these concepts, see Karen Offen, "Liberty, Equality, and Justice for Women: The Theory and Practice of Feminism in Nineteenth-Century Europe," in *Becoming Visible: Women in European History*, 2nd ed. Renate Bridenthal, Claudia Koonz, and Susan Stuard (Boston: Houghton Mifflin, 1987), 335–73.

12. See Pamela M. Potter, *Most German of the Arts: Musicology and Society from the Weimar Republic to the End of Hitler's Reich* (New Haven: Yale University Press, 1998).

13. Most importantly, Johannes Köffler, "Über orchestrale Koloristik in den symphonischen Werken von Felix Mendelssohn-Bartholdy" (Ph.D. diss., University of Vienna, 1923).

14. See, for example, Alfred Einstein's view: "What Mendelssohn lacked, for the attainment of true greatness, is the courage to say the ultimate in love, or in tragedy.... While Wagner was thinking about 'Siegfried's Death' and Verdi of *Macbeth*, Mendelssohn was thinking about the *Loreley* of the tender-souled and patriotic phrase-maker Emanuel Geibel" (*Greatness in Music*, trans. César Saerchinger [New York: Oxford University Press, 1941], 580). See also Paul Henry Lang's verdict that "There can be no doubt that in many of Mendelssohn's works there is missing that real depth that opens wide perspectives, the mysticism of the unutterable" (*Music in Western Civilization* [New York: W. W. Norton, 1941], 811).

15. See, for example, John Garratt's essay on "Mendelssohn's Babel: Romanticism and the Poetics of Translation" (no. 769)—an article that may represent one of the most important conceptual breakthroughs since Mintz's dissertation (1960) or Werner's biography (1963).

16. There are some useful items in Dutch, Polish, and Russian which could not be included here. For a bibliographic inventory that includes these items, the reader is encouraged to consult the "Literaturanhang" to Ralf Wehner, *Studien zum geistlichen Chorschaffen des jungen Felix Mendelssohn Bartholdy* (no. 903), or *idem*, "Bibliographie des Schrifttums zu Felix Mendelssohn Bartholdy von 1972 bis 1994" (no. 468).

1. Life-and-Works Studies

I.   Collections of Specialized Essays, Conference Reports
II.   Surveys of Mendelssohn's Life and Works
III. Special Aspects of Mendelssohn's Biography

I.   COLLECTIONS OF SPECIALIZED ESSAYS, CONFERENCE REPORTS

1. Botstein, Leon, ed. *Felix Mendelssohn—Mitwelt und Nachwelt: Bericht zum 1. Leipziger Mendelssohn-Kolloquium am 8. und 9. Juni 1993*. Wiesbaden: Breitkopf & Härtel, 1996. 134 p. ISBN 3765103063. ML410.M5 L25 1993.

    A report from a symposium, focusing on disparities between FMB's contemporary and posthumous reception histories.

2. Cooper, John Michael, and Julie D. Prandi, eds. *The Mendelssohns: Their Music in History*. Oxford: Oxford University Press, [forthcoming].

    Slated for release in 2001. Topically organized into five main groups: sources and source problems, discussions of individual works, repertoires, Felix and Fanny, and reception history.

3. Dahlhaus, Carl, ed. *Das Problem Mendelssohn*. Studien zur Musikgeschichte des 19. Jahrhunderts, Bd. 41. Regensburg: Gustav Bosse, 1974. 212 p. ISBN 3764920939. ML410.M5 P76.

    A collection of papers from a symposium of the same name held in Berlin in 1972, this is a seminal volume in the latest stage of Mendelssohn research (see the Introduction in this book, p. 6).

4.   Elvers, Rudolf, and Hans-Günter Klein, eds. *Die Mendelssohns in Berlin:*
      Eine Familie und ihre Stadt. Staatsbibliothek Preußischer Kulturbesitz,
      Ausstellungskataloge   20.   Berlin: Staatsbibliothek   Preußischer
      Kulturbesitz, 1983. 266 p. ISBN 3882261854. DD857.A2 M46 1983.

      A collection of essays on various biographical aspects of the
      Mendelssohn family, accompanying a catalogue of an exhibit by the
      Mendelssohn-Archiv of the Staatsbibliothek Preußischer Kulturbesitz,
      Berlin. The exhibit was first shown in Bonn-Bad Godesberg on 14
      October–27 November 1983, and subsequently in Düsseldorf and Berlin.

5.   Finson, Jon W., and R. Larry Todd, eds. *Mendelssohn and Schumann:*
      Essays on Their Music and Its Context. Durham: Duke University Press,
      1984. 189 p. ISBN 0822305690. ML410.M5 M48 1984.

      Papers from a conference hosted jointly by Duke University and the
      University of North Carolina at Chapel Hill in 1982.

6.   Gerhartz, Leo Karl, ed. *Felix Mendelssohn Bartholdy: Repräsentant*
      und/oder Außenseiter? Fünf Vorträge zu den "Kasseler Musiktagen 1991."
      Kassel: Kasseler Musiktage, 1993. 102 p.

      The volume (like the festival from which it was derived) takes as its
      starting points the facts that (1) most of the institutions central to modern
      musical life were established during Mendelssohn's career, many of them
      under his leadership; and (2) one crucial change involved in the establish-
      ment of these institutions concerned the relationship between public and
      private art and life. The essays are all attempts to identify the issues and
      questions that have made Mendelssohn's contemporary and posthumous
      reception histories so complex (e.g., "Mendelssohn and Berlin: Also a
      Question of Religion"). The volume provides little documentation or other
      scholarly apparatus; some of the essays include a bibliography, but most
      are simply undocumented remarks.

7.   Heyder, Bernd, and Christoph Spering, eds. *Blickpunkt FELIX*
      Mendelssohn Bartholdy: Programmbuch Drei Tage für Felix vom 30.10 bis
      1.11.1994. Cologne: Dohr, 1994. 194 p. ISBN 3925366369. ML410.M5
      D75 1994.

      Based on a symposium held in Cologne, 30 October–1 November
      1994.

8.   Leonardy, Robert, ed. *Felix Mendelssohn Bartholdy: Leben und Werk—*
      Musikfestspiele Saar 1989. Edition Karlsberg, Bd. 6. Lebach: Joachim
      Hempel, 1989. 97 p. ISBN 3925192417.

A handy volume of thoughtful general essays, originally presented as papers in the context of the *Musikfestspiele Saar.*

9. *Mendelssohn-Studien: Beiträge zur neueren deutschen Kultur-und Wirtschaftsgeschichte.* Berlin: Duncker & Humblot, 1972--

    An invaluable venue for scholarship pertaining to all aspects of the lives and works of the many distinguished members of the Mendelssohn family. There is a supplemental volume (issued between vols. 10 and 11) which thoroughly indexes the contributions in volumes one through ten.

10. Metzger, Heinz-Klaus, and Rainer Riehn, eds. *Felix Mendelssohn Bartholdy.* Musik-Konzepte, Bd. 14/15. Munich: edition text + kritik, 1980. 176 p. ISBN 3883770558. MLCM 91/02638 (M).

    An important, if somewhat uneven, resource.

11. *The Musical Quarterly 77* (December 1993).

    Although the entire issue of this important English musicological journal is not devoted to the Mendelssohns, the bulk of it is—in the words of editor Leon Botstein—a "forum."

12. Schmidt, Christian Martin. *Felix Mendelssohn Bartholdy: Kongreß-Bericht Berlin 1994.* Wiesbaden: Breitkopf & Härtel, 1997. 351 p. ISBN 3765103047. ML410.M5 I65 1994.

    Based on a conference held in Berlin on 12–15 May 1994[1] and edited by the editor-in-chief of the new Mendelssohn *Gesamtausgabe,* this is in many ways a successor to Dahlhaus's *Das Problem Mendelssohn*; indeed, the substantive importance of its contributions is arguably even greater, and the geographic scope of provenance for the contributors is likewise superior. The essays are in the respective languages of the contributors (mostly in German, with four essays in English).

13. Schuhmacher, Gerhard. *Felix Mendelssohn Bartholdy.* Wege der Forschung, Bd. 494. Darmstadt: Wissenschaftliche Buchgesellschaft, 1982. 448 p. ISBN 3534071093. ML410.M5 F4 1982.

    A collection of original and reprinted essays, some presented in German translation for the first time.

14. Seaton, Douglass, ed. *The Mendelssohn Companion.* Westport, Connecticut: Greenwood, [forthcoming].

Slated for release in 2001. Each contribution except the work-list is followed by a selection of "Historical Views and Documents" that complement the observations in the essay and provide valuable information for studies of reception history.

15. Todd, R. Larry, ed. *Mendelssohn and His World.* Princeton: Princeton University Press, 1991. 401 p. ISBN 0691091439. ML410.M5 M47 1991.

Geared to the Bard College Mendelssohn Festival in 1991, this is another of the cardinal achievements of latter-day Mendelssohn scholarship. Divided into four parts: original essays, copiously annotated excerpts (in translation, as appropriate) from important memoirs, translations of correspondence between Mendelssohn and important contemporaries, and criticism and reception. Parts II–IV make accessible a number of important documents that were generally obscure prior to this book's publication (due to their age and the rarity of the sources in which they are found), or were accessible only to German speakers. Susan Gillespie's translations are quite readable, and the editor's annotations and introductions to the material in Parts II–IV are exemplary in their thoroughness and usefulness.

Rev.: D. Seaton in *Current Musicology* 52 (1993): 108–10; R. Wehner in *Die Musikforschung* 45 (1992): 421–22.

16. Todd, R. Larry. *Mendelssohn Studies.* Cambridge: Cambridge University Press, 1992. 261 p. ISBN 0521417767. ML410.M5 M63 1992.

Another significant collection of mostly new English-language Mendelssohn studies. Coverage ranges from biographical and *rezeptionsgeschichtliche* issues to studies of FMB's aesthetics and of individual works.

II. SURVEYS OF MENDELSSOHN'S LIFE AND WORKS

Remarks: See also the collections of reminiscences edited by Irene Hempel (no. 252) and Roger Nichols (no. 262).

17. Barbedette, Hippolyte. *Felix Mendelssohn (Bartholdy): Sa vie et ses oeuvres.* Paris: Huegel, 1868. 167 p.

A standard biography that drew upon various otherwise neglected writings in order to paint a picture of a cosmopolitan, multidisciplinary FMB that would resonate with the contemporary Parisian reading public.

The centrality of religious music in Mendelssohn's oeuvre is recognized, and works like *Antigone* and *Oedipus* are seen to form a transition between the sacred and the secular. Addresses the contemporary music-historical conundrum by referring to the suggestion of Wilhelm von Lenz that FMB seemed destined to be "Beethoven's successor," but then concludes: "It must be said that the hope was not realized." [DM/JMC]

18. Bartels, Bernhard. *Mendelssohn-Bartholdy: Mensch und Werk.* Bremen: Walter Dorn, 1947. 302 p. ML410.M5 B27.

    Standard—perhaps deliberately cautious—in many ways, but important as one of the first FMB biographies after the Second World War. Very little here is new, but the author does shy away from the prewar views that were most obviously shaped by the anti-Semitic ideologies adopted by the Nazis.

19. Bellaigue, Camille. *Mendelssohn.* Paris: Félix Alcan, 1907. 4th ed., 1920. 227 p. ML410.M5 B29.

    A life-and-works study with some insights concerning the musico-poetic alliance implied by the generic designation of the Songs without Words and FMB's thematic and developmental techniques.

20. Benedict, Julius. *Sketch of the Life and Works of the Late Felix Mendelssohn Bartholdy: Being the Substance of a Lecture Delivered at the Camberwell Literary Institution, in December, 1849.* London: J. Murray, 1850. 61 p. 2nd ed. (rev. and enl.), 1853. 66 p. ML410.M5 B3.

    Though Benedict had known FMB since 1821, the book is in the form of a narrative *Leben und Werke*, with only occasional personal references of the sort that characterize most contemporary memoirs. The book's significance derives in part from the fact that it was written during a crucial stage in FMB reception history, precisely the years in which a number of important works were receiving their first publication. Thus, there is no mention of the "Reformation" Symphony (which remained unpublished until 1868), and the A-major ("Italian") Symphony (first published in 1851) is absent from the 1850 version but described and associated with Italy in the book's 1853 revision.

21. Blaze de Bury, Ange Henri. *Musiciens contemporains.* Paris: Michel Lévy Frères, 1856. Rpt. Paris: Éditions d'Aujourd'hui, 1982. 289 p. ISBN 2730702792. ML385 .B64.

    Mendelssohn, Niels W. Gade, Jenny Lind, and Chopin on pp. 89–120. Another early biography significant for the ways in which it differs from views that were standard in writings about FMB after ca. 1870. De Bury's classifications are clearly derived from art-historical (rather than musicological or music-theoretical) literature. Thus, Mozart, Haydn, and Weber are "naturalists," while Bach, Beethoven, and Cherubini, by contrast, are "idealists." Against this backdrop, FMB is not classified according to the now-conventional dichotomy between "classic" and "romantic"; instead, he represents the link between the naturalists and the idealists: a realist.

22. Blunt, Wilfred. *On Wings of Song*. London: Hamish Hamilton, 1974. 288 p. ISBN 0684136333. ML410.M5 B62. Trans. Polish (Warsaw: Panstwowy Instytut Wydawniczy, 1979). ISBN 8306001796.

    A popular life-and-works study, richly illustrated but otherwise derivative in the material used to paint its portrait. Nevertheless illuminating because of its commitment to producing a reasonably realistic picture of FMB rather than the enduring "happy Felix" view. [DM]

    Rev.: E. Sams, in *The Musical Times* 115 (1974): 849; E. Werner, in *Notes* 32 (1975): 39–41.

23. Bölliger, Max. "Das Wunderkind: Felix Mendelssohn Bartholdy, 1809–1847." In *Was soll nur aus dir werden? Sechs Lebensbilder*, 36–59. Stuttgart: Hubert Frauenfeld, 1977. ISBN 3719305589.

    A conventional but usefully focused review of FMB's prodigious youth, combining biographical information with references to works.

24. Buenzod, Emmanuel. *Musiciens*. Musiciens et leurs œvres, 6. Lausanne: F. Rouge,1945. 220 p. ML410.M5 B62.

    FMB in Vol. 1, p. 139–149, in a section titled "Mendelssohn ou le bonheur." The section title says it all: because of the family life of privilege, FMB's music suffers from "softness" and "is deprived of the vigor that comes from struggle." Only his talent kept him from staying too long in "the no man's land between art and academicism." [DM]

25. Colson, Percy. *Victorian Portraits*. London: Rich & Cowan, 1932. Rpt. Freeport, New York: Books for Libraries Press, 1968. 256 p. DA562 .C7 1968.

    "Mendelssohn, a Fallen Idol" on p. 227–253. The title seems to promise a bit of reception history, but the essay is thoroughly typical in its bland admixture of anti-Semitic assumptions and stereotypes with post-Shaw anti-Victorianism. Instructive as an example of the decline Mendelssohn scholarship had experienced by the 1930s. [DM/JMC]

26. Comettant, Oscar. *Les compositeurs illustres de notre siècle: Rossini, Meyerbeer, Mendelssohn, Halévy, Gounod, Félicien David.* Paris: Ch. Delagrave, 1883. 173 p.

Comettant presents FMB in company that seems unlikely at best to today's readers, but provides useful insight because of his emphasis on the (perceived) qualities of Mendelssohn's music that both appealed to late-nineteenth-century French partisans (whose anti-Germanic sentiments were understandable after the Franco-Prussian War) and offended Wagnerians and German nationalists.

27. Crowest, Frederick James. *The Great Tone Poets: Being Short Memoirs of the Greater Musical Composers.* London: Bentley, 1874. 7th edn., 1891. 373 p. Rpt. Freeport, New York: Books for Libraries Press, [1972]. ISBN 0836926412. ML390 .C95 1972.

A classic example of the standard late-nineteenth-century view that Jews were like children in the evolutionary hierarchy of races:[2] "Mendelssohn's was a noble nature; spurning all that was base, mean, and insincere; full of fiery energy, yet as simple and lovable as a child's." [DM]

28. Dahms, Walter. *Mendelssohn.* Berlin: 1st–5th installments: Berlin: Schuster & Loeffler, 1919; rpt. 1976. 6th–9th installments, 1922. 202 p. ML410 .M5014.

A life-and-works study, obviously written at a period in which persons sympathetic to FMB's music felt defensive against New German School and anti-Semitic views: FMB is referred to as a "Romantic tone-poet," and the issue of his German nationality and his Jewishness is raised almost immediately ("Mendelssohn is . . . the only great and serious master whose work will endure for all time whom the Jews have given to music. His music has German character" [p. 14]). This study also evokes the "naturalist realist idealist" stylistic classifications employed by some other FMB biographies (e.g., no. 21), while adopting the by-then-standard view of Beethoven's three creative periods and applying it to FMB's works. It treats his life first (with references to works in their appropriate chronological positions), and then his works (a genre-by-genre summary-evaluation, introduced by a chapter entitled "Genie oder Epigone?" and followed by one entitled "Mendelssohn und die Zeit.")

29. Donner, Eka. *Felix Mendelssohn Bartholdy: Aus der Partitur eines Musikerlebens.* Düsseldorf: Droste, 1992. 160 p. ISBN 3770009894. ML410.M5 D7 1992.

An eminently readable and well-illustrated popular life-and-works study, written in the present tense.

30. Elvers, Rudolf. "Frühe Quellen zur Biographie Felix Mendelssohn Bartholdys." In *Felix Mendelssohn Bartholdy: Kongreß-Bericht Berlin 1994*, ed. Christian Martin Schmidt, 17–22. Wiesbaden: Breitkopf & Härtel, 1997.

This article inventories and describes the earliest known familial and official references to FMB, as well as the initiation of the family's contact with Zelter and Goethe; their trip to Paris in 1816; and the beginnings of Felix's and Fanny's private education. It also includes the earliest known portrait of FMB—one that dates from 1813 (three years earlier than the one usually considered earliest).

31. Ernouf, Alfred August. *L'Art musical du XIXè siècle, Compositeurs célèbres: Beethoven—Rossini—Meyerbeer—Mendelssohn—Schumann.* Paris: Perrin, 1888. 351 p.

FMB on p. 193–261. This study is generally sympathetic and utterly free of the stereotype of FMB's supposedly typically Jewish artistic decline—but there is also some suggestion that his character and his attitudes toward art were more important than his works. The book's chronological focus makes it possible to beg the aesthetic and historical questions of whether "importance" resides primarily in the quality of one's work or the extent of one's posthumous influence.

32. Fétis, F. J. *Biographie Universelle des Musiciens.* 8 vols. Brussels: Meline, Cans & Cie, 1840. ML105 .F414.

An article on FMB in vol. 6, p. 366–69. Straightforward biography with integrated references to works. Provides useful insights concerning the FMB reception at the early heights of his international fame: "this young artist . . . is incontestably at this point the musician who offers the most hope to Germany, and he represents the future schools of that country" (p. 369).

33. Foss, Hubert J. "Felix Mendelssohn-Bartholdy (1809–1847)." In *idem, The Heritage of Music*, 2: 151–74. London: Humphrey Milford, 1927. ML390 .F7.

"Even if it is allowed that in romanticism Mendelssohn falls behind and that in originality he is a small figure, he may be called not only a product but also a type of his age. There is a conspicuous lack of originality about Mendelssohn's technique. One can of course point to small virtues.

Otherwise we can find only efficiency displayed in the very earliest of his compositions, but not surprising in so clever a Jew." [DM]

34. García Pérez, Jesús. *Los Románticos Alemanes.* Barcelona: Monsalvat, 1973. 122 p. ISBN 8485243005. ML196 .R64

FMB in the chapter on "Romantismo del Concierto" (p. 73–92). A standard biography, largely derived from the 1963 version of Eric Werner's life-and-works study (no. 96). One of relatively few studies (if such it is) of FMB in Spanish.

35. Gleich, Ferdinand. *Charakterbilder aus der neueren Geschichte der Tonkunst.* 2 vols. in 1. Leipzig: Merseburger, 1863. ML390 .G53.

Clearly an early representative of the "happy Felix" myth: claims that "an artistic nature so tenderly strung and of such fine feeling as Mendelssohn's could flourish only in sunshine." Stresses the modernity of the sacred works. [DM/JMC]

36. Grove, George. "Mendelssohn." Article in *Grove's Dictionary of Music and Musicians*, ed. George Grove, 2: 253–310. London: Macmillan, 1880.

Although obviously dated in some of its particulars, this article still stands as one of the finest achievements of Mendelssohn scholarship. The quantity of Grove's publications on FMB clearly bespeaks a measure of sympathy for the composer (as the several contributions listed in this book attest), but the method and tone of his writings remains objective, with an emphasis on philological analysis and biographical documentation. The length of the essay in the nineteenth century's first major English lexicon of music—it runs to some 76 pages—also bespeaks the esteem with which FMB was regarded in that country at the time, especially in comparison with the articles on other major composers (such as J. S. Bach, Beethoven, Wagner, and Robert Schumann). Also draws extensively on contemporary reports (e.g., on FMB's abilities as a pianist). Another valuable aspect is the annotations to the bibliography: the problems of the editions of the FMB letters are noted and the glaring inadequacies of Lady Wallace's widely circulated English translation of the *Reisebriefe* are duly pointed out in the commentaries on the published correspondence.

37. Grove, George. *Beethoven, Schubert, Mendelssohn.* London: Macmillan, 1951. ML390 .G95 1951.

FMB treated on p. 253–394. A reprint—in a more reader-friendly font—of the Mendelssohn article from Grove's *Dictionary* (no. 36).

38. Gumprecht, Otto. *Musikalische Charakterbilder: Schubert, Mendelssohn, Weber, Rossini, Auber, Meyerbeer.* Leipzig: Adolf Gumprecht, 1869. 341 p. ML390 .G97. Partially rpt., rev., in *idem, Musikalische Lebens- und Charakterbilder, [v. 3–4]: Neuere Meister*, Vol. 1. Leipzig: H. Haessel, 1886. ML390 .G975.

   FMB on p. 84–181. FMB best reflects the "silver age" of German music (whereas Wagner represents the "golden age"). Similar to many contemporary writings in its emphasis on the composer's fine character; different, however, in that it sees *St. Paul* not as seeking refuge in an older, less dramatic genre than opera, but as turning away from the oratorio style of Graun and toward that of Bach and Handel—thus setting the path for the proper development of the genre. [DM/JMC]

39. Hadden, J[ames] C[uthbert]. *Life of Mendelssohn.* London: Keliher, 1882. 2nd ed., 1904. 174 p.

   The "Classical Romantic" FMB is emphasized in this late-nineteenth-century biography through the apollonian imagery used to describe his life: "Mendelssohn's way through life lay, as it were, among pleasant meads, and by the side of pure, sparkling rivers." Despite that consilience with the views of Mendelssohn's more overt detractors, however, the author makes few gestures to suggest a compositional decline after ca. 1836; in fact, *Elijah* quite clearly ranks as a more masterly oratorio than *St. Paul.* [DM/JMC]

40. Horton, John. *Some Nineteenth Century Composers.* London: Oxford University Press, 1950. 106 p. Rpt. Freeport, New York: Books for Libraries Press, 1971. ISBN 0836980689. ML390 .H78 1971.

   FMB on p. 1–11. A sensible, though relatively traditional, appreciation. [DM]

41. Hurd, Michael. *Mendelssohn.* London: Faber, 1970. 87 p. ISBN 0571086403. ML410.M5 H9. Rpt. New York: T. Y. Crowell, 1971. 0690531052. ML410.M5 H9 1971. Trans. Japanese Reiko Fujiwara (Tokyo: Zenon-gakufusyuppansa, 1974).

   A straightforward popular account, lavishly illustrated.

42. Jacob, Heinrich Eduard. *Felix Mendelssohn und seine Zeit: Bildnis und Schicksal eines Meisters.* Stuttgart: Deutscher Bücherbund, 1959. ML410.M5 J3. Rpt. Frankfurt am Main: Fischer, 1981. 432 p. ISBN 3596250234. Trans. Richard and Clara Winston as *Felix Mendelssohn and His Times.* London: Barrie, 1959; Englewood Cliffs: Prentice Hall, 1963.

Rpt. Westport, Conn.: Greenwood, 1973. ISBN 0837168236. ML410.M5 J33 1973.

A life-and-works study, reiterating and reexamining standard sources without recourse to unpublished materials. A good example of how spin-off biographies continued to proliferate concurrently with the revival of credible biographical and stylistic scholarship after the Second World War.

Rev.: Rassegna musicale 31 (1961): 76–77.

43. Jacobs, Rémi. *Mendelssohn*. Paris: Éditions de Seuil, 1977. 191 p. ISBN 2020046849.

In contrast to nineteenth-century French FMB biographies, which generally viewed the composer and his significance with enthusiasm, this book suggests stereotypical Gallic restraint. The post-1910 pseudo-truisms are almost all present. Most of the credit is reserved for FMB's revival of earlier composers' works and for his own earlier compositions; his life was too simple and happy to foster for spiritual growth and artistic greatness; and so on.

Rev.: C. Chamfray, in *Courier musical de France* 66 (1977): 158.

44. Kaufman, Schima. *Mendelssohn: A Second Elijah*. New York: Thomas Y. Crowell, 1934, and New York: Tudor, 1936. Rpt. Westport, Conn.: Greenwood, 1971. 353 p. ISBN 0837132290. ML410.M5 K3 1971.

The Greenwood edition is a reprint of the 1934 edition. This book claims to be "the first full-length biography of a great composer, one whose shielded existence was not the life of unsullied happiness gossip would have us believe." While it does avoid the pitfalls of the "happy Felix" myth, it can hardly be called the "first full-length biography" of FMB, or even the first to surmount that myth. There are also numerous errors (e.g., " L[ass] e[s] g[elingen] G[ott]" is misread as "L. v. g. G"[3]) and the book is full of made-up dialogue. [DM/JMC]

45. Köhler, Karl-Heinz. *Felix Mendelssohn Bartholdy*. Reklams Universal-Bibliothek, Bd. 301. Leipzig, Reklam, [1966]. ML410.M5 K6. 285 p. 2nd ed., 1972. 275 p. ML410.M5 K6 1972. Trans. Polish (Kraków: PWM, 1980).

A general life-and-works book written by a scholar intimately connected with the Mendelssohn revival, with substantial recourse to primary sources. Contains a fine section on the changes in orchestral performance practice that took place under Wagner and how inimical these were to

Mendelssohn, both as conductor and composer. There is a good summary of Mendelssohn's relations with Wagner and of Wagner's anti-Mendelssohn and anti-Semitic writings after Mendelssohn's death. [DM/JMC]

46. Köhler, Karl-Heinz. "Mendelsssohn(-Bartholdy), (Jacob Ludwig) Felix." Article in *The New Grove Dictionary of Music and Musicians*, ed. Stanley Sadie, 12: 134–59. London: Macmillan, 1980. Work-list and bibliography by Eveline Bartlitz. Revised and reprinted with more reader-friendly font, index, and revised work-list by Eveline Bartlitz and R. Larry Todd in *The New Grove Early Romantic Masters 2* (New York: W. W. Norton, 1985), 197–301. ISBN 0393016927.

By virtue of Köhler's command of Mendelssohn sources—for years he was head librarian of the most important depository of Mendelssohn family manuscripts, the Staatsbibliotek Preußischer Kulturbesitz—and of its venue of publication, one of the central resources for Mendelssohn scholars since 1980. The article is divided into three sections: (1) a periodic overview of FMB's life (including references to major compositions), (2) a generic overview of the works, and (3) "heritage" (conspicuously brief in comparison to the other parts of the essay). The work-list and bibliography by Eveline Bartlitz in the original *New Grove* are seriously lacking in several regards (see Elvers, no. 458, in this book); their revised versions are decidedly more accurate, useful, and complete.

47. Konold, Wulf. *Felix Mendelssohn Bartholdy und seine Zeit.* Laaber: Laaber, 1984. 375 p. ISBN 3921518822. ML410.M5 K69 1984.

Despite a sizable bibliography fraught with virtually every type of bibliographic error, this is a semi-popular biography—not so much a *Leben und Werke* in the sense of Eric Werner's (no. 96), but rather a topically organized set of style-and-influence studies. Also includes a non-thematic work list and a "Chronik" stretching from 1729 (the year of the birth of Moses Lessing and Moses Mendelssohn and the first performance of the *St. Matthew Passion*) to 1963 (the publication year of the English version of Werner's book about Mendelssohn). The liturgical and religious music is dealt with in a chapter called "The Renewal of Church Music." A final chapter deals with "Mendelssohn and Posterity," and consists of separate sections devoted to a general discussion of the Mendelssohn reception, the Mendelssohn reception in the press, "Mendelssohn in the Third Reich," "The Mendelssohn Reception Today," and "Mendelssohn's Work in German Musical Life."

Rev.: S. Großmann-Vendrey, in *Musica* 39 (1985): 489–490; G. Schuhmacher in *Musik und Kirche* 62 (1992): 281–22.

48. Krinitz, Elise. *La Musique en Allemagne: Mendelssohn*. Paris: G. Baillière, 1867. 156 p.

A book that, like many other early French FMB biographies, paints a more favorable picture of him than contemporaneous German biographies do.

49. Kupferberg, Herbert. *The Mendelssohns: Three Generations of Genius*. London: W. H. Allen, 1972. 272 p. ISBN 0491007329. ML410.M5 K88. Also published as *Felix Mendelssohn: His Life, His Family, His Music*. New York: C. Scribner's Sons, 1972. 176 p. ISBN 0684129523. ML3930.M44 K9. Trans. German Klaus Leonhardt as *Die Mendelssohns*. Tübingen: Rainer Wunderlich, 1972. 2nd ed., 1977. 302 p. ISBN 0491007329.

A widely circulated and largely derivative popular biography with extensive information about the family, particularly Moses Mendelssohn. Except for this familial aspect (which is largely based on an uncritical reading of Sebastian Hensel's family memoir [no. 355 in this book]), the book's authority rests on its readability. Despite its late date, there is no effort to deal with the immense amount of primary source-material neglected by most earlier FMB biographers; in this sense, it belongs to an earlier stage in the development of FMB research.

Rev.: S. Großmann-Vendrey in *Die Musikforschung* 28 (1975): 125–26.

50. Lampadius, Wilhelm Adolf. *Felix Mendelssohn Bartholdy: Ein Denkmal für seine Freunde*. Leipzig: Hinrichs, 1848. 218 p. ML410.M5 L19. Trans. English William Leonard Gage as *Life of Felix Mendelssohn Bartholdy*. New York: F. Leopoldt, 1865. ML410.M5 L2. 2nd ed., with supplementary sketch by Ignaz Moscheles of Mendelssohn's character, Boston: O. Ditson, 1872. ML410.M5 L205 1872. 2nd ed. also published as *Memoirs of Felix Mendelssohn Bartholdy,* Boston: Ditson, 1865; includes supplementary sketches by Julius Benedict, Henry F. Chorley, Ludwig Rellstab, Bayard Taylor, R. S. Willis, and J. S. Dwight. 2nd ed. with additional notes by C. L. Gruneisen, London: W. H. Reeves, 1877).

The most extensive version of this popular book is the second (1877) edition of the *Memoirs* (first published Boston, 1865). Emphasizes the influence of Goethe and offers extensive discussions of *St. Paul* and the

Lobgesang as well as of other works that were celebrated in the late nineteenth century but are less so today (e.g., *Die erste Walpurgisnacht* and the
incidental music to *Antigone*). Like most contemporary FMB biographies,
devotes considerable attention (the entire penultimate chapter) to his
appearance and his outstanding personality. The final chapter is a pane-
gyrical summary of his artistic greatness. See also Lampadius's
Gesammtbild (no. 51).

51. Lampadius, Wilhelm Adolf. *Felix Mendelssohn Bartholdy: Ein
     Gesammtbild seines Lebens und Wirkens*. Leipzig: Leuckart, 1886. Rpt.
     Walluf: Martin Sändig, 1978. 379 p. ISBN 3500306608. ML410.M5 L21.

     An expansion of the author's *Ein Denkmal* (no. 50). Makes use of the
     extensive published material—all of it accessible to the modern reader
     without recourse to this volume—that had appeared since that book was
     written. The book is generally useful but contains many errors and incon-
     sistencies to balance its few commendable features.

52. Lewinski, Wolf-Eberhard von. "Felix Mendelssohn Bartholdy: Hinweise
     auf Leben und Werk." In *Felix Mendelssohn Bartholdy: Leben und Werk—
     Musikfestspiele Saar 1989*, ed. Robert Leonardy, 31–47. Edition Karlsberg,
     Bd. 6. Lebach: Joachim Hempel, 1989.

     A general life-and-works study that, like Müller-Blattau's essay in the
     same volume (no. 67) views FMB as caught between his own "spirited and
     by no means emotionally deprived" style and the pathos of Beethoven's
     late style. General references to many well-known works, with more detail
     in comments on the *Midsummer Night's Dream Overture*, Op. 21, and
     Elijah. Also discusses FMB's activities as conductor.

53. Lipsius, Maria [La Mara]. M*usikalische Studienköpfe, Band II*. Leipzig: H.
     Schmidt, 1868. 10th ed., Leipzig: Breitkopf & Härtel, 1911. ML60 .L47.

     FMB on p. 159–212. As the publication history suggests, the
     Musikalische Studienköpfe were popular books, intended primarily to offer
     compact life-and-works studies to musical amateurs; there was little to
     encourage real research or serious scholarly and musical contemplation.
     Given that, the character of the Mendelssohn chapter is predictable: the
     "happy Felix" approach raised to unimaginable heights of bombast.
     [DM/JMC]

54. Lobe, Johann Christian. *Musikalische Briefe: Wahrheit über Tonkunst und
     Tonkünstler*. 2 vols. Leipzig: Baungärtner,1852. 2nd ed., 1860.

     FMB in vol. 2, p. 105–16. A very early *Leben und Werke* best understood as a complement to Lobe's memoir of FMB (no. 255), and a testament to the importance of the 1848 revolutions in the composer's reception history[4]: Mendelssohn lived during an artistically calm period "when art rests and gathers its strength for a further climb"; he "stood at the height of his time but could not exceed it." The works singled out as most influential are the concert overtures (which of course anticipated the symphonic poems of Liszt, though Lobe does not make this connection explicit), while FMB's music generally is criticized for its "flacidity" *(Weichheit)*. Many works—especially the sacred ones—are criticized as being unduly influenced by Zelter.

55. Loeper, G. von. "Felix Mendelssohn Bartholdy." Article in *Allgemeine deutsche Biographie*, 21: 324–45. Leipzig: Duncker & Humblodt, 1885. Rpt. Berlin: Duncker & Humblodt, 1967–71.

    A careful overview, the first part of which is drawn largely from the essay in Grove's *Dictionary* (no. 36). Loeper credits FMB with having been the person who successfully initiated the German *Nationalbildung* intended with the Prussian state's founding of the Berlin Akademie der Künste in 1809, as well as discussing his activities as conductor (including durations for certain works under his baton). [DM]

56. Lyser, Johann Peter. "Felix Mendelssohn Bartholdy." *Allgemeine Wiener Musik-Zeitung* 154 (24 December 1842). Rpt. in *Ein unbekanntes Mendelssohn-Bildnis von Johann Peter Lyser*, ed. Max F. Schneider, 37–43. Basel: Internationale Felix-Mendelssohn-Gesellschaft, 1958.

    Johann Peter Lyser—a member of Schumann's *Davidsbündler* who is likely familiar to many readers for his posthumous pen-and-ink drawing of Beethoven on a stroll—produced a portrait of FMB in 1835, followed by a glowing assessment of his artistic greatness in 1842. Both are useful as documents of contemporary reception history. See also his "Zur Biographie Felix Mendelssohn Bartholdys" (no. 57).

57. Lyser, Johann Peter. "Zur Biographie Mendelssohn Bartholdys." *Sonntagsblätter* [Vienna] (1847): 592–97.

    Not available for examination. One of the earliest biographical memoirs for FMB.

58. Mackerness, E. B. "Mendelssohn und Charles Auchester." In *Bericht über den siebenten internationalen musikwissenschaftlichen Kongreß Köln 1958*, ed. Gerald Abraham, Suzanne Clercx-LeJeune, Hellmut Federhofer, and Wilhelm Pfannkuch, 188. Kassel: Bärenreiter, 1959.

One indication of the excesses of the English Mendelssohn cult was the enormous popularity of Elizabeth Shephard's fictional biography *Charles Auchester* (London, 1853), in which the main character, Seraphael, is overtly (but not explicitly) based on FMB. This study surveys the parallels between (what was then known about) FMB's life and Shephard's hero, and discusses the significance.

59. Marek, George. *Gentle Genius: The Story of Felix Mendelssohn*. New York: Funk and Wagnalls, 1972. 365 p. ISBN 0815203748. ML410.M5 M15.

A general and popular book by an author well-versed in the literature. There are good sections on Moses and Abraham Mendelssohn. [DM]

60. Mariotti, Giovanni. *Mendelssohn*. Roma: Edizione latine, 1937. 227 p. ML410.M5 M17.

An important book because of its origin in fascist Italy in the most troubled years of FMB reception history. See also the author's study on FMB's Italy (no. 177).

61. [Marx, Adolph Bernhard]. "Mendelssohn-Bartholdy, Dr. Felix." Article in *Encyclopädie der gesammten musikalischen Wissenschaften, oder Universal-Lexikon der Tonkunst*, ed. Gustav Schilling, Vol. 4, p. 654–55. Stuttgart: Franz Heinrich Köhler, 1837.

An unusually personal contribution to the lexicographic literature on FMB, almost certainly by A. B. Marx, who is credited among the contributors to the encyclopedia, whose prose style resembles that of the article, and whose lifelong friendship with FMB came to an end in the later 1830s. The author visited with FMB in Frankfurt am Main in the summer of 1836, and speaks in considerable detail about the composer's education and background as a musician. The generally respectful tone gives way to grave reservations: despite his strong ear, sharp memory, and almost incomprehensible ability as a sight-reader, FMB had been constrained by the practicality of Zelter's education and certain directions in the contemporary arts, and so was unable, thus far, to fulfill hopes that he would be a "second Mozart." Expresses reservations whether FMB will ever be able to surmount these limitations on the "soulful depth" of his music, and concludes: "it would be wonderful, inestimably valuable, if we were to be compelled to confess that we had arrived at and pronounced this view misguidedly and with undue haste."

62. Mascheroni, Anna Maria. *Classic Composers*. Wigston, Leicestershire:

Magna, 1991. 194 p. ISBN 1854222465.

Material on FMB is derived primarily from Werner's biography (nos. 96 and 97) and Köhler's *New Grove* essay (no. 46). Volume also includes Bach, Vivaldi, Handel, Haydn, Mozart, Beethoven, Schubert, Berlioz, Chopin, Schumann, Verdi, Liszt, Wagner, Brahms, Tchaikovsky, Mahler, Debussy, Stravinsky, Shostakovich, and Gershwin.

63. Meloncelli, Raoul. "Mendelssohn-Bartholdy, Felix." Article in *Dizionario enciclopeico universale della musica e dei musicisti*, ed. Alberto Basso, Vol. 5, p20–39. Torino: UTET, 1988.

An overview of FMB's life and his orchestral, keyboard, and chamber works, in Italian. There is no mention of the organ works, sacred works, or other vocal music. The bibliography is useful and more comprehensive than one might expect on the basis of the article itself.

64. Mendel, Hermann, and August Reissmann. "Mendelssohn, Felix." In *Musikalisches Conversations-Lexikon: Eine Encyclopädie der gesammten musikalischen Wissenschaften für Gebildeten aller Stände*. Berlin: Robert Oppenheim, 1877. Vol. 7, p. 119–26.

A carefully balanced but generally sympathetic assessment, written at a troubled juncture in FMB's reception history. The anonymous author portrays FMB as a composer who synthesized the Romantic era's historicist aspects (especially its interest in the music of Handel and J. S. Bach, as cultivated in FMB by Zelter) with its more modern proclivities, especially the contributions to drama made by Weber. Nevertheless, the sacred works are criticized as "long [having] counted as true expressions of Protestant piety precisely because they lack even a trace of religious coloration." [DM/JMC]

65. Morin-Labrecque, Albertine. *Félix Mendelssohn, 1809–1847*. Montréal: Éditions de l'Étoile, 1943. 30 p.

A short popular biography seemingly derived largely from the family memoir by Sebastian Hensel (although no reference to any source is provided). FH figures somewhat more prominently than one might expect, but otherwise the book is thoroughly traditional in its portrayal of FMB as a composer whose importance resides primarily in his role in the Bach revival.

66. Moshansky, Mozelle. *Mendelssohn: His Life and Times*. Neptune City, New Jersey: Paganiniana Publications, 1981; and Tunbridge Wells: Midas, 1982. 144 p. ISBN 3500306608. ML410.M5 M84 1984.

A richly illustrated and sympathetic popular biography. Among such books, it also contains perhaps the best material on the situation of Jews in late-eighteenth- and early-nineteenth-century Germany.

Rev.: R. Anderson in *The Musical Times* 124 (1983): 35–36.

67. Müller-Blattau,   Wendelin.   "Felix   Mendelssohn   Bartholdy   im Spannungsfeld europäischer Musik." In *Felix Mendelssohn Bartholdy: Leben und Werk—Musikfestspiele Saar 1989*, ed. Robert Leonardy, 9–29. Edition Karlsberg, Bd. 6. Lebach: Joachim Hempel, 1989.

A general overview contesting the oft-repeated notion that "there seemingly is no happier fate for a musician than that of Felix Mendelssohn Bartholdy" (p. 9). Includes familiar background information about the Mendelssohn family before FMB, and surveys FMB's activities as conductor and pianist as well as composer. Pays special attention to his relationship—musical and personal—with Berlioz, especially by comparing the *Walpurgisnacht* with the *Symphonie fantastique*.

68. Neumayr, Anton. *Musik und Medizin, II: Am Beispiel der deutschen Romantik*. Vienna: J & V Edition, 1988. 2nd ed., 1991. ISBN 3850580075. ML390 .N385 1988. 2nd ed. Trans. English Bruce Cooper Clarke as *Music and Medicine, II: Hummel, Weber, Mendelssohn, Schumann, Brahms, Bruckner—Notes on Their Lives, Works, and Medical Histories*. Bloomington, IL.: Medi-Ed, 1994. 600 p. ISBN 0936741074. ML390 .N38513 1994.

This book is dated, but useful. (See also nos. 131 and 132, below.)

69. Neunzig, Hans A. *Lebensläufe der deutschen Romantik: Komponisten*. Munich: Kindler, 1984. 336 p. ISBN 3463008793. ML390 .N4 1984.

A useful biography, derived almost exclusively from Eric Werner's FMB book (nos. 96 and 97) and Sebastian Hensel's family memoir (no. 352).

70. Petitpierre, Jacques. *Le Mariage de Mendelssohn, 1837–1937*. Lausanne: Payot, 1937. 209 p. ML410.M5 P4. Trans. G. Micholet-Coté as *The Romance of the Mendelssohns*. New York: Roy, 1937. Rpt. 1950, and London: D. Dobson, [1947]. 251 p. ML410.M5 P412.

A very sympathetic popular biography, nicely illustrated and with extensive recourse to little-known primary sources. A book about Mendelssohn via a biography of Cécile. The book contains some errors (many of which are corrected in Peter Ward Jones's edition of the couple's honeymoon diary [no. 232]), but is laudable for the scope and integrity of its contribution to the biographical literature.

71. Pitrou, Robert. *Musiciens romantiques: Beethoven, Weber, Schubert, Chopin, Mendelssohn, Schumann, Berlioz, Liszt, Wagner.* Paris: A. Michel, 1946. 195 p. ML390 .P56. Trans. German Lolo Kraus, with revisions by H. Halm, as *Musiker der Romantik.* Lindau im Bodensee: Frisch & Perneder, 1946. 254 p.

    FMB on p. 97-107 of French, p. 113–31 of German.

72. Polko, Elise. *Meister der Tonkunst: Ein Stück Musikgeschichte in Biographien.* Wiesbaden: Lützenkirchen & Bröcking, 1897.

    See also the author's memoir (no. 264). A largely fanciful biography, representative of the late-Victorian version of the Mendelssohn cult.

73. Prod'homme, Jacques Gabriel. *Félix Mendelssohn Bartholdy (1809–1847): Avec une notice biographique et une introduction historique.* Brussels: n.p., 1950.

    Not available for examination. The author is a prodigious scholar, having published biographical notices on composers ranging from Lassus onward, and translated the writings of various New German School composers (most prominently, Wagner and Liszt) into French.

74. Radcliffe, Philip. *Mendelssohn.* London: J. M. Dent & Sons, 1954; rpt. 1957. 208 p. ML410.M5 R25. New York: Collier, 1963. 224 p. 2nd ed., New York: J. M. Dent, 1967. 210 p. ML410.M5 R25 1967. 2nd ed., reissued, London: Dent, 1976. 214 p. ISBN 0460031236. ML410.M5 R25 1976. 3rd ed., revised Peter Ward Jones, London: Dent, 1990. 188 p. ISBN 0460860291.

    A life-and-works study with more musical insights than most works of that variety. The 1990 revision by Peter Ward Jones offers useful annotations and corrections of factual errors, as well as a revised work-list.

75. Ranft, Peter. *Felix Mendelssohn Bartholdy: Eine Lebenskronik.* Leipzig: Deutscher Verlag für Musik, [1972]. ML410.M5 R28.

    As the title says, an event-by-event sketch of the principal events in and around FMB's life. Includes numerous quotations from letters.

    Rev.: E. Sams in *The Musical Times* 114 (1973): 265–66; S. Großmann-Vendrey in *Die Musikforschung* 28 (1975): 123–24.

76. Reich, Willi. *Felix Mendelssohn im Spiegel eigener Aussagen und zeit-*

genössicher Dokumente. Zürich: Manesse, 1970. 443 p. ML410.M5 R35. 2nd ed., 1987. 447 p. ISBN 3717512803.

A documentary biography comprising carefully edited documents from Mendelssohn and his circle. An introductory chronological table is followed by a chapter on FMB's "early youth" (through spring 1829); one on his *Wanderjahre* (mid 1829 through August 1835); and a surprisingly short one on his *Meisterjahre* (late 1835 until his death). See also the documentary biographies by Max Schneider (no. 84) and Hans Christoph Worbs (nos. 100 and 101).

Rev.: H. C. Worbs in *Musica* 24 (1970): 492–93.

77. Reinicke, Carl. *Meister der Tonkunst: Mozart, Beethoven, Haydn, Weber, Schumann, Mendelssohn.* Berlin: W. Spemann, 1903.

FMB on p. 441–80. The most credible of the life-and-works studies that assert that, for modern times, FMB was too close to the classics who overshadow him. Also suggests that his reputation had suffered because he has been imitated so much.

78. Reissmann, August. *Felix Mendelssohn-Bartholdy: Sein Leben und seine Werke.* Berlin: J. Gutentag, 1867. 317 p. 2nd ed., rev. and enl., 1872. 320 p. 3rd ed., rev. and enl., Leipzig: List und Francke, 1893.

Evidently an attempt—largely successful—to do better what Lampadius had attempted with his *Denkmal* (no. 50), but still a life-and-works overview that is easily susceptible to charges of facile superficiality. Ernst Wolff's assessment in the "Vorwort" to his outstanding biography (no. 98) is appropriate: having noted that there was still no German-language biography of FMB worthy of the designation, Wolff states that "a clear organization of the material, objective evaluations of Mendelssohn's works, and reliable handling of the facts are all too easily missed" in Reissman's book.[5]

79. Rellstab, Ludwig. *Biographien berühmter Männer.* Leipzig: F. A. Brockhaus, [1850]. Rpt. in *Ludwig Rellstab, Gesammelte Schriften: Neue Ausgabe*, Bd. 24, T. 4. Leipzig: F. A. Brockhaus, [1861].

A careful biographical sketch, one of the earliest of its type. Like the other life-and-works studies of FMB that appeared prior to the 1870s, this one is interesting because its evaluation is based only on the works that FMB himself chose to release—not the posthumously published ones that he had suppressed or left unpublished.

80. Riehl, W. H. "Bach und Mendelssohn aus dem socialen Gesichtspunkte." *Musikalischen Charakterköpfe* 1 (1853): 65–107.

   A look at two of Leipzig's greatest musical personalities, important because of its early date. Although FMB's greatness was not as universally accepted as Bach's was, his prestige, based on his versatility and his character, are exemplary.

81. Rockstro, William S. *Mendelssohn*. The Great Musicians. London: Sampson Low, Marston Searle, and Rivington, 1884. 147 p. 3rd ed., 1890. ML410.M5 R8.

   A popular biography, valuable (like Benedict's [no. 20]) as a biographical testimony by a man old enough to have had a brief contact with Mendelssohn. Like other early biographies, the book makes much of FMB's private character and of his exemplary devotion to good public works. His assessments of FMB's music, on the other hand, differ from most other contemporary biographies in that they cohere with Robert Schumann's assessments in recognizing FMB's importance in maintaining and re-defining high compositional standards in an age in which the music shops were deluged with tripe.

82. Rockstro, William S. "*Felix Mendelssohn-Bartholdy*." Article in *Encyclopedia Britannica*, 11th ed. and earlier (Cambridge: Cambridge University Press, 1911). Vol. 18; p. 121–24.

   This article overlaps considerably, not surprisingly, with the author's book on FMB. The article in the eleventh edition is the same as that in the earlier ones, but contains a telling note appended by Donald Francis Tovey, explaining that Mendelssohn "was a man whom even his contemporaries knew to be greater than his works. . . . [a man whose] reputation, except as the composer of a few inexplicably beautiful and original orchestral pieces, has vanished."[6]

83. Saint-Saëns, Camille. *Les grands maitres de la musique: Jusqu'à Berlioz*. Paris: Lafitte, [1907]. 347 p.

   Mendelssohn treated on p. 247–54. Suggests that FMB is widely disdained because his music is simple and candid—qualities consistent with stereotypically Gallic attitudes at the turn of the century, and definitely at odds with the overwhelmingly Wagnerian cultural mores of the day. The essay's main interest lies in its turn-of-the-century view—part defense, part not—and the name of its author.

84. Schneider, Max F. *Felix Mendelssohn Bartholdy: Denkmal in Wort und*

Bild, mit einer biographischen Einführhung von Willi Reich. Basel: Internationale Felix Mendelssohn-Gesellschaft, 1947. 150 p. ML410.M5 A4.

Published at the centennial of FMB's death, this book is an affectionate but scholarly counterpart to the books by Willi Reich (no. 76) and Hans Christoph Worbs (no. 100).

85. Schuhmacher, Gerhard. "Felix Mendelssohn Bartholdys Bedeutung aus sozialgeschichtlicher Sicht: Ein Versuch." In *Felix Mendelssohn Bartholdy,* ed. Gerhard Schuhmacher, 138–73. Wege der Forschung, Bd. 494. Darmstadt: Wissenschaftliche Buchgesellschaft, 1982.

86. Schwingenstein, Christoph. "Mendelssohn." Article in *Neue Deutsche Biographie*, ed. Historische Kommission bei der Bayrischen Akademie der Wissenschaften, 17: 53–58. Berlin: Duncker & Humblot, 1994.

A complete and straightforward biography, based on a good knowledge of FMB research.

87. [Stierlin, Leonhard]. *Biographie von Felix Mendelssohn-Bartholdy.* Zürich: Orell Fässli, [1849]. 26 p. ML5.N48 no. 37.

The author, a pastor in the Canton of Zurich, offered this little biography as "a New Year's gift for the youth of Zurich"—an indication of the approach of the volume, which holds FMB up as an exemplary musician, citizen, educator, and student. Stierlin also authored short biographies of several other important composers (including Palestrina, Hasse, Gluck, Graun, Cherubini, and Spohr).

88. Stratton, Stephen S. *Mendelssohn.* London: J. M. Dent, 1901. 306 p. ML410.M5 S9. 2nd ed., 1921. 3rd ed., rev. Eric Blom, 1934. 233 p. ML410.M5 S9 1934.

Although FMB's reception in England had become a problem by the early 1930s, this book reveals the substance (rather than just the ebullience, as was usual) of the English reverence for FMB. As in Lampadius's biography (nos. 50 and 51), the penultimate chapter is devoted to "Mendelssohn: The Man" and the final chapter to "Mendelssohn: The Musician."

89. Stresemann, Wolfgang. *Eine Lanze für Felix Mendelssohn.* Berlin: Stapp, 1984. ISBN 3877762751. ML410.M5 S94 1984

Rev.: F. Krummacher in *Musica* 39 (1985): 197–98.

90. Stückenschmidt, H. H. "Mendelssohn." Article in *Die großen Deutschen*, 3: 152–62. Berlin: Propyläen, 1956.

91. Subira, José. *Musicos románticos: Schubert, Schumann, Mendelssohn.* Biblioteca de artistas celebres, II. Madrid: [A. Marzo], 1925. 219 p.

92. Tiénot, Yvonne. *Mendelssohn: Musicien complet.* Paris: H. Lemoine, [1972]. 246 p. ML410.M5 T55.

   Rev.: C. Chamfray in *Le Courier musical de France* 41 (1973): 30; R. Viollier, in *Schweizerische Musikzeitung* 113 (1973): 180.

93. Todd, R. Larry. "Mendelssohn." *The Heritage of Music*, ed. Michael Raeburn and Alan Kendall, 2-p. 182–93. Oxford: Oxford University Press, 1989.

   An optimal combination of compactness, authority, and illustrations. Discussion tends to favor the instrumental works, but includes references to vocal (especially choral/orchestral) compositions as well.

94. Werner, Eric. "Mendelssohn." Article in *Die Musik in Geschichte und Gegenwart*, ed. Friedrich Blume, 9: 59–98. Kassel: Bärenreiter, 1961.

   An important article that anticipates much of the material in the author's biography (nos. 96 and 97). The work-list was the most complete and accurate up to that point. Extensive bibliography.

95. Werner, Eric. "Mendelssohn Bartholdy, Felix Jacob Ludwig." Article in *Rizzoli Ricordi: Enciclopedia della musica*. Milan: Rizzoli Editione, 1972. Vol. 4, 172–77.

   An abbreviated and updated version of the MGG article (no. 94).

96. Werner, Eric, trans. Dika Newlin. *Mendelssohn: A New Image of the Composer and His Age*. London: Free Press of Glencoe, 1963. 545 p. ML410.M5 W37. Rpt. Westport, Conn.: Greenwood, 1978. ISBN 0313203024. ML410.M5 W37 1978.

   A seminal, but deeply problematical, contribution to the biographical literature on FMB. Among the volume's many strengths are its use of archival sources (particularly previously unpublished documents from the Mendelssohns' family correspondence) and its sympathetic and detailed exploration of the importance of Jewish issues in FMB's life and works. Unfortunately, its integrity on both fronts has been seriously questioned. Several authors (most prominently, Marian Wilson Kimber [no. 239], Wolfgang Dinglinger [no. 743], Jeffrey L. Sposato [nos. 391 and 392], and Peter Ward Jones [no. 230]) have demonstrated that Werner fabricated or otherwise misrepresented some of the unpublished documents he cites, and numerous otherwise unpublished documents can be neither traced nor checked for accuracy. In addition, the volume may be considered to place too much emphasis on Jewish issues—perhaps overcompensation for the failure of previous biographies to explore those issues sufficiently. See the substantial discussion over the existence or extent of this problem in the *Musical Quarterly* articles mentioned as well as the responses by Leon Botstein (nos. 374 and 376) and Michael P. Steinberg (no. 369).

English-language readers should also be aware of the idiosyncracies of the book's publication history. Although the book was originally written in German, only the English translation by Dika Newlin was published in 1963; publication of the German text—in an extensively revised and enlarged version, which is still plagued by problems of the sort described above—occurred only in 1980 (no. 97). That revised version, unfortunately, has never been released in English translation. Readers are therefore advised to use the German text, and whenever possible to verify the information provided in it through other, more reliable sources.

Rev.: H. Eppstein in *Svensk Tidskrift für Musikforskning* 48 (1966): 255–59; A. L. Ringer in *The Musical Quarterly* 51 (1965): 419–25; M. Carner in *Music and Letters* 45 (1964): 395–97.

97.　Werner, Eric. *Mendelssohn: Leben und Werk in neuer Sicht*. Zurich: Atlantis, 1980. 635 p. ISBN 3761105711. ML410.M5 W35 1980.

The significantly revised and expanded German version of no. 96. Despite extensive reworkings (at least some of them in response to reviews of the 1963 edition), the volume includes numerous substantial errors and remains liable to criticisms of scholarly accuracy and authorial prejudice (see the articles by Wilson, Sposato, and Botstein listed in the annotation to no. 96).

Rev.: M. Hansen in *Musik und Gesellschaft* 33 (1983): 625–26.

98.　Wolff, Ernst. *Felix Mendelssohn Bartholdy*. Berlin: Harmonie, 1906. 2nd ed., enl., 1909. ML410.M5 W82.

Still among the finest biographies of FMB, especially in its 1909 revision. The approach is strictly biographical (i.e., chronological) and documentary, with only brief descriptive references to the compositions; there are few gestures of critical evaluation. Accurately adduces considerable evidence from otherwise unpublished letters, and includes several fascimiles and rare drawings. Drawing substantially on Sir George Grove's outstanding FMB article (no. 36), Wolff conscientiously endeavors to avoid the pitfalls to which the principal German-language biographies then available had succumbed.[7] The result is a biographical overview of singular thoroughness, clarity, and objectivity.

99. Worbs, Hans Christoph. *Felix Mendelssohn Bartholdy*. Musikbücherei für Jedermann, 10. Leipzig: Breitkopf & Härtel, 1956. 2nd ed., 1957. 71 p. ML410.M5 W85 1957.

A short, mostly accurate (if also somewhat dated), and objective life-and-works study.

100. Worbs, Hans Christoph. *Felix Mendelssohn Bartholdy: Wesen und Wirken im Speigel von Selbstzeugnißen und Berichten der Zeitgenossen*. Leipzig: Köhler und Amelang, 1958. 255 p.

A predecessor to the author's contribution to the Rowohlt's Monographien series (no. 101). See also Reich (no. 76), and Schneider (no. 84).

101. Worbs, Hans Christoph. *Felix Mendelssohn Bartholdy in Selbstzeugnissen und Bilddokumenten*. Rowohlt's Monographien, 215. Rheinbek: Rowohl, 1974. 151 p. ML410.M5 W86. ISBN 3499502151. 10th ed., 1994. 152 p. ISBN 3499502151.

An invaluable resource, and for most English speakers the most easily accessible of the triumvirate of documentary biographies. See also Reich (no. 76) and Schneider (no. 84).

III. SPECIAL ASPECTS OF MENDELSSOHN'S BIOGRAPHY

Coverage: Mendelssohn's relationships with specific persons, places, and contemporary topics. See also "The Mendelssohn Family," "Studies of Jewish Issues," and "Reception History," in Chapter 3.[8]

102. Alexander, Boyd. "Felix Mendelssohn and the Alexanders." *Mendelssohn-Studien* 1 (1972): 81–105.

In English with German abstract. Among FMB's many London friends was the Alexander family, whose three daughters (Mary, Joanna, and Margaret) found the composer personally fascinating, and who promoted his music in the British capital. Article includes on p. 102–05 the first publication of a detailed English report of FMB's death (probably an English translation of a letter from Charlotte Moscheles to Karl

Klingemann), as well as two facsimiles.

103. Alexander, Boyd. "Felix Mendelssohn and Young Women." *Mendelssohn-Studien 2* (1975): 71–102.

In English with German abstract. A sequel to the author's contribution in the previous issue of the *Mendelssohn-Studien*, this study focuses on FMB's relationship with Mary Alexander (1806–67), the youngest of the three sisters in the Alexander family in London. The two were of similar political tendencies, and (on the basis of the documents examined here, some of which were previously unpublished) it appears that Mary Alexander felt an abiding love for FMB, while his own feelings for her vacillated between strong affection and cool restraint. Like the previous article, this one documents Felix's appreciation for the company of young women.

104. Alf, Julius. *Geschichte und Bedeutung der Niederrheinischen Musikfeste in der ersten Hälfte des neunzehnten Jahrhunderts.* Düsseldorfer Jahrbuch: Beiträge zur Geschichte des Niederrheins, 42. Düsseldorf: Ed. Lintz, 1940.

As a document of the vagaries of FMB reception history in Germany ca. 1940, an outstanding document; as a chronicle of FMB's numerous important contributions to that festival, more bizarre than accurate. Omits, seemingly systematically, most references to FMB by name while referring clearly and accurately to the works he programmed and/or conducted.

105. Bailbé, Joseph-Marc. "Mendelssohn à Paris en 1831–32." In *Music in Paris in the Eighteen-Thirtees: Conference Smith College,* 1982, ed. Peter A. Bloom, 23–39. Stuyvesant, N.Y.: Pendragon, 1987.

FMB's third Parisian sojourn has been poorly represented in most of the biographical literature: it was not only the sojourn in which his feelings about Parisian musical life and musical style were solidified, but also the locus of some important compositional work (e.g., the writing of the overture to *Die erste Walpurgisnacht* and the "Intermezzo" that replaced the Minuet originally composed for the A-major String Quintet). This article offers a tidy overview of these activities.

106. Biba, Otto. "Mendelssohn in Wien." *Musikblätter der Wiener Philharmonike*r 35 (1981): 232–34.

A study of reception history: in a city virtually synonymous with the musical styles of Mozart, Haydn, and Beethoven, how does FMB (who is often explicitly associated with "the" Classical style) fare?

107. Bischoff, Bodo. *Monument für Beethoven: Die Entwicklung der Beethoven-Rezeption Robert Schumanns.* Cologne-Rheinkassel: Dohr, 1994. 564 p. ISBN 3925366261. ML410.S4 B57 1994.

Adapted from the author's dissertation (Freie Universität Berlin, [1992]). FMB on p. 171–84, in section titled "Zur Beethoven-Pflege in Schumanns Freundeskreis: Mendelssohn." Relates to the *Variations sérieuses*, Op. 54.

108. Bledsoe, Robert Terrell. *Henry Fothergill Chorley: Victorian Journalist.* Aldershot: Ashgate, 1998. 365 p. ISBN 184014257X. ML423.C55 B54 1998.

"Elizabeth Barrett and Mendelssohn" on p. 73–117. The respected composer/critic Chorley was one of Mendelssohn's most influential advocates in England during the critical period that witnessed the institutionalization of the English Mendelssohn cult. Study draws upon letters from FMB to Chorley and reminiscences provided in the latter's memoirs (nos. 244 and 245) to chronicle their relationship and its aesthetic foundations.

109. Blumner, Martin. *Geschichte der Sing-Akademie zu Berlin.* Berlin: Horn und Raasch, 1891. 256 p.

FMB on p. 71–79. An important survey of the history of the institution that dealt FMB his single most embarrassing professional defeat. States that FMB's version of Bach's *St. Matthew Passion* was still in use at the time (i.e., the early 1890s), and includes a list of FMB works performed in 1827–29. Discusses the choice of a successor to Zelter as director of the Sing-Akademie and Mendelssohn's unsuccessful candidacy for the post. Blumner's take on the Sing-Akademie affair differs somewhat from the standard (but now questioned) account by Eduard Devrient: whereas Devrient attributes the defeat largely to the composer's Jewishness, Blumner suggests that the election of Carl Friedrich Rungenhagen was simply an act of "Respect for age [and] gratitude for loyal, well-intentioned work." [DM/JMC]

110. Blozan, Claudio. "'Il paese celestiale': Sul soggiorno veneziano e sul viaggio in Italia di Mendelssohn." *Rassegna veneta di studi musicali* 2–3 (1986–87): 207–16.

The most thorough study yet of FMB's time in Italy. See also Norbert Miller's essay on the subject (no. 312).

111. Bowles, Edmund A. "Mendelssohn, Schumann, and Ernst Pfundt: A Pivotal Relationship Between Two Composers and a Timpanist." *Journal of the*

American Instrument Society 24 (1998): 5–26.

The Leipzig timpanist Ernst Pfundt (1806–71), praised by Mendelssohn, Schumann, Berlioz, and other contemporary greats, is credited with having been the agent of change that led to the frequent use of three rapid-tuning "machine" timpani in German orchestras after ca. 1836.

112. Brodbeck, David L. "A Winter of Discontent: Mendelssohn and the *Berliner Domchor.*" In *Mendelssohn Studies*, ed. R. Larry Todd, 1–32. Cambridge: Cambridge University Press, 1992.

A thoughtful and carefully documented study of one of most problematical areas of FMB's life and works: his appointment in 1842 as *Generalmusikdirektor* to the court of the new King Friedrich Wilhelm IV— an appointment that revolved not least of all around the reform of music in the German Protestant churches. Examines a number of unpublished and otherwise obscure primary sources and other archival documents. See also the studies by Wolfgang Dinglinger (nos. 115 and 744).

113. Cherington, Michael, Richard Smith, and Peter J. Nielson. "The Life, Legacy and Premature Death of Felix Mendelssohn." *Seminars in Neurology* 19 (1999): 47.

This essay examines the probable causes of FMB's death.

114. David, Ernest. *Les Mendelssohn-Bartholdy, et Robert Schumann.* Paris: Calmann Lévy, 1886. 359 p. ML410.M5 D18.

Written in an age of fervent Mendelssohnism in a France deeply riven over the case of Mendelssohn's nemesis Wagner, this book is an important document of reception history. Draws liberally on the French translation of Sebastian Hensel's family memoir (no. 352).

115. Dinglinger, Wolfgang. "Mendelssohn: General-Musik-Direktor für kirchliche und geistliche Musik." In *Felix Mendelssohn Bartholdy: Kongreß-Bericht Berlin 1994*, ed. Christian Martin Schmidt, 23–37. Wiesbaden: Breitkopf & Härtel, 1997.

An important complement to David L. Brodbeck's similar study (no. 112). Proceeds from the paradoxical observation that while the greater share of biographical significance in FMB's return to Berlin in the early 1840s resided in his activities on behalf of liturgical music, the works that have claimed the greatest musical significance are the dramatic ones (e.g., the incidental music to *Antigone* and *A Midsummer Night's Dream*). Draws extensively on unpublished archival documents.

116. Dörffel, Alfred. *Geschichte der Gewandhausconcerte zu Leipzig vom 25. November 1781 bis 25. November 1881.* Leipzig: Im Auftrag der Concert-Direction, 1884. Rpt. Leipzig: Deutscher Verlag für Musik, 1980.

FMB in "Die Concerte unter Felix Mendelssohn-Bartholdy, Ferdinand Hiller, Niels W. Gade 1835–1848"(p. 83–137). Like Foster's *History of the Philharmonic Society of London* (no. 130), an invaluable documentary resource. Includes descriptions of individual programs and season overviews, as well as transcriptions of documents, programs, and reviews. Part II (not reproduced in all available exemplars) is a "Chronik" that gives a program-by-program overview.

117. Droysen, G[ustav]. "Johann Gustav Droysen und Felix Mendelssohn-Bartholdy." *Deutsche Rundschau* 111 (1902): 107–26, 193–215, 386–408.

Essay chronicles the relationship between the poet and the composer, with extensive quotations from family documents. The author figured already in Sebastian Hensel's family history (no. 352), but the extent and nature of artistic productivity involved in the friendship become fully evident here. He provides important (and seemingly accurate) information to supplement, correct, and complement the memoirs of Marx (no. 257) and Devrient (no. 248), as well as corroboration for some points in Hiller's recollections (no. 297). In addition to providing the texts for many of FMB's Lieder (e.g., "Frage," Op. 9, no. 2 and "Ferne," Op. 9 no. 9), Droysen also collaborated with FMB on the incidental music for *Antigone*.

118. Elvers, Rudolf. "Eine Schwede besucht die Mendelssohns: Aus den Reisebriefen des Hendrik Munktell 1829/30." In *Neue Musik und Tradition: Festschrift Rudolf Stephan zum 65. Geburtstag*, ed. Josef Kuckertz, Helga de la Motte-Haber, Christian Martin Schmidt, and Wilhelm Seidel, 233–37. Laaber: Laaber, 1990.

German translation of excerpts from a Swedish letter describing life in the Berlin Mendelssohn household ca. 1830. A valuable and vivid portrayal of the family at a critical point in its history.

119. Elvers, Rudolf. "Über das 'Berlinsche Zwitterwesen': Felix Mendelssohn Bartholdy in Briefen Über Berlin." In *Die Mendelssohns in Berlin: Eine Familie und ihre Stadt*, ed. Rudolf Elvers and Hans-Günter Klein, 31–42. Berlin: Staatsbibliothek Preußischer Kulturbesitz, 1983.

Though it was the residence of many friends and family, Berlin consistently elicited an emotional response from the composer that was at best ambivalent, at worst hostile. This essay culls passages from Mendelssohn's personal correspondence that document his enduring ambivalence toward the Prussian capital, dispelling the widely held assumption that the composer's negative feelings stemmed largely from his unsuccessful bid for the directorship of the Singakademie after the Zelter's death in 1832. See also Wm. A. Little's related essay, on the subject (no. 172).

120. Esser, Joseph. "Felix Mendelssohn Bartholdy und die Rheinlande." Ph.D. diss., Universität Bonn, 1923. 106 p.

   Perhaps the most thorough and extensive summary of FMB's relationship to Düsseldorf, Cologne, and other parts of the Rhineland. Draws upon a variety of published sources (including early nineteenth-century newspaper clippings) and some archival documents, and includes the only examination in print of FMB's first incidental music (for Karl Immermann's adaptation of Caldéron de la Barca's *The Steadfast Prince*), composed and performed in the spring of 1833.

121. Feuchte, Andreas. "Felix Mendelssohn Bartholdy als Lehrer und Freund von Eduard Franck." *Mendelssohn-Studien* 10 (1997): 57–76.

   Eduard Franck, whose older brother Hermann was a friend and pupil of FMB from ca. 1830 and was a reasonably well-known and respected composer in nineteenth-century Germany, studied with FMB after mid-1833. This essay chronicles the early stages of the professional relationship between FMB and the younger Franck. Derived from the author's dissertation (no. 122). Draws extensively on unpublished documents and letters of FMB and others.

122. Feuchte, Paul, and Andreas Feuchte. *Die Komponisten Eduard Franck und Richard Franck: Leben und Werk, Dokumente, Quellen.* Stuttgart: n.p., 1993. 310 p. ML390 .F42 1993.

   An important examination of Mendelssohn's pedagogical, personal, and professional relationship with and influences on two of his students. Extensive recourse to unpublished primary sources.

123. Fischer, Wilhelm Hubert. "Felix Mendelssohn-Bartholdy, sein Leben und Wirken in Düsseldorf." In *idem, 95. Niederrheinischen Musikfest, Düsseldorf 1926: Festschrift mit Angaben der Konzerte des Städt. Musikvereines und seiner Geschichte [. . .] nebst einer Schilderung der Düsseldorfer Musikfeste 1833 und 1836 unter Leitung von Felix Mendelssohn-Bartholdy, sein Leben und Schaffen in Düsseldorf.* Düsseldorf: F. Dietz, 1926.

   Though dated in some specific information, this remains a valuable resource for persons interested in FMB's activities in the Rhineland (see also Fischer's other study, below, as well as Joseph Esser's 1923 dissertation on the subject [no. 120]. Includes reproductions and transcriptions of little-known archival documents, including some FMB correspondence held in the Stadtarchiv Düsseldorf. Traces the composer's relationship with Düsseldorf from its commencement in the early 1830s to the end of his life.

124. Fischer, Wilhelm Hubert. "Der Musikverein unter Leitung von Felix Mendelssohn Bartholdy von 1833 bis 1835." In *Festschrift zur hundertjährigen Jubelfeier des Städtischen Musikvereins Düsseldorf und zum hundertjährigen Bestehen der Niederrheinischen Musikfeste [. . .].* Düsseldorf: F. Dietz, 1918.

The most important and detailed published chronicle of FMB's first independent professional engagement (as Municipal Music Director in Düsseldorf from 1833–1835).[9] Draws on archival as well as published sources to trace FMB's association with Düsseldorf, and presents transcriptions and facsimiles of little-known documents. Includes a Rhinelander's appreciation of FMB.

125. Fiske, Roger. *Scotland in Music: A European Enthusiasm*. Cambridge: Cambridge University Press, 1983. 234 p. ISBN 0521247721. ML3655 .F56 1983.

An indispensable starting point for those interested in FMB's role in the nineteenth-century obsession with Scotland and things Scottish. FMB and Chopin are treated separately in the chapter titled "Scotland as a Reality" (p. 116–55). Discussion of FMB focuses on biographical connections, but there are references to the "Sonate Écossaise" (Op. 28), the *Hebrides* Overture, the "Scottish" Symphony, and *Heimkehr aus der Fremde* as well. Includes facsimiles of several drawings made by FMB while in Scotland. See also Goldhan (no. 137) and Jenkins (no. 148) and Todd (no. 636).

126. Flaschar, Hellmut. "August Böckh und Felix Mendelssohn Bartholdy." In *Disiecta membra: Studien, Karlfried Gründer zum 60. Geburtstag*, ed. W. Schmidt-Biggemann, 66–81. Basel: Schwabe, 1989. Rpt. in Hellmut Flaschar, *Eidola: Ausgewählte kleine Schriften*, ed. Manfred Kraus, 581–96. Berlin: Akademie-Verlag, 1989.

127. Forchert, Arno. "Adolf Bernhard Marx und seine 'Berliner Allgemeine musikalische Zeitung.'" In *Studien zur Musikgeschichte Berlins im frühen 19. Jahrhundert*, ed. Carl Dahlhaus, 381–404. Studien zur Musikgeschichte des 19. Jahrhunderts, Bd. 56. Regensburg: Gustav Bosse, 1980.

The author discusses the ways in which Marx's critical and aesthetic agenda was influenced by Hegel's concept of the "idea" of an artwork, and the ways in which this understanding shaped Marx's responses to various composers, including Beethoven and FMB.

128. Forner, Johannes, ed. *Die Gewandhauskonzerte zu Leipzig 1781–1981: Mit einem zusammenfassenden Rückblick von den Anfängen bis 1781*. Leipzig: Deutscher Verlag für Musik, 1981. 560 p.

    An expanded and richly illustrated version of Dörffel's history of the Gewandhaus concerts (no. 116). Includes floor plans, a survey of Mendelssohn's accomplishments and programs, and a section on the founding of the conservatory. There are also details about the destruction of the Mendelssohn monument by the Nazis. [DM]

129. Forner, Johannes. "Mendelssohns Mitstreiter am Leipziger Konservatorium." *Beiträge zur Musikwissenschaft* 14 (1972): 185–204. Rpt. in *Felix Mendelssohn Bartholdy*, ed. Gerhard Schuhmacher, 64–99. Wege der Forschung, Bd. 494. Darmstadt: Wissenschaftliche Buchgesellschaft, 1982.

    As founder and director of the Leipzig Conservatory for Music (today the Leipzig Hochschule für Musik), FMB exerted considerable influence on the pedagogy of applied music, music history, and music theory in the mid- and later nineteenth century. This important article examines his relationship with six of the professional colleagues who helped to establish the Conservatory as a leading institution of music: Moritz Hauptmann, Robert Schumann, Ignaz Moscheles, Niels W. Gade, Julius Rietz, and Ferdinand David. Includes overviews of the student body and the programs of the concerts and recitals. See also Newman (no. 184) and Phillips (no. 187).

130. Foster, Myles Birket. *History of the Philharmonic Society of London, 1813–1912: A Record of a Hundred Years' Work in the Cause of Music*. London: John Lane, 1913. 610 p. ML286.8.L52 P54.

    Like Dörffel's study of the Gewandhaus (no. 116), this is an invaluable documentary resource concerning an orchestra that played a central role in Mendelssohn's professional prestige from 1829 on. The chapters include a description of the highlights of each season, followed by the programs of the individual concerts. The index includes not only individual works and composers, but also inventories of how often they were represented over given periods of time.

131. Franken, Franz Hermann. *Das Leben großer Meister im Spiegel der Medizin: Schubert, Chopin, Mendelssohn.* Stuttgart: Enke, 1959. 99 p. ML390 .F83.

     This is the predecessor to his *Krankheiten und Tod* (no. 132).

132. Franken, Franz Herman. *Krankheit und Tod großer Komponisten.* Baden-Baden: Sitzstrock, 1979. 280 p. ISBN 387921123X. ML390 .F82.

     Mendelssohn discussed on p. 159–179. Subarachnoid hemorrhage from the basal artery is the diagnosis. The judgment was corroborated by Dr. E. Bedord in Franken's earlier book (no. 131) (Bedford is quoted in Bennett's article, R. Sterndale, [no. 218]). It is also possible that Mendelssohn had high blood pressure and possibily a brain tumor and that he may have suffered an unreported head trauma in the accident that caused his well-known knee injury (London, 1829). [DM/JMC]

133. Franken, Franz Hermann. *Die Krankheiten großer Komponisten, Band I: Joseph Haydn, Ludwig van Beethoven, Vincenzo Bellini, Felix Mendelssohn Bartholdy, Frederic Chopin, Robert Schumann.* Taschenbucher zur Musikwissenschaft no. 104. Wilhelmshaven: Heinrichshofen, 1986. ML390 .F825 1986. 2nd ed., revised,1991. 303 p. ISBN 3795904196. Trans. by Karel B. Absolon as *Diseases of Famous Composers: Twenty-two Pathographies from Bach to Bartók.* Rockville, Maryland: Kabel, 1996. 361 p. ISBN 1575290103

     An examination of the probable causes of FMB's demise. The book is an expanded revision of no. 132, but the overall discussion of FMB is similar.

134. Galley, Ursula. "Bilder aus Düsseldorfs musikalischer Vergangenheit." *Niederrheinisches Musikfest, Düsseldorf* 110 (1956): 33–40.

     A simple but essentially accurate account of FMB's stay in Düsseldorf, focusing on his relationship with Immermann.

135. Gates, Eugene. "Felix Mendelssohn: Virtuoso Organist." *Journal of the American Liszt Society* 37 (1995): 13–25.

     A survey of FMB's activities as an organist and the ways in which the Bach tradition influenced his performances and programming. Emphasis is on FMB's performances of others' works rather than the difficulty of FMB's own organ compositions.

136. Ghislanzoni, Antonio. "I rapporti fra Spontini e Mendelssohn." *In*

Congresso Internationale di Studi Spontiniani 1951: Atti, 94–103. Fabriano: Arti grafiche "Gentile," 1954. 142 p.

FMB biographers have made much of the intrigues Spontini instigated against the public reception of the last of FMB's early opera, *Die Hochzeit des Camacho*, Op. 10, and one can easily envision how the politics of Berlin musical life might have made the Italian Berliner uneasy at the thought of an FMB success. This is an examination that is more sympathetic to Spontini, based largely on Devrient (no. 248).

137. Goldhan, Wolfgang, and Peter Kaubisch. *Schottische Skizzen: Eine Reise nach Aufzeichnungen von Felix Mendelssohn Bartholdy*. Berlin: edition q, 1992. 100 p. ISBN 3928024949.

This book contains valuable reproductions of the sketches and drawings FMB made during his tour of Scotland in 1829. See also Fiske (no. 125) and Jenkins (no. 148).

138. Gresham, Carolyn Denton. "Ignaz Moscheles: An Illustrious Musician in the Nineteenth Century." Ph.D. diss., University of Rochester, 1980. 378 p.

FMB esp. on p. 118–23.

139. Gülke, Peter. "Mendelssohn und Leipzig: Vielleicht vor allem eine Frage der Musik." In *Felix Mendelssohn Bartholdy: Repräsentant oder Außenseiter? Fünf Vorträge zu den "Kasseler Musiktagen 1991,"* ed. Leo Karl Gerhartz, 55–63. Kassel: Kasseler Musiktage, 1993.

Gülke explores the importance of public life in Leipzig for FMB's sense of professional and personal identity.

140. Häfner, Klaus. "Felix Mendelssohn Bartholdy in seinen Beziehungen zu König Friedrich August II. Von Sachsen: Ein Beitrag zur Biographie Mendelssohns." *Mendelssohn-Studien* 7 (1990): 219–68.

This essay supplements the frequent biographical looks at FMB's ties to monarchs Friedrich Wilhelm III and IV of Prussia with a look at his "own" king (i.e., the king of Saxony, where Mendelssohn was employed for the last thirteen years of his life).

141. Harwell, Anna H. "'Unsre Kunst heisst Poesie': Niels W. Gade's Early Compositions and Their Programmatic Origins." Ph.D. diss., Duke University, 1996. 478 p.

The Danish composer Gade (1817–1890) studied with FMB at the Leipzig Conservatory from 1843 and stood in for him as conductor of the

Gewandhaus Orchestra in 1844, before becoming second director of the ensemble. Dissertation draws upon otherwise unpublished correspondence to examine the personal and musical relationships between the two composers. See also Spitta (no. 217).

142. Hellmundt, Christoph. "Anton Christanell und seine Beziehungen zu Felix Mendelssohn Bartholdy." *Mendelssohn-Studien* 11 (1999): 77–102.

Christanell (1801–82) was a well-to-do amateur musician who lived in Schwyz (in the Tyrol, near Innsbruck, Austria), and for whom FMB composed a *Festgesang* that was discovered and published only in 1997 (see Appendix B). Article describes the relationship between the composer and the commissioner, drawing on archival materials and otherwise unpublished correspondence. See also Hellmundt's essay on the *Festgesang "Möge das Siegeszeichen"* (no. 619).

143. Henneberg, Fritz. "Mendelssohn in Leipzig." In *Felix Mendelssohn Bartholdy: Leben und Werk—Musikfestspiele Saar 1989*, ed. Robert Leonardy, 49–71. Lebach: Joachim Hempel, 1989.

A straightforward and largely traditional overview of FMB's activities in Leipzig and the significance of his contribution to the city's musical life. Begins with a pre-history of the Leipzig appointment (from 1833, when FMB competed to succeed Zelter for the directorship of the Berlin Singakademie); then includes substantial sections devoted to the Gewandhaus Orchestra, Leipzig Conservatory, and the programming of the Leipzig concerts.

144. Hermann, Marcelle. "J.-J. B. Laurens' Beziehungen zu deutschen Musikern." *Schweizerische Musikzeitung* 105 (1965): 257–66.

The article contains a little-known letter from FMB to Laurens (a friend and colleague who was a composer as well as a painter and writer).

145. Hexelschneider, Erhard. "Wilhelm Küchelbecker: Ein frühes ausländisches Urteil über Felix Mendelssohn Bartholdy." *Mendelssohn-Studien* 8 (1993): 131–40.

A discussion and reproduction of an 1820 diary entry by Wilhelm Karowitsch Küchelbecker, a Russian poet who encountered the young FMB in Berlin.

146. Holtzmann, Sigrid, ed. *Carl Friedrich Zelter im Spiegel seines Briefwechsels mit Goethe*. Weimar: Kiepenheuer, 1957. 285 p. ML390 .F83

An overview and analysis of Zelter's and Goethe's views of the young FMB, including the troubling implicit Semitic stereotypes in some of the letters.

147. Hueffer, Francis. *Half a Century of Music in England, 1837–87.* London: Chapman and Hall, 1889. 240 p. ML286.4 .H8. Rpt. Boston: Longwood, 1977. ISBN 089341025X. ML286.4 .H8 1977.

The first chapter ("Introduction: General Music during the Queen's Reign in England") leads to the main essays about Wagner, Liszt, and Berlioz in England. It looks back on the "limited efforts of our grandfathers"—meaning the events of the first quarter of the century—and is interesting mainly because of its patronizing tone. There is, however, good material about Mendelssohn and Victoria and Albert. [DM/JMC]

148. Jenkins, David, and M. Visocchi. *Mendelssohn in Scotland.* London: Chappell, 1978. 116 p. ISBN 090344318X. ML410.M5 J5.

A coffee-table book, but well illustrated and generally reliable. For a more scholarly approach to the same subject, see the books by Fiske (no. 125) and Goldhan (no. 137).

149. Jullien, Adolphe. "Mendelssohn à Paris." In *Airs variés: Histoire, critique, biographies musicales*, 65–156. Paris: G. Charpentier, 1877. ML60 .J85.

An overview of FMB's activities and relationships during his Parisian sojourns, including discussions of his relationships with Cherubini and Heine. Most of the material is digested from the *Reisebriefe* (nos. 309 and 310) and Hensel's family memoir (no. 352), but a focused study is convenient.

150. Keller, Hans. "The Classical Romantics: Mendelssohn and Schumann." In *Of German Music: A Symposium*, ed. Hans-Hubert Schönzeler, 179–218. London: Oswald Wolff, 1976. ISBN 0854964010.

As the title indicates, a study unquestioningly founded on the view that the composers who lived and worked after 1850 were the "true" Romantics, while FMB and Schumann represented an earlier, more classical approach to Romanticism (in which FMB, of course, was the more classical and therefore less historically advanced).

151. Kemp, Friedhelm. "Mendelssohns Berliner Umwelt." In *Das Problem Mendelssohn*, ed. Carl Dahlhaus, 11–21. Regensburg: Gustav Bosse, 1974.

An important, if now somewhat dated, study of the personages and institutions with which FMB lived during his stays in Berlin.

152. Kerner, Dieter. *Krankheiten grosser Musiker.* 2 vols. Stuttgart: F. K. Schattauer, 1963. 2nd ed., 1967. ML390 .K37. 3rd ed., rev., 1973. ISBN 3794503597.

   FMB in vol. 2. The book includes extended citations from letters spanning the composer's life. Concludes that the cause(s) of his death "can hardly be satisfactorily explained" (p. 45 of the 1st and 2nd eds.).

153. Kestner-Boche, Ruth. "Zum Profil der Streicherausbildung an der Leipziger Musikhochschule seit 1843 unter besonderer Berücksichtigung der Kinngeiger." In *Festschrift 150 Jahre Musikhochschule 1843–1993*, ed. Johannes Forner, 190–228. Leipzig: Kunst und Touristik, 1993.

154. Kirchmeyer, Helmut. "Richard Wagner und Felix Mendelsson-Bartholdy." *Bayreuther Festspiele 1981, Programmheft 3: "Der fliegende Holländer,"* 26–33, 56–66, 71, 88–92.

   A detailed and careful, but (given its venue) somewhat biased assessment of the Mendelssohn-Wagner relationship.

155. Klein, Hans-Günter. "'Wir erleben einige Freude an diesem jungen Mann': Die Briefe von Abraham Mendelssohn Bartholdy vom Niederrheinischen Musikfest 1833 nach Berlin." *Mendelssohn-Studien* 11 (1999): 49–76.

   An important study providing new evidence concerning FMB's impact at the Lower Rhine Music Festival in 1833—the event that secured his first professional appointment and enhanced his prominence as a conductor, interpreter of Handel, and performer around the German-speaking world. Includes generously annotated critical transcriptions of six letters from Abraham to the family, reporting on the events surrounding the festival and FMB's role in them.

156. Kneschke, Emil. *Das Conservatorium der Musik in Leipzig: Seine Geschichte, seine Lehrer und Züglinge. Festgabe zum 25jährigen Jubileum am 2. April 1868.* Leipzig: Breitkopf & Härtel, 1868. 70 p. MT5.L5 L257.

   This book contains Mendelssohn's famous letter of 8 April 1840 stating his reasons for suggesting the establishment of the conservatory, the most important being to deepen artist's interest in their art. Details about the founders and the first faculty of six; extensive quotations from the first prospectus and details about the early curriculum. Contains a list of all students up to 1868 including a breakdown of their geographical origins. (There were 68 males and 17 females from "North America" and one male and one female from "South America and California.") [DM]

157. Kneschke, Emil. *Zur Geschichte des Theaters und der Musik in Leipzig.*
Leipzig: Fr. Fleisher, 1864. 330 p. ML280.8.L3 K63.

158. Kneschke, Emil. *Die Hundertfünfzigjhrige Geschichte der Leipziger
Gewandhausconzerte, 1743–1893.* Leipzig: Internationale Verlags- und
Kunstanstalt, [1893]. 160 p. ML280.8.L3 K6.

This study includes a review of Mendelssohn's seasons with the
orchestra with an emphasis on his programs.

159. Kneschke, Emil. *Das Königliche Conservatorium der Musik zu Leipzig
1843–1893.* Leipzig: Internationale Verlags- und Kunstanstalt, [1893]. 86
p. MT5.L5 L259.

The author quotes the letters about the founding of the conservatory
contained in the 1918 Festschrift and gives further details about the founding. Contains a useful review of the older literature about the institution,
much of it quite rare. There is a survey of the history of the conservatory
to date, useful not only in itself, but also because of the inferences about
artistic and intellectual orientation that can be drawn from its straightforward prose. Yet another source of Mendelssohn's letter of 8 April 1840
advocating the founding of the conservatory.

160. Kobbé, Gustav. *The Loves of Great Composers.* New York: Crowell, 1905.
175 p.

"Mendelssohn and His Cécile" on p. 47–70. Conventional account of
FMB's relationship with Cécile,[10] evidently derived mostly from Eduard
Devrient's late and problematical FMB memoir (no. 248); what little is
substantiated is conjecture based on the numerous late-Victorian effusions
about FMB's exemplary character combined with anti-Mendelssohnian
complaints about his ostensible lack of passion.

161. Köhler, Karl-Heinz. *Der unbekannte junge Mendelssohn.* Basel:
Internationale Mendelssohn-Gesellschaft, 1960. 25 p. ML410.M5 K65.

Though dated in some particulars, this is one of the most substantial
explorations of FMB's early life and works.[10] Observes that while FMB
evidently began composing at an appreciably later age than the child prodigy Mozart, his growth as a composer was much more rapid. Chronicles the
persons, compositions, and activities that made up the world in which this
prodigious development occurred.

162. Konold, Wulf. "Mendelssohn und London: Nicht zuletzt eine Frage der
Identität." In *Felix Mendelssohn Bartholdy: Repräsentant und/oder
Außenseiter? Fünf Vorträge zu den "Kasseler Musiktagen 1991,"* ed. Leo

Karl Gerhartz, 11–18. Kassel: Kasseler Musiktage, 1993.

Konold provides thoughtful observations about the significance of the difference between public and private life for FMB, proceeding from Schumann's characterization of FMB as "the person who was able to resolve the contradictions of [their time]." Ironically (given the title), the essay devotes little discussion specifically to London or to FMB's workings there.

163. Kopitz, Klaus. *Der Düsseldorfer Komponist Norbert Burgmüller: Ein Leben zwischen Beethoven, Spohr, Mendelssohn.* Kleve: B.o.s.s., 1998. 384 p. ISBN 3980593169. ML410.B956 K83 1998.

Burgmüller, a promising composer who died prematurely in 1836, was an acquaintance of Mendelssohn from 1833; he won the praises of Robert Schumann, among many other contemporary critics. Kopitz chronicles the relationship between Mendelssohn and Burgmüller and correlates the two composers' works chronologically and generically.

164. Krauskopf, Gunther. "Felix Mendelssohn Bartholdy 1844 und 1845 in Bad Soden." *Hessische Heimat* [Marburg] 40 (1990): 60–65.

This book contains remarks on FMB's trips to Bad Soden (near Frankfurt am Main, where his in-laws lived). Includes facsimiles of several of the composer's characteristically elegant drawings of the area.

165. Krauskopf, Gunther. "'Mit Notenpapier und Zeichenbuch': Felix Mendelssohn-Bartholdy 1844 u. 1845 in Bad Soden." *Soden (Taunus): Jahreschronik (1984)*: 63–70.

Krauskopf includes facsimiles of ten FMB drawings of Bad Soden and Neuhain (both located near Frankfurt am Main).

166. Krellmann, Hanspeter. "Felix Mendelssohns Wirken im Rheinland." *Musica* 30 (1977): 511–15.

A brief but thorough and (on the basis of the documents then available) accurate survey of FMB's contributions to the musical life of Düsseldorf, Cologne, and Aachen from 1833 onward.

167. Krellmann, Hanspeter. "Junges Genie am Rhein: Felix Mendelssohn Bartholdys Düsseldorfer Jahre." *Düsseldorfer Hefte* 17 (1972): 5–7, 10–12, 14–16.

A less scholarly, but still surprisingly substantive, version of no. 166. Examines FMB's relationship with the city from his earliest contacts with its artists through the end of his stay there in 1835. Suggests that Düsseldorf essentially missed its opportunity to gain fame through FMB because it was incapable of being decisive at the right moment.

168. Kretschman, L. von. "Felix Mendelssohn-Bartholdy in Weimar: Aus dem Nachlass der Baronin Jenny von Gustedt, geb. Von Pappenheim." *Deutsche Rundschau* 69 (1891): 304.

169. Kruse, Joseph A. "Mendelssohn und Düsseldorf: Nebenbei eine Frage der Literatur." In *Felix Mendelssohn Bartholdy: Repräsentant und/oder Außenseiter? Fünf Vorträge zu den "Kasseler Musiktagen 1991,"* ed. Leo Karl Gerhartz, 41–54. Kassel: Kasseler Musiktage, 1993.

Kruse proceeds from the observation that because of Düsseldorf's cultural history and its position in FMB's biography, FMB's experience there can serve as a lens through which to view his ideas on literature, artistic creativity, and the role of the artist in public life. Useful insights concerning his relationships with Immermann, Heine, and (to a lesser extent) Goethe in life and in reception history.

170. Lester, Joel. "Substance and Illusion in Schumann's 'Erinnerung,' Op. 68: A Structural Analysis and Pictorial (*Geistliche*) Description." *In Theory Only* 4 (1978): 9–17.

A Schenkerian and quasi-hermeneutic analysis of an important piece from Schumann's *Album für die Jugend*. Suggests that the structure of the piece reflects the date of FMB's death.

171. Little, Wm. A. "Mendelssohn and Liszt." In *Mendelssohn Studies*, ed. R. Larry Todd, 106–25. Cambridge: Cambridge University Press, 1992.

A complicated amicability characterized this not-quite-friendship, which has largely eluded scholarly investigation because of the politics of Liszt's writings on FMB after the latter's death (see no. 386) and the difficulty of access to primary sources for Liszt. Draws upon numerous unpublished letters and carefully examines the correspondence and several biographical/artistic episodes.

172. Little, Wm. A. "Mendelssohn and the Berlin *Singakademie*." In *Mendelssohn and His World*, ed. R. Larry Todd, 65–85. Princeton: Princeton University Press, 1991.

The author proposes that the conventional wisdom (first reported in Devrient's memoirs [no. 248] and repeated in countless subsequent sources, including Werner's biography [nos. 96 and 97]) concerning

FMB's failed candidacy for the directorship of the *Singakademie* is misguided. Instead, FMB seems to have approached the candidacy halfheartedly, with the realization that it was doomed—not because of his Jewishness, but because of his youth and his principal opponent's established position and respect.

173. Locke, Ralph P. "Mendelssohn's Collision with the Saint-Simonians." In *Mendelssohn and Schumann: Essays on Their Music and Its Context*, ed. Jon W. Finson and R. Larry Todd, 109–22. Durham: Duke University Press, 1984.

Adapted from the author's dissertation/book (no. 174).

174. Locke, Ralph P. *Music, Musicians, and the Saint-Simonians*. Chicago: University of Chicago, 1986. 399 p. ISBN 0226489019. ML410.B956 K83 1998. Trans. French Malou Haine and Philippe Haine as *Les Saint-Simoniens et la musique*. [Liège]: Mardaga, 1992. 493 p.

An adaptation of the author's Ph.D. dissertation ("Music and the Saint-Simonians: The Involvement of Félicien David and Other Musicians in an Utopian Socialist Movement," 2 vols. [University of Chicago, 1980]). FMB on p. 107–14 of the University of Chicago book.

175. Lowenthal-Hensel, Cécile. "Der vergessene Felix: Nachtrag zu einem Beitrag." *Mendelsson-Studien* 11 (1999): 103–04.

This article corrects the author's assertion in an earlier issue of the journal that a certain portrait of FMB could not be found.

176. Maegaard, Kirsten. "Hans Christian Andersen's travel album." *Fontes artis musicae* 42 (1995): 82–84.

A brief article that includes an interesting document of FMB's acquaintance with the Danish writer: a two-part canon in C minor dated 11 November 1840.

177. Mariotti, Giovanni. *L'Italia di Felix Mendelssohn-Bartholdy*. N. p. : Consalvo, 1934. 210 p.

Not available for examination. See also the author's general FMB biography (no. 60).

178. Matthews, B. "Mendelssohn and the Crosby Hall Organ." *The Musical Times* 114 (1973): 641–43.

Matthews discusses the organ used for the first performance of *Hear

My Prayer and provides the specifications of the organ used.

179. Mendelssohn-Bartholdy, Karl. *Goethe und Felix Mendelssohn-Bartholdy.* Leipzig: S. Hirzel, 1871. 51 p. Trans. English M. E. von Glehn as *Goethe and Mendelssohn, 1821–1831.* London: Macmillan,1872. 2nd ed., with additional letters, 1874. 198 p. Rpt. New York: Haskell House, 1970. ISBN 083830902X. ML410.M5 M53 1970.

The "Vorwort" provides an important clue as to the perspective of the book's author (the younger son of FMB): it is a written version of a presentation commissioned by the "Gesellschaft für Geschichtskunde" of Freiburg on the eve of German unification. Consequently FMB and his cultural godfather are presented as persons who collectively shaped and articulated a German cultural identity in an age well before any such political identity existed. Chronicles the relationship in edited letters and reveals the artists' views on several issues that had become quite significant for Germany at the turn of the 1870s (most importantly, Schiller and his politics).

180. Middell, Elke. "Der 'schöne Zwischenfall' oder 'Wie ein Walzer zur Predigt': Das Problem Mendelssohn aus literaturhistorischer Sicht." In *Felix Mendelssohn—Mitwelt und Nachwelt: Bericht zum 1. Leipziger Mendelssohn-Kolloquium am 8. und 9. Juni 1993*, 117–22. Wiesbaden: Breitkopf & Härtel, 1996.

The author views the contradictions and complexities of the "Mendelssohn Problem" through the eyes of literary writers' reflections on FMB. See also Kruse (no. 169).

181. Mintz, Donald. "Mendelssohn as Performer and Teacher." In *The Mendelssohn Companion*, ed. Douglass Seaton. Westport, Conn. Greenwood. [Forthcoming]

182. Müller, Carl Heinrich. *Felix Mendelssohn, Frankfurt am Main und der Cäcilien-Verein.* Darmstadt: Volk und Scholle, 1925. 17 p.

Despite its modest length, an impressive biographical achievement. FMB's association with the Frankfurt Cäcilien-Verein and its director, Johann Nepomuk Schelble, dates from 1822. The association resulted in some important works (including the original invitation to write the oratorio that became *St. Paul*).

183. Musch, Hans. "Felix Mendelssohn Bartholdy in Freiburg und im Schwarzwald: Aus dem Tagebuch der Hochzeitsreise." In *Musik am Oberrhein*, ed. Hans Musch, 181–213. Hochschuldokumentation zu

Musikwissenschaft und Musikpädagogik, Musikhochschule Freiburg, no. 3. Regensburg: Gustav Bosse, 1993.

See also Peter Ward Jones's edition of the Mendelssohns' honeymoon diary (no. 232).

184. Newman, William S. "Three Intimates of Mendelssohn and Schumann in Leipzig: Hauptmann, Moscheles, and David." In *Mendelssohn and Schumann: Essays on Their Music and Its Context*, ed. Jon W. Finson and R. Larry Todd, 87–98. Durham: Duke University Press, 1984.

Newan examines the ways in which FMB and his colleagues in the Leipzig Conservatory constructed their curricula and relates these to the composers' philosophies and musical styles. See also Forner (no. 129) and Phillips (no. 187).

185. Niemöller, Klaus Wolfgang. "Felix Mendelssohn-Bartholdy und das Niederrheinische Musikfest 1835 in Köln." *Studien zur Musikgeschichte des Rheinlandes* 3 (1965): 46–64.

This article examines the program and execution of the 1835 Lower Rhine Music Festival in Cologne—an important event in FMB's biography because it signaled the end of his stay in Düsseldorf and the beginning of his transition to Leipzig.

186. Nowack, Natalie. "Felix Mendelssohn-Bartholdy und seine Bedeutung für das Kulturleben der Stadt Leipzig im 19. Jahrhundert." Ph.D. diss., Lüneberg [in progress].

187. Phillips, Leonard M. "The Leipzig Conservatory: 1843–1881." Ph.D. dissertation, Indiana University, 1979. 373 p.

An examination of the founding, personnel, programs, student rosters, and curriculum of the Leipzig Conservatory to 1881. See also Forner (no. 129) and Newman (no. 185).

188. Plantinga, Leon. "Schumann's Critical Reaction to Mendelssohn." *In Mendelssohn and Schumann: Essays on Their Music and Its Context*, ed. Jon W. Finson and R. Larry Todd, 11–19. Durham: Duke University Press, 1984.

Because of their chronological proximity and their stylistic similarities and differences, as well as Schumann's activities as a published music critic, FMB's and Schumann's critical opinions of each other's works are of obvious interest. Earlier studies (such as those of Brendel [no. 763] and Wasielewski [no. 233]) had already taken on this issue, but considerable damage was done by the publication in 1941 of Wolfgang Boetticher's Schumann biography, which (despite its apparent thoroughness and scholarly rigor) consistently falsified documents in order to present a view of the relationship that was consistent with Nazi ideology. Plantinga's essay, although brief and focused on Schumann's side of the picture, represents a much-needed step towards revision and clarification of the relationship.

189. Plesske, Hans-Martin. "Das Leipziger Musikverlagswesen und seine Beziehungen zu einigen namhaften Komponisten: Ein Beitrag zur Geschichte des Musikalienhandels im 19. und zu Beginn des 20. Jahrhunderts." Diss., University of Leipzig, 1974.

　　　FMB on p. 141–48. Examines the composer's publishing relationships with several Leipzig firms, most notably Breitkopf & Härtel, Hofmeister, and Kistner. Overlooks the 1842 publication of *Lord Have Mercy upon Us* (1833) by Bösenberg, and the information concerning the publication of some works released independently and in musical albums is sometimes confused. Still, a useful and generally accurate overview.

190. Porter, Cecelia Hopkins. "The Reign of the Dilettanti: Düsseldorf from Mendelssohn to Schumann." *The Musical Quarterly* 73 (1989): 476–512.

　　　FMB esp. on p. 482–90. Asserts that music in Düsseldorf "was undergoing several profound transitions reflecting fundamental historical processes . . .: the shift from dilettantism to professionalism and virtuosity; from music within a court establishment to its incorporation as an urban institution; and from music as a somewhat elitist pursuit to a broadened role as a function of *Vokstümlichkeit*." Attributes FMB's growing dissatisfaction with his position there in the years 1833–35 largely to the prominence of dilettantism in cultural life.

191. Reich, Nancy B. "The Correspondence between Clara Weick Schumann and Felix and Paul Mendelssohn." In *Schumann and His World*, ed. R. Larry Todd, 205-32. Princeton: Princeton University Press, 1994.

　　　An important study of FMB's warm artistic collaborations with Clara Schumann. Includes a little-known letter from Paul Mendelssohn Bartholdy (younger brother to the composer) written shortly after FMB's death, as well as programs, reviews, and information regarding the pianos used for the performances.

192. Reininghaus, Frieder. "Mendelssohn und Berlin: Auch eine Frage der Religion." In *Felix Mendelssohn Bartholdy: Repräsentant und/oder Außenseiter? Fünf Vorträge zu den "Kasseler Musiktagen 1991,"* ed. Leo Karl Gerhartz, 19–39. Kassel: Kasseler Musiktage, 1993.

An examination of the role of FMB's Jewish heritage in his difficulties with the *Singakademie* and his reappointments by Friedrich Wilhelm IV to reform the music of the protestant church.

193. Reininghaus, Frieder. "Zwei Emanzipationswege aus Berlin: Anmerkungen zum Verhältnis Meyerbeers und Mendelssohns." In *Giacomo Meyerbeer— Musik als Welterfahrung: Heinz Becker zum 70. Geburtstag*, ed. Sieghart Döhring and Jürgen Schläder, 223–35. Munich: Ricordi, 1995.

The author compares and contrasts the ways in which the two composers dealt with the realities of Jewish assimilation.

194. Reissner, H. G. "Felix Mendelssohn-Bartholdy und Eduard Gans: Gans' Vorlesungen über die Geschichte der französischen Revolution, nach der Niederschrift von Felix Mendelssohn-Bartholdy." *Publications of the Leo Baeck Institute* 4 (1959): 92–110.

One of precious few studies providing substantive insight into FMB's political views, important also as a document of an unfortunately overlooked acquaintance of the composer. A frequent visitor in the Mendelssohn household in Berlin, Eduard Gans (1797–1839) was a professor of history at the University of Berlin in 1828/29, when FMB was a student there; because of his political views and his popularity as an academic orator, he was forced to suspend his political lectures after the July Revolution of 1830. The content of his inflammatory lecture series on "The History of the French Revolution" remained unknown until this article, which discusses FMB's notes from the lectures and contextualizes the relationship within the backgrounds and careers of the composer and the professor.

195. Richter, Arnd. "'Mendelssohn der Ausländer, durchaus undeutsch': Das Verhältnis Mendelssohn—Wagner." In *Blickpunkt FELIX Mendelssohn Bartholdy: Programmbuch Drei Tage für Felix vom 30.10 bis 1.11.1994*, ed. Bernd Heyder and Christoph Spering, 45–51. Cologne: Dohr, 1994.

Was FMB German (as he believed he was) or was he, as a Jew, a foreigner (as Wagner asserted)? An overview of the arguments, with an examination of FMB's own statements about Germanness and *Nationalmusik*.

196. Richter, Arnd. *Mendelssohn: Leben, Werke, Dokumente*. Serie Musik Piper no. 8202. Mainz: Schott, 1994. 425 p. ISBN 3795782023. ML410.M5 R57 1994.

A largely conventional popular biography that draws upon some lesser-known documents and strives for a considerable measure of objectivity.

197. Richter, Brigitte. *Frauen um Felix Mendelssohn Bartholdy: In Texten und Bildern vorgestellt.* With a Foreword by Johannes Forner. Insel-Bücherei, no. 1178. Frankfurt am Main: Insel, 1997. 141 p. ISBN 345819178X. ML410.M5 R59 1997.

A useful book that complements Boyd Alexander's studies on FMB and young women (nos. 102 and 103) and Marian Wilson [Kimber]'s study of FMB and Cécile (no. 239). Although there is no real documentation and the information seems mostly derived from standard sources, the volume can serve as a convenient reference. Contains short chapters describing the following female figures in FMB's life and his relationship to them: Lea Mendelssohn Bartholdy, Fanny Hensel, Rebecka Mendelssohn Bartholdy, Henriette Voigt, Ottilie von Goethe, Adele Schopenhauer, Wilhelmine Schröder-Devrient, Rahel Varnhagen von Ense, Pauline von Schätzel, Charlotte Moscheles, Maria Malibran, Delphine von Schauroth, Josephine Lang, Dorothea von Ertmann, Clara Schumann, Clara Novello, Henriette Grabau, Livia Frege, Sophie Schloß, Cécile Mendelssohn Bartholdy, Elisa Meerti, Queen Victoria, Jenny Lind, and Elise Polko.

198. Rieschel, Hans-Peter. *Komponisten und ihre Frauen.* Düsseldorf: Droste, 1994. 234 p. ISBN 3770010280. ML390 .R425 1994.

A conventional account of FMB's relationship with Cécile, generally consistent with those of Kobbé, Marek, Kupferberg, and Werner. This view has been challenged in Marian Wilson [Kimber]'s essay (no. 239).

199. Riethmüller, Albrecht. "Gade, Mendelssohn und Schumann empfehlen Robert Franz der Alma mater Halensis." In *Festschrift fur Winfried Kirsch zum 65. Geburtstag,* ed. Peter Ackermann, Ulrike Kienzle, and Adolf Nowak, 303–310. Frankfurter Beiträge zur Musikwissenschaft, Bd. 24. Tutzing: Hans Schneider, 1996.

The FMB portion of this essay focuses on a letter of recommendation he wrote for Robert Franz in 1845. The recommendation was something of a dilemma: the references (who also included Gade and Schumann) were familiar with Franz as a composer, but they were to recommend him for a professorship in music theory.

200. Rudolph, Eberhard. "Mendelssohns Beziehungen zu Berlin." *Beiträge zur Musikwissenschaft* 14 (1972): 205–14.

Rudolph comments on how FMB's progressive and liberal (but not radical) political sympathies were shaped by Moses Mendelssohn, Karl Ritter, Eduard Gans, and Zelter, and examines how they relate to his theater music of the early 1840s (the Incidental Music to *A Midsummer Night's Dream, Antigone, Athalie*, and *Oedipus*).

201. Rychnovsky, E. "Aus Felix Mendelssohn Bartholdys letzen Lebenstagen." *Die Musik* 8 (1908–09): 141–46.

A review of the events of the last days of FMB's life—less thorough than that in Wolff's biography (no. 98) but useful nevertheless.

202. Rudolf, E. "Der junge Felix Mendelssohn: Ein Beitrag zur Musikgeschichte der Stadt Berlin." Diss., Humboldt-Universität Berlin, 1964.

Not available for examination.

203. Schmidt, Christian Martin. "Zwei große Komponisten aus Berlin." In *Konzerthaus Berlin, Schauspielhaus am Gendarmenmarkt: Das Buch über Gestern und Heute*, ed. Dieter Götze and Frank Schneider, 71–81. Berlin: Museums- und Galerie-Verlag, 1994.

On FMB and Meyerbeer.

204. Schneider, Max F. "Felix Mendelssohn Bartholdy: Herkommen und Jugendzeit in Berlin." *Jahrbuch der Stiftung Preussischer Kulturbesitz 1963*, 157–68. Berlin: Staatsbibliothek Preussischer Kulturbesitz, 1963.

One of several important studies dealing with FMB's early years in the Prussian capital.

205. Schneider, Max F. *Mendelssohn oder Bartholdy? Geschichte eines Familiennamens*. Basel: Internationale Felix-Mendelssohn-Gesellschaft, 1962. 28 p.

Rev.: G. Schweizer in *Musica* 17 (1963): 93.

206. Schneider, Max F. "Mendelssohn und Schiller in Luzern." *Die Ernte* 51 (1960): 125–27.

Not available for examination.

207. Schönfelder, Gerd. "Mendelssohn einerseits, Wagner andererseits: Mendelssohn und Wagner zusammen." In *Felix Mendelssohn—Mitwelt und Nachwelt: Bericht zum 1. Leipziger Mendelssohn-Kolloquium am 8. und 9. Juni 1993*, 89–96. Wiesbaden: Breitkopf & Härtel, 1996.

A thoughtful examination of the personal and professional relationship between FMB and his eventual detractor, focusing on the development of Wagner's negative views.

208. Schottländer, Johann-Wolfgang. "Zelters Beziehungen zu den Komponisten seiner Zeit." *Jahrbuch der Sammlung Kippenberg* 8 (1930): 134–248.

209. Schünemann, Georg. *Carl Friedrich Zelter, der Begründer der preussischen Musikpflege.* Berlin: Hesse, 1932. 52 p. ML410.Z4 S3. Enlarged as *Carl Friedrich Zelter: Der Mensch und sein Werk.* Berlin: Bibliophillenabend, 1937. 100 p.

   A source of undeniable importance that, unfortunately, suffers from serious ideological bias because of its chronological and geographic points of origin.

210. Siebenkäs, Dieter. *Ludwig Berger: Sein Leben und seine Werke unter besonderer Berücksichtigung seines Liedschaffens.* Berliner Studien zur Musikwissenschaft, Bd. 4. Berlin: Merseburger, 1963. 316 p. ML410.B496 S5.

   FMB studied piano with Berger beginning in 1815, and Berger, as a leading composer of the Second Berlin School approach to text-music relationships in Lieder, naturally assumes a position of importance in understanding FMB's own song aesthetic. The book (adapted from the author's dissertation [Berlin, 1962]) focuses on the relationship between the two composers.

211. Siegfried, Christina. "'Der interessanteste und problematischste seiner Freunde': Adolf Bernhard Marx." In *Blickpunkt FELIX Mendelssohn Bartholdy: Programmbuch Drei Tage für Felix vom 30.10 bis 1.11.1994,* ed. Bernd Heyder and Christoph Spering, 35–44. Cologne: Dohr, 1994.

   A theorist of considerable importance but far less respected as a composer, Marx occupies an especially problematical position in FMB's biography and reception history. The two were inseparable boyhood friends; FMB recommended Marx for the chair in music at the University of Berlin when he himself declined it; and Marx was an important early advocate of FMB's music in early reviews. Sometime in the later 1830s, however, the two suffered a serious falling-out, and after the friendship ended Marx's remarks on FMB became increasingly more condescending and less sympathetic. Marx published his memoirs of the relationship in 1865 (no. 257), and complaints of bias and distortion prompted his widow to publish her own defense of her husband (no. 258).

212. Sietz, Reinhold. "Mendelssohn ging nicht nach Weimar." *Neue Zeitschrift*

für Musik 120 (1959): 72–74.

This article concerns the process by which FMB was invited to succeed Hummel as Kapellmeister in the prestigious musical establishment of Weimar in 1837 and his reasons for declining the invitation. Useful as a document of the regard in which he was held by contemporaries and the reasons for his professional prestige.

213. Sietz, Reinhold. "Beiträge zur Rheinischen Musikgeschichte des 19. Jahrhunderts: Felix Mendelssohn und Ferdinand Hiller." *Jahrbuch des Kölnischen Geschichtsvereins* 41 (1967): 96–117; 43 (1971): 101–30.

An important study of the personal friendship and professional interactions between FMB and one of his most important lesser-known contemporaries, author of one of the finest memoirs of FMB (no. 297). Includes reliable, thoroughly annotated editions of otherwise unpublished correspondence to supplement the generally good letters printed in Hiller's other writings.

214. Sietz, Reinhold. "Das Stammbuch von Julius Rietz." *Studien zur Musikgeschichte des Rheinlandes* 52 (1962): 219–34.

An important documentary study of the friend and colleague of FMB who became editor-in-chief of the *Sämtliche Werke*.

215. Sittard, Josef. "Felix Mendelssohn Bartholdy." In *Paul Graf Waldersee: Sammlung musikalischer Vorträge, dritte Reihe*, 255–288. Leipzig: Breitkopf & Härtel, 1881.

A thoughtful and generally sympathetic, but somewhat biased overview. Initially appears to rank Mendelssohn with Schubert and Schumann as a Lieder composer, but then says that the three are equal only in popularity though the latter two are far more important as song composers. He maintains that the Songs without Words are not novel creations but rather extensions of Field's nocturnes. [DM/JMC]

216. Smidak, Emil F. *Isaak-Ignaz Moscheles: Das Leben des Komponisten und seine Begegnungen mit Beethoven, Liszt, Chopin, Mendelssohn*. Vienna: Edition Wien, 1988. 213 p. ISBN 3850580229. ML410.M84 S5 1988. Trans. as *Isaak-Ignaz Moscheles: The Life of the Composer and His Encounters with Beethoven, Liszt, Chopin, and Mendelssohn*. Aldershot, Hampshire: Scolar Press, 1989. 237 p. ISBN 0859678210. ML410.M84 S6 1989.

A student of Beethoven and respected composer/performer in

England, France, and Germany, Moscheles was one of the more important friends and musical mentors of FMB. Drawing on a variety of published resources, this book presents a clear portrait of the composer's personal and professional relationships.

Rev.: N. Temperley in *Music and Letters* 72 (1991): 303; D. Seaton in *Notes* 48 (1991): 62–64.

217. Spitta, Philip. "Niels W. Gade." In *Zur Musik: Sechszehn Aufsätze,* [355]–83. Berlin: Gebrüder Paetel, 1892.

An early overview of the recently deceased Gade's work which discusses FMB's influences on the Danish composer. See also Harwell (no. 141).

218. Sterndale Bennett, R. "The Death of Mendelssohn." *Music and Letters* 36 (1955): 374–76.

This article draws on a previously unpublished letter (in English translation) from Ferdinand David and cites the judgment of Dr. Evan Bedford of the Middlesex Hospital that the cause of FMB's death was likely subarachnoid hemorrhage from a congenital condition.

219. Sternfeld, Frederick W. *Goethe and Music: a List of Parodies and Goethe's Relations to Music, with a List of References.* New York: New York Public Library, 1954.

Elementary and incomplete, but useful as a starting point in preparing an inventory of FMB's musical settings of Goethe's poems. See also Lawrence Kramer's studies on the relationship between the two (nos. 779 and 780).

220. Stevens, Denis. "Mendelssohn in Switzerland." *The Musical Times* 132 (1991): 413–16.

This article is informal but informative. Surveys FMB's encounters with Switzerland and draws on a detailed description in a letter of 24 August 1831 in order to reconstruct an organ improvisation FMB gave at the Benedictine Abbey at Engelberg.

221. Straeten, Erich van der. "Mendelssohns und Schumanns Beziehungen zu J. H. Lübeck und Johann J. H. Verhulst: Aus meist unveröffentlichten Briefen." *Die Musik* 3 (1903–04): 8–20.

A useful study of FMB's professional relationship with two respected contemporary composer/conductors. Includes little-known letters discussing his own works and critiquing theirs.

222. Straeten, Erich van der. "Streiflichter auf Mendelssohns und Schumanns Beziehungen zu zeitgenössischen Musikern." *Die Musik* 4 (1904–05): 25, 105.

An insightful study, culled from a careful reading of the composers' letters and other documents.

223. Tappolet, Willy. *Begegnungen mit der Musik in Goethes Leben und Werk.* Bern: Bentelli, 1975. 136 p. ISBN 3716500461. ML80.G5 T36.

A useful and thorough overview.

224. Thiele, Siegfried. "Mendelssohn und das Leipziger Konservatorium." In *Felix Mendelssohn—Mitwelt und Nachwelt: Bericht zum 1. Leipziger Mendelssohn-Kolloquium am 8. und 9. Juni 1993*, ed. Leon Botstein, 127–30. Wiesbaden: Breitkopf & Härtel, 1996.

225. Thomä, Hellmut. "Felix Mendelssohn Bartholdy und der Taunus." *Wiesbadener Leben* 32/2 (1983): 22–24.

Thomä discusses FMB's stays in Eppstein and Bad Soden, 1839–47.

226. Todd, R. Larry. *Mendelssohn's Musical Education: A Study and Edition of His Exercises in Composition.* Cambridge: Cambridge University Press, 1983. 260 p. ISBN 0521246555. ML410.M5 T65 1983.

Adapted from the author's dissertation (no. 933), this is one of the most important studies of FMB's early life and works,[11] focused on a manuscript held in the Bodleian Library, Oxford. The Introduction includes a study of the Berlin Bach tradition and an overview of how it influenced FMB's study of composition; Part I includes a description and analysis of various aspects of this composition course along with a section on "Some Unknown *Juvenilia*"; and Part II is an inventory and critical transcription of the Oxford manuscript.

227. Vetter, Walther. *Res severa verum gaudem: Die Tradition des Gewandhauses. Festschrift zum 175jährigen Bestehens der Gewandhauskonzerte, 1781–1956.* Leipzig: Deutscher Verlag für Musik, 1956.

FMB on p. 25–35. Discussion focuses on his humanistic orientation and its influence on the Gewandhaus concerts. [DM]

228. Vogt, Franz-Josef. "Felix Mendelssohn-Bartholdy und die Orgel der

Düsseldorfer St. Lambertuskirche." *Der Niederrhein* 49/2 (1982): 50–55.

Not available for examination.

229. Wanner, Gustaf Adolf. *Felix Mendelssohn Bartholdy und Basel*. Basel: Edition Bartholdy, 1974. 31 p. ML410.M5 W27.

An important study of FMB's Swiss connections.

230. Ward Jones, Peter. "Letter to the Editor." *The Musical Quarterly* 83 (1999): 27–30.

A response to Leon Botstein's defense (no. 374) of Jeffrey L. Sposato's critique (no. 391) of Eric Werner's FMB biography (nos. 96 and 97). See also Michael P. Steinberg's "intervention" (no. 369) and Botstein's "final word" (no. 376). Points out several examples of Werner's fabricated or otherwise inaccurate reproductions of important documents.

231. Ward Jones, Peter. "Mendelssohn and His English Publishers." In *Mendelssohn Studies,* ed. R. Larry Todd, 240–55. Cambridge: Cambridge University Press, 1992.

A detailed and extremely useful chronicle of FMB's complicated relationships with the English publishing houses of Clementi, Collard & Collard; Cramer, Addison & Beale; Mori & Lavenue; Novello; and Ewer. Examines the correspondence (much of it previously unpublished) between the composers and these firms, as well as the most important publications involved in the relationships, including the Op. 19[b] *Original Melodies for the Pianoforte*, the *Capriccio brillant*, the G-minor Piano Concerto, and especially the *Lobgesang* and the Op. 65 Organ Sonatas.

232. Ward Jones, Peter, ed. and trans. *The Mendelssohns on Honeymoon: the 1837 Diary of Felix and Cécile Mendelssohn Bartholdy, together with Letters to Their Families*. Oxford: Clarendon, 1997. 225 p. ISBN 0198165978. ML410.M5 A3 1997. Trans. German by Thomas Schmidt-Beste as *Felix und Cécile Mendelssohn Bartholdy: Das Tagebuch der Hochzeitsreise, nebst Briefen an die Familien*. Zurich: Atlantis, 1997. ISBN 3254002245.

Important not only as a scholarly and lavishly illustrated compendium of primary sources, but also as a rich and authoritative source of documentation for the most controversial period in FMB's career as a composer (the year of his ostensible compositional decline). In addition to a carefully translated and copiously annotated text of the couple's honeymoon diary, it includes a sizable appendix of family letters from the period, likewise well-annotated and critically reproduced.

233. Wasielewski, Wilh[elm] Jos[eph] von. "Felix Mendelssohn-Bartholdy und Robert Schumann: Eine künstlerische Parallele mit Einflechtung persönlicher Erinnerungen." *Deutsche Revue* 13 (1894): 329–41.

An important early comparison because of the author's personal acquaintance with his subjects and because it articulates the philosophical basis for the pairing of Mendelssohn and Schumann (and other composers)—a pairing that many subsequent studies have assumed is necessary and valid, without any clear philosophical basis for the pairing. For Wasielewski (and many nineteenth-century thinkers), Mendelssohn and Schumann (like Bach and Handel, Mozart and Beethoven, Goethe and Schiller) formed a dialectic of personalities, each taking its own direction (one in the direction of the Ideal and the other in the direction of the Real) and complementing the other in such a fashion that ultimately the artistically beautiful was produced through synthesis. As the title states, the essay is "inflected" with memoir-like elements because Wasielewski draws upon his personal recollections; on the whole, however, it was intended to situate the two composers in what nineteenth-century historians and aestheticians considered to be the ongoing historical dialectic of artistic progress.

234. Wauer, Wilhelm. "Felix Mendelssohn-Bartholdy und Dr. Eduard Krüger." *Neue Berliner Musik-Zeitung* 4 (23 January 1850): 25–27.

An important study concerning the treatment of FMB in the writings of one of his most important early critics.

235. Wehnert, Martin. "Das Leipziger Konservatorium und die nordischen 'nationalen' Schulen." *Beiträge zur Musikwissenschaft* 17 (1975): 317–22.

The early student population of the Leipzig Conservatory (an institution founded with FMB as Director) reveals a conspicuously high number of Scandinavian students, including Gade. This article discusses the situation and examines the ways in which some distinctive features of the Conservatory's curriculum and philosophy influenced Scandinavian musical life and institutions via those students.

236. Weiss, Hermann F. "Neue Zeugnisse zu Felix Mendelssohn Bartholdy und Johann Paul von Falkenstein." *Mendelssohn-Studien* 9 (1995): 53–88.

Closely related to Häfner's study (no. 140) of FMB's relationship to King Friedrich August II of Saxony, this study draws upon little-known correspondence: twenty-six letters from Falkenstein to FMB; FMB's drafts for answers to four of them; and two previously unpublished letters from FMB. Like Häfner, Weiss asserts that the Saxon monarch's warm reception of FMB was decisive in the composer's decision to resume his full-time work there rather than in Prussia in the early 1840s, and also suggests that Falkenstein and FMB shared a similar agenda for cultural politics.

237. Werner, Eric. "Mendelssohn—Wagner: Eine alte Kontroverse in neuer Sicht." In *Musica Scientiae Collectanea: Festschrift Karl Gustav Fellerer zum 70. Geburtstag*, ed. Heinrich Hüschen, 640–58. Cologne: Arno Volk, 1973.

A detailed exploration—with some little-known documents—of the development of the relationship between the two composers. Proposes that the principal difference between the two was not religious or racial *per se*, but national—that while Wagner was in theory (if not always in practice) fixated on the musical articulation of a specifically German national past, drawing on specifically German *Volkstümlichkeit*, FMB disdained the concepts of nationalism and made recourse to German folk music only in his chorale treatments.

238. Whistling, Karl. *Die Statistik des Königlichen Conservatorium der Musik zu Leipzig, 1843–1893*. Leipzig: Breitkopf & Härtel, 1893. 82 p.

Brief but useful documentation concerning the conservatory FMB founded in 1843.

239. Wilson [Kimber], Marian. "Mendelssohn's Wife: Love, Art and Romantic Biography." *Nineteenth Century Studies* 6 (1992): 1–18.

An important survey of biographical treatments and study of how they reflect fallacies and skewed methodologies in FMB research generally. Points out a seemingly deliberate fabrication concerning Cécile and the Op. 40 Piano concerto in Eric Werner's biography (no. 96).

240. Wilson Kimber, Marian. "'For Art Has the Same Place in Your Heart as in Mine': Friendship, Family, and Community in the Life of Felix Mendelssohn." In *The Mendelssohn Companion*, ed. Douglass Seaton. Westport, Conn.: Greenwood, [forthcoming].

241. Wolschke, Martin. *Von der Stadtpfeiferei zu Lehrlingskapelle und Sinfonieorchester: Wandlungen im 19. Jahrhundert*. Studien zur Musikgeschichte im 19. Jahrhundert, 59. Regensburg: Gustav Bosse, 1981. ISBN 3764922206. ML275.4 .W64.

Although the Leipzig Conservatory was founded under FMB's directorship in 1843, it did not begin to train orchestral musicians until 1881. Consequently, traditional methods of producing these musicians necessarily continued until nearly the end of the nineteenth century. Wolschke supplies the background essential to understanding all of Mendelssohn's dealings with his orchestras in Düsseldorf and Leipzig. [DM/JMC]

NOTES

1. For a review of the conference, see Wolfgang Hanke, "Internationaler Mendelssohn-Kongreß," *Musik und Kirche* 65 (1995): 233–34; further, Thomas Christian Schmidt, "Berlin, 12. bis 15. Mai 1994: Internationaler Mendelssohn-Kongreß," *Die Musikforschung* 48 (1995): 54–55.

2. See the essay by Marian Wilson Kimber on "Gender and Race in the Biography of Felix Mendelsson" (447).

3. FMB typically inscribed "L.e.g.G." ("let it work [succeed], God") or "H.D.m." ("help me, [Lord]") at the beginning of a manuscript for a new compositional undertaking. "L.e.g.G." is more common in the earlier manuscripts (to ca. 1832).

4. See also Donald Mintz's study of this issue (no. 426).

5. Ernst Wolff, Felix Mendelssohn Bartholdy (no. 1.98), [7].

6. See Donald M. Mintz, "1848, Anti-Semitism, and the Mendelssohn Reception" (no. 426).

7. See the studies by Lampadius (nos. 50 and 51) and Reissmann (no. 78).

8. Mercer-Taylor, Peter. *The Life of Mendelssohn*. Cambridge: Cambridge University Press, 2000. 238 p. ISBN 0521630258. ML 410.M5 M66 2000.

    This book is probably the most important general biography of FMB since Eric Werner's 1963/1980 study (nos. 96 and 97) and Karl-Heinz Köhler's article in the *New Grove* (no. 46). There is extensive discussion situating the family in the cultural context of the Restoration (especially with regard to Jewish issues), and references to the works are primarily for biographical purposes.

9. See also Joseph Esser's dissertation (no. 120).

10. See Marian Wilson [Kimber]'s article on "Mendelssohn's Wife" (no. 239).

11. See also R. Larry Todd's study of FMB's musical education (no. 226).

12. See also Köhler's *Der unbekannte junge Mendelssohn* (no. 161).

2. Memoirs, Recollections, and Editions of Letters

I. Memoirs and Recollections
II. Editions of Letters

I. MEMOIRS AND RECOLLECTIONS

Prefatory Note: The memoirs and reminiscences of FMB that appeared in the second half of the nineteenth century vividly reflect the highly politicized vacillations in the composer's posthumous reception discussed in the Introduction. It is therefore appropriate to caution the reader of the dangerous beauties offered by such sources. On the one hand, they transmit first-hand reminiscences of a subject whose biography otherwise rests largely on secondary sources. On the other hand, because those reminiscences typically were recorded only years after the actual encounters they discuss, and because they therefore tend to view contemporary facts through the lens of the author's later experiences and opinions, they can seldom be taken at face value despite their first-hand authority.

Two examples will suffice to make the point. Eduard Devrient was a close friend of FMB throughout the composer's life and therefore was in an excellent position to provide meaningful insights into his life and works. But Devrient's memoirs (no. 248) were not written and published until 1869. By that time Devrient had been a collaborator of Wagner for nearly fifteen years, and the New German School's evaluation of FMB as a boyish prodigy who failed as a *Zukunftsmusiker* because of his ostensibly underdeveloped dramatic proclivities was well established. Thus, Devrient's memories of FMB, clearly recorded for the musical public of the late 1860s, were almost certainly influenced by issues and ideas that were irrelevant to the composer and many others prior to 1847, and his presentation of the correspondence has been shown to be quite corrupt;[1] the reader can therefore hardly afford to take Devrient's account of *Die Hochzeit des Camacho* and its merits at face value. Similarly, Julius Schubring's memoirs (no. 267) were written at a time when the oratorio as a genre was under severe criticism. Because of this, Schubring's perspective is probably skewed toward the defensive rather than critical side—even though his fidelity to the texts of the documents and his overall accuracy are demonstrably superior to those in

Devrient's memoirs.

In short, the reader should use these sources eagerly but also cautiously, giving careful consideration (whenever possible) to the biases or agendas evident in the respective authors' other writings and activities.

***

242. Berlioz, Hector. *Mémoires de Hector Berlioz, comprenant ses voyages en Italie, en Russie et en Angleterre, 1803–1865.* 2 vols. Paris: Calmann Lévy, 1870. Numerous eds. after 1878–1900. New ed., ed. Pierre Citron, [Paris:] Flammarion, 1991. 631 p. ISBN 2080665189. Trans. English Ernest Newman as *Memoirs of Hector Berlioz from 1803 to 1865, comprising his travels in Germany, Italy, Russia, and England.* New York: Alfred A. Knopf, 1932. ML410.B5 A42 1932. New English trans. David Cairns as *A Life of Love and Music: The Memoirs of Hector Berlioz 1803–1865.* London: Folio Society, 1987. 461 p.

Along with FMB and Robert Schumann, Berlioz was one of those nineteenth-century composers whose brilliant prose often rivaled the brilliance of their music. The *Memoirs* are thus eminently readable, written by a composer who—despite significant differences in upbringing, philosophy, and musical style—was in every way FMB's peer. One could hardly wish for more entertaining first-hand accounts from a more reputable source. But because the memoirs were written nearly twenty years after FMB's death and in the wake of profound changes in the musical life and musical style of the century, they can hardly afford to be taken at face value: after all Berlioz is not known for his reticence to shun fanciful exaggeration.

243. Bode, Wilhelm. *Goethes Schauspieler und Musiker: Erinnerungen von Eberwein und Lobe.* Berlin: Mittler, 1912. 231 p. ML80.G5 E2.

244. Chorley, Henry Fothergill, ed. H. G. Hewlett. *Autobiography, Memoir and Letters.* London: Richard Bentley & Son, 1873. 118 p.

The English composer, writer, and music critic Henry Chorley (1808–72) was a close friend of FMB from early on, and one of his important advocates in England in the third quarter of the nineteenth century. This volume is an enlarged and edited version of no. 245. See also Robert Terrell Bledsoe's biography of Chorley (no. 108) for an overview of his relationship with FMB.

245. Chorley, Henry Fothergill. *Modern German Music: Recollections and Reflections*. 2 vols. London: Smith, Elder and Co., 1854. Rpt., with new introduction and index by Hans Lenneberg. New York: Da Capo, 1973. ISBN 0306719118. ML275.4 .C55 1973.

"The Last Days of Mendelssohn" in Vol. 2, p. 383–418. Chorley was with FMB in Interlachen during a critical point in his life, on 28–31 August 1847—a period in which the composer was trying to recover from his grief at the death of FH and was trying to make plans for the coming years. This essay is a touching and informative account of that period: in addition to recounting FMB's improvisation of an organ fugue in C minor at the cathedral in Freiburg and discussing his general disposition, it identifies important topics of conversation such as FMB's plans to compose an opera and his thoughts on Donizetti, Handel, Rossini, and Wordsworth. See also p. 48–52 of Vol. 1 for reports of FMB's skills as virtuoso pianist in 1839

246. Chorley, Henry Fothergill. *Thirty Years' Musical Recollections*. 2 vols. London: Hurst and Blackett, 1862. Rpt. New York: Da Capo, 1984. ISBN 0306762161. ML1731 .C58 1984. Also reissued in 1 volume, edited and with introduction by Ernest Newman. New York: Alfred A. Knopf, 1926. 411 p. ML423.C55 C5 1926.

This book recounts many of the author's direct personal encounters as well as recording his impressions of FMB's relationships with his contemporaries. Includes little-known correspondence of FMB.

247. Davison, Henry, ed. *From Mendelssohn to Wagner: Being the Memoirs of J. W. Davison, Forty Years Music Critic of "The Times."* London: Wm. Reeves, 1912. 539 p. ML423 .D18.

The author's father, James William Davison (1813–85), was a highly influential critic and a close friend of FMB from ca. 1836, when the two met after the Düsseldorf premiere of Mendelssohn's *St. Paul*. These posthumously assembled recollections are based on a draft for a memoir left by the elder Davison, supplemented some of his various essays for the London *Times* and previously unpublished correspondence. Davison's career is divided into three periods, the first of which (to ca. 1842) was inspired by FMB's position at the forefront of contemporary German music and characterized by an agenda to found an English "national school" of composition. Afterwards Davison grew skeptical of the potential for an English school, and ultimately he rejected the nationalistic agendas of Wagner and the "New German School" in favor of the nationalism of Mendelssohn and his followers.

248. Devrient, Eduard. *Meine Erinnerungen an Felix Mendelssohn-Bartholdy*

und seine Briefe an mich. Leipzig: J. J. Weber, 1869. 290 p. ML410.M5 D4. 3rd ed., 1891. 284 p. ML410.M5 D41. Trans. English Natalia MacFarren as *My Recollections of Felix Mendelssohn-Bartholdy, and His Letters to Me.* London: Richard Bentley, 1869. 307 p. ML410.M5 D5. Rpt. New York: Vienna House, 1972. ISBN 0844300020. ML410.M5 D5 1972.

Devrient (1801–77) was a close friend and acquaintance of FMB and, after 1849, a friend and collaborator of Richard Wagner. Published in 1869, his memoirs reveal his affection and sympathy for FMB as well as the likely influence of Wagner's views; they have also been shown by J. Rigbie Turner to be disturbingly unfaithful in their documentation of the author's relationship with FMB. The same issues arise in Devrient's other writings, which include a series of "Dramatische und dramaturgische Schriften" (1846) and a widely disseminated *Geschichte der deutschen Schauspielkunst* (5 vols., 1848).

249. Devrient, Hans, ed. *Briefwechsel zwischen Eduard und Thérèse Devrient.* Stuttgart: Carl Krabbe, 1910. 456 p. PN2655.D4 A3.

First-hand observations concerning FMB's relationship with the actor and his wife (1803–82), a singer and friend of the family from the time she joined the Berlin *Singakademie* in 1822.

250. Eckardt, Johannes. *Ferdinand David und die Familie Mendelssohn-Bartholdy: Aus hinterlassenen Briefschaften.* Leipzig: Duncker & Humblot, 1888. 289 p.

An important—and, for the day, surprisingly reliable—reproduction of the correspondence between the Mendelssohn family and the violinist, composer, and music editor Ferdinand David (1810–73), integrated in an account of David's long relationship with the Mendelssohns. David was in many ways at the center of FMB's musical activities: from 1836 he was concertmaster of the Gewandhaus Orchestra; from 1843, head of violin studies at the Leipzig Conservatory—and it was with him in mind that FMB wrote and revised the Violin Concerto, Op. 64.

251. Edwards, F. G. "Reminiscences of Mendelssohn." *The Musical Times* 33 (1892): 465–67.

An annotated distillation from the recollections Julius Benedict had presented at Camberwell in 1849 and published in 1851 (no. 20). Omits the style-critical material in order to present a more focused memoir; also more easily accessible than Benedict's book itself.

252. Hempel, Irene, ed. *Erinnerungen an Felix Mendelssohn Bartholdy, aus zeit-*

genössischen Beiträgen zusammengestellt. Leipzig: Deutscher Verlag für
Musik, 1984. 335 p.

A valuable collection of contemporary documents, organized by
author and then by chronology.

253. Holland, Henry Scott, and William S. Rockstro, eds. *Memoir of Mme Jenny
Lind-Goldschmidt: Her Early Art-Life and Dramatic Career.* London: John
Murray, 1891. 2 vols. ML420.L7 H6. 2nd ed., abridged, as *Jenny Lind the
Artist, 1820–1851: a Memoir of Madame Jenny Lind Goldschmidt, Her
Art-life and Dramatic Career: from Original Documents, Letters, Ms.
Diaries, &c.* London: J. Murray, 1893. 473 p. ML420.L7 H7. Trans.
German Hedwig I. Schoell as *Jenny Lind: Ihre Laufbahn als Künstlerin,
1820 bis 1851.* 2 vols. Leipzig: F. A. Brockhaus, 1891. ML420.L7 H72.

One of the leading sopranos of the day, Jenny Lind (1820–87) possessed a measure of artistic acclaim comparable to that of FMB. She sang
under FMB's direction at a Gewandhaus concert in 1845, and as an artist
was well placed to remark on his personality and his conducting habits.
Volume includes unpublished correspondence as well as references to collections of primary sources (most importantly, the "Green Books" collection now held in the Bodleian Library, Oxford;(see no. 480, 487, and 516).

254. Horsley, Charles Edward. "Reminiscences of Mendelssohn by His English
Pupil." *Dwight's Journal of Music* 32 (1872): 345–47, 353–55, 361–63.
Rpt., annotated by R. Larry Todd, in *Mendelssohn and His World*, ed. R.
Larry Todd, 237–51. Princeton: Princeton University Press, 1991.

Charles Edward Horsley's (1822–76) acquaintance with FMB dated
from 1832; he studied with FMB from 1841–43, and in his subsequent
career in London acquired considerable reputation as a composer. His
"Reminiscences" exemplify the bombast of the FMB cult in the last third
of the century—Mendelssohn was "in all relations of life . . . humanly
speaking[,] perfect"—but they also provide important glimpses into FMB's
activities as conductor, organist, and pianist, as well as into contemporary
concert life.

255. Lobe, Johann Christian. "Gespräche mit Felix Mendelssohn." *Fliegende
Blätter für Musik* 1 (1855): 280–96. Trans. English Susan Gillespie and
annotated by R. Larry Todd as "Conversations with Felix Mendelssohn," in
Mendelssohn and His World, ed. R. Larry Todd, 187–205. Princeton:
Princeton University Press, 1991.

Modeled on Johann Peter Eckermann's widely disseminated
Gespräche mit Goethe, this is a useful but slightly problematical source. As

in the case of Eckermann's memoir, much of the purportedly quoted dialog may well be fabricated, and some of the material seems suspiciously close to anecdotes already relayed in early biographies. Still, Lobe's reference to some items and facts that were not yet generally known—such as the still-unpublished numbers composed for *St. Paul* and then removed—suggest that he had at least some reasonably direct access to information otherwise unavailable.

256. Lobe, J[ohann] C[hristian]. "Ein Quartett bei Goethe: Erinnerung aus Weimars großer Zeit." *Die Gartenlaube* 1 (1867): 4–8.

   Lobe recalls the occasion in November 1821 at which three members of the Weimar Hofkapelle gathered together at Goethe's home with the young FMB and his teacher, Zelter.

257. Marx, Adolf Bernhard. *Erinnerungen aus meinem Leben*. Berlin: Otto Janke, 1865. ML423 .M39. Excerpts trans. English Susan Gillespie and annotated by R. Larry Todd as "From the Memoirs of Adolf Bernhard Marx," in *Mendelssohn and His World*, ed. R. Larry Todd, 206–20. Princeton: Princeton University Press, 1991.

   The theorist, aesthetician, and composer Adolf Bernhard Marx (ca. 1795–1866) ranks among the most problematical of FMB's personal and professional acquaintances. He was a boyhood friend of FMB and one of his earliest advocates, especially in the *Berliner Allgemeine musikalische Zeitung*, which he edited from 1824–30; the same journal also served as forum for some of Marx's earliest advocacies of Beethoven's late works. FMB and Marx suffered a serious break in the late 1830s, and Marx destroyed his correspondence with FMB. In successive writings, as he expanded his early views on the historical and stylistic significance of Beethoven's compositions, Marx grew increasingly dismissive and patronizing toward FMB; it is difficult to know how much of his critical stance was the consequence of personal differences and professional envy or of legitimate philosophical and aesthetic differences. In any case, Marx's 1855 memoir was written long after he ceased to be public about the merits or importance of FMB's music. Consequently, it should be approached enthusiastically but used cautiously. See also Therése Marx's response (no. 258) to Devrient's sympathetic (if also somewhat condescending) portrayal of the relationship (no. 248), as well as Christina Seigfried's study (no. 211).

258. Marx, Therese. *Adolf Bernhard Marx' Verhältniß zu Felix Mendelssohn-Bartholdy, in Bezug auf Eduard Devrient's Darstellung*. Leipzig: Dürr, 1869. 24 p. ML410.M5 M2.

As the title suggests, this short book by Marx's widow is a response to Eduard Devrient's portrayal of the Marx/FMB friendship (no. 248)—specifically to Devrient's perceived "partisanship" favoring FMB over Marx (who, according to his widow, "exerted a significant influence on the education and development" of FMB).

259. Moscheles, Charlotte, ed. *Aus Moscheles' Leben: Nach Briefen und Tagebüchern*. Leipzig: Duncker & Humblodt, 1872. 2 vols. in 1. Trans. English A. D. Coleridge as *Recent Music and Musicians, as Described in the Diaries and Correspondence of Ignatz Moscheles*. New York: H. Holt, 1873. 434 p. Rpt. New York: Da Capo, 1970. ISBN 0306700220. ML410.M84 M82 1970.

The FMB-Moscheles correspondence (no. 313) is one of the most important documents of FMB's life and activities, and these materials assembled from diaries and journals form an important supplement. Although they are understandably affectionate for Ignaz Moscheles (1794–1870), one of FMB's closest friends, they also maintain a reasonably objective stance and transmit important information concerning little-known but relevant events, concerts, and so on.

260. Müller, F. Max. *Auld Lang Syne*. New York: C. Scribner's Sons, 1898. 325 p. PJ64.M8 A3 1898. Excerpts rpt. and annotated in *Mendelssohn and His World*, ed. R. Larry Todd, 252–58. Princeton: Princeton University Press, 1991.

Müller (1823–1900) was the son of Wilhelm Müller (poet of *Die schöne Müllerin* and *Die Winterreise*), a notable philologist, and an educated musical connoisseur of conservative taste. This memoir reflects back on his encounters with the personages who by 1900 had come to epitomize the century's struggle for artistic progress, focusing on FMB, Schumann, and Liszt.

261. Naumann, Emil. "Erinnerungen an Felix Mendelssohn-Bartholdy." In *Nachklänge: Eine Sammlung von Vorträgen und Gedenkblättern aus dem Musik-, Kunst- und Geistesleben unserer Tage*. Berlin: R. Oppenheim, 1872. ML60 .N29.

FMB treated on p. 22–24. A professor at the University of Bonn, Naumann (1827–88) received informal instruction in composition from FMB in 1842–44, and was active as an author of general music histories.

262. Nichols, Roger. *Mendelssohn Remembered*. London: Faber and Faber, 1997. 258 p. ISBN 057117860X; 0571178618 (pbk).

Certainly the most important general source for reminiscences of FMB. Draws extensively on the recollections available in print, as well as some unpublished and otherwise hard-to-come-by items. Documents are well-annotated.

Rev.: J. Daverio in *Music & Letters* 79 (1998): 281–83.

263. Planché, James Robinson. *The Recollections adn Reflections of J.R. Planché (Somerset Herald): A Professional Biography.* London: Tinsley Brothers, 1872. 2 vols. Rev. ed. in 1 vol. London: S. Low, Marston & Co., 1901. 464 p. PN2598.P5 A3 1901. Rpt. New York: Da Capo, 1978. ISBN 0306775019. PR5187.P2 A827 1978.

FMB in Vol. 1. Planché (1798–1880) was a leading librettist in London in the early nineteenth century—most significantly, the librettist for Weber's *Oberon*. Also a playwright, antiquary, and heraldic scholar (author of *A History of British Costumes*, 1834), he worked with FMB on a libretto project in 1838, but the endeavor came to nothing. This memoir provides important insight into the expectations FMB faced from the English opera-going public.

264. Polko, Elise. *Erinnerungen an Felix Mendelssohn-Bartholdy: Ein Künstler- und Menschenleben.* Leipzig: F. A. Brockhaus, 1868. 216 p. ML410.M5 P64 1868. Trans. English Lady [Grace Stein Don] Wallace as *Reminiscences of Felix Mendelssohn-Bartholdy: A Social and Artisitic Biography.* London: Longmans, Green & Co., 1869; and New York: Leopoldt & Holt, 1869. 222 p. ML410.M5 P643 1869. Leopoldt ed. rpt., with new introduction by James A. Keene, Macomb, Ill.: Glenbridge, 1987.

In R. Larry Todd's words, a "freely embroidered biographical account."[2] Polko (1823–99) was a prolific popular biographer (see no. 72) and an acquaintance of FMB from 1845. Nevertheless, her fanciful tone and unabashedly glowing affection for her subjects render her reliability questionable and her veracity doubtful. This memoir would be valuable as a document of reception history at the least, had Polko not also waxed equally poetic about virtually every other composer whom she happened to describe.

265. Reich, Nancy B., ed. and trans. "From the Memoirs of Ernst Rudorff." In *Mendelssohn and His World*, ed. R. Larry Todd, 259–71. Princeton: Princeton University Press, 1991.

Ernst Rudorff (1840–1916) was a composer, conductor, and editor, and was head of the piano department at the Königliche Hochschule für Musik in Berlin from 1869 to 1910. His posthumously published memoirs

(*Aus den Tagen der Romantik: Ein Bildnis einer deutschen Familie* [Leipzig: L. Staackmann, 1938]) omitted the pages on the Mendelssohn family; the memoirs were based on reminiscences, published letters, family records, and the diaries of his father, Adolph Rudorff (1802–73)—who, together with Ernst's mother, Betty, knew FMB.

266. Rellstab, Ludwig. Aus meinin Leben. Berlin: F. Guttinteg, 1861. 2 vols. in 1. FMB in vol. 2, ch. 11. Headed "Medelssohn im Goetheschen Hause," the chapter concerns an evening in which FMB played some of Mozart's, Beethoven's, and his own works for Zelter.

267. Schubring, Julius. "Erinnerungen an Felix Mendelssohn Bartholdy." *Daheim* 2 (1866): 373–76. Trans. English (anonymously) as "Reminiscences of Felix Mendelssohn Bartholdy. On His 57th Birthday, February 3rd, 1866," in *The Musical World* 31 (12 and 19 May 1866). Trans. newly printed and annotated by R. Larry Todd as "Reminiscences of Felix Mendelssohn-Bartholdy," in *Mendelssohn and His World*, ed. R. Larry Todd, 206–20. Princeton: Princeton University Press, 1991.

FMB's principal consultant for the librettos to *St. Paul* and *Elijah*, Julius Schubring (1806–89) was a pastor in Dessau, and a regular correspondent of the composer (see no. 322). His twenty-two year friendship with FMB provided him with many glimpses into FMB's personal life. This memoir contains some anecdotes that, while unverifiable, have the ring of truth about them. Nevertheless, some (such as his recollection concerning the chorale at the end of the piano fugue Op. 35, no. 1) have been questioned with good reason—not so much as fabrications, but as instances in which the pastor's interpretation of an event unduly tempered his memory of what happened.

268. Schumann, Robert. *Erinnerungen an Felix Mendelssohn Bartholdy*. Ed. Georg Eismann (Zwickau: Predella, 1947; 2nd ed., enlarged, 1948). Trans. James A. Galston as *Memoirs of Felix Mendelssohn-Bartholdy: from Private Notes and Memoranda, Letters, and Dairies [sic] of Robert Schumann*. Rochester: n.p., 1951. 83 p. New, critical edition of German text by Heinz-Klaus Metzger and Rainer Riehn in *idem, Felix Mendelssohn Bartholdy*. Musik-Konzepte 14/15. Munich: edition text + kritik, 1980.

A vital document concerning the relationship between Schumann and FMB, and one that was seriously misrepresented in Wolfgang Boetticher's seemingly authoritative Schumann biography (Berlin, 1941). Not a published memoir *per se*, but aphoristic sketches that may have been intended to serve as the basis of such. The first complete publication (1947) rectified many of the distortions and falsifications in Boetticher's text, but the first critical edition was that in the FMB volume of the *Musik-Konzepte* series (see no. 10).

269. Webern, Emil von. "Felix Mendelssohn Bartholdy aus den Erinnerungen des Generalleutnants Karl Emil von Webern." *Die Musik* 12 (1912–13): 67–74.

   Not available for examination.

II. EDITIONS OF LETTERS

Prefatory Note: In the last third of the nineteenth century, the burgeoning cult of individualism (nourished by the contemporary evolutionary philosophy that the natural course of history was a development from the general and typical to the individual, so that the most individualistic representatives of a species, a nation, or an art represented the most highly developed) combined with the historicist movement to produce a prodigious number of editions of letters from eminent figures in virtually every area of endeavor. The most important positive conse-quence of the flood of epistolary collections was that primary sources were avail-able to the reading public in unprecedented quantities. Unfortunately, however, the concept of textual fidelity and source-critical reproduction were in an embry-onic state. Because of this, virtually all of the letters were heavily (and, for the most part, tacitly) edited for content—partly to shield individuals and families who had been subject to negative or inappropriately personal remarks, and part-ly to make the text of the document read in a fashion that was optimally consis-tent with the way the editor perceived the author of the letters.[3] Mendelssohn was no exception to this situation—indeed, the heavily edited and bowdlerized late-nineteenth-century editions of his letters in many ways epitomize the problem.

   Because of this situation, and because of the enormous number of entries that would be required to provide a comprehensive overview of editions of FMB correspondence, entries will be limited to the most important (and, where possible, most critical) editions.

   For other extensive collections of letters, see also Thomas Schmidt-Beste's book on the aesthetics of FMB's instrumental music (no. 790), as well as many of the memoirs cited earlier in this chapter and a number of the biograph-ical studies cited in chapter 1.

***

270. Anacker, Wilhelm. "Zwei Briefe von Felix Mendelssohn Bartholdy." *Musik und Gesellschaft* 9 (1972): 654–58.

   Letters from FMB dated 5 April 1838 and 15 August 1841.

271. Sterndale Bennett, James Robert. *The Life of William Sterndale Bennett.*

Cambridge: Cambridge University Press, 1907. 471 p. ML410.B45 B4.

This book includes a substantial number of little-known letters from Mendelssohn.

272. Boetticher, Wolfgang. *Briefe und Gedichte aus dem Album Robert und Clara Schumanns*. Leipzig: Deutscher Verlag für Musik, 1979. 2nd ed., 1981.

This study includes a number of FMB documents.

273. Citron, Marcia J., ed. and trans. *The Letters of Fanny Hensel to Felix Mendelssohn*. [Stuyvesant, N.Y.]: Pendragon, 1987. 687 p. ISBN 0918728525. ML410.H482 A4 1987.

Although it presents only just over half of the extant letters from FH to FMB, this is an invaluable resource for their correspondence, much of it otherwise unpublished; also presents plentiful excerpts from FMB's letters to FH, including unpublished ones. Includes an introductory essay on "The Relationship between Fanny and Felix." It presents letters first in an extensively annotated English translation and then in the original German (with some errors) (see no. 951).

274. Cox, H. Bertram, and C.L.E. Cox *Leaves from the Journals of Sir George Smart*. London: Longmans, Green & Co., 1907. Rpt. New York: Da Capo, 1971. 355 p. ISBN 0306701642. ML410.S6 A3 1971.

Contains a number of important FMB letters.

275. Dahlgren, L., ed. *Bref till Adolf Fredrick Lindblad från Mendelssohn, . . . och andra*. Stockholm: Albert Bonnier, 1913. 212 p.

Lindblad (1801–78)—a composer who commanded considerable respect well into the nineteenth century—studied with FMB, and the two conducted a lively correspondence that includes FMB's comments and criticisms of some of Lindblad's works, as well as reports on FMB's own activities, plans, and compositions. The correspondence with FMB is on p. 9–52.

276. Dibdin, Edward Rimbault. "Some Letters of Mendelssohn." *The Musical Quarterly* 5 (1949): 494–98.

The author's father, Henry Edward Dibdin, heard FMB perform in Birmingham in 1837 or 1840, and extended an invitation to him for a professorship at Edinburgh University. This article contains FMB's response to the invitation, as well as a facsimile of the manuscript for a posthumously published Prelude in C Minor dated 9 July 1841.

277. Elvers, Rudolf. "Acht Briefe von Lea Mendelssohn an den Verleger Schlesinger in Berlin." In *Das Problem Mendelssohn*, ed. Carl Dahlhaus, 47–53. Studien zur Musikgeschichte des 19. Jahrhunderts, Bd. 41. Regensburg: Gustav Bosse, 1974.

Although some gaps are inevitable because of on-site and oral communications, these eight letters chronicle part of the means by which FMB established his relationship with his first publisher. Includes a characteristically thorough introduction by Rudolf Elvers.

278. Elvers, Rudolf. "Bilder-Briefe von und an Felix Mendelssohn Bartholdy." In *Festschrift Hans-Peter Schmitz zum 75. Geburtstag*, ed. Andreas Eichhorn, 81–84. Kassel: Bärenreiter, 1992.

Elvers examines the form and function of one "picture-letter" by FMB (dated 1 January 1847) and one sent to him in 1839 by Ernst Benedikt Kietz. Includes facsimiles of the letters' respective illustrations.

279. Elvers, Rudolf. *Felix Mendelssohn Bartholdy: Briefe an deutsche Verleger*. Felix Mendelssohn Bartholdy: Briefe, 1. Berlin: Walter de Gruyter, 1968. 399 p.

An indispensable source for inquiries into the history of the works published during FMB's lifetime, not only because of the insights it provides into the works' genesis and publication history, but also because of its illumination of FMB's compositional process and the acuity of his ear in effecting revisions. The 431 letters include correspondence with the following German publishing houses: Breitkopf & Härtel (Leipzig), N. Simrock (Bonn), A. M. Schlesinger (Berlin), Friedrich Hofmeister (Leipzig), Pietro Mechetti (Vienna), Kistner (Leipzig), B. Schott's Söhne (Mainz), Bote & Bock (Berlin), J. P. Spehr (Braunschweig), R. Friese (Leipzig), and B. Tauchnitz (Leipzig). Also includes two appendices: the first traces the publication history of a complicated item, the "Romanze" from the *Incidental Music to Victor Hugo's Ruy Blas*; the second is a bibliographic survey of the "thematic catalogs" published during FMB's lifetime.

280. Elvers, Rudolf. "Die Ausgabe der Briefe Felix Mendelssohns." In *Quellenforschung in der Musikwissenschaft*, ed. Georg Feder in collaboration with Wolfgang Rehm and Martin Ruhnke, 71–73. Wolfenbüttler Forschungen, Bd. 15. Wolfenbüttel: Herzog August Bibliothek, 1982.

281. Elvers, Rudolf, ed. *Felix Mendelssohn Bartholdy: Briefe*. Frankfurt: Fischer Taschenbuch, 1984. 276 p. ISBN 3596221420. ML410.M5 A2839 1984. Trans. Englin Craig Tomlinson as *Felix Mendelssohn: A Life in*

Letters. New York: Fromm International, 1986. 334 p. ISBN 088064060X. ML410.M5 A4 1986.

Rev.: C. Brown in *Music and Letters* 69 (1988): 88–89.

282. Elvers, Rudolf. "Ein Jugendbrief von Felix Mendelssohn." In *Festschrift für Friedrich Smend zum 70. Geburtstag*, 91–92. Berlin: Merseburger, [1963].

A letter of 1 November 1819 from the ten-year-old FMB to "Signore Rudolph"—the Waldhorn player Rudolph Gugel.

283. Elvers, Rudolf. "Der letzte Familienbrief: Rebecka Dirichlet an Felix Mendelssohn Bartholdy." In *Festschrift Wolfgang Rehm zum 60. Geburtstag*, ed. Dietrich Berke and Harald Heckmann, 193–96. Kassel: Bärenreiter, 1989.

Elvers provides an overview of problems and editions surrounding FMB's correspondence before turning to what evidently is the last, previously unpublished installment in the long series of "family letters" that have been widely disseminated since the late 1860s, including a letter from Rebecka Dirichlet to FMB written on 21 October 1847.

284. Feder, Georg, and Peter Hübner. "Felix Mendelssohns Briefe an Pauline und Julius Hübner." In *Festschrift Rudolf Elvers zum 60. Geburtstag*, ed. Ernst Herttrich and Hans Schneider, 157–97. Tutzing: Hans Schneider, 1985.

A carefully annotated critical edition of twenty letters written by FMB between 1840 and 1847 to his painter friend Julius Hübner and Hübner's wife. Abundant references to the programming and performances of Bach, Handel, Haydn, Mozart, and Beethoven, as well as FMB's own compositional activities.

285. Federhofer-König, Renate. "Der unveröffentlichte Briefwechsel Alfred Julius Becher (1803–1848)—Felix Mendelssohn Bartholdy (1809–1847)." *Studien zur Musikwissenschaft* 41 (1992): 7–94.

A longtime friend of FMB from the latter's Düsseldorf years, Becher (1803–48) was active as a music critic and chronicler. Some of FMB's letters to him were published previously, but several were not. Those letters are combined with Becher's side of the correspondence in this critically transcribed and extensively annotated article.

286. Ferguson, Faye. "Unknown Correspondence from Felix Mendelssohn Bartholdy to His Leipzig Publisher Friedrich Kistner." In *Festschrift*

Wolfgang Rehm zum 60. Geburtstag, ed. Dietrich Berke and Harald Heckmann, 197–206. Kassel: Bärenreiter, 1989.

An important supplement to Rudolf Elvers's 1968 edition of FMB's correspondence with his German publishers (no. 279). Descriptions and annotated transcriptions of six little-known letters, with facsimiles of four of the letters. Mentioned are the Incidental Music to *Antigone* (Op.55), the *Erste Walpurgisnacht* (Op. 60), Ferdinand David's arrangement for violin of the Second Cello Sonata (Op. 58), and the Incidental Music to *A Midsummer Night's Dream* (Op. 61), as well as a "Liedchen."

287. Friedländer, Max. "Briefe an Goethe von Felix Mendelssohn-Bartholdy." *Goethe-Jahrbuch* 12 (1891): 77, 110.

288. Friedländer, Max. "Ein Brief Felix Mendelssohns." *Vierteljahrsschrift für Musikwissenschaft* 5 (1889): 483–89.

First printing of a letter of 26 June 1838 in which FMB declines to forward to the recipient (Franz von Piatkowski) the score to "the symphony for the celebration of the Reformation festival" (*"die Symphonie zur Feier des Reformationsfestes"*) because it was "such a childish work of [his] youth," with further rejections of Op. posth. 107.

289. Gilbert, Felix. *Bankiers, Künstler und Gelehrte: Unveröffentlichte Briefe der Familie Mendelssohn aus dem 19. Jahrhundert.* Tübingen: J.C.B. Mohr, 1975. 328 p. ISBN 3168363626. DS135.G5 A12.

290. Gilbert, Felix. "Ein Brief von Cécile Mendelssohn Bartholdy an Sophia Horsley in London aus dem Jahre 1849." *Mendelssohn-Studien* 5 (1992): 131–33.

291. Gotch, Rosamund Brunel. *Mendelssohn and His Friends in Kensington: Letters from Fanny and Sophy Horsley Written 1833–36.* London: Oxford University Press, 1934. 289 p. ML410.M5 T5.

The Horsleys were close friends of the Mendelssohn family, recipients of a number of autographs, and witnesses to and participants in many of the composer's London activities. Gotch's book provides valuable insights into this aspect of FMB's English persona.

292. Hake, Bruno. "Mendelssohn als Lehrer: Mit bisher ungedruckten Briefen Mendelssohns an Wilhelm v. Boguslawski." *Deutsche Rundschau* 140 (1909): 453–70. Abridged, trans. English Susan Gillespie as "Mendelssohn as Teacher, with Previously Unpublished Letters from Mendelssohn to Wilhelm v. Boguslawski." In *Mendelssohn and His World*, ed. R. Larry Todd, 310–37. Princeton: Princeton University Press, 1991.

An important study of FMB's activities as a teacher, drawing on the little-known correspondence between the composer and a musically gifted civil servant based in Breslau. The correspondence, which extends from 1823 to 1845, may be considered some of the earliest and most extensive documentation of FMB's pedagogical philosophies. The abridged translation by Susan Gillespie is well-annotated and easily accessible to non-German speakers.

293. Hallé, C. E., and Marie Hallé, eds. *The Life and Letters of Sir Charles Hallé*. London, Smith, Elder, 1896. 432 p. Abridged and ed. Michael Kennedy as *The Autobiography of Charles Hallé, with Correspondence and Diaries*. London: Elek, 1972. 215 p. ISBN 0236154486. ML422.H18 A3 1972. Rpt. New York: Da Capo, 1981. ISBN 0306760940. ML422.H18 A3 1981.

"Mendelssohn's [piano] playing was not exactly that of a 'virtuoso,' not to be compared to that of a Liszt or a Thalberg (he himself called it *'en gros spielen'*), but it was remarkably perfect, and one felt the great musician, the great composer, in every bar he played. He was also a great organist, and I had the privilege of hearing him improvise." There are anecdotes about Mendelssohn's memory. On Mendelssohn's famous letter to Souchay in which he says that music is more definite than words: "the letter seems to be more ingenious than true." Hallé met Mendelssohn only once, in Frankfurt in 1842. [DM]

294. Hanslick, Eduard. "Briefe von F. Mendelssohn." *Aus neuer und neuester Zeit: Musikalische Kritiken und Schilderungen*. Berlin: Allgemeiner Verein für deutsche Literatur, 1900. Rpt. Farnborough: Gregg, 1971. 377 p. ISBN 0576281891.

The Viennese music critic celebrated for his influential book *Vom Musikalisch-Schönen* (1854) was also a correspondent with FMB, and an avid collector of composers' autographs (letters and scores alike). This article presents a number of letters for the first time, with introductions that reflect Hanslick's fastidious approach to documenting and interpreting composers' works.

295. Hanslick, Eduard. "Briefe von Felix Mendelssohn-Bartholdy an Aloys Fuchs." *Deutsche Rundschau* 57 (1888): 65–85. Trans. English Susan Gillespie as "Letters from Felix Mendelssohn-Bartholdy to Aloys Fuchs." In *Mendelssohn and His World*, ed. R. Larry Todd, 275–309. Princeton: Princeton University Press, 1991.

A remarkable collection that includes a characteristically vivid introduction by Hanslick. Letters reveal FMB's activities as a collector of autographs of Beethoven, Clementi, Gluck, Handel, Moscheles, Mozart, Righini, and Rossini, among others. It also chronicles his purchase of a new fortepiano.

296. Hase, Oskar von. *Breitkopf und Härtel: Gedenkschrift und Arbeitsbericht.* Leipzig, Breitkopf und Härtel, 1917. 2 vols.

This book contains a section about Mendelssohn, "der frühreife Edeljude," whose correspondence with the firm was "nearly complete" in its archives at the time von Hase wrote. Many letters are printed, one in facsimile, in the course of a discussion of Mendelssohn's relations with the firm. There is also a facsimile of the *Neujarhslied*, Op. 88/no. 1. [DM/JMC]

297. Hiller, Ferdinand. *Félix Mendelssohn-Bartholdy: Lettres et souvenirs.* Paris: J. Baur, 1867. 357 p. ML410.M5 H57. German as *Felix Mendelssohn-Bartholdy: Briefe und Erinnerungen.* Cologne: M. DuMont-Schauberg'sche Buchhandlung, 1874. 196 p. ML410.M5 H59. Trans. M. E. von Glehn as *Mendelssohn: Letters and Recollections.* London: Macmillan, 1874. 223 p. ML410.M5 H593. Rpt., with introduction by Joel Sachs. New York: Vienna House, 1972. ISBN 0844300039. ML410.M5 H593 1972.

A widely respected and influential composer in his own right, Hiller (1811–85) was also a longtime confidant of FMB. Because of his longevity as a composer, critic, and chronicler of musical life in Germany and France, he was also unusually well qualified to situate FMB in the various stylistic currents of nineteenth-century music. His recollections, while decidedly affectionate, reveal nothing of the wholesale idolatry that characterized many other contemporary reminiscences, and his presentation of the letters is likewise more accurate than was customary in such nineteenth-century editions.

298. Hogarth, George. *The Birmingham Festival of 1852.* Birmingham: Hall, 1852. 57 p. ML38.R67 H6.

This book includes a memoir of FMB.

299. Hübner, Rudolf. *Johann Gustav Droysen: Briefwechsel.* Stuttgart: Deutsche Verlags-Anstalt, 1929. Deutsche Geschichtsquellen des 19. Jahrhunderts, Bd. 25–26. Rpt. Osnabrück: Biblio-Verlag, 1967. ML38.R67 H6.

See no. 117.

300. Hasubek, Peter, ed. *Karl Lebrecht Immermann, Briefe: Textkritische und*

kommentierte Ausgabe. 3 vols. Munich: Hänser, 1978–82. ISBN 3446124446. ML38.R67 H6.

Immermann (1796–1840) was, along with A. B. Marx, one of the most troubling figures in FMB's professional and personal life. An accomplished playwright, director, and author, he transformed the Düsseldorf theater from a minor epigonal stage to a leading center of theater in the German-speaking countries, and his ambitious artistic agenda (including the celebrated *Musterbühne*) was part of FMB's attraction to that city when he assumed the position of its Municipal Music Director in 1833. By late in 1834, however, the two were at odds with each other (in part because of controversies surrounding their collaborative production of Mozart's *Don Giovanni*), and the correspondence chronicling the decline in their friendship provides useful insights into FMB's early conduct of his professional relationships. This edition includes transcriptions of letters from FMB to Immermann as well as the playwright's letters to the composer.

301. Hasubek, Peter, ed. *Karl Lebrecht Immermann, zwischen Poesie und Wirklichkeit: Tagebücher 1831–1840.* Munich: Winkler, 1984. 1071 p. ISBN 3538051216.

A valuable complement to Immermann's letters, also useful for filling in some blanks in the events surrounding FMB's Düsseldorf activities.

302. Joachim, Johannes, and Andreas Moser, eds. *Briefe von und an Joseph Joachim.* 3 vols. Berlin: Julius Bard, 1911–13. ML418.J6 J6. Abridged, trans. English Nora Bickley with a preface by J. A. Fuller-Maitland, as *Letters from and to Joseph Joachim.* London: Macmillan, 1914. 470 p. ML418.J6 B5. Rpt. New York: Vienna House, 1972. 470 p. ISBN 0844300438. ML418.J6 A43 1972.

This study contains a facsimile of a letter from Mendelssohn to the Leipzig publisher C. F. Kistner about the Austro-Hungarian Joachim (1831–1907), a respectable composer and perhaps the greatest violinist of the late nineteenth and early twentieth centuries. FMB advised him on his general and compositional education.

303. Klingemann, Karl [jr.], ed. *Felix Mendelssohn-Bartholdys Briefwechsel mit Legationsrat Karl Klingemann in London.* Essen: G. D. Baedecker, 1909. 371 p. ML410.M5 A353.

Klingemann was an official at the Hanoverian legation to London, a trusted lifelong friend and artistic collaborator of FMB, and (along with Moscheles) one of the composer's principal London contacts and intermediaries. His son's edition of the correspondence is a central source of information regarding FMB's activities and works, and more reliable than most contemporary editions (though some of the letters contain minor infidelities to the autograph sources).

304. Krause, Peter. "Ein unbekannter Brief von Mendelssohn." *Musik und Gesellschaft* 26 (1976): 429–33.

This article provides both discussion and text of FMB's letter of 3 February 1840 to the Leipzig City Councilman Carl Wilhelm August Porsche, documenting FMB's activities on behalf of the city's performers.

305. Krautwurst, Franz. "Ein unbekannter Brief Felix Mendelssohn Bartholdys an Heinrich Dörrien in Leipzig." In *Augsburger Jahrbuch für Musikwissenschaft*, ed. Franz Krautwurst, 107–12. Tutzing: Hans Schneider, 1985.

Letter of 5 October 1835.

306. Kruse, Joseph A. "'Verzeiht den schändlich schlechten Brief . . .': Felix Mendelssohn Bartholdy als Briefschreiber." In *Festschrift Rudolf Elvers zum 60. Geburtstag*, ed. Ernst Herttrich and Hans Schneider, 331–47. Tutzing: Hans Schneider, 1985.

Kruse argues that the complete corpus of FMB's letters permits a more revealing portrait of his life and works than is possible from the music alone (given the complicated and highly politicized reception history of his music). Divides the letters into two literary genres: (1) letters to publishers and businesses; (2) letters to family and friends. Also recognizes chronological groups, and suggests (following Devrient's [no. 248] description of FMB's musical personality) that the composer's drive for perfection, responsible representation of reality, and appropriateness correspond exactly to his artistic conscience.

307. Mecklenburg, Klaus. "Neue Mendelssohn-Briefe, oder: Schön wär's ja?" In *Festschrift Rudolf Elvers zum 60. Geburtstag*, ed. Ernst Herttrich and Hans Schneider, 365–57. Tutzing: Hans Schneider, 1985.

308. Meloncelli, Raoul, ed. *Felix Mendelssohn Bartholdy: Lettere dall' Italia*. Turin: Fògola, 1985. 268 p.

A carefully annotated transcription of the 1958 edition of Peter Sutermeister's book of *Reisebriefe* (no. 329).

309. Mendelssohn-Bartholdy, Paul, ed. *Felix Mendelssohn Bartholdy: Reisebriefe aus den Jahren 1830 bis 1832*. Leipzig: Hermann

Mendelssohn, 1861. 520 p. ML410.M5 A29. Multiple eds. after 1862. Revised and enlarged ed. by Paul Hübner (Bonn: R. Piper, 1947). Trans. Lady [Grace Stein Don] Wallace, with a biographical introduction by Julie de Marguerittes, as *Letters from Italy and Switzerland by Felix Mendelssohn Bartholdy*. Boston: O. Ditson, 1862. 360 p. ML410.M5 A314. 3rd ed., 1863, rpt. Freeport, New York: Books for Libraries Press, 1970. ISBN 0836952715. ML410. M5 A316 1970.

Like Werner's biography (nos. 96 and 97), a seminal contribution to public knowledge of FMB, but one that creates almost as many problems as it solves. The composer was a brilliant correspondent, able to pen lively, eloquent, and accurate descriptions of the events, persons, works, and activities he described, and his remarkable prose combined with his renown to make these collections of letters best-sellers of their day. But the editions are heavily edited and sometimes conflate individual letters (as well as tacitly omitting potentially objectionable references to persons who were still alive). The unconscionably free English translation by Lady Grace Stein Don Wallace only contributes to the misrepresentation that is liberally admixed with the representation. For reliable texts of the letters readers must consult the editions by Peter Sutermeister (no. 329) and Rudolf Elvers (no. 281), or the English translation of Elvers' edition.

310. Mendelssohn-Bartholdy, Paul, and Carl Mendelssohn-Bartholdy, eds. *Briefe aus den Jahren 1833 bis 1847 von Felix Mendelssohn Bartholdy . . . nebst einem Verzeichnisse der sämmtlichen musikalischen Compositionen von Felix Mendelssohn Bartholdy, zusammengestellt von Dr. Julius Rietz.* Leipzig: Hermann Mendelssohn, 1863. 520 p. ML410.M5 A32 vol. 2. Multiple subsequent eds. Trans. Lady [Grace Stein Don] Wallace as *Letters of Felix Mendelssohn Bartholdy, from 1833 to 1847 . . . with a Catalogue of All His Musical Compositions Compiled by Julius Rietz.* London: Longman, Green, Longman, Roberts & Green, 1862. ML410.M5 A33. Numerous subsequent eds.

Originally vol. 2 of the *Reisebriefe aus den Jahren 1830 bis 1832* (no. 309). The same importance and difficulty applies to this source.

311. Mendelssohn-Bartholdy, Paul, and Carl Mendelssohn-Bartholdy, eds. *Felix Mendelssohn Bartholdy: Briefe aus den Jahren 1830 bis 1847.* Leipzig: Hermann Mendelssohn, 1864. 2 vols. Numerous eds. after 1864. Facsimile rpt., with new foreword by Beatrix Borchard, as *Felix Mendelssohn Bartholdy: Briefe.* Potsdam: Verlag für Berlin-Brandenburg, 1997. 2 vols. ISBN 3930850680. ML410.M5 A4 1997.

A combination of nos. 309 and 310. The same importance and difficulty applies to this source.

312. Miller, Norbert. "Felix Mendelssohn Bartholdys italienische Reise: Notizen zu seinen Reisebriefen." In *Das Problem Mendelssohn*, ed. Carl Dahlhaus, 23–34. Studien zur Musik des 19. Jahrhunderts, Bd. 41. Regensburg: Gustav Bosse, 1974.

An overview of the celebrated *Reisebriefe* from a literary as well as biographical standpoint. Suggests that FMB's Italian letters were not simply a personalized chronicle, but also a trope on his mentor Goethe's *Italienische Reise*.

313. Moscheles, Felix, ed. *Briefe von Felix Mendelssohn-Bartholdy an Ignaz und Charlotte Moscheles*. Leipzig: Duncker & Humblot, 1888. 287 p. ML410.M5 A358. Rpt. Walluf-Nendeln: Martin Sändig, 1976. Trans. Karl Klingemann [jr.], as *Letters of Felix Mendelssohn to Ignaz and Charlotte Moscheles*. London: Trübner, and Boston: Ticknor, 1888. 306 p. ML410.M5 A36. Rpt. Freeport, New York: Books for Libraries, 1970. ISBN 0836952170. Also rpt. [New York]: B. Blom, 1971, and Boston: Ticknor, 1979.

A student of Beethoven and close lifelong friend to FMB, Moscheles (1794–1870) was a widely respected composer, conductor, and pianist, and (along with Klingemann) one of FMB's principal London contacts. Because of the friendship between the two, the correspondence is quite free and largely devoid of formalities. The letters are replete with references to FMB's compositions and professional activities, as well as descriptions of the family and mutual friends. Editions are not error-free, but are better than those edited by the composer's brother and nephew (nos. 309, 310, and 311).

314. Nohl, Ludwig. *Musiker-Briefe: Eine Sammlung Briefe von C. W. von Gluck, Ph. E. Bach, Jos. Haydn, Carl Maria von Weber und Felix Mendelssohn-Bartholdy*. Leipzig: Duncker & Humblot, 1867. 354 p. 2nd ed., enlarged, 1873. Trans. English Lady [Grace Stein Don] Wallace as *Letters of Distinguished Musicians: Gluck, Haydn, P. E. Bach, Weber, Mendelssohn*. London: Longmans, Green & Co., 1867. 467 p.

Thirty FMB letters on p. 297–346 of German edition, 389–458 of English edition.

315. Postolka, Milan. "Musikerbriefe in der Musikabteilung des Nationalmuseums in Prag." In *Beiträge zur Musikdokumentation: Festschrift Franz Grasberger zum 60. Geburtstag*, ed. Günther Brosche, 363–90. Tutzing: Hans Schneider, 1975.

316. Reich, Willi. "Mendelssohn sucht einen Operntext: Fünf unbekannte Briefe des Komponistens." *Musica* 13 (1959): 366–77.

    First publication of five letters to the German author/actress Charlotte Birch-Pfeiffer (1800–68). Useful insights into the issues involved in FMB's lifelong quest for a suitable opera libretto.

317. Rolland, Abraham-Auguste, ed. *Lettres inédites de Mendelssohn.* Paris: J. Hetzel, 1864. 344 p. Reissued with foreword by Rémi Jacobs, as *Felix Mendelssohn Bartholdy: Voyage de jeunesse—Lettres européenes (1830–1832).* Paris: Stock, 1980. 375 p.

318. Rothe, Hans-Joachim, and Reinhard Szeskus, eds. *Felix Mendelssohn Bartholdy: Briefe aus Leipziger Archiven.* Leipzig: Deutscher Verlag für Musik, 1972. 290 p. ML410.M5 A2838. 2nd ed., 1976. 290 p.

    An important collection of 146 critically transcribed letters housed in various archives in Leipzig and organized according to designated recipients. Includes letters to Eduard Bendemann, Ferdinand David, the directors of the Leipzig Gewandhaus and the Leipzig Conservatory, the Leipzig City Council, and various other individuals.

319. Schirmer, Eduard. "Briefe Felix Mendelssohns an J. W. Schirmer." *Die Musik 2* (1902–03): 83–88.

    [Annotation for no. 319:] Schirmer (1807–63) taught FMB painting while the composer lived in Düsseldorf. This article presents five little-known letters. Mentioned: Psalm 114, Op. 51.

320. Schmidt-Beste, Thomas. "'Alles von ihm gelernt?': Die Briefe von Carl Friedrich Zelter an Felix Mendelssohn Bartholdy." *Mendelssohn-Studien* 10 (1997): 25–56.

    A significant contribution to our somewhat mythologized understanding of FMB's relationship to his composition teacher—or, more specifically, of what Zelter imparted to his young student. In addition to FMB's oft-cited "protestant work-ethic," traces certain views regarding the aesthetics of composition and Beethoven. Includes copiously annotated critical editions of twelve letters.

321. Schnapp, Friedrich. "Felix Mendelssohns Brief an seine Schwester Fanny Hensel vom 26./27. Juni 1830." *Schweizerische Musikzeitung* 99 (1959): 85–91.

    A single letter, but an intriguing one—not only containing the earliest version of the *Lied ohne Worte* in B-flat Minor, Op. 30, no. 2, but also refer-

ring to Munich's interest in an opera by FMB (and his interest in composing one), as well as references to Haydn, Beethoven, and Delphine von
Schauroth, and a lively description of the going-ons in the Bavarian capital.

322. Schubring, Julius, [Jr.] *Briefwechsel zwischen Felix Mendelssohn
Bartholdy und Julius Schubring: Zugleich ein Beitrag zur Geschichte und
Theorie des Oratoriums.* Leipzig: Duncker & Humblot, 1892. 227 p.
ML410.M5 A37. Rpt. Wiesbaden: Martin Sändig, 1973. ISBN
3500282105. ML410.M5 A37 1973.

Like Klingemann and Moscheles, the Dessau pastor Julius Schubring
(1806–89) was a close personal friend as well as professional collaborator
of FMB; among other things, he was the principal librettist for *St. Paul* and
Elijah. The volume's subtitle derives from the fact that the correspondence
reveals much about the issues and opportunities the composer and pastor
confronted in creating two of the nineteenth century's most important contributions to the oratorio genre.

323. Schultz, Günter. *Glückliche Jugend: Briefe des jungen Komponisten Felix
Mendelssohn-Bartholdy.* Bremen: Jacobi, 1971. 252 p. ML410.M5 A2836.

324. Selden-Goth, G., ed. and trans. *Felix Mendelssohn: Letters.* [New York]:
Pantheon, [1945]. 372 p. ML410.M5 A28. Rpt. New York: Vienna House,
[1973]. ISBN 0844301086. ML410.M5 A28 1973.

In general, a good and reasonably reliable selection of letters by a
scholar whose work with other composers (most notably, Busoni) well
qualified her for the task of creating an epistolary biography. The translations are reliable, and the collection includes some letters that are otherwise
quite difficult to come by.

325. Sietz, Reinhold. *Aus Ferdinand Hillers Briefwechsel (1826–1885):
Beiträge zu einer Biographie Ferdinand Hillers.* 7 vols. Beiträge zur
rheinischen Musikgeschichte, Hfte. 28, 48, 56, 60, 65, 70, 92. Cologne:
Arno Volk, 1958, 1970. ML410.H654 A4.

A valuable supplement to Hiller's memoir (no. 297), critically annotated and introduced.

326. Sterndale Bennett, J. R. *The Life of William Sterndale Bennett.* Cambridge:
University Press, 1907. 471 p. ML410.B45 B4.

The English composer William Sterndale Bennett (1816–75) was a
good friend of FMB.

327. Suhr, Norbert. "Felix Mendelssohn Bartholdy und Philipp Veit:

Unveröffentlichte Briefe." *Mendelssohn-Studien* 2 (1975): 107–50.

Veit (1793–1877) was one of FMB's Frankfurt cousins—a developer of a new theory of portraits and a member of the "Nazarene" painters with whom the composer had numerous other ties. Although Veit was not musically educated, FMB's interest in the visual arts made for a lively relationship, and there are indications that Veit may have been directly involved with the stage production of FMB's 1843 incidental music for *A Midsummer Night's Dream* (Op. 61).

328. Sutermeister, Peter, ed. *Felix Mendelssohn Bartholdy: Lebensbild mit Vorgeschichte*. Zurich: Ex Libris, 1949. 351 p. ML410.M5 A286.

The first critical edition of the many bowdlerized *Reisebriefe* edited by Paul and Carl Mendelssohn Bartholdy (nos. 309, 310, 311) in the late nineteenth century. There are still some significant errors and omissions, however; most of these are corrected in Sutermeister's next edition of the travel letters (no. 329).

329. Sutermeister, Peter, ed. *Felix Mendelssohn Bartholdy: Briefe einer Reise durch Deutschland, Italien und die Schweiz, und Lebensbild . . . mit Aquarellen und Zeichnungen aus Mendelssohns Reiseskizzenbüchern.* Zurich: M. Niehans, 1958. 384 p. ML410.M5 A286 1958. Rpt. Tübingen: Heliopolis, 1979. ISBN 3873240491.

An indispensable tool for FMB research, not least of all because it represents the single most reliable and complete edition of the letters long known through heavily edited sources (see esp. nos. 309, 310, 311).

330. Tank, Ulrich. "Felix Mendelssohn Bartholdy: Briefe an Sophie Schloss." *Mitteilungen der Arbeitsgemeinschaft für rheinische Musikgeschichte* 48 (1975): 126–28.

331. Tank, Ulrich. *Die Geschwister Schloss: Studien zur Biographie der Kölner Altistin Sophie Schloss (1822–1903) und zur Geschichte des Musikalienverlages ihres Bruders Michael (1823–1891).* Beiträge zur rheinischen Musikgeschichte, Heft 115. Cologne: Arno Volk, 1976. 97 p.

FMB first encountered Sophie Schloss in 1836, and she participated in the premieres of many of his compositions (most importantly, the revised version of the *Walpurgisnacht*). The letters presented here are, unfortunately, taken from Elise Polko's reminiscences (no. 264), but the narrative connecting tissue is more reliable, and provides useful insights.

332. Thompson, H. "Some Mendelssohn Letters." *The Musical Times* 64 (1923):

461–64, 605–08.

A collection of otherwise unpublished letters from FMB to G. A. Macfarren (1813–87), a critic, conductor, and composer who agitated actively in the British FMB cult after 1848.

333. Tiersot, Julien. *Lettres de musiciens écrites en français du XVe au XXe siè-cle*. Paris: Félix Alcan, 1924. 2 vols. ML90 .T5.

FMB in vol. 2.

334. Turner, J. Rigbie. "Mendelssohn's Letters to Eduard Devrient: Filling in Some Gaps." In *Mendelssohn Studies*, ed. R. Larry Todd, 200–39. Cambridge: Cambridge University Press, 1992.

An essential resource. Devrient's memoir on FMB (no. 248) has long been a staple of biographical and critical literature on the composer, but it is seriously flawed as a source because of numerous "gaps" (most of them tacit) that substantively alter the texts of the letters. This article begins with a biographical overview of the friendship between composer and actor, then compares Devrient's presentation of the surviving letters with the manuscripts. Provides annotations, corrections, and supplemental text in German and English.

335. Wehmer, C. *Ein tief gegründet Herz: Der Briefwechsel Felix Mendelssohn-Bartholdys mit Johann Gustav Droysen*. Heidelberg: Lambert Schneider, 1959. 118 p. ML410.M5 A345.

336. Wells, David Arthur. "Letters of Mendelssohn, Schumann and Berlioz in Belfast." *Music and Letters* 60 (1979): 180–85.

Wells includes a letter from FMB to Hermann Franck dated 1 January 1840 on p.180 ff.

337. Werner, Eric. "The Family Letters of Felix Mendelssohn Bartholdy." *Bulletin of the New York Public Library* 65 (1960): 5–20.

338. Wolff, Ernst. *Meister-Briefe: Felix Mendelssohn Bartholdy*. Berlin: B. Behr, 1907. 237 p.

A collection of letters (some of them previously unpublished, some newly released) carefully organized and annotated to produce an epistolary biography. A worthy complement to Wolff's outstanding FMB biography (no. 98).

339. Wolff, Ernst. "Sechs unveriffoutliehte Brife Felix Mendelssohn Bartholdys an Wilhelm Taubert," *Die Musik* 8 (1908–09): 165–70.

NOTES

1. See J. Rigbie Turner's study (no. 337).

2. R. Larry Todd, "The Unfinished Mendelssohn," in *Mendelssohn and His World*, ed. R. Larry Todd (Princeton: Princeton University Press, 1991), 158.

3. For an overview and case-study of these problems, see Stephen Jay Gould, "Flaws in a Victorian Veil," in *The Panda's Thumb: More Reflections in Natural History* (New York: W. W. Norton, 1980), 169–76.

3. Sociological and Cultural Studies

I.   The Mendelssohn Family
II. Studies of Jewish Issues
III. Reception History

I.   THE MENDELSSOHN FAMILY

Prefatory Note: Although this unit is devoted primarily to items that treat Felix Mendelssohn's immediate and avuncular familial relationships, it also includes studies dealing with more remote issues in prior generations, especially when these concern Moses Mendelssohn (with whose writings Felix and Fanny were familiar). There is no attempt to deal with such issues when they deal with persons such as Arnold Mendelssohn who belong to generations later than that of Felix and Fanny and were not part of their immediate family.

See also the contributions by Eckardt (no. 250) and Gilbert (no. 289).

340. Blankenburg, Elke Mascha. "Gedanken über eine Geschwisterliebe: Fanny und Felix Mendelssohn." *Neue Zeitschrift für Musik* 159 (May–June 1998): 50–52.

341. Cai, Camilla. "Fanny Hensel's 'Songs for Pianoforte of 1836–37': Stylistic Interaction with Felix Mendelssohn." *Journal of Musicological Research* 14 (1994): 55–76.

An important essay focusing on the major cycle of works for piano solo that Hensel considered publishing in 1836–37. It suggests that despite some substantial differences between the two siblings' styles (e.g., Hensel's cultivation of expansive length, developmental techniques, and multiple themes), there are also telling similarities in harmonic, rhythmic, and melodic material.

342. Elbe, Joachim von. "Paul Mendelssohn Bartholdy (1812–1874)." In *Die Mendelssohns in Berlin: Eine Familie und ihre Stadt*, ed. Rudolf Elvers and Hans-Günter Klein , 43–54. Staatsbibliothek Preußischer Kulturbesitz, Ausstellungskataloge 20. Berlin: Staatsbibliothek Preußischer Kulturbesitz, 1983.

A brief portrait of the younger son of Abraham Mendelssohn. He possessed some musical talent (he was reportedly a fine cellist, and in 1829 Felix wrote the Adagio and Allegro published posthumously as Op. 70 with him in mind). Paul left the Mendelssohn home in Berlin in 1831 to study banking in London; in 1833 he entered the firm of Mendelssohn & Co. Elbe's portrait of Paul as highly intelligent, conservative, elegant, and warm-hearted is further supported by Paul's generous assistance to Clara Schumann after Robert Schumann's hospitalization and death; see Nancy Reich's essay on the Schumanns' relationships with the Mendelssohn family (no. 191).

343. Elvers, Rudolf. "Der fingierte Brief Ludwig van Beethovens an Fanny Mendelssohn Bartholdy." *Mendelssohn-Studien* 10 (1997): 97–100.

An epistolary documentation of a marvelous brother-sister gag: a letter supposedly written to Fanny by Beethoven on 8 November 1825, actually written by FMB, with joking references to the family friend Adolf Bernhard Marx's enthusiasm for hermeneutic interpretations of Beethoven's late style (especially the adagios). It focuses especially on the Piano Sonata in B-flat Major, Op. 106.

344. Elvers, Rudolf, and Hans-Günter Klein. "Wilhelm und Fanny Hensel und ihre Nachfahren." In *Die Mendelssohns in Berlin: Eine Familie und ihre Stadt*, ed. Rudolf Elvers and Hans-Günter Klein, 55–57. Staatsbibliothek Preußischer Kulturbesitz, Ausstellungskataloge 20. Berlin: Staatsbibliothek Preußischer Kulturbesitz, 1983.

A list of the descendants of the five children of Wilhelm and Fanny Hensel (also displayed in the family-tree fold-out included in the volume), also providing their places of residence.

345. Elvers, Rudolf, and Hans-Günter Klein. "Sebastian Hensel: Briefe an seine Kinder 1881." In *Die Mendelssohns in Berlin: Eine Familie und ihre Stadt*, ed. Rudolf Elvers and Hans-Günter Klein, 74–76. Staatsbibliothek Preußischer Kulturbesitz, Ausstellungskataloge 20. Berlin: Staatsbibliothek Preußischer Kulturbesitz, 1983.

346. Elvers, Rudolf. "Schenkungen und Stiftungen der Mendelssohns." In *Die Mendelssohns in Berlin: Eine Familie und ihre Stadt,* ed. Rudolf Elvers and Hans-Günter Klein, 94–109. Staatsbibliothek Preußischer Kulturbesitz, Ausstellungskataloge 20. Berlin: Staatsbibliothek Preußischer Kulturbesitz, 1983.

347. Feilchenfeldt, Konrad. "Karl August Varnhagen von Ense: Sieben Briefe an Rebecka Dirichlet." *Mendelssohn-Studien* 3 (1979): 51–79.

   Sheds useful light on familial relations during the generation of FMB and Fanny Hensel. This is one of relatively few studies that deals substantively with the family's younger sister, Rebecka Dirichlet.

348. Feilchenfeldt, Konrad, and Lieselotte Kinskofer. "Rebecka Dirichlet: Briefe—Aus der Varnhagen von Enseschen Sammlung." *Mendelssohn-Studien* 6 (1986): 121–50.

   The previously unknown correspondence between Rebecka Dirichlet, Frederike Robert, Rahel Varnhagen von Ense, Karl August Varnhagen von Ense, and Ludmilla Assign presents not only the development of the personality of FMB's younger sister, but also the development of the relationship between two close-knit families over nearly three decades. This article includes nine letters from "Beckchen" (as she was known to family and friends) to these family members, as well as a letter from Fanny Hensel to Frederike Robert.

349. Gantzel-Kress, Giesela. "Karl Mendelssohn Bartholdy, 1838–1897." *Mendelssohn-Studien* 8 (1993): 197–225.

   Traces the life of FMB's son Karl, who evidently suffered from schizophrenia.

350. Gilbert, Felix. "Paul Mendelssohn Bartholdy (1841–1880)." *Die Mendelssohns in Berlin: eine Familie und ihre Stadt,* ed. Rudolf Elvers and Hans-Günter Klein, 80–86. Staatsbibliothek Preußischer Kulturbesitz, Ausstellungskataloge 20. Berlin: Staatsbibliothek Preußischer Kulturbesitz, 1983.

   The most important biographical study of FMB's younger son.

351. Haufe, Veronika. "Die Paten der Familie Mendelssohn." *Friede und Freiheit: Monatsblatt der Evangelisch-Reformierten Kirche in Sachsen (Dresden)* 39, no. 7 (1984): 10–14.

   The only article to examine the minor but too neglected issue of godmother and godfather relationships in the Mendelssohn family.

352. Hensel, Sebastian. *Die Familie Mendelssohn 1729–1847: Nach Briefen und Tagebüchern.* Berlin: Behr, 1879. 3 vols. Numerous subsequent editions (18th in 1924), most of them in 2 vols. Trans. Karl Klingemann [jr.] and an American collaborator as *The Mendelssohn Family (1729–1847): From Letters and Journals.* New York: Harper, 1881. 2nd ed., with a notice by George Grove, 1882. 2 vols. Numerous subsequent eds. after 1891. Rpt. New York: Greenwood, 1968. ML385 .H542 1968. Rpt. New York: Haskell House, 1969. ISBN 0838303048. ML385 .H542 1969.

This book remains a central source for research concerning virtually every aspect of FMB's life and works, and of the lives of the remarkable Mendelssohn family; however, it must be used in close consultation with other sources. Fanny Hensel's son, Sebastian, originally wrote the book only as a memoir for the family, and when it was prepared for publication many changes were necessary. Some re-writings of original sources were undertaken (in Hensel's words) to eradicate "gossip which would amuse the immediate circle of acquaintances [but] would have no interest for the general public," while others stem from Hensel's other objective in publishing the family memoir: to present to an increasingly anti-Semitic and unappreciative public a vivid portrait of the Mendelssohns as a good German family whose lives and works would refute the anti-Semitic stereotypes that pervaded the popular literature of the day. However understandable his reasoning may have been, the book also conflates letters, makes tacit omissions, and contains numerous minor factual errors—problems which compromise its usefulness but in no way negate it.

353. Heuberger, Richard. *Musikalische Skizzen.* Musikalische Studien, 6. Leipzig: Seemann Nachfolger, 1901. ML60 .H499. Rpt. Nendeln/Liechtenstein: Kraus Reprint, 1976. ML60 .H499 1976.

"Felix Mendelssohn-Bartholdy (Zu seinem fünfzigsten Todestag)" on p. 66–74. "In recent times Mendelssohn has had to endure many an attack. He has been accused of softness and sentimentality; indeed, attempts have even been made to interpret his formal perfection as a shortcoming." Heuberger then mounts an attack on "dandified" ("vergilgert") modern music that, he says, stutters. Therefore, "who speaks clearly is scorned." Mendelssohn's conducting is described and Joseph Joachim is quoted in its praise. Mendelssohn's piano playing is likewise praised. [DM]

354. Klein, Han-Günter. "Joseph Mendelssohn." In *Die Mendelssohns in Berlin: eine Familie und ihre Stadt,* ed. Rudolf Elvers and Hans-Günter Klein, 20–30. Staatsbibliothek Preußischer Kulturbesitz, Ausstellungskataloge 20. Berlin: Staatsbibliothek Preußischer Kulturbesitz, 1983.

A sketch of the life and business affairs of Felix Mendelssohn's uncle Joseph, who in 1795 established the first of the banks run by members of the Mendelssohn family. (For an overview of these banks, see the illustration on p. 16–17 of the volume.)

355. Klein, Hans-Günter. "Parallels and Differences in the Artistic Development of Fanny and Felix Mendelssohn Bartholdy." In *The Mendelssohns: Their Music in History*, ed. John Michael Cooper and Julie D. Prandi. Oxford: Oxford University Press, [forthcoming].

356. Kleßmann, Eckardt. *Die Mendelssohns: Bilder aus einer deutschen Familie. Zurich: Artemis*, 1990. ISBN 3760810209. ML390 .K62 1990. 3rd ed. 1997. 192 p. ISBN 3760810209. 2nd ed. Frankfurt am Main: Insel, 1993. Insel Taschenbuch no. 1523. 315 p. ISBN 3458332235.

A lavishly illustrated family history, drawn from popular sources but devoid of the dismissive generalizations that characterize much of even the sympathetic popular literature on FMB.

357. Kühm, Helga-Maria. "'In diesem ruhigen Kleinleben geht so schrecklich viel vor': Rebecka Lejeune Dirichlet, geb. Mendelssohn Bartholdy, in Göttingen 1855–1858." *Mendelssohn-Studien* 11 (1999): 145–56.

One of comparatively few biographical studies dealing with Rebecka.

358. Lepsius, Sabine. "Das Haus Hensel." In *Die Mendelssohns in Berlin: eine Familie und ihre Stadt*, ed. Rudolf Elvers and Hans-Günter Klein, 77–79. Staatsbibliothek Preußischer Kulturbesitz, Ausstellungskataloge 20. Berlin: Staatsbibliothek Preußischer Kulturbesitz, 1983.

359. Lowenthal-Hensel, Cécile. "Mutter und Sohn: Fanny und Sebastian Hensel." In *Die Mendelssohns in Berlin: eine Familie und ihre Stadt*, ed. Rudolf Elvers and Hans-Günter Klein, 58–73. Staatsbibliothek Preußischer Kulturbesitz, Ausstellungskataloge 20. Berlin: Staatsbibliothek Preußischer Kulturbesitz, 1983.

A thoughtful biographical sketch of Fanny and her son, written by the great-granddaughter of the composer. It is prefaced by an explanation of the names employed and preferred by both.

360. Lowenthal-Hensel, Cécile. "Wilhelm Hensel: Fanny und Felix im Porträt." *Mendelssohn-Studien* 10 (1997): 9–24.

361. Lowenthal-Hensel, Cécile. "Wilhelm Hensel in England." *Mendelssohn-Studien* 2 (1975): 203–14.

Fanny's husband, the Prussian court painter, visited England twice, in

1838 and 1843. Like FMB, he was received by the English royal family (perhaps both Victoria and Albert, perhaps only Albert). This essay explores that dimension of the Mendelssohn family's relationships with England, and also provides reproductions of Wilhelm Hensel's portraits of Queen Victoria, Prince Albert, and Edward, Prince of Wales.

362. Lowenthal-Hensel, Cécile. "Wilhelm Hensels 'Lebenslauf' von 1829." *Mendelssohn-Studien* 3 (1979): 175–79.

Wilhelm Hensel became a member of the Royal Academy of Arts on 21 February 1829 and, in compliance with the requirements of the Academy, submitted a prose curriculum vitae of his life and works up to that point—the year in which he also became engaged to and married Fanny. Article features a transcription of this previously unpublished document.

363. Mygdalis, Lampros. "Unbekannte Gedichte von Wilhelm Hensel." *Mendelssohn-Studien* 5 (1982): 135–40.

Wilhelm Hensel was also a poet—one whose works found some reception and publication in the nineteenth century. The five little-known poems reproduced here exemplify these poetic proclivities (also evident in the texts of some of Fanny Hensel's songs), as well as providing literary documentation of Wilhelm's philhellene interests.

364. Rabien, Ilse. "Die Mendelssohns in Bad Reinerz: Zur Familie Nathan Mendelssohns." *Mendelssohn-Studien* 7 (1990): 153–70.

365. Rothe, Hans-Joachim. "Famliäre Bindungen und gesellschaftliche Leistungen der Mendelssohns im 18./19. Jahrhundert." *Sächsische Heimatblätter* 35 (1989): 18–25.

366. Sabean, David Warren. "Fanny and Felix Mendelssohn-Bartholdy and the Question of Incest." *The Musical Quarterly* 77 (1993): 709–17.

This article is not as inflammatory as the title suggests, but it is a thoughtful consideration of the closeness of the relationship (artistic as well as personal) between FMB and Fanny.

367. Schroeder, Johann Karl v[on]. "Um das Eiserne Kreuz von 1813: Wilhelm Hensel in den Freiheitskriegen." *Mendelssohn-Studien* 3 (1979): 163–73.

As an ambitious and adventurous nineteen-year-old painter, Hensel participated in various German campaigns in the wars of rebellion against Napoleon. Article includes Hensel's surviving notes on these campaigns.

368. Steinberg, Michael P. "Culture, Gender, and Music: A Forum on the Mendelssohn Family (Introduction)." *The Musical Quarterly* 77 (1993): 648–50.

    A rather staid introduction to a series of essays that have generated much controversy (see no. 11).

369. Steinberg, Michael P. "Mendelssohn's Music and German-Jewish Culture: An Intervention." *The Musical Quarterly* 83 (1999): 31–44.

    See also the contributions by Jeffrey L. Sposato (no. 391 and 392), Leon Botstein (nos. 374 and 376), and Peter Ward Jones (no. 230).

370. Stolzenberg, Ingeborg. "Paul Mendelssohn-Bartholdy nach dem Tode seines Bruders Felix: Ein Brief vom 10. Dezember an Karl Klingemann nebst drei Briefen von Eduard Magnus." *Mendelssohn-Studien* 8 (1993): 179–95.

    An important study documenting the impact of FMB's death on his immediate family and closest friends through little-known correspondence. It is carefully annotated and critically transcribed.

371. Wilcke, Gero von. "Die Mendelssohns in Leipzig—Vorfahren und Nachkommen: Zur Eröffnung des Neuen Gewandhauses." *Geneaologie, Neustadt/Aisch* 32 (1983): 497–519.

372. Wollney, Peter. "Sara Levy and the Making of Musical Taste in Berlin." *The Musical Quarterly* 77 (1993): 651–88.

    An important contribution to the literature concerning FMB's great-aunt Sara Levy (1761–1864). The essay examines Levy's activities up to 1800, focusing on her role as collector and patron of music, particularly music by members of the Bach family. Includes an appendix identifying musical sources (manuscript and printed) formerly owned by members of Levy's family.

II. STUDIES OF JEWISH ISSUES

373. Blessinger, Karl. *Judentum und Musik: Ein Beitrag zur Kultur- und Rassenpolitik.* Berlin: B. Hahnefeld, 1944. 156 p.

    A revised and expanded version of Blessinger's *Mendelssohn, Meyerbeer, Mahler: Drei Kapitel Judentum in der Musik als Schlüssel zur Musikgeschichte des 19. Jahrhunderts* (Berlin: B. Hahnefeld, [1939]). By the time of the earlier volume's publication, Blessinger had established his position as a vehement (if also eloquent) advocate of anti-Semitic historiography and criticism; those who dare might also consult his *Die musikalische Probleme der Gegenwart und ihre Lösung* (Stuttgart: B. Filser, [1920]). The deplorableness of his several published compositions is consistent with that of these writings.

374. Botstein, Leon. "Mendelssohn and the Jews." *The Musical Quarterly* 82 (1998): 210–19.

A response to Sposato's criticisms (no. 391) of Eric Werner's handling of FMB's Jewishness in the major biographical studies (nos. 96 and 97), and a cautious defense of Werner based on the challenges he faced in raising the issues in general. See also Sposato's response (no. 392), Bostein's counter-response (no. 376), and Michael P. Steinberg's "intervention" (no. 369).

375. Botstein, Leon. "Mendelssohn, Mahler und Schönberg: Die gesellschaftliche Rolle von Sprache und Kultur." In *Judentum und Modernität: Essays zur Rolle der Juden in der deutschen und österreichischen Kultur 1848 bis 1938*, 44–54. Vienna: Böhlau, 1991.

A thoughtful and thought-provoking essay situating the three titular figures amid three broad societal developments: (1) Jews had participated in the profits that most of society reaped from the economic developments and industrialization of the continent; (2) over the course of the centuries the legitimacy of the ideals of education (*Bildung*) had become recognized, providing a mechanism for Jews to enter into society; and (3) new forms of anti-Semitism had emerged as a result of increasing nationalist sentiments combined with Enlightenment logic. Suggests that FMB's belief in a true, normative, and communicable capacity for Jewish assimilation is represented in the symphony-cantata *Lobgesang*, Op. 52.

376. Botstein, Leon. "Mendelssohn, Werner, and the Jews: A Final Word." *The Musical Quarterly* 83 (1999): 45–50.

See Botstein's previous contribution to this discussion (no. 374) and the essay by Jeffrey L. Sposato that provoked it (no. 391), as well as Peter Ward Jones's response (no. 230) and Michael P. Steinberg's "intervention" (no. 369).

377. Botstein, Leon. "Songs without Words: Thoughts on Music, Theology, and the Role of the Jewish Question in the Work of Felix Mendelssohn." *The Musical Quarterly* 77 (1993): 561–78.

A characteristically thoughtful examination of ways in which specifically Jewish aspects of FMB's upbringing shaped his views on his obligations as a composer and influenced his compositions.

378. Bourel, Dominique. "Bendavids Trinkspruch auf Moses Mendelssohn, Berlin 1829 (übersetzt von Michael S. Collins)." *Mendelssohn-Studien* 6 (1986): 41–47.

379. Bourel, Dominique. "Moses Mendelssohn, Markus Herz und die Akademie der Wissenschaften zu Berlin." *Mendelssohn-Studien* 4 (1979): 223–34.

380. Bücken, Ernst. *Musik der Nationen: eine Musikgeschichte.* Körners Taschenausgabe, Bd. 131. Leipzig: Körner, 1937. 494 p. ML160.B92 M9. 2nd ed., rev. Jürgen Völckers, as *Geschichte der Musik.* Körners Taschenausgabe, Bd. 131. Stuttgart: Körner, 1951. 392 p.

381. Reinharz, Jehuda, and Walter Schatzberg, eds. *The Jewish Response to German Culture from the Enlightenment to the Second World War (Conference, Clark University, 1983).* Hanover, New Hampshire: Clark University Press of New England, 1985. 362 p. ISBN 0874513456. DS135.G33 J47 1985.

382. *Juden in Berlin, 1671–1945: Ein Lesebuch.* Berlin: Nicolai, [1988]. 350 p. ISBN 3875842502. DS135.G4 B45445 1988.

A reader that contains several illuminating remarks on FMB and responses to writings about the composer.

383. Katz, Jacob. *The Darker Side of Genius: Richard Wagner's Anti-Semitism.* Hanover: University Press of New England, 1986. 158 p. ISBN 0874513685. ML 410 .W19 K3313.

An important study by a leading scholar of the history of anti-Semitism. Unlike many studies that discuss Wagner's anti-Semitic imagination, this book does not proceed from biographical concerns; instead, it situates Wagner's ideas against the backdrop of European intellectual and cultural history. The chapter on "Wagner's 'Philo-Semitism'" traces the emergence of Wagner's anti-Semitic denigrations of FMB and offers useful observations concerning the immediate causes.

384. Katz, Jacob. "Die Enstehung der Judenassimilation in Deutschland und deren Ideologie." Diss., Frankfurt am Main, 1935. Rpt. (in German) in *Emancipation and Assimilation: Studies in Modern Jewish History.* Farmborough: Gregg, 1972. 293 p. DS135.G33 K32. Also rpt. in *idem, Zur Assimilation und Emanzipation der Juden: Ausgewählte Schriften.* Darmstadt: Wissenschaftliche Buchgesellschaft, 1982. ISBN 3534084284.

DS135.G33 K33 1982.

Katz (b. 1904) is one of the leading authorities on the history of anti-Semitism and ideologies concerning Jewish assimilation; as the citation indicates, much of his later work proceeds from his important dissertation (written at a time when such a study placed the author in peril in Germany). This study is included here because of its centrality to much later research on such issues, and because of the importance of these themes in FMB's own biography and historiography.

385. Kaufman, Wanda. *Deutsche und Juden: Studien zur Geschichte des deutschen Judentums*. Frankfurt: Fischer, 1979. 449 p.

386. Liszt, Franz. *Des Bohémiens et de leur musique en Hongroie*. Paris: A. Bourdilliat, 1859. Rpt. Paris: Marval, 1999. 221 p. ISBN 2862342831. 2nd ed. Leipzig: Breitkopf & Härtel, 1881. 538 p. Rpt. Bologna: Forni, 1972. ML410.L7 A18 1881. Rpt. Walluf [bei Wiesbaden]: Martin Sänding, 1973. ISBN 3500283705. Trans. German Peter Cornelius as *Die Zigeuner und ihre Musik in Ungarn*. Budapest: G. Heckenast, 1861. 259 p. Trans. English Edwin Evans as *The Gipsy in Music, by Franz Liszt: the Result of the Author's Life-long Experiences and Investigations of the Gipsies and Their Music*. London: W. Reeves, 1926. Rpt. London: W. Reeves, [1960]. 369 p. ML410 .L7A181.

Although not as well-known as Wagner's notorious essay on "Judaism in Music" (no. 394), this essay is equally essential as a document of the repugnant anti-Semitic views that strongly influenced the late nineteenth century's assessment of FMB's life, works, and artistic significance. In this work, the Jews are compared unfavorably to Gypsies, with whom they typically share a nomadic life-style and a position on the periphery of "civilized" society. Like Wagner, however, Liszt concludes that the Jews' homelessness, language, and innate repulsiveness have prevented them from achieving anything more than talent in the arts. FMB, of course, is presented as a case-study in the power of these racially based fatal flaws to undermine any potential for true artistic greatness.

387. Martens, Helen. Mendelssohn's Faith and Works: *The Spiritual Odyssey of a Composer*. Waterloo, Ontario: Conrad Grebel College, 1989. 22 p. ML410.M5 M185 1990.

388. Mayer, Hans. "Felix Mendelssohns geschichtlicher Augenblick." In *Der Widerruf: Über Deutsche und Juden*, 25–49. Frankfurt am Main: Suhrkamp, 1994. 467 p. ISBN 3518405829. 2nd ed. (not so designated) 1996. ISBN 3518390856. Rpt. in *Felix Mendelssohn—Mitwelt und*

Nachwelt: Bericht zum 1. Leipziger Mendelssohn-Kolloquium am 8. und 9. Juni 1993, ed. Leon Bostein, 5–14. Wiesbaden: Breitkopf & Härtel, 1996.

389. Ringer, Alexander L. "Felix Mendelssohn oder das Judentum in der Musik." In *Felix Mendelssohn Bartholdy: Repräsentant und/oder Außenseiter? Fünf Vorträge zu den "Kasseler Musiktagen 1991,"* ed. Leo Karl Gerhartz, 67–91. Kassel: Kasseler Musiktage, 1993.

A thoughtful history of the anti-Semitic elements of FMB reception history and the ways in which they related to general racial thinking in late-nineteenth-century culture (emphasizing figures such as Wagner and Uhlig), followed by an overview of some aspects of FMB's life and works which he himself probably would have described as Jewish. The disparities between nineteenth- and twentieth-century perspectives are remarkable.

390. Ringer, Alexander L. "Mendelssohn, ein Problem?" In *Felix Mendelssohn—Mitwelt und Nachwelt: Bericht zum 1. Leipziger Mendelssohn-Kolloquium am 8. und 9. Juni 1993,* ed. Leon Botstein, 97–103. Wiesbaden: Breitkopf & Härtel, 1996.

This article questions the nature and existence of "The Mendelssohn Problem" (see no. 3).

391. Sposato, Jeffrey S. "Creative Writing: The [Self-]Identification of Mendelssohn as Jew." *The Musical Quarterly* 92 (1998): 190–209.

A controversial essay, but one that offers a much-need critique of some falsehoods created and/or propagated by Eric Werner in his FMB biography (nos. 96 and 97). Reveals that Werner seemingly deliberately distorted and misrepresented the text of several documents in which FMB's Jewishness was an issue, and suggests that subsequent scholars' almost unquestioning acceptance of Werner's view of the role of Jewishness in FMB's life and works has led to misunderstandings concerning the nature and extent of the assimilation that (in Sposato's view) the composer greatly prized. It has long been known that Werner's biography contains extensive errors with regard to some factual matters, transcriptions of documents, and representations of otherwise unpublished manuscripts, but this is by far the most extensive and systematic treatment of those problems.

392. Sposato, Jeffrey S. "Mendelssohn, *Paulus*, and the Jews: A Response to Leon Botstein and Michael Steinberg." *The Musical Quarterly* 83 (1999): 280–91.

Perhaps the final installment in the protracted dispute . . . See nos. 369, 374, and 376, and also Sposato's dissertation (no. 900).

393. Stolle, Thomas Leon . "Zwischen Ausgrenzung und Vereinnahmung: Vom Umgang mit jüdischen Komponisten." In *Der jüdische Beitrag zur Musikgeschichte Böhmens und Mahrens*, ed. Torsten Fuchs, Ingrid Hader, and Klaus-Peter Koch, 54–70. Veröffentlichungen des Sudetendeutschen Musikinstituts: Allgemeine Reihe, Nr. 2. Regensburg: Sudetendeutsches Institut, 1994.

> A survey of nineteenth-century written opinions about Mendelssohn, Meyerbeer, and Mahler. Demonstrates that the attribution "Jewish" was used either to isolate the composer and his music from the mainstream, or to acknowledge positively certain characteristics in their music.

394. [Wagner, Richard.] "Das Judenthum in der Musik." *Neue Zeitschrift für Musik* 33, no. 19 (3 September 1850): 101–07, and no. 20 (6 September 1850): 109–12. Revised ed., 1869. Rev. ed. rpt. in *Richard Wagner: Gesammelte Schriften und Dichtungen*, 4th ed., 5: 66–85. Leipzig: C.F.W. Giegel, 1907. Trans. English by W. Ashton Ellis as "Judaism in Music." In *Richard Wagner's Prose Works, Vol. III: The Theatre* (London: Kegan Paul, Trench, Trübner & Co., 1894), 75–122.

> This essay—one of the most notorious chapters in the anti-Semitic reception history of FMB—was originally issued under the ironically pseudonymous authorship of "K. Freigedank" (roughly, K[arl] Free-Thought). The main tenets of Wagner's thoughts are by now all too familiar: gentiles (especially Germans, as is emphasized in the later essay "Was ist deutsch?") are naturally and involuntarily repulsed by the nature and personality of the Jew; the "be-Jewing" (*Verjüdung*) of modern art had worked to the detriment of all the arts, especially the poetic ones (and, among those, especially music); the Jew is incapable of great artistic utterance because his language is incapable of producing poetry; the Jew's mercantile and mercenary instincts prevented a true understanding of non-commercial art; and so on. FMB is presented as a case-study of a Jew who, despite the amplest store of "specific talents," was unable "to call forth in us that deep, that heart-searching effect which we await from art."

395. Weiner, Marc A. *Richard Wagner and the Anti-Semitic Imagination.* Lincoln, Nebraska: University of Nebraska Press, 1995.4 39 p. ISBN 0803247753. ML 410 .W19 W23 1995.

> Although Weiner mentions FMB only a few times, this book is distinctively useful as a tool because of the manner in which it dissects the ideas and the cultural baggage of Wagner's infamous essay on "Judaism in Music" (no. 394). The organization proceeds from Wagner's own usual

means for discussing society and the future of art: the metaphor of the body. Thus, the main chapters are dedicated to "The Eyes of the Volk"; "Voices: Coloratura vs. *tief und innig*"; "Smells: The Teutonic *Duft and the foetor*"; and "Feet: Clubfoot, Heroic Foot." The final two chapters, titled "Icons of Degeneration" and "Epilogue: Wagner and the Embodiment," offer considerable insights into the means by which pseudo-scientific racial stereotypes infected one of the nineteenth century's greatest musical minds and libelled another one.

396. Werner, Eric. "Felix Mendelssohn—Gustav Mahler: Two Border-line Cases of German-Jewish Assimilation." *Yuval: Studies of the Jewish Music Research Centre Israel* 4 (1982): 240–64.

397. Wolter, Günter. "Der Weg der Verheissung: Über jüdische Assimilation und Antisemitismus im deutschen Musikleben." *Das Orchester: Zeitschrift für Orchester- und Rundfunk-Chorwesen* 43/7–8 (1995): 15–22.

The title is taken from a musical by Weill. This essay discusses the emancipation and assimilation of German Jews, including Mendelssohn, Meyerbeer, Offenbach, and Mahler. Reviews the consequences of the anti-Semitic views that so characterized the late-nineteenth- and early-twentieth-century literature on these composers.

III. RECEPTION HISTORY

398. Adorno, Theodor. *Versuch über Wagner.* Berlin: Suhrkamp, 1952. ML410.W1 A595. 2nd ed. 1974. 145 p. 2nd ed. reissued 1981. ISBN 3518366777. Trans. English Rodney Livingstone as *In Search of Wagner.* London: NLB, 1981. Rpt. 1991. 159 p. ISBN 0860910377 (cloth), 0860917967 (pbk.). ML410.W1 A5953 1991. NLB ed. reissued London: Verso, 1984. 160 p. ISBN 0860917967.

An important (if also ideologically charged) attempt, in part, to come to terms with Wagner's critique of FMB.

399. Ambros, August Wilhelm. *Die Grenzen der Musik und der Poesie: eine Studie zur Ästhetik der Tonkunst.* Leipzig: Matthes, 1855. 187 p. Rpt. Hildesheim: G. Olms, 1976. ISBN 3487060310. ML3849 .A46 1976. 2nd ed., 1878. 193 p.

This book provides contemporary perspective on the mid-century debates concerning potentials and limitations of music and poetry, and attempts to situate FMB's concert overtures (especially the *Hebrides*

Overture and *Calm Sea and Prosperous Voyage*) in relationship to programmatic works of Spohr (*Die Weihe der Töne*), Berlioz (*Symphonie fantastique, Roméo et Juliette*), and Wagner, as well as aesthetic theories of
Adolph Bernhard Marx and Eduard Hanslick.

400. Berlioz, Hector. *Les Soirées de l'orchestre.* Paris: Calmann Lévy, 1852. 436
p. ML3849 .A46 1976. 2nd ed., fully revised, Paris: Michel Lévy, 1854.
435 p. ML410.B5 A53 1854. Numerous subsequent eds. Ed. Léon
Guichard, with introduction by Henri Barraud, Paris: Librairie Gründ,
1968. 653 p. ML410.B5 A53 1968. Rpt. 1998. Trans. English Charles E.
Roche, with introduction by Ernest Newman, as *Evenings in the Orchestra*.
New York: Alfred A. Knopf, 1929. 366 p. ML410.B5 A533 1929. New
Eng. trans. Jacques Barzun, New York: Alfred A. Knopf, 1956. 376 p.
ML410.B5 A533 1956. Reissued Chicago: University of Chicago Press,
1973. 381 p. Rpt., with new introduction by Peter Bloom, 1999. ISBN
0226043746. ML410.B5 A533 1999. Trans. C. R. Fortescue, with intro-
duction and notes by David Cairns, Baltimore: Penguin, 1963. 342 p.
ML410.B5 A533 1963.

Although literally a memoir, this eminently readable and often entertaining book is, *au fond*, a document of reception history. See also Berlioz's
Memoirs (no. 242).

401. Bloom, Peter A. "Berlioz and the Critic: La Damnation de Fétis." In *Studies
in Musicology in Honor of Otto E. Albrecht,* ed. John Walter Hill, 240–60.
Kassel: Bärenreiter, 1980.

This essay is important as one of precious few systematic explorations of the politics of FMB's relationships with Berlioz, Fétis, and the
French musical public in general. Bloom documents the faultiness of
Berlioz's memory (as recorded in the *Memoirs* [no. 242]) with regard to
certain events, examines the history of his increasingly hostile relationship
to the respected critic Fétis, and shows how FMB was unwittingly (and
unhappily) drawn into the feud that left the two French partisans with
formidable lists of enemies.

402. Botstein, Leon, ed., and Susan Gillespie, trans. "Heinrich Heine on
Mendelssohn." In *Mendelssohn and His World,* ed. R. Larry Todd, 352–63.
Princeton: Princeton University Press, 1991.

Like FMB, Heine was Jewish—but unlike FMB, he never converted
to Christianity. Despite their friendship in Berlin and Paris, Heine harbored
lifelong suspicions about the motives for FMB's conversion, and he (also
unlike FMB) always considered himself an outsider. Article presents

Heine's views on FMB's significance as an artist and a cultural phenomenon.

403. Brodbeck, David L. "Brahms's Mendelssohn." *The American Brahms Society Newsletter* 15/2 (1997): 1–3.

A brief but insightful overview of numerous instances in which Brahms drew upon FMB's works in his own compositions.

404. Burg, Josef. "Widor et l'Allemagne: Charles-Marie Widor, ses voyages et ses contacts avec la vie musicale et intellectuelle en Allemagne." *L'orgue francophone: Bulletin de liaison de la Fédération Francophone des Amis de l'Orgue* 11 (November 1991): 42–70.

405. Burkholder, Samuel R. "The Oratorio: Its Development since the Time of Mendelssohn." Ph.D. diss., Northwestern University, 1939.

Not available for examination.

406. Busch, Hermann J., and Werner Kleuppelholz. *Musik—gedeutet und gewertet: Texte zur musikalischen Rezeptionsgeschichte.* DTV Dokumente, Nr. 2937. Kassel: Bärenreiter, 1983. 309 p. ISBN 3423029374.

407. Cooper, Jeffrey H. "The Rise of French Instrumental Music and Concert Series in Paris, 1828–1871." Ph.D. diss., Cornell University, 1981. 387 p. Reissued under same title, Ann Arbor, Mich.: UMI Research Press, 1983. Studies in Musicology, no. 65. 387 p. ISBN 0835714039. ML497.8.P4 C6 1983.

408. Crawford, Chris Reagan. "Felix Mendelssohn-Bartholdy and His Music as Reported in *Dwight's Journal of Music.*" M.A. thesis, Stephen F. Austin State University, 1983. 110 p.

A laudable attempt to study FMB's place in the musical tastes of mid-nineteenth-century listeners, performers, and critics, unfettered by the erraticisms and vicissitudes of anti-Semitic and anti-Victorian reception history. The focus is on the leading American music periodical, *Dwight's Journal of Music* (a journal that included four hundred articles devoted to FMB during its operational years, 1852–81). Includes chapters on music by FMB that was performed in the U.S.; the composer's musical style as reviewed in *Dwight's*; material concerning his biography and personal appearance; and one on miscellaneous materials.

409. Cupers, Jean-Louis. "De la nécessité de la sympathie critique ou quelques considérations sur des opinions émises à propos de Félix Mendelssohn." *International Review of the Aesthetics and Sociology of Music* 5 (1974):

313–25.

410. Drechsler, Nanny. "Felix Mendelssohn im 'Dritten Reich.'" In *Felix Mendelssohn Bartholdy: Leben und Werk—Musikfestspiele Saar 1989*, ed. Robert Leonardy, 77–92. Edition Karlsberg, Bd. 6. Lebach: Joachim Hempel, 1989.

411. Ellis, Katharine. *Music Criticism in Nineteenth-Century France: 'La Revue et Gazette musicale de Paris,' 1834–80*. Cambridge: Cambridge University Press, 1995.

>   One of comparatively few systematic explorations of FMB's reception in France. Shows that French critics responded particularly to the F-minor String Quartet, Op. posth. 80, the piano music as a whole, and the Mendelssohnian scherzo in general.

412. Frisius, Rudolf. "Ein Gedenkjahr im Schatten der 'Unbewältigten Vergangenheit': Die Karlsruher Mendelssohn-Tage 1984." *Neue Zeitschrift für Musik* 145/9 (1984): 37–38.

413. Gömann, Silke. "Zur Funktion von Mendelssohn-Bildern in der Musikgeschichte: Rezeptionsästhetische und gattungstheoretische Untersuchungen zu den Sinfonien Felix Mendelssohns." Ph.D. diss., University of Bonn, [in progress].

414. Haweis, Rev. Hugh Reginald. *Music and Morals*. London: Strachan, 1871. 576 p. Rpt. New York: Harper & Brothers, 1872. L60 .H39. Revised ed., London: Harper, [1897]. 503 p.

>   The first book, "Philosophy," is about "Music, Emotion, and Morals" and seeks to show the relationship of these three. Suggests that "music is pre-eminently the art of the nineteenth century because it is in a supreme manner responsive to the emotional wants, the mixed aspirations, and the passionate self-consciousness of The Age," and that the moral qualities of a work of art depend on the intentions of its author rather than any characteristic directly observable in it. The section about Mendelssohn emphases his way of "finely calculating the capacities of the ordinary, music-loving mind." Includes a long discussion of *Elijah*. [DM/JMC]

415. Heiduk, Franz. "Zur Mendelssohn-Transkiption von Franz Liszt." *Aurora* 48 (1988): 154–67.

416. Hiller, Ferdinand. *Aus dem Tonleben unserer Zeit: Gelegentliches*. Leipzig: Hermann Mendelssohn, 1868. 2 vols. ML60 .H65. 2nd ed., Leipzig: F.E.C. Lenchast, 1971. 194 p.

>   Vol. 1 contains a review of Marx's *Die Musik des 19ten Jahrhunderts*

und ihre Pflege (p. 210–29), as well as a commentary/review fo the recently released edition of FMB's letters (p. 277–305). According to Hiller, Marx loses his objectivity when dealing with Mendelssohn and "casts a shadow on the purity of Mendelssohn's artistic character." Hiller also remarks that "all will agree that ancient Greek tragedy can no longer be comfortable on our stage," but that Mendelssohn's attempt to revive it was noble in intent. A review of the publication of the first volume of Mendelssohn's *Reisebriefe* contains a comment, apparently added later, about the second official volume of letters: "Among the many perfected works of art that Mendelssohn gave to the world, his life is the most beautiful." [DM/JMC]

417. Huschke, Konrad. *Unsere Tonmeister unter Einander.* [Bd. 3]: *Robert Schumanns Beziehungen zu Felix Mendelssohn-Bartholdy, Richard Wagner und Franz Liszt.* Pritzwalk: Tienken, 1928. 132 p.

   A study of reception history by effect rather than by design. "Robert Schumann, the most German and noble of those in art, had as artist the tragic fate to find in Felix Mendelssohn-Bartholdy a friend who despite great talent was by tendency and development totally unable to understand him in his most individual, his profound German manner. Through Mendelssohn, to whose influence he in romantic enthusiasm far too much submitted, he was led to paths that did not conform to his individuality, and moreover, was brought into lamentable dissension with two great contemporaries, Wagner and Liszt, to whom, granted all the differences in artistic goals, his art meant far more than to Mendelssohn." [DM] See also Huschke's *Musiker, Maler und Dichter als Freunde und Gegner* (Leipzig: Heilingsche Verlagsanstalt, 1939). [JMC]

418. Josephson, Nors S. "Westeuropäische Stilmerkmale in der Musik Borodins (1833–1887)." *Jahrbuch des Staatlichen Instituts fur Musikforschung Preussischer Kulturbesitz* 27 (1994): 278–303.

   The author explores the ways in which Borodin's music was influenced by Western European stylistic prototypes (especially FMB and Liszt), as well as by Musorgski.

419. Konold, Wulf. "Mendelssohn und Brahms: Beispiele schöpferischer Rezeption im Lichte der Klaviermusik." In *Brahms-Analysen: Referate der Kieler Tagung 1983*, ed. Friedhelm Krummacher and Wolfram Steinbeck, 81–90. Kieler Studien zur Musikwissenschaft, Bd. 28. Kassel: Bärenreiter, 1984.

   After the requisite nod to Brahm's oft-quoted derision of "reminiscence-seekers" (*Reminszenzenjäger*), this essay explores an obvious but too-seldom-undertaken issue: the extensiveness of Brahms's compositional indebtedness to FMB—a composer whom he unabashedly respected. The introductory section discusses formal and orchestrational similarities between FMB's *Walpurgisnacht* and Brahms's *Rinaldo*; other ties between the slow movements of FMB's "Italian" and Brahms's Second Symphony, and between FMB's "Scottish" Symphony and Brahms's Third Symphony; and still more ties between FMB's Op. 12 String Quartet and Brahms's Horn Trio and FMB's Op. 66 Piano Trio and Brahms's Op. 60 Piano Quartet. The bulk of the essay, however, focuses on extensive parallels between FMB's *Lied ohne Worte* in B-flat major, Op. 67, no. 4, and Brahms's Intermezzo in the same key (Op. 76, no. 4).

420. Krummacher, Friedhelm. "Epigones of an Epigone? Concerning Mendelssohn's String Quartets—and the Consequences." In *The Mendelssohns: Their Music in History*, ed. John Michael Cooper and Julie D. Prandi. Oxford: Oxford University Press, [forthcoming].

421. Krummacher, Friedhelm. "Komponieren als Anpassung? Über Mendelssohns Musik im Verhältnis zu England." In *Deutsch-englische Musikbeziehungen: Referate des wissenschaftlichen Symposions im Rahmen der Internationalen Orgelwoche "Musica Brittanica,"* ed. Wulf Konold, 132–56. Munich: Katzbichler, 1985. Trans. English John Michael Cooper as "Composition as Accommodation? On Mendelssohn's Music in Relation to England." In *Mendelssohn Studies*, ed. R. Larry Todd, 80–105. Cambridge: Cambridge University Press, 1982.

An exploration of the perpetually thorny issues of FMB's influence on English music and the nature of the significance of English musical life for his music. (On these questions, see also the study by Nicholas Temperley [no. 441].) This article focuses on the Op. 65 organ sonatas, *Elijah*, and the hymn *Hear My Prayer*. The English translation reveals a little too clearly the complexity of Krummacher's German prose.

422. Krummacher, Friedhelm. "Aussichten im Rückblick: Felix Mendelssohn Bartholdy in der neueren Forschung." In Christian Martin Schmidt, ed., *Felix Mendelssohn Bartholdy: Kongreß-Bericht Berlin* 1994, 279–96. Wiesbaden: Breitkopf & Härtel, 1997.

An extensive and perceptive overview of issues and developments in FMB research to 1997 (focusing on the period 1972–97).

423. Little, Wm. A. "Mendelssohn's Place in the Organ World of the Early Nineteenth Century." In *The Mendelssohns: Their Music in History*, ed.

John Michael Cooper and Julie D. Prandi. Oxford: Oxford University Press, [forthcoming].

424. Mackenzie, Sir Alexander. "Gedächtnisrede auf Mendelssohn." In *International Musical Society. Haydn-Zentenarfeier: III Kongreß der Internationalen Musikgesellschaft. Bericht Wien 25–29 May, 1909.* 60–66. Vienna: Artaria, 1909.

A discussion of Mendelssohn's influence in Britain beginning with a disquisition on the high state of organ playing in England in the first few decades of the nineteenth century and of British knowledge of Bach's organ works. The article contains interesting remarks about *Elijah* and its continuing influence as well as its place in the religiosity of the mid-nineteenth century. Mackenzie suggests that the current tendency to patronize Mendelssohn does modern times no credit: "Underestimation follows on the heels of overestimation." [DM]

425. Mackerness, E. B. "Mendelssohn und Charles Auchester." In *International Musicological Society. Berichtüber den internationalen musikwissenschaftlichen Kongreß Köln 1958: Cologne 23–28 June 1958*, ed. G. Abraham, S. Clercx-LeJeune, 188. Kassel: Bärenreiter, 1958.

A brief explanation of the ways in which Elizabeth Shephard's widely read novel was based on the life, works, and circle of FMB, and thus functions as a fictional document of reception history.

426. Mintz, Donald. "1848, Anti-Semitism and the Mendelssohn Reception." In *Mendelssohn Studies*, ed. R. Larry Todd, 126–48. Cambridge: Cambridge University Press, 1992.

One of surprisingly few studies to link the increasingly anti-Semitic climate of post-revolutionary Europe with the concurrent decline in FMB's reputation. It includes an overview of the dynamics of FMB reception history, followed by a case-by-case study of shifting views from those articulated by Robert Schumann to arid dismissals such as those by Eduard Krüger, Franz Brendel (see no. 763), and Heine (see no. 402).

427. Möhler, Philip. "Die Vergabe des Mendelssohn-Preises aus der Sicht der Jury." *Jahrbuch Preußischer Kulturbesitz* 10 (1972): 161–67.

428. Niecks, Frederick. "On Mendelssohn and Some of His Contemporary Critics." *Monthly Musical Record* 5 (1875): 162–64. Rpt., annotated by R. Larry Todd, in *Mendelssohn and His World*, ed. R. Larry Todd, 382–89. Princeton: Princeton University Press, 1992.

Best known for his extensive study of the history of program music (no. 871), Niecks (1845–1924) was a violinist and Reid Professor of Music at the University of Edinburgh, and author of biographies on Chopin and Schumann. This article—written in the context of the strife between the "New German School" and other forces in contemporary music—accuses FMB's critics of losing sight of the fact that musical criticism (like criticism in general) is essentially an expression of likes and dislikes that have their origins in "temperament, habit, and education." It situates FMB's Piano Sonata in E Major, Op. 6, the *Lieder ohne Worte,* and the concert overtures among the ideas and works of Schumann, Wagner, and Liszt, and argues that we should not forget FMB's "many excellencies" simply because he does not "possess all."

429. Nofze, Mathias. "Mendelssohn-Rezeption im 19. Jahrhundert." Ph.D. diss., University of Detmold, [forthcoming].

430. Nowack, Leopold. "Mendelssohns 'Paulus' und Anton Bruckner." *Österreichische Musik-Zeitung* 31 (1976): 574–77.

431. Oelmann, Klaus Henning. *Edvard Grieg als Streichquartettkomponist: Eine konzeptionelle und wirkungsgeschichtliche Studie.* Essen: Blaue Eule, 1992. 117 p. ISBN 3892064628. ML410.G9 O37 1992.

 Adapted from the author's dissertation ("Die Streichquartette Edvard Griegs: Quellen und formale Konzeption im Vergleich" [Freie Universität Berlin, 1972]). This study identifies FMB's quartets (esp. Opp. 12, 13, and 44) as an important influence on Grieg's string quartets.

432. Pachnicke, Peter. "Fragen eines Außenseiters nach der Modernität des Felix Mendelssohn Bartholdy." In *Felix Mendelssohn—Mitwelt und Nachwelt: Bericht zum 1. Leipziger Mendelssohn-Kolloquium am 8. und 9. Juni 1993,* ed. Leon Bostein, 71–78. Wiesbaden: Breitkopf & Härtel, 1996.

433. Rensis, Raffaelo de. *Critiche e cronache musicale di Arrigo Boito (1862–1870).* Milan: Treves, 1931. 201 p. ML410.B694 A3.

 This book includes "Mendelssohn in Italia" on pp. 1–51.

434. Schinkröth, Thomas. "'Es soll hier keine Diskussion über den Wert der Kompositionen angeschnitten werden': Felix Mendelssohn Bartholdy im NS-Staat." *Mendelssohn-Studien* 11 (1999): 177–205.

 A documentary study of the mechanics of FMB's vilification in the German-speaking countries during the Hitler years. It includes sections dealing with the destruction of the Leipzig Gewandhaus's Mendelssohn monument; the judgments of musical scholars; the role of Wagner's "Judentum in der Musik" essay in publicizing the Nazi view of FMB; the systematic removal of FMB's music from concerts, recitals, and recordings; and the means by which some few popular works in his oeuvre (such as the songs for male chorus, Op. 50 and Opp. posth. 75 and 76) were kept: by disguising his authorship and declaring the song a "Volkslied."

435. Schinkröth, Thomas. *Jüdische Musik in Leipzig, 1855–1945.* Altenburg: Klaus-Jürgen Kamprad, 1994. 310 p. ISBN 3930550008.

> See esp. pp. 227–35.

436. Schuhmacher, Gerhard. "Profis und Dilettanten im Wandel der Maßstabe." *Neue Zeitschrift für Musik* 144/3 (1983): 4–7.

> Schuhmacher discusses FMB's importance for middle-class musical life and the ways in which the musical world since the 1830s has moved increasingly away from amateur music-making towards professional and specialized performance and composition. The implication: FMB's music is less suited to the latter-day sociology of music than it was to the real world of the *Vormärz.*

437. Schweikert, Uwe. "'Der schöne Zwischenfall der deutschen Musik'? Gedanken zu Felix Mendelssohn Bartholdys 175. Geburtstag." In *Musik, Deutung, Bedeutung: Festschrift Harry Goldschmidt zum 75. Geburtstag,* ed. Hanns-Werner Heister and Hartmut Lück, 86–90. Dortmund: Pläne, 1986.

438. Silbermann, Alphons. "Kunst, aus vielfältigem Zwiespalt geboren: Über Felix Mendelssohn Bartholdy." In *Blickpunkt FELIX Mendelssohn Bartholdy: Programmbuch Drei Tage für Felix vom 30.10 bis 1.11.1994,* ed. Bernd Heyder and Christoph Spering, 11–16. Cologne: Dohr, 1994.

439. Solliers, Jean de. "Zur Mendelssohn-Rezeption in Frankreich." *Beiträge zur Musikwissenschaft* 15 (1973): 209–12.

> Prompted by the upswing in credible FMB scholarship in the 1960s and early 1970s, this is an exploration of FMB's reception in France (specifically Paris). Asserts that FMB was better known and understood in France during his lifetime and for some years thereafter than he has been more recently, and further suggests that composers (especially Gounod, Saint-Saëns, and Alcan) understood him better than musicologists have (from Fétis on).

440. Stephan, Rudolf. "Über einige Ansichten, Felix Mendelssohn Bartholdy betreffend." In *Felix Mendelssohn Bartholdy: Kongreß-Bericht Berlin 1994,* ed. Christian Martin Schmidt, 12–16. Wiesbaden: Breitkopf &

Härtel, 1997.

A brief but insightful essay concerning FMB's contemporary reception and the ways in which it reflected his views of his own position vis-à-vis the musical public; his Germanness, his position in history, and his Christianity.

441. Temperley, Nicholas. "Mendelssohn's Influence on English Music." *Music and Letters* 43 (1962): 224–33.

Temperley argues convincingly that the oft-reiterated claims that English composers' reliance on Mendelssohnian idioms exerted a detrimental effect on English music of the middle and late nineteenth century are greatly exaggerated. He examines works by Cramer, Crotch, and Sterndale Bennett to reassess the extent and nature of FMB's influence.

442. Tillard, Françoise. "Felix Mendelssohn and Fanny Hensel as Standards of a Bourgeois Perfection." In *The Mendelssohns: Their Music in History*, ed. John Michael Cooper and Julie D. Prandi. Oxford: Oxford University Press, [forthcoming].

443. Todd, R. Larry. "Strauss before Liszt and Wagner: Some Observations." In *Richard Strauss: New Perspectives on the Composer and His Work,* ed. Bryan Gilliam, 3–40. Durham: Duke University Press, 1992.

An exploration of ways in which FMB's music influenced Richard Strauss before his self-described "conversion" to the aesthetics of the Zukunftsmusik.

444. Webster, James. "Ambivalenzen um Mendelssohn: Zwischen Werk und Rezeption." In Christian Martin Schmidt, ed., *Felix Mendelssohn Bartholdy: Kongreß-Bericht Berlin 1994,* 257–78. Wiesbaden: Breitkopf & Härtel, 1997.

A consideration of the nature of the "Mendelssohn problem" more than twenty-five years after Dahlhaus's conference on that theme (see no. 3). This article analyzes the major problematical themes of FMB reception history. It includes close analytical remarks concerning the *Hebrides* Overture.

445. Wessely, Othmar. "Bruckners Mendelssohn-Kenntnis." In *Bruckner-Studien*, ed. Franz Grasberger, 81–112. Veröff entlichungen der Kommission für Musikforschung, ed. Franz Grasberger, Heft. 16. Vienna: Verlag der Österreichischen Akademie der Wissenschaften, 1975.

446. Wiegandt, Matthias. "Shakespeare, Mendelssohn, Raff—und ein

verkappter *Sommernachtstraum?" Musik-Theorie* 9 (1994): 195–209.

447. Wilson Kimber, Marian. "The Composer as Other: Gender and Race in the Biography of Felix Mendelssohn." In *The Mendelssohns: Their Music in History*, ed. John Michael Cooper and Julie D. Prandi. Oxford: Oxford University Press, [forthcoming].

448. Wolff, Hellmuth Christian. "Zum Singspiel 'Dichterliebe' von Mendelssohn." *Mendelssohn-Studien* 6 (1986): 151–62.

> The compilation in question (by Emil Stern) is a surprising and in some ways impressive indication of how popular FMB's music was at the turn of the twentieth century.

449. Worbs, Hans Christoph. "Mendelssohn: Ein Komponist wird wiederentdeckt." *Musik und Medizin* 1/8 (1975): 70–71.

450. Worbs, Hans Christoph. "Zur Rezeption von Mendelssohns Musik in der 2. Hälfte des 19. Jahrhunderts." In *Gesellschaft für Musikforschung: Bericht über den internationalen musikwissenschaftlichen Kongreß Berlin 1974*, ed. Hans Hellmut Kühn and Peter Nitsche, 387–389. Kassel: Bärenreiter, 1980.

> In 1877, when the copyright on Mendelssohn's works expired, many publishers speculated on "more-or-less complete editions." This article raises the question of the extent to which the public ignored the critical strictures of Mendelssohn then being made. [DM]

451. Worbs, Hans Christoph. "Zwischen Kult und Verdikt: Zu Felix Mendelssohn Bartholdys 150. Todestag." *Das Orchester: Zeitschrift für Orchester- und Rundfunk-Chorwesen* 45/11 (1997): 2–7.

> A brief but exceptionally thoughtful overview of how FMB's contemporary fame has risen and plummeted over the years (see the Introduction in this book, pp. 3–7.). The essay includes sections on Wagner's "Judaism in Music" (no. 394), the ban on performances of FMB's music during Hitler's "Third Reich," and on the fallacious assumption of his facility and superficiality in composing.

452. Zimdars, Richard Louis, and Theodor Pfeiffer, ed. and trans. *The Piano Master Classes of Hans von Bülow: Two Participants' Accounts*. Bloomington: Indiana University Press, 1992. 192 p. ISBN 0253368693.

4. Documentary Studies

I.   WORK-LISTS AND LITERATURE CONCERNING COLLECTED-WORKS EDITIONS

453. Bartlitz, Eveline. "Works." In *The New Grove Dictionary of Music and Musicians*, ed. Stanley Sadie, 12: 152–59. London: Macmillan, 1980. Revised by R. Larry Todd in *The New Grove Early Romantic Masters 2*, ed. Stanley Sadie, 270–83. New York: W. W. Norton, 1985.

   The *New Grove Early Romantic Masters 2* revision should be used whenever possible; see Elvers's essay on Bartlitz's work-list (no. 458) and this book's comments on the original *New Grove* article (no. 46).

454. Becher, Alfred Julius. "Vollständiges Verzeichniss der Compositionen von Dr. F. Mendelssohn-Bartholdy." *Orpheus: Musikalisches Album für das Jahr 1842 3* (1842): iii–viii.

455. Bernhard, W. "Gesammtausgabe von Mendelssohn's Werken." *Neue Zeitschrift für Musik* 71 (1875): 41–42, 312; 72 (1876): 89; 73 (1877): 81.

   A review of the (then) just-published *Sämtliche Werke* of FMB's works, edited by Julius Rietz (the edition that still provides the scores for most libraries).

456. Chrysander, Friedrich. "Mendelssohn's Werk: Gesamtausgabe von Breitkopf & Härtel." *Allgemeine Musikalische Zeitung* (Leipzig), Neue

Folge, 12 (1877): col. 273–80.

An important early comment on the "Collected Works" edited by Julius Rietz, not least of all because of the insights it provides into contemporary awareness of the emerging "Mendelssohn problem." Chrysander points out that the publishers had gone to considerable lengths to avoid making this edition one that was "only for libraries," and also questions whether FMB, despite his prestige, was deserving of such an edition because he represented a "transitional" period in the history of the art.

457. Cooper, John Michael. "Mendelssohn's Works: Prologomenon to a Comprehensive Inventory." In *The Mendelssohn Companion*, ed. Douglass Seaton. Westport, Conn.: Greenwood, [forthcoming].

458. Elvers, Rudolf. "Verlorgegangene Selbstverständlichkeiten: Zum Mendelssohn-Artikel in *The New Grove*." In *Festschrift Heinz Becker zum 60. Geburtstag am 26. Juni 1982*, ed. Jürgen Schläder and Reinhold Quandt, 417–21. Laaber: Laaber, 1982.

Eveline Bartlitz's work-list in *The New Grove* (no. 453) contains numerous serious errors and problems, ranging from omitted works and sources to misidentified poets. This essay also includes an explanation of the composer's name and reasons for the proper spelling and non-hyphenation of it. (The list was substantially revised by R. Larry Todd in *The New Grove Early Romantic Masters* 2.)

459. "Felix Mendelssohn-Bartholdy." *Allgemeine Musikalische Zeitung* [Leipzig] 34 (1837): col. 845–51.

Preceded by a biographical sketch, this is an inventory of FMB's works published with opus numbers up to that point (including the Opus 39 motets). It indicates whether the materials were available in score, parts, or arrangements.

460. Riehn, Rainer. "Werkverzeichnis." In *Felix Mendelssohn Bartholdy*, ed. Heinz-Klaus Metzger and Rainer Riehn, 147–52. Musik-Konzepte 14/15. Munich: edition text + kritik, 1980.

461. Rietz, Julius. "Verzeichnis der sämmtlichen musicalischen Compositionen von Felix Mendelssohn Bartholdy." In *Felix Mendelssohn Bartholdy: Briefe aus den Jahren 1833–1847*, ed. Paul and Carl Mendelssohn Bartholdy. Leipzig: Hermann Mendelssohn 1863.

Reprinted, with additions and corrections, in subsequent editions of the *Briefe* (see discussion above, no. 312).

462. Schmidt, Christian Martin. "Konzeption und Stand der Mendelssohn-Gesamtausgabe." In *Felix Mendelssohn—Mitwelt und Nachwelt: Bericht zum 1. Leipziger Mendelssohn-Kolloquium am 8. und 9. Juni 1993*, ed. Leon Botstein, 131–34. Wiesbaden: Breitkopf & Härtel, 1996.

463. "Systematisches Verzeichnis der in Deutschland im Druck erschienenen Compositionen von Felix Mendelssohn Bartholdy." *Musikalisches Wochenblatt 1* (1870), supplement.

464. *Thematisches Verzeichnis der im Druck erschienenen Compositionen von Felix Mendelssohn-Bartholdy.* "First installment" (*Auflage*) Leipzig: Breitkopf & Härtel, [1846]. 2nd edn. of first installment *idem*, [1853]. 2nd installment of 2nd edn., 1873. 3rd edn, 1882. 99 p. Rpt. Wiesbaden: Martin Sändig, 1973. ML134.M53 A2 1973. Also rpt. 1976 and 1982.

II. BIBLIOGRAPHIES, BIBLIOGRAPHIC ESSAYS, AND DISCOGRAPHIES

465. Bartlitz, Eveline. ""Bibliography." In *The New Grove Dictionary of Music and Musicians*, ed. Stanley Sadie, 12: 156–59. London: Macmillan, 1980. Revised and updated by R. Larry Todd in *The New Grove Early Romantic Masters 2*, ed. Stanley Sadie, 284–303. New York: W. W. Norton, 1985.

   The *New Grove* bibliography features some unfortunate omissions; every effort should be made to consult the revised and updated list in The *New Grove Early Romantic Masters 2*.

466. Konold, Wulf. "Auswahldiskographie." In *Felix Mendelssohn Bartholdy*, ed. Heinz-Klaus Metzger and Rainer Riehn, 153–59. Musik-Konzepte 14/15. Munich: editon text + kritik, 1980.

   Despite some annoying bibliographic errors, this article is useful as a document of FMB's discographic reception history to 1979.

467. Riehn, Rainer. "Auswahlbibliographie." In *Felix Mendelssohn Bartholdy*, ed. Heinz-Klaus Metzger and Rainer Riehn, 160–76. Musik-Konzepte 14/15. Munich: edition text + kritik, 1980.

   This article is plagued by bibliographic errors of every variety (especially in non-German names and titles), but comprehensive in its coverage.

468. Wehner, Ralf. "Bibliographie des Schriftums zu Felix Mendelssohn Bartholdy von 1972 bis 1994." In Christian Martin Schmidt, ed., *Felix Mendelssohn Bartholdy: Kongreß-Bericht Berlin 1994, 297–351.*

Wiesbaden: Breitkopf & Härtel, 1997.

A state-of-the-art bibliography by the leader of the FMB *Forschungsstelle* in Leipzig, well organized and containing only a few bibliographic errors.

III.   THE MENDELSSOHN ESTATE *NACHLAβ*

469. Caspar, Hellmut. "Nachlaß der Familie Mendelssohn: Attraktion des Museums für Geschichte der Stadt Leipzig." *Neue Zeit* 41/54 (1985): 3–4.

Not available for examination.

470. Elvers, Rudolf. "Auf den Spuren der Autographen von Felix Mendelssohn Bartholdy." In *Beiträge zur Musikdokumentation: Festschrift Franz Grasberger zum 60. Geburtstag*, ed Günter Brosche, 83–91. Tutzing: Hans Schneider, 1975.

One of the most extensive and detailed essays dealing with the problems presented by FMB's posthumous estate. It begins with a history of the "Green Books" compiled over many years by FMB and donated after his death to the Königliche Bibliothek in Berlin, then traces (as far as possible) the fate of several missing volumes and works, referring to the archives of publishers such as N. Simrock (Bonn), Friedrich Kistner (Leipzig), and Breitkopf & Härtel (Leipzig).

471. Elvers, Rudolf. "Felix Mendelssohn Bartholdys Nachlaß." In *Das Problem Mendelssohn*, ed. Carl Dahlhaus, 35–46. Studien zur Musikgeschichte des 19. Jahrhunderts, Bd. 41. Regensburg: Gustav Bosse, 1974.

A chronicle of the processes by which FMB's estate was gathered, catalogued, and deposited in the Königliche Bibliothek in Berlin, including previously unpublished official letters. It also discusses the inventory of his library that FMB made before his return to Leipzig from Berlin in November 1844 (no. 517), and discusses some of the problematical volumes of the Mendelssohn *Nachlaß*.

472. Elvers, Rudolf. "Mendelssohn in der Staatsbibliothek Preußischer Kulturbesitz: Zur wachsenden Mendelssohn-Sammlung und zur Geschichte des Nachlasses von Felix Mendelssohn Bartholdy." *In* ". . . gefördert von der Stiftung Volkswagenwerk": Dokumentation, 81–84. Göttingen: Vandenhoeck & Ruprecht, 1982.

473. Elvers, Rudolf. "Schenkungen und Stiftungen der Mendelssohns." In *Die*

Mendelssohns in Berlin: Eine Familie und ihre Stadt, ed. Rudolf Elvers and Hans-Günter Klein, 94–109. Staatsbibliothek Preußischer Kulturbesitz, Ausstellungskataloge 20. Berlin: Staatsbibliothek Preußischer Kulturbesitz, 1983.

IV. DOCUMENTARY INVENTORIES AND OVERVIEWS OF EDITIONS, EXHIBITIONS, MUSIC MANUSCRIPTS, AND PAPERS

474. Abraham, Gerald. "The Scores of Mendelssohn's *Hebrides.*" *Monthly Musical Record 78* (1948): 172–76.

This study is an attempt to come to terms with the complex source-situation of the *Hebrides* Overture (See also the studies by Walker [no. 514] and Todd [nos. 604 and 605]).

475. Albrecht, Otto E. *A Census of Autograph Music Manuscripts of European Composers in American Libraries*. Philadelphia: University of Pennsylvania Press, 1953. 331 p. ML135.A2 A4.

FMB on p. 186–90.

476. Angermüller, Rudolph. "Die Autographensammlung des Alois Taux." *Mitteilungen der Internationalen Stiftung Mozarteum* 1–4 (1989): 177–85.

Taux (1817–61) owned an autograph of a two-part canon in B minor dated 5 September 1845.

477. Appel, Bernard R. "Musikbeiträge im Album der Constanze Erdmunde Jacobi." In *Das Stammbuch der Constanze Dawison geb. Jacobi*, ed. Joseph A. Kruse, [9–14]. Berlin: Kulturstiftung der Länder, 1991. 20 p.

478. Bill, Oswald. "Unbekannte Mendelssohn-Handschriften in der Hessischen Landes- und Hochschulbibliothek Darmstadt." *Die Musikforschung* 26 (1973): 345–49.

An inventory and brief description of an impressive collection of FMB autographs. Covered: numerous Lieder, as well as the Organ Fugue in C Minor, Op. 37, no. 1; the arioso "Doch der Herr, er leitet die Irrenden recht" (Op. posth. 112, no. 1); the unfinished concert aria *O laßt mich einen Augenblick noch hier;* and the chorale cantata *O Haupt voll Blut und Wunden.*

479. Brosche, Günter, and Karin Breitner, eds. *Österreichische Nationalbibliothek Wien, Musiksammlung: Katalog der Sammlung*

Anthony van Hoboken in der Musiksammlung der Österreichischen Nationalbibliothek, musikalische Erst- und Frühdrucke, X: Franz Liszt, Felix Mendelssohn Bartholdy. Tutzing: Hans Schneider, 1994. 189 p. ISBN 3795207878. ML136.V6 N34 1982.

FMB on p. 55–179.

480. Crum, Margaret. *Catalogue of the Mendelssohn papers in the Bodleian Library, Oxford, Volume I: Correspondence of Felix Mendelssohn Bartholdy and Others.* Musikbibliographische Arbeiten Bd., 7. Tutzing: Hans Schneider, 1980. 374 p. ISBN 3795202639. ML134.M53 C8.

During his lifetime FMB systematically collected and had bound his manuscripts and his incoming correspondence; he also kept detailed diaries. Many of these are now in the possession of the Bodleian Library, Oxford. This volume, together with no. 481, provides an invaluable annotated index to that wealth of still largely untapped documents. See also Peter Ward Jones's inventory of the Oxford materials (no. 517).

481. Crum, Margaret. *Catalogue of the Mendelssohn Papers in the Bodleian Library, Oxford, Volume II: Music and Papers.* Musikbibliographische Arbeiten, Bd. 8. Tutzing: Hans Schneider, 1983. 337 p. ISBN 3795202639.

Includes a tree of the Mendelssohn family and descendants. See also Vol. I of Crum's Catalogue (no. 480) and Peter Ward Jones's inventory of the Oxford materials (no. 516).

482. Crum, Margaret. *Felix Mendelssohn Bartholdy.* Bodleian Picture Books Special Series, No. 3. Oxford: Oxford University Press, 1972. 22 p. ISBN 900177152.

This book comprises three main parts: Preface (a compact but remarkably substantive biographical sketch); Description of Plates (the exhibit catalog, providing appropriate details and source information for thirty-six items displayed); and the plates (high-quality facsimiles of drawings, programs, letters, and music manuscripts by FMB and his circle, including Goethe and Eduard Bendemann).

483. Currie, Norman. "Hector Berlioz, Robert Schumann, Felix Mendelssohn: Three Early Romantic Composers and Their Publishers." Ph.D. diss., City University of New York, [forthcoming].

484. Elvers, Rudolf. *Felix Mendelssohn Bartholdy: Dokumente seines Lebens. Ausstellung zum 125. Todestag im Mendelssohn-Archiv der Staatsbibliothek Preußischer Kulturbesitz vom 1. bis 30. November 1972.*

Staatsbibliothek Preußischer Kulturbesitz, Ausstellungskataloge 3. Berlin: n.p., [1972]. ML141.B3 M45.

A generously illustrated descriptive catalog of an exhibit mounted by the library in possession of the world's largest single collection of Mendelssohniana. It includes an overview of the family on p. 18.

485. Elvers, Rudolf. "Felix Mendelssohns Beethoven-Autographe." In *Bericht über den Internationalen Musikwissenschaftlichen Kongreß Bonn 1970*, ed. Carl Dahlhaus, Hans Joachim Marx, Magda Marx-Weber, and Günther Massenkeil, 380–82. Kassel: Bärenreiter, [1973].

Mendelssohn's enthusiasm as a collector of music autographs is well known (see, e.g., Hanslick's collections of letters [nos. 294 and 295]). This study focuses on the issue of which autographs of Beethoven he probably possessed, examining the possibility that a number of them eventually passed into the hands of Heinrich Beer (brother of Giacomo Meyerbeer) before being donated to FMB's son Paul and his grandson Ernst von Mendelssohn-Bartholdy.

486. Elvers, Rudolf. "Mus. Hs. 40.499." In *Beiträge zur musikalischen Quellenkunde: Katalog der Sammlung Hans P. Wertitsch in der Musiksammlung der Österreichischen Nationalbibliothek*, ed. Günter Brosche, 249–51. Tutzing: Hans Schneider, 1989.

This article studies the manuscript source for three songs (nos. 1, 2, and 4) of Op. 57.

487. Elvers, Rudolf. "Neuerwerbungen für das Mendelssohn-Archiv der Staatsbibliothek 1965–69." *Jahrbuch der Stiftung Preußischer Kulturbesitz* (1969): 308–20.

Elvers identifies and briefly describes items acquired from the Mendelssohn collection of Lili Wach (family portraits, paintings, and water colors); the album of Fanny Hensel; the estate of Arnold Mendelssohn; the estate of Albrecht von Mendelssohn Bartholdy; and various other letters and documents.

488. Elvers, Rudolf. "Neuerwerbungen für die Musikabteilung der Staatsbibliothek." *Jahrbuch der Stiftung Preußischer Kulturbesitz* 4 (1966): 240–46.

489. Elvers, Rudolf. "Verzeichnis der von Felix Mendelssohn Bartholdy herausgegebenen Werke J. S. Bachs." In *Gestalt und Glaube: Festschrift für Vizepräsident Prof. Dr. Oskar Söhngen*, 145–49, 238. Witten: Luther, 1960.

An inventory of FMB's various editions of J. S. Bach's works, including the Orchestrial Suite in D Major and the "Chaconne."

490. Elvers, Rudolf, and Peter Ward Jones. "Das Musikalienverzeichnis von Fanny und Felix Mendelssohn Bartholdy." *Mendelssohn-Studien* 8 (1993): 85–104.

This study concerns an inventory of music held in the Mendelssohn household and prepared between ca. 1823 and ca. 1833. It is extremely useful for identifying at least some of the music that was available to FMB and FH during these years. See also Peter Ward Jones's essay on "The Library" (no. 517).

491. Evans, David R. A. "The Powell Collection of Music Manuscripts." *Current Musiocology* 52 (1993): 64–74.

A history and inventory of the Nanteos music manuscript collection housed in the University College of Wales (Aberystwyth), which contains an autograph score of *Calm Sea and Prosperous Voyage* Overture, Op. 27.

492. Flindell, E. F. "Ursprung und Geschichte der Sammlung Wittgenstein im 19. Jahrhundert." *Die Musikforschung* 22 (1969): 300–14.

A history of an important collection of music manuscripts and musicians' papers, including a number of letters from FMB.

493. Grumbacher, Rudolf, and Albi Rosenthal. "'Dieses einziges Stückchen Welt . . .': Über ein Albumblatt von Felix Mendelssohn Bartholdy." In *Totum me libris dedo: Festschrift zum 80. Geburtstag von Adolf Seebass*, ed. Alain Moirandat, Heide Spilker, and Verene Tammann, 53–61. Basel: Haus der Bücher, 1979. Rpt. in *Mendelssohn-Studien* 5 (1982): 123–29.

On an *Albumblatt* dated 29 September 1842 that includes a Swiss *Geißreihen* (a kind of yodeled folk song best known to English speakers by the French term *ranz des chèvres*) transcribed by FMB during his 1831 grand tour.

494. Hartmann, Günter. "Ein Albumblatt für Eliza Wesley: Fragen zu Mendelssohns Englandaufenthalt 1837 und eine spekulative Antwort." *Neue Zeitschrift für Musik* 150/1 (1989): 10–14.

An examination of a puzzle canon written on an Albumblatt for Eliza Wesley (1815–95) on the eve of the death of Reverend Samuel Wesley, a close friend of FMB. Solves the canon with the chorale tune "O Haupt voll Blut und Wunden," which FMB also used in one of his string-quartet fugues, the eponymous chorale cantata, and the 1840 Leipzig organ concert for the raising of Leipzig's first monument to J. S. Bach.

495. King, Alec Hyatt. "The Royal Library in the British Museum." In *Beiträge zur Musikdokumentation: Franz Grasberger zum 60. Geburtstag*, ed. Günter Brosche, 193–201. Tutzing: Hans Schneider, 1975.

   King discusses the growth of the Royal Library from the 1760s to 1927, and refers to Mendelssohn's involvement with and contributions to the collections.

496. Kinsky, Georg. *Manuscripte, Briefe, Dokumente von Scarlatti bis Stravinsky: Die Musikautographen-Sammlung L. Koch.* Stuttgart: Hoffmansche Buchdruckerei Felix Krais, 1953. 360 p. ML138 .K63.

   An inventory of an important collection that is now dispersed. FMB manuscripts described on p. 203–14.

497. Kinsky, Georg. *Musikhistorisches Museum von Wilhelm Heyer in Cöln. Katalog 4. Band: Musikerautographe.* Cologne: Wilhelm Heyer, 1916.

   The author includes a facsimile of an early score of *The Hebrides* and the String Quartet in D Major, Op. 44, no. 1.

498. Klein, Hans-Günter, with Cécile Lowenthal-Hensel and Ernst Thamm. *"25 Jahre Mendelssohn-Gesellschaft Berlin e. V.: Ausstellung im Ausstellungsraum des Mendelssohn-Archivs der Staatsbibliothek zu Berlin—Preußischer Kulturbesitz, 28. Oktober 1992–9. January 1993."* Berlin: n.p., 1992.

499. Klein, Hans-Günter. "Verzeichnis der im Autograph überlieferten Werke Felix Mendelssohn Bartholdys im Besitz der Staatsbibliothek zu Berlin." *Mendelssohn-Studien* 10 (1997): 181–214.

   This article provides essential documentation of the world's largest collections of FMB music autographs. The works known by opus numbers (posthumously or in FMB's lifetime) are given first, followed by the works with no assigned opus number, grouped by genre and scoring. The article includes dates given in the manuscripts as well as page numbers for manuscripts contained within larger collections of manuscripts.

500. Krause, Peter. *Autographe, Erstausgaben und Frühdrucke der Werke von Felix Mendelssohn Bartholdy in Leipziger Bibliotheken und Archiven.* Bibliographische Veröffentlichungen der Musikbibliothek der Stadt Leipzig, Bd. 6. Leipzig: Deutscher Verlag für Musik, 1972.

501. Kröll, Christina. *Felix Mendelssohn Bartholdy zum 125. Todestag: Eine Ausstellung des Goethe-Museums Düsseldorf Anton-und-Katharina-Kippenberg-Stiftung, 4. November 1972–16. Januar 1973.* Düsseldorf: Stiftung Anton und Katharine Kippenberg, 1972. ML141.D83 M4 1972.

502. Leibintz, Thomas, and Agnes Ziffer. *Katalog der Sammlung Anton Dermota: Musikerhandschriften und Musikerbriefe.* Publikationen des Instituts für Österreichische Musikdokumentation, ed. Günter Brosche, 12. Tutzing: Hans Schneider, 1988. 190 p. ISBN 3795205344. ML138 .D47 1988.

503. Leven, Louise W. "An Unpublished Mendelssohn Manuscript." *The Musical Times* 78 (1948): 361.

   Leven discusses the manuscript for a two-voice canon in B minor dated 7 April 1841.

504. Riedel, Friedrich W. *Musikalische Schätze aus neun Jahrhunderten: Ausstellung des Musikarchivs, der Bibliothek und des Graphischen Kabinetts des Stiftes Göttweig.* [Steinweg]: Stift Gottweg, 1979. 100 p. ML141.S73 S77 1979.

   FMB on p. 52–55. Riedel includes a facsimile of a letter to Aloys Fuchs dated 11 December 1845.

505. Rokseth, Yvonne. "Manuscrits de Mendelssohn à la Bibliothèque du Consertoire." *Revue de musicologie* 15 (1934): 103–06.

   Despite some errors and ambiguities, the only systematic inventory of FMB autographs held in the Bibliothèque du Consertoire (now part of the Bibliothèque national in Paris).

506. Reich, Nancy B. "The Rudorff Collection." *Notes* 31 (1974): 247–61.

   Ernst Rudorff (1840–1916) was a pianist, conductor, and head of the piano department of the Berlin Hochschule für Musik from 1859 to 1910. He inherited a sizable collection of musical and literary autographs of works by Mozart, Weber, Schubert, Mendelssohn, Brahms, and Bruch. This article discusses the history of the collection and inventories its contents.

507. Schultz, Klaus. *Felix Mendelssohn Bartholdy—"der schöne Zwischenfall in der deutschen Musik": Zur Ausstellung anlässlich des XX. Internationalen Musikfestes der Wiener Konzerthausgesellschaft im Rahmen der Wiener Festwochen 1981.* Vienna: Wiener Konzerthausgesellschaft, 1981. 42 p. ML410.M5 F44 1981.

508. Schneider, Max F. "Eine Mendelssohn-Sammlung in Basel." *Der*

Amerbache Bote: Almanach (Basel, 1947): 200–28.

Not available for examination.

509. Schneider, Max F. *Die Wach'sche Mendelssohn-Sammlung auf dem Ried in Widerswill bei Interlaken*. Berlin: n.p., [1966]. ML410.M5 S14.

510. Seebass, Tilman. *Musikhandschriften in Basel, aus verschiedenen Sammlungen: Ausstellung im Kunstmuseum Basel vom 31. Mai bis zum 13. Juli 1975*. Basel: Basler Berichthaus, [1975]. 99 p. ML141.B22 O47.

> The introductory essay on "Musik und Musikhandschrift" provides useful observations on the iconographic as well as compositional interests of music manuscripts. FMB manuscripts (music and letters) on p. 56–59. Includes facsimiles.

511. Smith, Carleton. "Music Manuscripts Lost During World War II." *The Book Collector* 17, no. 1 (1968): 26–36.

> Smith provides an overview of the numerous important manuscripts that were held in the Staatsbibliothek Preußischer Kulturbesitz before they disappeared during the Second World War. Some of the FMB manuscripts are identified on p. 34–35. (Almost all of them now known to be in the Biblioteca Jagiellońska, Kraków.).

512. Staehelin, Martin. "Musikalien aus dem Besitz von Mendelssohns Freund Karl Klingemann." In *Festschrift Rudolf Elvers zum 60. Geburtstag*, ed. Ernst Herttrich and Hans Schneider, 483–90. Tutzing: Hans Schneider, 1985.

513. Turner, J. Rigbie. "Nineteenth-Century Autograph Music Manuscripts in the Pierpont Morgan Library: A Check List." *Nineteenth-Century Music* 4 (1980): 49–69. Also published separately under the same title (New York: The [Pierpont Morgan] Library, 1982). 53 p. ISBN 0875980775. ML136.N5 P56 1982.

> FMB on p. 165–67 in the periodical publication and p. 35–37 in the book.

514. Walker, Ernest. "Mendelssohn's *Die einsame Insel*." *Music and Letters* 26 (1945): 148–50.

> An examination of an early autograph score for the *Hebrides* Overture and a comparison of the variants with the published version.

515. Walker, Ernest. "An Oxford Collection of Mendelssohniana." *Music and Letters* 19 (1938): 426–28.

A description of the sizable collection of FMB autographs in the possession of Margaret Deneke. See also Margaret Crum's and Peter Ward Jones's catalogs of the Oxford Mendelssohniana (nos. 480, 481, and 516).

516. Ward Jones, Peter. *Catalogue of the Mendelssohn Papers in the Bodleian Library, Oxford, Volume III: Printed Music and Books.* Musikbibliographische Arbeiten, Bd. 9. Tutzing: Hans Schneider, 1989. 133 p. ISBN 3795205417. ML134.M53 C8.

The third and final volume in the series initiated by Margaret Crum (see nos. 480 and 481). Includes a list of errata for the previous volumes.

517. Ward Jones, Peter. "The Library of Felix Mendelssohn Bartholdy." In *Festschrift Rudolf Elvers zum 60. Geburtstag*, ed. Ernst Herttrich and Hans Schneider, 289–328. Tutzing: Hans Schneider,1985.

An invaluable tool for documenting the considerable library of one of the nineteenth century's most culturally versatile composers. At the core of the article is an inventory FMB prepared in the autumn of 1844 as he prepared to return to Leipzig from his frustrating tenure as Generalmusikdirektor in the service of Prussian King Friedrich Wilhelm IV. Divided into four main lists: (1) Mendelssohn's books in the 1844 list; (2) books in an 1835 inventory which do not appear in the 1844 list; (3) other extant books known to have belonged to FMB; and (4) books known only from a list of books lent in 1839. Where possible, complete bibliographic information and the present location of the items are given.

518. Ward Jones, Peter. *Mendelssohn: An Exhibition to Celebrate the Life of Felix Mendelssohn Bartholdy (1809–1847).* Oxford: Bodleian Library, 1997. ISBN 1851240527. 68 p.

519. Ward Jones, Peter. "Mendelssohn Scores in the Library of the Royal Philharmonic Society." In *Felix Mendelssohn Bartholdy: Kongreß-Bericht Berlin 1994*, ed. Christian Martin Schmidt, 64–75. Wiesbaden: Breitkopf & Härtel, 1997.

The author discusses FMB manuscripts preserved in the library of the Philharmonic Society of London, an orchestra central to FMB's English career. In addition to three scores widely known and easily accessible since 1914—those for the the C-minor Symphony, Op. 11; the "Trumpet" Overture; and the *Fair Melusine* Overture—Ward Jones discusses eight further non-autograph scores that provide significant source material. These "new" scores pertain to the *Hebrides* Overture, the A-major ("Italian") Symphony, the *Fair Melusine* Overture, the still-unpublished 1834 concert aria *Infelice!/Ah, ritorna, età dell' oro*, the 1846 concert aria *On Lena's Gloomy Heath* (likewise still unpublished), the Violin Concerto (Op. 64), the Overture to *Die Hochzeit des Camacho*, and a bass aria from *Elijah*.

520. Wehner, Ralf. "'It Seems to Have Been Lost': on Missing and Recovered Mendelssohn Sources." In *The Mendelssohns: Their Music in History*, ed. John Michael Cooper and Julie D. Prandi. Oxford: Oxford University Press, [forthcoming].

521. Wehner, Ralf. "'. . . ich zeigte Mendelssohns Albumblatt vor und Alles war gut.' Zur Bedeutung der Stammbucheintragungen und Albumblätter von Felix Mendelssohn Bartholdy." In *Felix Mendelssohn Bartholdy: Kongreß-Bericht Berlin 1994*, ed. Christian Martin Schmidt, 37–63. Wiesbaden: Breitkopf & Härtel, 1997.

This article concerns the significance of *Albumblätter* in FMB sources. Focuses on the *Lied ohne Worte* Op. 62, no. 3.

522. Werner, Eric. "The Family Letters of Felix Mendelssohn Bartholdy." *Bulletin of the New York Public Library* 65 (1960): 5–20. Rpt. in *idem*, *Three Ages of Musical Thought: Essays on Ethics and Aesthetics*, 351–65. New York: Da Capo, 1981.

523. Werner, Eric. "Mendelssohn Sources." *Notes* 12 (1954/55): 201–04.

An appropriate critical review of the misinformation propagated by the Rietz "Collected Works" edition and a plea for a serious return to primary sources.

524. Werner, Eric. "Mendelssohniana: Dem Andenken Wilhelm Fischers." *Die Musikforschung* 27 (1975): 19–33. Rpt. in Felix Mendelssohn Bartholdy, ed. Gerhard Schuhmacher, 376–98. Wege der Forschung, Bd. 494. Darmstadt: Wissenschaftliche Buchgesellschaft, 1982.

Written in the early prime of the ongoing FMB revival, this is an articulation of vital issues confronting FMB scholars, including: a return to primary sources; clarification and correction of biographical information; a critique of the composer's overall oeuvre; a critique of individual works; and a serious confrontation of the difficulties of the FMB reception history (especially as concerns the FMB/Wagner controversy).

525. Werner, Eric. "Mendelssohniana II: Den Manen Egon Wellesz', des Freundes und des Mentors."*Die Musikforschung* 30 (1977): 492–501. Rpt. in *Felix Mendelssohn Bartholdy*, ed. Gerhard Schuhmacher, 399–418. Wege der Forschung, Bd. 494. Darmstadt: Wissenschaftliche

Buchgesellschaft, 1982.

This article comments on information provided by new investigations of primary sources, then launches into a summary/review of Dahlhaus's seminal *Das Problem Mendelssohn* (no. 3).

526. Wolff, Hellmuth Christian. "Zur Erstausgabe von Mendelssohns Jugendsinfonien." *Deutsches Jahrbuch für Musikwissenschaft* 12 (1967): 96–115.

FMB's early string *sinfonie* were omitted from the so-called "Collected Works" edited by Julius Rietz in the 1870s, and they remained unpublished until the 1960s, when they appeared in the early volumes of the new *Leipziger Ausgabe der Werke Felix Mendelssohn Bartholdys* under Wolff's editorship. This article explores a number of issues raised by the works' first publication, as well as surveying the source-situation and a description of some aspects of the music.

527. Zappalà, Pietro. "Autografi mendelssohniani a Milano." *Musica e cultura* 2 (1988): 91–98.

528. Zappalà, Pietro. "Autografi mendelssohniani in Italia." Cremona: [private publication], 1991. Expanded version as "Autographe von Felix Mendelssohn Bartholdy in Italien." *Mendelssohn-Studien* 10 (1997): 77–96.

Ironically (given the important role played by Italy in studies of FMB's life and works) there has been little work on sources currently preserved in Italian libraries. This article is a crucial first step, although other important manuscripts doubtless remain to be located. Includes an inventory of the autographs, transcriptions of ten letters (to Friedrich Hofmeister, Luigi Rossi, Michelangelo Russo, Louis Spohr, and Breitkopf & Härtel, among others), as well as descriptions of four music autographs (Op. 37 and 93, as well as two canons).

V.   MENDELSSOHN AND THE VISUAL ARTS

NB: The subject of this lamentably small section of this chapter may represent one of the most pressing needs for future Mendelssohn scholarship. Commentators have long referred to Mendelssohn's remarkable ability as a draftsman and aquarellist (indeed, few popular studies miss an opportunity to reproduce at least one of his many drawings and watercolors), and the numerous contemporary drawings and portraits of the composer likewise provide valuable insights into his public and private persona as he rose to international fame over the course of his lifetime. Because of the complementary insights provided by FMB's own visual artworks and visual artworks concerning him, this section is simply headed "Mendelssohn and the Visual Arts."

529. Crum, Margaret. "Mendelssohn's Drawing and the Doubled Life of Memory." In *Festschrift Albi Rosenthal,* ed. Rudolf Elvers, 87–103. Tutzing: Hans Schneider, 1984.

An insightful exploration of the ways in which FMB's drawings, far from representing simply accomplished amateur sketching, are commemorative of "little certain moments which Mendelssohn himself thought worth remembering." The drawings thus lend insight into the events and people considered significant by the composer himself.

530. Klein, Hans-Günter. "Felix Mendelssohn Bartholdy als Zeichner auf Reisen." In *Mendelssohn,* ed. Reiko Koyanagi, 5–9 in supplement (German) and 24–30 in text (trans. Japanese). Oneiros, 7. Tokyo: Iwasaki Bijutsusha, 1992.

See also Larry Todd's essay in the same volume (no. 533).

531. Koyanagi, Reiko. Mendelssohn. Oneiros No. 7. Tokyo: Iwasaki Bijutsusha, 1992. 71 p. ISBN 4753413063.

The most lavishly illustrated volume of FMB's drawings and watercolors. See also the essays by Hans-Günter Klein and R. Larry Todd (nos. 530 and 533).

532. Schneider, Max F. *Ein unbekanntes Mendelssohn-Bildnis von Johann Peter Lyser* (see no. 56). Basel: n.p., 1958. 57 p. ML410.M5 L9.

533. Todd, R. Larry. "Felix Mendelssohn Bartholdy." In *Mendelssohn,* ed. Reiko Koyanagi, 1–5 in supplement (English) and 62–67 in text (trans. Japanese). Oneiros, 7. Tokyo: Iwasaki Bijutsusha, 1992.

See also Hans-Günter Klein's essay in the same volme (no. 531).

534. Ward Jones, Peter. "Felix und Cécile Mendelssohn Bartholdy als bildende Künstler." In *Blickpunkt FELIX Mendelssohn Bartholdy: Programmbuch Drei Tage für Felix vom 30.10 bis 1.11.1994,* ed. Bernd Heyder and Christoph Spering, 27–33. Cologne: Dohr, 1994.

535. Worbs, Hans Christoph. "Von Komponisten, die malen, und Malern, die komponieren." *Musik und Medizin* 1/8 (1975): 70–71.

536. Worbs, Hans Christian. "Mendelssohn as Maler und Zeichner und sein

Verhltnis zur bildenden Kunst." In *Felix Mendelssohn Bartholdy*, ed. Gerhard Schuhmacher, 100–37. Wege der Forschung, Bd. 494. Darmstadt, Wissenschaftliche Buchgesellschaft, 1982.

In contrast to Chopin, who was a caricaturist, Mendelssohn was at first primarily a landscape painter who painted to maintain a recollection rather than for an artist purpose. Later, painting became for him "a private amusement but also a passion." After Fanny's death, he drew comfort from drawing and watercolor. His more serious works are studio productions; that is, they are not painted *al fresco* but in the studio from sketches or recollection. The article contains information about Mendelssohn's relations with visual artists: Horace Vernet, Berthel Thorwaldsen, Wilhelm von Schadow, Julius Hübner, and other artists in Düsseldorf. There is also a discussion of Mendelssohn's relation to the visual arts of the past. [DM/JMC]

VI.   THE MENDELSSOHN HOMES AND MENDELSSOHN MONUMENTS

537. Cullen, Michael. "Leipziger Straße Drei: Eine Baubiographie." *Mendelssohn-Studien* 5 (1982): 9–77.

An important "building history" of the celebrated edifice that in 1825 became the Mendelssohn family home in Berlin. This article traces the property's ownership and plans from the late seventeenth century into the early twentieth century. Includes numerous illustrations, among them two drawings by FMB; the plans for the remodeling undertaken when Abraham Mendelssohn acquired the property in 1825; and several photographs.

538. Dümling, Albrecht. "Licht in die Dunkelkammer: Pläne für das Leipziger Wohn- und Sterbehaus von Felix Mendelssohn Bartholdy." *Neue Zeitschrift für Musik* 153/2 (1992): 20–21.

The author outlines plans for the restoration of the FMB house in Leipzig, as well as those for the recovery and resurrection of the Gewandhaus's Mendelssohn monument (destroyed by the Nazis). The plans have now come to fruition, of course, but in some ways differently than envisioned.

539. [Elvers, Rudolf.] "Leipziger Straße 3." In *Die Mendelssohns in Berlin: Eine Familie und ihre Stadt,* ed. Rudolf Elvers and Hans-Günter Klein, 169–179. Staatsbibliothek Preußischer Kulturbesitz, Ausstellungskataloge 20. Berlin: Staatsbibliothek Preußischer Kulturbesitz, 1983.

Not a *Baubiographie*, but an overview of the personages,

performances, and works that populated the remarkable life of the family's palatial Berlin domicile.

540. Kliem, Manfred. "Die Berliner Mendelssohn-Adresse Neue Promenade 7: Zeitliche Zuordnung und soziales Umfeld als Forschungsanliegen." *Mendelssohn-Studien* 7 (1990): 123–40.

A thorough and useful study of the building that was the Berlin home to the Mendelssohn family from their move to the Prussian capital in 1811 until the move to Leipziger Straße 3 in 1825. It is an important complement to Michael Cullen's and Cécile Lowenthal Hensel's studies of the latter address (nos. 537 and 541).

541. Lowenthal-Hensel, Cécile. "Neues zur Leipziger Straße Drei." *Mendelssohn-Studien* 7 (1990): 141–51.

A complement to Michael Cullen's study of the house, focusing on financial aspects of the construction. This article includes facsimiles of four drawings by FMB.

542. Meyer-Krahmer, Marianne. "Carl Goerdeler und das Mendelssohn-Denkmal." In *Felix Mendelssohn—Mitwelt und Nachwelt: Bericht zum 1. Leipziger Mendelssohn-Kolloquium am 8. und 9. Juni 1993*, ed. Leon Bostein, 60–63. Wiesbaden: Breitkopf & Härtel, 1996.

543. Reich, Ines. "In Stein und Bronze: Zur Geschichte des Leipziger Mendelssohn-Denkmals 1868–1936." In *Felix Mendelssohn—Mitwelt und Nachwelt: Bericht zum 1. Leipziger Mendelssohn-Kolloquium am 8. und 9. Juni 1993*, ed. Leon Bostein, 31–53. Wiesbaden: Breitkopf & Härtel, 1996.

544. Richter, Brigitte. "Das 'Mendelssohn-Zimmer'' in Leipzig." *Musik und Gesellschaft* 22 (1972): 646–52.

545. Wehner, Ralf. 'Das Ende des Mendelssohn-Denkmals: Eine Dokumentation.' Ph.D. diss., Universität Leipzig, 1991.

5. Studies Of Individual Works and Repertoires

I.   SECULAR WORKS

A. Stage Works (Including Incidental Music)

546. Andraschke, Peter. "Felix Mendelssohns *Antigone*." In *Felix Mendelssohn Bartholdy: Kongreß-Bericht Berlin 1994*, ed. Christian Martin Schmidt, 141–66. Wiesbaden: Breitkopf & Härtel, 1997.

> FMB's incidental music to Sophocles's *Antigone* was premiered on 18 October 1841 in the context of a production of J. J. C. Donner's German translation of the play, and this music played a central role for many years in FMB's reputation. This article is a thorough introduction to the circumstances surrounding the production, the issues involving the translation into German, and the musical styles represented in the work.

547. Bischoff, Heinrich. *Ludwig Tieck als Dramaturg*. Brussels: Office de publicité, 1897. 124 p. PT2540 .B6

> This pulication includes a discussion of *Oedipus at Colonos, Antigone*, and *Athalia*.

548. Böckh, Phillip August. *Über die Antigone des Sophocles und ihre Darstellung auf dem königlichen Schloßtheaters im neuen Palais bei Sansouci.* Berlin: E. H. Schroeder, 1842. 97 p.

549. Büssinger, J. J. *Über Felix Mendelssohn und seine Musik zur Antigone.* Basel: n.p., 1862.

550. Didion, Robert. "Heimkehr aus der Fremde." In *Pipers Enzyklopädie des Musiktheaters*, ed. Carl Dahlhaus and Sieghart Döhring, 4: 52–53. Munich: Piper, 1991.

551. *Rudolf Elvers, "Nichts ist so schwer gut zu componiren als Strophen": Zur Entstehungsgeschichte des Librettos von Felix Mendelssohns Oper "Die Hochzeit des Camacho,"* . . . *mit dem Faksimile eines Briefes von Mendelssohn.* Berlin: Mendelssohn-Gesellschaft, 1976. 16 p.

     FMB's early opera based on Cervantes's *Don Quixote* played an important role in his early public persona: the first performance was a striking success; the second, a victim of several serious handicaps. Although FMB released the work as his Opus 10, he distanced himself from it quickly. The ambivalence of the success of both the music and the performances may have accounted for FMB's later reluctance to commit to and complete an opera. This book includes a facsimile and transcription of a long and detailed letter concerning the libretto, as well as commentary.

552. Hennemann, Monika. "'So kann ich es nicht componiren': Mendelssohn and Opera—A Libretto Problem?" In *The Mendelssohns: Their Music in History*, ed. John Michael Cooper and Julie D. Prandi. Oxford: Oxford University Press, [forthcoming].

553. Köhler, Karl-Heinz. "Das dramatische *Jugendwerk* Felix Mendelssohn Bartholdys: Basis seiner Stil- und Persönlichkeitsentwicklung." In *The International Musicological Society: Report of the Eleventh Congress Copenhagen 1972*, ed. Henrik Glahn, Søren Sørensen, and Peter Ryom, II: 495–99. Copenhagen: Wilhelm Hansen, 1974.

     This article offers a broad survey of Mendelssohn's *Jugendwerk* (the compositions to ca. 1825), and uses these (still) little-known early dramatic works as a springboard to challenge the (still-) prevalent image of him as lacking the characteristically Romantic dramatic sensitivities. It asserts that the ongoing rediscovery and reappraisal of his works encourages a recognition that drama pervades his compositions, even those in seemingly undramatic genres. Refers to the *Midsummer Night's Dream* Overture, *Elijah, Die Lorelei,* the *Calm Sea and Prosperous Voyage* Overture, *Die erste Walpurgisnacht,* and the "Scottish" Symphony.

554. Köhler, Karl-Heinz. "Zwei rekonstruierbare Singspiele von Felix Mendelssohn-Bartholdy." *Beiträge zur Musikwissenschaft* 2 (1960): 86–93.

> On *Die Soldatenliebschaft* (1820) and *Die beiden Pädagogen* (1821).

555. Krettenauer, Thomas. *Felix Mendelssohn Bartholdys "Heimkehr aus der Fremde": Untersuchungen und Dokumente zum Liederspiel op. 89.* Collectanea musicologica, Bd. 5. Augsburg: Bernd Wißner, 1994. ISBN 3928898280. ML410.M5 K76 1994.

> Adapted from the author's dissertation ("Felix Mendelssohn Bartholdys Liederspiel 'Heimkehr aus der Fremde' Op. 89— Voraussetzungen, Entstehungsgeschichte, Stil und Rezeption" [University of Augsburg, 1993]). An extensive study of the sources, text, and music for the posthumously published *Liederspiel.*

556. Krummacher, Friedhelm. "'. . . fein und geistreich genug': Versuch über Mendelssohns Musik zum Sommernachtstraum," in *Das Problem Mendelssohn*, ed. Carl Dahlhaus, 89–117. Studien zur Musikgeschichte des 19. Jahrhunderts, Bd. 41. Regensburg: Gustav Bosse, 1974.

> The author uses the seventeen-year span between the *Midsummer Night's Dream* Overture (Op. 21) and the complete incidental music (Op. 61) as a foil for testing the notion that in remaining stylistically "true to himself" (Riemann) FMB effectively became an epigone of himself in his later years (i.e., lost his originality). Focuses on FMB's approach to the form and drama of Shakespeare's play, as well as to musical form, and discerns substantial differences between the early overture and the late incidental music.

557. Little, Arthur Mitchell. *Mendelssohn's Music to the Antigone of Sophocles.* Washington, D.C.: Gibson, 1893. 91 p. ML410.M15 L4.

558. Liszt, Franz. "Über Mendelssohns Musik zum 'Sommernachtstraum,'" *Neue Zeitschrift für Musik* 40 (1854): 233–37.

> This article is useful as a case-study in the criticisms Liszt and other members of the New German School leveled at FMB after about 1850. It asserts that despite its originality, sensitivity, nuance, and appeal, FMB's music does not participate fully in the drama, and thus represents an approach to incidental music that belonged to a stage in that genre's development earlier than Beethoven's *Egmont*. (But see also Krummacher [no. 556].)

559. Macfarren, G. A. Mendelssohn's *Antigone*. London: n.p., 1865.

Although Macfarren is notorious for inaccuracy and misrepresentation in details of almost every variety, he was an acquaintance of FMB; his writings offer additional insight because of his prominence as a music critic during the years that witnessed the zenith of the English FMB cult. The status of *Antigone* as a work that was formerly an acclaimed masterpiece but now largely forgotten renders Macfarren's remarks on it particularly useful.

560. Schünemann, Georg. "Mendelssohns Jugendopern." *Zeitschrift für Musikwissenschaft* 5 (1923): 506–45.

An important survey of Mendelssohn's youthful Singspiele and Liederspiele, generously illustrated with music examples. It includes the Lustspiel *Ich, J. Mendelssohn*; the comic opera *Die Soldatenliebschaft*; the Singspiel *Die beiden Pädagogen*; and the comic operas *Die wandernden Komödianten* and *Die beiden Neffen, oder Der Onkel aus Boston*.

561. Sietz, Reinhold. "Die musikalische Gestaltung der Loreleysage bei Max Bruch, Felix Mendelssohn und Ferdinand Hiller." In *Max-Bruch-Studien: Zum 50. Todestag des Komponisten*, ed. Dietrich Kamper, 14–45. Beiträge zur rheinischen Musikgeschichte, Hft. 87. Cologne: Arno Volk, 1970.

Despite a lifelong search for a suitable opera project, FMB was able to commit to such an undertaking only in the last year of his life; the product was *Die Lorelei*, based on a libretto by Emmanuel Geibel and left unfinished at FMB's death. This essay examines the issues articulated in letters documenting the collaboration between composer and librettist, and compares FMB's approach to that in Hiller's cantata (1854) and Bruch's opera (1863) on the same subject. It concludes that all three works were swept away in the flood of "modern" German music. (See also Todd [no. 563].)

562. Steinberg, Michael P. "The Incidental Politics to Mendelssohn's *Antigone*." In R. Larry Todd, *Mendelssohn and His World* , 137–57. Princeton: Princeton University Press, 1991.

A thoughtful essay situating the highly visible success of the incidental music to *Antigone* within FMB's professional development and contemporary trends in German cultural life, and speculating that FMB's call to Berlin and to the court of the new king may have reactivated the composer's youthful "rebellious individualism" in his setting of the political, ethical, and psychological ambivalence of Sophocles's play.

563. Todd, R. Larry. "On Mendelssohn's Operatic Destiny: *Die Lorelei* Reconsidered." In *Felix Mendelssohn Bartholdy: Kongreßbericht Berlin*

1994, ed. Christian Martin Schmidt, 113–40. Wiesbaden: Breitkopf & Härtel, 1997.

The most extensive investigation of FMB's incomplete late opera, *Die Lorelei*, including some numbers omitted when the work was posthumously published. This article examines the genesis and musical style of FMB's music, as well as his approach to the dramatic content. It includes a list of FMB's unfinished or contemplated operatic projects (spanning the period 1824–47).

564. John Warrack, "Mendelssohn's Operas." In *Music and Theatre: Essays in Honour of Winton Dean*, ed. Nigel Fortune, 263–97. Cambridge: Cambridge University Press, 1987.

An overview of the four early operas, with information concerning what can be discerned of their plots.

565. Wirth, Helmut. "Natur und Märchen in Webers *Oberon*, Mendelssohns *Sommernachtstraum* und Nicolais *Die lustige Weiber von Windsor*." In *Festschrift Friedrich Blume zum 70. Geburtstag*, ed. Anna Amalie Abert und Wilhelm Pfannkuch, 389–397. Kassel: Bärenreiter, 1963.

This article proceeds from the observations that (1) nature and fairy tales were intimately related in the nineteenth century, and (2) the importance of nature in Shakespeare's *A Midsummer Night's Dream* grants a special tone to that play. This article comments on the musical structure of the Overture (Op. 21) and its relationship to Weber's music, as well as the links between the Overture and the remainder of the incidental music. It views the three titular works as representing three stages in the Romantic view of nature and Romantic techniques for dealing with symbols and allegories of nature.

B. Orchestral Works (Symphonies, Overtures, Concertos)

566. Barnes, Marilyn Hodt. "Developmental Procedures in the Sonate Form Movements of the Symphonies of Beethoven, Schubert, Mendelssohn, and Schumann." Ph.D. diss., Case Western Reserve University, 1978. 359 p.

567. Botstiber, Hugo. *Geschichte der Ouvertüre und der freien Orchesterformen*. Kleine Handbücher der Musikgeschichte nach Gattungen, vol. 4. Leipzig: Breitkopf & Härtel, 1913. 274 p. ML1261 .B68. Rpt. Wiesbaden: Martin Sändig, [1969]. ML1261 .B68 1969

FMB discussed on p. 176–82. Mendelssohn was the first to use the term "concert overture." His works in this genre are "true, unqualified program music. Mendelssohn is a program musician in almost all his works."

But "subordination to a program does not prevent Mendelssohn from giving form all its rights." The relationship of *Calm Sea and Prosperous Voyage* to the Goethe poems is discussed. [DM]

568. Boyd, John Pretz. "Ouvertüre für Harmoniemusik op. 24 by Felix Mendelssohn Bartholdy: An Edition for Contemporary Wind Band." D.M.A. diss., University of Missouri at Kansas City, 1981. 169 p.

Boyd discusses the autograph of 1826, the original version for eleven winds of 1824, and the final version of 1838.

569. Cooper, John Michael. "'Aber eben dieser Zweifel': A New Look at Mendelssohn's 'Italian' Symphony." *Nineteenth-Century Music* 15 (1992): 169–87.

An overview of the sources and compositional history for the A-major Symphony, including the first published consideration of the manuscript fragments held in the Bodleian Library, Oxford. Cooper argues that the undated manuscript long assumed to be a draft for the work actually represents a revision of the published version.

570. Cooper, John Michael. "Felix Mendelssohn Bartholdy and the *Italian* Symphony: Historical, Musical, and Extramusical Perspectives." Ph.D. diss., Duke University, 1994. 454 p.

The author considers the compositional history, sources, music, and programmatic content of the A-major Symphony, as well as its posthumous reception history. Asserts that the then-unpublished manuscript version of the symphony represents the revised version of the familiar work rather than an early draft.

571. Cooper, John Michael. "Words without Songs? Of Texts, Titles, and Mendelssohn's *Lieder ohne Worte*." In *Musik als Text? Bericht über den internationalen Kongreß der Gesellschaft für Musikforschung, Freiburg im Breisgau 1993*, ed. Hermann Danuser and Tobias Plebuch, 2: 341–46. Kassel: Bärenreiter, 1999.

The essay draws on little-known correspondence to explore FMB's views on the issues involved in publishing texted versions or programmatic interpretations of originally untexted music.

572. Dinglinger, Wolfgang. "Felix Mendelssohn Bartholdys Klavierkonzert a-moll: Umgang mit einer Modellkomposition." *Mendelssohn-Studien* 8 (1993): 105–30.

This article concerns the little-known Piano Concerto in A Minor

(1822) and suggests that FMB may have taken Hummel's Piano Concerto in A Minor, Op. 85, as a point of departure. It suggests that while the young Mendelssohn's concerto contains obvious emulations of specific aspects of Hummel's work, it also reveals the composer struggling to find his own voice.

573. Dinglinger, Wolfgang. "The Program of Mendelssohn's 'Reformation' Symphony, Op. 107." In *The Mendelssohns: Their Music in History*, ed. John Michael Cooper and Julie D. Prandi. Oxford: Oxford University Press, [forthcoming].

574. Ehrenforth, Karl Heinrich. "Das Trauerspiel von Vergangenheit und Gegenwart . . . Deutungsperspektiven des 2. Satzes der 'Italienischen Symphonie.'" *Musik und Bildung* 20 (1988): 486–94.

Ehrenforth proceeds from Werner's assertion that the main theme of the slow movement of the A-major Symphony is modeled after a song by Zelter on a text by Goethe.

575. Ehrle, Thomas. *Die Instrumentation in den Symphonien und Ouvertüren von Felix Mendelssohn Bartholdy*. Neue musikgeschichtliche Forschungen, Bd. 13. Wiesbaden: Breitkopf & Härtel, 1983. 259 p. ISBN 3765101923. ML410.M5 E3 1983.

Adapted from the author's Ph.D. diss. by the same title (Goethe-Universität Frankfurt am Main, 1983). Except for the 1923 Vienna dissertation by Josef Köffler, *Über orchestrale Koloristik in den symphonischen Werken von Felix Mendelssohn Bartholdy*, which has apparently been lost, there is very little about this subject. Emphasis is placed on the extreme novelty of Mendelssohn's instrumentation within the limits of Beethoven's orchestra: "In the case of Mendelssohn, what is particularly striking is the realization of new effects within the stated borders." Changes in the construction and techniques of orchestra instruments during Mendelssohn's lifetime are discussed. Mendelssohn's viola parts are particularly demanding. Related to this is the liberation of the cellos from the bass part. The development of string writing in the early symphonies for strings is emphasized, as is string writing in general. Another section is devoted to wind writing in general; the fifteen works are examined individually. Krummacher's thesis about Mendelssohn's "turn away from motivic working out and fragmentation of thematic material" is accepted and the consequences for orchestral technique discussed. [DM]

576. Eichhorn, Andreas. *Felix Mendelssohn-Bartholdy: Die Hebriden— Ouvertüre für Orchester op. 26*. Meisterwerke der Musik, Hft. 66. Munich:

Fink, 1998. 91 p. ISBN 3770532740. MT130.M35 E53 1998.

A handbook that complements R. Larry Todd's book on the programmatic concert overtures. The bulk of Eichhorn's study consists of a thorough discussion of the genesis of the overture (along with a list of the surviving sources), followed by a substantial analytical study (including conventional music-theoretical perspectives as well as hermeneutic ones). To these are appended a compilation of "Dokumente" (quotations from letters, reviews, and other primary sources), a selective discography, and an overview of the edition history, as well as a good bibliography.

577. Gerlach, Reinhard. "Mendelssohns schöpferische Erinnerung der 'Jugendzeit': Die Beziehungen zwischen dem Violinkonzert, op. 64, und dem Oktett für Streicher, op. 20." *Die Musikforschung* 25 (1972): 142–52. Rpt. in *Felix Mendelssohn Bartholdy*, ed. Gerhard Schuhmacher, 248–62. Wege der Forschung, Bd. 494. Darmstadt: Wissenschaftliche Buchgesellschaft, 1982.

The author finds that the nostalgic tone of several of FMB's letters to Johann Gustav Droysen in the early 1840s is the result of the composer's longing for the "freshness" and "liveliness" of the time that FMB, Droysen, and A. B. Marx shared before the composer's painful break in friendship with the theorist. The composition of Op. 64 represented a bridging of the two poles represented by the composer's erstwhile friend (Marx) and the librettist who remained his friend (Droysen).

578. Grove, George. "Mendelssohn's 'Hebrides' Overture." *The Musical Times* 45 (1905): 531–33.

Grove's essay on the *Hebrides* was the first to reproduce in facsimile the composer's original sketch for the beginning of the piece (from a letter to his family dated 7 August 1829). This essay focuses on changes between the original and published versions.

579. Grove, George. "Mendelssohn's Overture to 'A Midsummer Night's Dream.'" *The Musical Times* 44 (1903): 728–38.

A typically thorough and insightful Grove essay, drawing attention to circumstances of the work's composition and specific musical features.

580. [Grove, George.] "Mendelssohn's Unpublished Symphonies." *Monthly Musical Record* 1 (1871): 159–60.

The first study of the thirteen string sinfonie, still useful despite the lengthier and more detailed studies by Wolff (no. 526) and Konold (no. 586).

581. Grove, George. "Mendelssohn's Violin Concerto." *The Musical Times* 47 (1906): 611–15.

    The first important essay on this major work. It provides information on the first performance, as well as a descriptive analysis and information regarding the changes evident in the autograph score.

582. Heuß, Andreas."Das 'Dresdener Amen' im ersten Satz von Mendelssohns Reformationssinfonie." *Signale für die musikalische Welt* 62 (1904): 281–84, 305–6.

    An important early analytical commentary on the posthumously published "Reformation" Symphony. Heuß traces the thematic evolution of the "Dresden Amen" in the main subjects of the first movement, also commenting on the tune's religious and cultural associations and describing its treatments as "typical of Mendelssohn's essence."

583. Kieland, Marianne. "Sketches after an Overture: Presented Musical Spans as Structural Models in Mendelssohn's *Hebrides* Overture." *In Theory Only* 1 (1975): 6–10.

    An abstract from a master's thesis, this intern provides an interpretation of Op. 26 proceeding from the assumption that the model according to which one perceives sound-data will determine the mode of analysis that seems to work best. It coordinates a four-level "perception diagram" with a middleground and background-level reduction.

584. Konold, Wulf. *Felix Mendelssohn Bartholdy: Symphonie Nr 4 A-Dur Op. 90, "Die Italienische."* Meisterwerke der Musik, Hft. 48. Munich: Fink, 1987. 62 p. ISBN 3770524543. MT130.M35 K6 1987.

    A compact and eminently readable reference source on the familiar (1833) version of the A-major Symphony. An introductory chapter on the compositional history is followed by a descriptive commentary.

585. Konold, Wulf. "Felix Mendelssohn Bartholdys Rondo brillant op. 29: Ein Beitrag zur Geschichte des einsätzigen Konzertstücks im 19. Jahrhundert." *Die Musikforschung* 38 (1985): 169–82.

    Konold examines the repertoire of one-movement "concerto pieces" (because of the genre-reference a better translation than the usual "concert piece") and the aesthetic and performance-related issues they entail, followed by an examination of FMB's five contributions to the genre (Opp. 22, 29, 43, 113, and 114, along with the *Konzertstück* on Weber's *Preziosa*).

586. Konold, Wulf. "Mendelssohns Jugendsymphonien: Eine analytische Studie." *Archiv für Musikwissenschaft* 46 (1989): 1–41, 155–83.

Perhaps the most important study of FMB's string *sinfonie* (see also Grove [580] and Wolf [526]). Konold surveys the corpus as a whole, then classifies the works into three separate groups that reflect FMB grappling with several important issues within his own developing style.

587. Konold, Wulf. "Opus 11 und Opus 107: Analytische Bemerkungen zu zwei unbekannten Sinfonien Felix Mendelssohn Bartholdys." In *Felix Mendelssohn Bartholdy*, ed. Heinz-Klaus Metzger and Rainer Riehn, 8–28. Musik-Konzepte 14/15. Munich: edition text+kritik, 1980.

Despite the rather peculiar title (by now the "Reformation" Symphony hardly counts as "unknown"; nor was it "unknown" in 1976, when the essay was written), an insightful discussion of the first two of FMB's mature symphonies. (Op. posth. 107 was composed *before* the "Scottish" and "Italian" symphonies.) The author's observations center around structure, but there is also an attempt to come to terms with the programmaticism of Op. posth. 107. The discussion of Op. 11 is one of the most thorough currently available (see also Vitercik [no. 801] and Todd [no. 606]).

588. Konold, Wulf. *Die Symphonien Felix Mendelssohn Bartholdys: Untersuchung zu Werkgestalt und Formstruktur.* Laaber: Laaber Verlag, 1992. 504 p. ISBN 3890072321. ML410.M5 K695 1992.

A monumental undertaking, including the early string *sinfonie* as well as the mature symphonies (Opp. 11, 52, 56, 60, 90, and 107). Much of the material is adapted from Konold's other writings, and the volume suffers from a lack of reference to any unpublished letters (as well as severe bibliographic problems). Still, a source that cannot be ignored, even if it must be used alongside other, more consistently reliable writings.

Rev.: J. M. Cooper in *Notes* 50 (1994): 1373–76; G. Dietel in *Neue Zeitschrift für Musik* 155, no. 1 (1994): 76–77.

589. Konold, Wulf. "Die zwei Fassungen der 'Italienischen Symphonie' von Felix Mendelssohn Bartholdy." In *Bericht über den Internationalen Musikwissenschaftlichen Kongress Bayreuth 1981*, ed. C.-H. Mahling and Sigrid Wiesmann, 410–15. Kassel: Bärenreiter, 1984.

A description and classification of the variants evident in the principal manuscript for the 1833 version of the A-major Symphony.

590. Kopf, René. "Felix Mendelssohn: *La grotte de fingal (ouverture)*." *L'Education musicale* 27 (1971): 183–85.

   Not available for examination.

591. Lehmann, Karen. "Der junge Mendelssohn und seine zwölf Jugendsinfonien." *Musikforum* 17/2 (1972): 21–22.

592. Longyear, Rey M. "Cyclic Form and Tonal Relationships in Mendelssohn's 'Scottish' Symphony." *In Theory Only* 4 (1979): 38–48.

   Even though Robert Schumann celebrated the extensive thematic unity of Op. 56 at the work's première, few subsequent commentators have explored it in any detail. This article examines the thematic content of the symphony and asserts that virtually all of them are derived from two basic ideas.

593. Mercer-Taylor, Peter. "Mendelssohn's 'Scottish' Symphony and the Music of German Memory." *Nineteenth-Century Music* 19 (1995): 68–82.

   Adapted from the author's dissertation, this article draws on melodic similarities between the thematic material of Op. 56 and the male chorus "Vaterland, in deinen Gauen" from the "Gutenberg" *Festgesang* (composed for Leipzig's 1840 celebration of the anniversary of Gutenberg's invention of the printing press) to suggest a kind of patriotic genre-discourse.

594. Pelto, William Lyle." Musical Structure and Extramusical Meaning in the Concert Overtures of Mendelssohn." Ph.D. diss., University of Texas at Austin, 1993. 316 p.

   A broad survey that entails a useful examination of nineteenth-century perspectives on issues involving music and extramusical content, followed by an examination of the four programmatic concert overtures (Opp. 21, 26, 27, and 32). This study compares those works to the *Ruy Blas* Overture, Op. posth. 95.

595. Reed, David F. "The Original Version of the *Overture for Wind Band* of Felix Mendelssohn-Bartholdy," *Journal of Band Research* 18 (1982): 3–10.

   Reed focuses on the little-known version of the *Overture* for ten winds (rather than the more familiar version for twenty-three winds), and reviews the genesis and publication history of the work (including arrangements).

596. Richter, Arnd. "Beethoven, Mendelssohn, Hegel & Marx: Zur Poetik der Ouvertüre 'Meeresstille und glückliche Fahrt.'" *Neue Zeitschrift für Musik* 149, no. 7–8 (1988): 18–23.

The author surveys instances of Beethoven's influence in FMB's early works and discusses relationships between Beethoven's cantata on Goethe's two poems "Meeresstille" and "Glückliche Fahrt" and FMB's concert overture on the poem-pair.

597. Richter, Christoph. "Zum langsamen Satz der 'Italienischen' von Felix Mendelssohn Bartholdy: Eine Annäherung durch Musizieren." *Musik und Bildung* 20 (1988): 497–506.

An experiential case-study in dimensions of musical meaning. Richter finds that one may experience the slow movement of the A-major Symphony in a variety of fashions, among them: as a ballad/processional; as a stylized dance; or as a Romantic study in emotional contrasts.

598. Roennfeldt, Peter John. "The Double Piano Concertos of Felix Mendelssohn." D.M.A. diss., University of Cincinnati, 1985. 163 p.

A routine but thorough study of the Concerto in D Minor for Piano and Violin with Strings (1823), the Concerto in E Major for Two Pianos and Orchestra (1823), and the Concerto in A-flat for Two Pianos and Orchestra (1824).

599. Schmidt-Beste, Thomas. "Just how 'Scottish' is the 'Scottish' Symphony? Thoughts on Poetic Content and Form in Mendelssohn's Opus 56." In *The Mendelssohns: Their Music in History*, ed. John Michael Cooper and Julie D. Prandi. Oxford: Oxford University Press, [forthcoming].

600. Silber [Ballan], Judith Karen. "Mendelssohn and His Reformation Symphony." *Journal of the American Musicological Society* 40 (1987): 310–36.

A compact but remarkably pithy article, adapted from the author's dissertation (601), then in progress. Silber corrects several oft-repeated errors concerning the D-minor Symphony and the circumstances of its composition and first performance.

601. Silber [Ballan], Judith. "Mendelssohn and the *Reformation* Symphony: A Critical and Historical Study." Ph.D. diss., Yale University, 1987.

The central document for any serious exploration of the D-minor Symphony. Silber examines the autograph score and draws extensively on unpublished documents to establish the personal and professional context for the Symphony's commission, creation, performance, and rejection. She also examines the programmatic dimensions and the ways in which the work reveals FMB's awareness of and concern with symphonic tradition (specifically the Beethovenian symphonic legacy). Aside from an evident unawareness of the 1837 Düsseldorf performance conducted by Julius Rietz, the documentation is exemplary

602. Steinbeck, Wolfram. "'Der klärende Wendepunkt in Felix' Leben': zu Mendelssohns Konzertouvertüren." In *Felix Mendelssohn Bartholdy: Kongreß-Bericht Berlin 1994*, ed. Christian Martin Schmidt, 232–56. Wiesbaden: Breitkopf & Härtel, 1997.

The springboard for this essay is Felix Weingartner's 1909 remark that "if Mendelssohn had given to his one-movement orchestral pieces the felicitous title 'symphonic poems,' which Liszt invented, he would likely be celebrated today as the inventor of program music and would be granted a position at the beginning of a new period in art rather than the end of an old one." Steinbeck argues that the four concert overtures opp. 21, 26, 27, and 32 represented a breakthrough not only in FMB's own compositional powers, but also for nineteenth-century programmatic composition in general.

603. Steinberg, Michael P. "The Incidental Politics to Mendelssohn's *Antigone*." In *Mendelssohn and His World*, ed. R. Larry Todd, 137–57. Princeton: Princeton University Press, 1991.

This article begins with the early and mid-nineteenth century's cults celebrating Sophocles' *Antigone*, exploring the ways in which important cultural figures such as Hegel, Hölderlin, Boeckh, and Johann Gustav Droysen contributed to these cults, and then adds that FMB's participation in such a "group dynamic" renders the work all the more interesting because "the group dynamic, together with the hidden voices of nonparticipants . . . informs themes and resonances that may not have clear lines of connection between an artist and his explicit artistic creation."

604. Todd, R. Larry. *Mendelssohn: "The Hebrides" and Other Overtures*. Cambridge: Cambridge University Press, 1993. 121 p. ISBN 0521407648.

Despite its compact scale, this (like most other volumes in the Cambridge Music Handbooks series) is a remarkably substantive resource, treating not only the *Hebrides*, but also the *Midsummer Night's Dream* Overture and *Calm Sea and Prosperous Voyage*. The introductory chapter on the background of the concert overture as a genre prior to FMB's foray into that realm is followed by a chapter on the genesis of each overture and chapters devoted to: musical influences, formal considerations, programmatic considerations, FMB's orchestration, and the works' influence and posthumous reception. *Rev.*: P. Ward Jones in *Music & Letters* 77 (1996): 128–29.

605. Todd, R. Larry. "Of Seagulls and Counterpoint: The Early Versions of Mendelssohn's *Hebrides* Overture." *Nineteenth-Century Music* 2 (1979): 197–213.

    Adapted from the author's dissertation. A compact introduction to the complicated source-situation for the work and the issues involved for FMB in reworking and successively retitling it. It includes a list of surviving and lost manuscripts as well as a reproduction of FMB's drawing of one of the islands. (See also Albrecht [no. 475] and Walker [no. 515].)

606. Todd, R. Larry. "Mendelssohn." In *The Nineteenth-Century Symphony,* ed. D. Kern Holoman, 78–107. New York: Schirmer Books, 1997.

    A survey of the early string *sinfonie* and Opp. 11, 21, 26, 27, 32, 52, 56, and 60, as well as the posthumous *opera* 90 and 107. Also includes the concert overtures.

607. Todd, R. Larry. "An Unfinished Piano Concerto by Mendelssohn." *The Musical Quarterly* 68 (1982): 80–101.

    This article concerns an unfinished piano concerto in E minor preserved in a manuscript miscellany in the Bodleian Library, Oxford. It suggests that some ideas from the concerto were rehabilitated in the Violin Concerto, Op. 64.

608. Todd, R. Larry. "An Unfinished Symphony by Mendelssohn." *Music and Letters* 61 (1980): 293–309.

    Todd discusses an unfinished symphony in C major held in the Bodleian Library, Oxford. (The symphony was first mentioned and discussed by Grove in his *Dictionary* [no. 36].)

609. Unger, Renate. "Ein Jugendwerk Felix Mendelssohn Bartholdys: Anmerkungen zum Konzert d-Moll für Violine und Streichorchester, 1. und 2. Fassung." *Musikforum* 17 (1972): 19–20.

    Stylistic comments on the two versions of the D-minor Violin Concerto (1822) by the scholar who edited the work for the Leipzig *Gesamtausgabe*.

610. Viertel, Matthias S. "Vom 'Blutenstaub der inneren Wahrheit': Überlegungen zu einer ästhetischen Betrachtung des 2. Satzes aus der Italienischen Symphonie von Mendelssohn." *Musik und Bildung* 20 (1988): 480–85.

    A discussion of the critical reception history of the slow movement of the A-major Symphony, focusing on the programmatic/characteristic elements, melodic structure, and the importance of orchestral timbres.

611. Weiss, Günther. "Eine Mozartspur in Felix Mendelssohn Bartholdys Sinfonie A-Dur op. 90 ('Italienische')." In *Mozart: Klassik für die Gegenwart*, ed. Constantin Floros, 87–89. Oldenburg: Stalling-Druck, 1978.

This article relates the third movement of FMB's A-major Symphony to Mozart's D-minor Piano Concerto, KV. 466.

612. Werner, Eric. "Two Unpublished Mendelssohn Concertos," *Music and Letters* 36 (1955): 126–38.

A study of the Concerto in E Major for Two Pianos (1823) and the Concerto in A-flat Major for Two Pianos (1824).

613. Witte, Martin. "Zur Programmgebundenheit der Sinfonien Mendelssohns." In *Das Problem Mendelssohn*, ed. Carl Dahlhaus, 119–27. Studien zur Musikgeschichte des 19. Jahrhunderts, Bd. 41. Regensburg: Gustav Bosse, 1974.

Of central importance in latter-day FMB research, even though many of the findings have been qualified or overturned by subsequent inquiries; this is a survey of the degree and nature of extramusical associations of the four purely instrumental mature symphonies (Opp. 11, 56, 90, and 107).

614. Wüster, Ulrich. "'Ein gewisser Geist': Zu Mendelssohns Reformations-Symphonie." *Die Musikforschung* 44 (1991): 311–30.

Wüster proposes that previous evaluations of the programmaticism of the D-minor Symphony are misguided because they assess the extramusical references only in terms of a synthesized product; a more appropriate criterion for understanding the extramusical gesture is the idea of *contrast*. Viewed in this fashion, the work emerges as a study in contrasts: between sonata form and chorale composition; modern and older musical styles; programmatic and absolute music; (implicitly) vocal and instrumental composition; and sacred and secular function.

C. Accompanied Secular Choral Works

615. Dahlhaus, Carl. "'Hoch symbolisch intoniert': Zu Mendelssohns *Erster Walpurgisnacht*." *Österreichische Musikzeitschrift* 36 (1981): 290–97.

The article focuses on the generic and compositional originality of the *Walpurgisnacht* and emphasizes the symbolic nature of the work's gradual melding-together of initially disparate thematic and motivic elements by a process of thematic transformation. It also examines generic and melodic links between it and the "Scottish" Symphony and the *Lobgesang*.

616. Edwards, F. G. *Hymn of Praise (Lobgesang): A Symphonia Cantata.* London, n.d.

617. Hatteberg, Kent Eutgene. "*Gloria* (1822) and *Große Festmusik zum Dürerfest* (1828): Urtext Editions of Two Unpublished Choral-Orchestral Works by Felix Mendelssohn, with Background and Commentary." D.M.A. diss., University of Iowa, 1995. 2 vols.

As per tradition, the text proper is in Volume 1 (comprising 223 pages). This text examines FMB's early youth and musical training leading up to the 1822 *Gloria*, then moves on to the composer's teenage years in Berlin leading up to the *Festmusik*.

618. Hauser, Richard. "'In rührend feierlichen Tönen': Mendelssohns Kantate *Die erste Walpurgisnacht*. Mit einem Exkurs: Goethes unvertonbarer Allvater." In *Felix Mendelssohn Bartholdy*, ed. Heinz-Klaus Metzger and Rainer Riehn, 75–92. Musik-Konzepte, Bd. 14/15. Munich: edition text + kritik, 1980.

This article emphasizes the seriousness of the *Walpurgisnacht* and draws parallels between the musical language FMB used to depict the "Allvater" in this work and the language used in his own setting of Psalm 95 and that in Schubert's *Ganymed*. See Metzger's response (no. 624) to this article.

619. Hellmundt, Christoph. "'Indessen wollte ich mich Ihnen gern gefällig Beweisen': on Some Occasional Works, with an Unknown Composition by Felix Mendelssohn Bartholdy." In *The Mendelssohns: Their Music in History*, ed. John Michael Cooper and Julie D. Prandi. Oxford: Oxford University Press, [forthcoming].

620. Hellmundt, Christoph. "Mendelssohns Arbeit an seiner Kantate *Die erste Walpurgisnacht*: Zu einer bisher wenig beachteten Quelle." In *Felix Mendelssohn Bartholdy: Kongreß-Bericht Berlin* 1994, ed. Christian Martin Schmidt, 76–112. Wiesbaden: Breitkopf & Härtel, 1997.

A careful study of the genesis of Op. 60, the first such study to focus on the autograph score that most clearly represents the version of the work used for the 1833 premiere. Essay includes facsimiles from that score and compares selected passages with their counterparts in the published version. There is a 34-item appendix of FMB's epistolary references to the work.

621. Kapp, Reinhard. "*Lobgesang*." In *Neue Musik und Tradition: Festschrift Rudolf Stephan*, ed. Josef Kuckertz, Helga de la Motte-Haber, Christian Martin Schmidt, and Wilhelm Seidel, 239–49. Laaber: Laaber, 1990.

A combination of descriptive analysis and reception history, focusing on the gestures of the chorale and the symphony-cantata and their influence on the subsequent development of the symphony as a genre. Contains substantial references to Beethoven, Berlioz, Liszt, Mahler, and especially Bruckner.

622. Mayer, Hans. "Emanzipation und Eklektizismus: Gedanken über den *Lobgesang* opus 52 von Mendelssohn Bartholdy." In *Felix Mendelssohn Bartholdy*, ed. Heinz-Klaus Metzger and Rainer Riehn, 29–33. Musik-Konzepte, Bd. 14/15. Munich: edition text + kritik, 1980.

Headed "a letter to [the editors]," this is a short meditation on the eclecticism of FMB's world-view and the extent to which his Protestant upbringing shielded him from the world-weariness evident in the works of some other contemporary German-Jewish artists (most notably, Heine).

623. Melhorn, Catherine Rose. "Mendelssohn's *Die erste Walpurgisnacht*." D.M.A. diss., University of Illinois at Urbana-Champaign, 1983. 232 p.

By far the most extensive treatment of a much-debated work whose presence in the realm of Mendelssohn scholarship continues to outstrip that in the concert repertoire. Melhorn assigns the work to the genre of the concert cantata. She begins with a discussion of FMB's relationship to Goethe; then explores the history of that genre prior to FMB's Op. 60; discusses the music and performance history of Op. 60; and finally discusses later contributions to the genre (works by Gade, Schumann, Hiller, Bruch, and Brahms). This dissertation also includes an appendix of nineteenth-century German concert cantatas of ballad character after the *Walpurgisnacht*, and a report on one modern performance of the work.

624. Metzger, Heinz-Klaus. "Noch einmal: *Die erste Walpurgisnacht*—Versuch einer anderen Allegorese." In *Felix Mendelssohn Bartholdy*, ed. Heinz-Klaus Metzger and Rainer Riehn, 93–96. Musik-Konzepte, Bd. 14/15. Munich: edition text + kritik, 1980.

A response (if not rebuttal) to Richard Hauser's observations on Op. 60 in the same volume (no. 618). It asserts that the *unvertonbarer Allvater* of the work is not a pagan, pantheistic, idealized, pseudo-celtic deity, but the God of the Jews — and therefore that the work centers around the theme of Jewish persecution.

625. Norris, James Weldon. "Mendelssohn's *Lobgesang* opus 52: An Analysis for Performance." D.M.A. diss., Indiana University, 1974.

626. Prandi, Julie D. "Kindred Spirits: Mendelssohn and Goethe, *Die Erste Walpurgisnacht.*" In *The Mendelssohns: Their Music in History*, ed. John Michael Cooper and Julie D. Prandi. Oxford: Oxford University Press, [forthcoming].

627. Rasmussen, M. "The First Performance of Mendelssohn's Festgesang *An die Künstler* op. 68." *Brass Quarterly* 4 (1961): 151–55.

> Although Op. 68 is actually mentioned only in the final two pages of the article, the previous material on the ways in which its composition and reception were influenced by the "emotional, textual, and social connotations of brass instruments" is worth reading.

628. Retallack, Diane Johnson. "A Conductor's Study for Performance of Mendelssohn's *Die erste Walpurgisnacht.*" D.M. diss., Indiana University, 1987. 413 p.

> Examines FMB's relationship with Goethe and traces the genesis of Op. 60 through FMB's published correspondence. Examines the structure of the work in descriptive analyses, emphasizing FMB's talent for "portraying the fantastic within Classical restraints."

629. Richter, Arnd. "Felix Mendelssohn Bartholdy: *Die erste Walpurgisnacht.*" *Neue Zeitschrift für Musik* 147/11 (1986): 33–40.

> This article grapples with the ambivalance of the reception history of the *Walpurgisnacht*, drawing upon musical similarities to two other important works: the "Hexenlied" Op. 8, no. 8; and the "Scottish" Symphony, Op. 56.

630. Schönewolf, Karl. "Mendelssohns Humboldt-Kantate." *Musik und Gesellschaft* 9 (1959): 408–11.

> Written shortly after Karl-Heinz Köhler's important essay introducing the existence of the Berlin "Green Books" to the general world (no. 862), this is the only essay to deal specifically with FMB's 1828 cantata written for the International Congress of Natural Scientists and Doctors headed by Alexander von Humboldt. It describes the music, but unfortunately provides no music examples.

631. Seaton, Douglass. "The Romantic Mendelssohn: The Composition of *Die erste Walpurgisnacht.*" *The Musical Quarterly* 68 (1982): 398–410.

> This article examines the ways in which the composition of the

Walpurgisnacht refutes the cliché of FMB as a formalist or mannerist and reveals instead his mastery of quintessentially Romantic compositional issues such as thematic/motivic transformation, cyclicity, overtly subjective textual reinterpretation, and so on.

632. Steinbeck, Wolfram. "Die Idee der Vokalsymphonie: Zu Mendelssohns *Lobgesang.*" *Archiv für Musikwissenschaft* 53 (1996): 222–33.

Steinbeck suggests that commentators from A. B. Marx onwards have generally been excessively fixated on the ways in which FMB's Op. 52 relates to Beethoven's Ninth Symphony, to such an extent that they have ignored its significance as a unique document in the history of composing.

633. Szeskus, Reinhard. "*Die erste Walpurgisnacht*, Op. 60, von Felix Mendelssohn Bartholdy." *Beiträge zur Musikwissenschaft* 17 (1975): 171–80.

This article discusses the extent of Goethe's influence on FMB, not only as a literary and aesthetic figure, but also as a model of the public reformer. It suggests that these ideals are evident in the choice of text and the musical style of the *Walpurgisnacht*.

634. Town, Stephen. "Mendelssohn's 'Lobgesang': A Fusion of Forms and Textures." *Choral Journal* 33 (1992): 19–26.

A narrative description of Op. 52. Argues that FMB went beyond the obvious model of Beethoven's Ninth Symphony, reaching back to Bach and Handel to create a work that "falls outside the classification system of musical genres" and "must be evaluated on its own merits" (25).

D. Concert Arias

635. Cooper, John Michael. "Mendelssohn's Two *Infelice* Arias: Problems of Sources and Musical Identity." In *The Mendelssohns: Their Music in History*, ed. John Michael Cooper and Julie D. Prandi. Oxford: Oxford University Press, [forthcoming].

636. Todd, R. Larry. "Mendelssohn's Ossianic Manner, with a New Source: *On Lena's Gloomy Heath.*" In *Mendelssohn and Schumann: Essays on their Music and Its Context*, ed. Jon R. Finson and R. Larry Todd, 137–60. Durham, N.C.: Duke University Press, 1984.

The first essay to discuss the still-unpublished concert aria *On Lena's Gloomy Heath*. It explains the work's relationship to the contemporary Ossianic cult, describes the ways in which its musical language evokes that background, and notes instances of similar musical language in other works.

E. Choral Songs

637. Abraham, Lars Ulrich. "Mendelssohns Chorlieder und ihre musikgeschichtliche Stellung." In *Das Problem Mendelssohn*, ed. Carl Dahlhaus, 79–87. Studien zur Musikgeschichte des 19. Jahrhunderts, Bd. 41. Regensburg: Gustav Bosse, 1974.

   This article begins with a general discussion of Mendelssohn's artistic reputation in the years since his death, based largely on various dictionary articles, and paying special attention to the anti-Semitic element to which strong impetus was given by Wagner's (at first pseudonymous) *Über das Judenthum in der Musik* (1850) [No. 394]. A new orientation to Mendelssohn's work must depend on analysis. In the case of the choral songs, it is difficult to find valid standards that can be applied to the large repertory; the general prejudice against the genre makes the task yet more difficult. As a beginning, attention is called to certain details of melody, rhythm, and form that can serve as points of comparison with other composers. [DM]

638. James M. Brinkman. "The German Male Chorus: Its Role and Significance From 1800–1850." Ed.D., University of Illinois, Urbana/Champaign, 1966. 204 p.

639. Goldhan, Wolfgang. "Felix Mendelssohn Bartholdys Lieder für gemischten und Männerchor." *Beiträge zur Musikwissenschaft* 17 (1975): 181–88.

   This is still the most extensive systematic survey of the choral songs. It considers the works' texts, approach to melody, harmony, form, and styles of text-setting and text/music relationships.

640. Ickstadt, Andrea. "Studien zu Felix Mendelssohn Bartholdys Chorliedern." Ph.D. diss., Hochschule für Musik, Frankfurt am Main, [in progress].

641. Kopfermann, Albert. "Zwei musikalische Scherze Felix Mendelssohns." *Die Musik* 8/2 (1908–9): 179–80.

   On *Der weise Diogenes* and *Musikantenprügelei*.

642. Robinson, Ray. "'Quis desiderio sit': A Newly Discovered Choral Work by Felix Mendelssohn." *Choral Journal* 35/10 (1994): 27–30.

   Unknown to Robinson, the "newly discovered choral work by Felix Mendelssohn" is actually a copy by FMB of a piece by Zelter.

F. Songs and Vocal Duets

643. Barr, Raymond Arthur. "Carl Friedrich Zelter: A Study of the Lied in Berlin

During the Late Eighteenth and Early Nineteenth Centuries." Ph.D. diss., University of Wisconsin at Madison, 1968. 290 p.

644. Berry, Corre. "Duets for Pedagogical Use." *NATS Bulletin* 34 (1977): 8–12.

Although it lags far behind latter-day scholarship in its techniques for approaching and interpreting texted music of the early nineteenth century, this article is one of only a few that deal specifically with FMB's vocal duets, pp. 63 and 77.

645. Heinrich Bunke. "Die Barform im romantischen Kunstlied bei Franz Schubert, Johannes Brahms, Hugo Wolf und Felix Mendelssohn-Bartholdy." Ph.D. diss., Bonn, 1955. 136 p.

646. Geck, Martin. "Sentiment und Sentimentalität im volkstümlichen Liede Felix Mendelssohn Bartholdys." In *Hans Albrecht in Memoriam: Gedenkschrift mit Beiträgen von Freunden und Schülern*, ed. Wilfried Brennecke and Hans Haase, 200–06. Kassel: Bärenreiter, 1962.

647. Hennemann, Monika. "Mendelssohn and Byron: Two Songs almost without Words." *Mendelssohn-Studien* 10 (1997): 131–56.

An insightful exploration of the compositional history of the *Two Byron Romances* ("There Be None of Beauty's Daughters" and "Sun of the Sleepless"). Hennemann includes analytical remarks and useful considerations of the significance of public vs. private venues of musical dissemination in FMB's oeuvre.

648. Leven, Louise W. "Mendelssohn als Lyriker, unter besonderer Berücksichtigung seiner Beziehungen zu Ludwig Berger, Bernhard Klein und Adolph Bernhard Marx." Ph.D. diss., Universität Frankfurt am Main, 1926.

Although it is not easily accessible in the U.S., this study remains an important resource in the critical literature concerning FMB's approach to song composition.

649. Leven, Louise W. "Mendelssohn's Unpublished Songs." *Monthly Musical Record* 88 (1958): 206–11. Trans. German Gerhard Schuhmacher as "Mendelssohns unveröffentlichte Lieder." In *Felix Mendelssohn Bartholdy*, ed. Gerhard Schuhmacher, 37–43. Wege der Forschung, Bd. 494. Darmstadt: Wissenschaftliche Buchgesellschaft, 1982.

This article discusses declamation, texture, form, and text/music relationships in eight of fifteen early unpublished songs: "Ave Maria," "Raste Krieger," "Die Nachtigall," "Der Verlassene," "Von allen deinen zarten Gaben," "Wiegenlied," "Sanft wehn im Hauch," and "Der Wasserfall."

650. Losse, Paul. "Ein bisher ungedrucktes Lied von Mendelssohn." *Musik und Gesellschaft* 9 (1959): 68–71.

    A study on the song "Ich flocht ein Kränzlein schöner Lieder" ("Lieben und Schweigen"), actually published in *Die musikalische Welt* (1872) (i.e., in contradiction to the titular assertion).

651. Schachter, Carl. "The Triad as Place and Action." *Music Theory Spectrum* 17 (1995): 149–69.

    Schachter examines the *Lied ohne Worte* in G Major, Op. 62, no. 1, along with Chopin's Prelude in E Minor, Op. 28, no. 4, and the fourth movement from Beethoven's "Pastoral" Symphony, as instances in which "expressive character relates to the specific tonal environment provided by the composing out of the tonic triad."

652. Seaton, Douglass. "The Cycles of Mendelssohn's Songs." In *The Mendelssohns: Their Music in History*, ed. John Michael Cooper and Julie D. Prandi. Oxford: Oxford University Press, [forthcoming].

653. Seaton, Douglass. "The Problem of the Lyric Persona in Mendelssohn's Songs." In *Felix Mendelssohn Bartholdy: Kongreß-Bericht Berlin 1994*, ed. Christian Martin Schmidt, 167–86. Wiesbaden: Breitkopf & Härtel, 1997.

    The author explores the aesthetics of FMB's Lieder, with an emphasis on the concept of voiced-ness: who speaks in poetry, vocal line, accompaniment, etc. The introductory section explores the ways in which FMB's Lieder relate to the aesthetics of Hegel and Schopenhauer, and the remainder of the essay focuses on "the Romantic persona in Mendelssohn's songs." Special attention is given to "Holder klingt der Vogelsang" (Op. 8, no. 1), "Es ist bestimmt in Gottes Rath" (Op. 47, no. 4), and the six songs of Op. 71.

654. Stoner, Thomas A. "Mendelssohn's Lieder Not Included in the *Werke*." *Fontes Artis Musicae* 26 (1979): 258–66.

    In the corpus of studies of FMB manuscript sources, perhaps the one that illustrates most compellingly the incompleteness of the so-called "Complete Works" edited by Julius Rietz and published by Breitkopf & Härtel in the 1870s. The author examines the source situation for thirty-five Lieder: some of them unpublished but surviving in autograph sources; some published during FMB's lifetime but not included in the *Werke*; some that seem to be only fragments; and some that are attributed but not definitely ascribable to FMB.

655. Stoner, Thomas Alan. "Mendelssohn's Published Songs." Ph.D. diss., University of Maryland, 1972. 428 p.

Stoner provides an overview of Lieder production in Berlin during the 1820s and 1830s, and describes FMB's Lieder as representing a transitional stage between Classical and Romantic schools of song composition. Discusses the musical style and textual content of the songs treated, as well as the societal milieu in which they were performed.

656. Tubeuf, André. *Le Lied allemand: Poètes et paysages*. Paris: Editions François Bourin, 1993.

FMB treated on p. 429–31. A thoroughly conventional survey with precious few references to actual songs. The perspective is evident from the essay's point of departure: the first heading is Richard Strauss's dismissive "born with a wig on" [*né coiffé*]. This suggests that FMB's Lieder do not succeed in performance because they were conceived for the salon, a performance venue that (for all practical purposes) has disappeared and is inconsistent with the exigencies of modern recital life. One telling sentence may account for the assessment—and the authority—of Tubeuf's views: "In the garden of the German Lied, Mendelssohn was not at home, like the child of the house: without having anything of the Jew about him, he also has nothing German, save his impeccability".

657. Woodward, Francis Lewis. "The Solo Songs of Felix Mendelssohn." D.M.A. thesis, University of Texas at Austin, 1972. 224 p.

G. Chamber Music

NB: See also Gerlach on Op. 64 and 20 (no. 577)

658. Austin, George Clifford. *Formal Procedures in Three Works for Chamber Ensemble by Felix Mendelssohn Bartholdy*. Ottowa: National Library of Canada, 1985. 72 p.

659. Cadenbach, Rainer. "Zum gattungsgeschichtlichen Ort von Mendelssohns letztem Streichquartett." In *Felix Mendelssohn Bartholdy: Kongreß-Bericht Berlin 1994*, ed. Christian Martin Schmidt, 209–31. Wiesbaden: Breitkopf & Härtel, 1997.

The musical style of FMB's Op. 80 represents a profound break with that of his earlier quartets, and one that likely would have rescued the genre from the quagmire it entered until the quartets of Brahms, had FMB lived to proceed further down the path he initiated with this work. This article analyzes several important revisions (see also Krummacher [nos. 666 and 667] and Klein [no. 663]). It also emphasizes that it took another half-century before other composers achieved a comparable balance between immediate expression and mastery of form.

660. Chittum, Donald. "Some Observations on the Pitch Structure in Mendelssohn's Octet Op. 20." Trans. German Gerhard Schuhmacher as "Einige Beobachtungen zur Ton- und Intervallstruktur in Mendelssohns Oktett op. 20." In *Felix Mendelssohn Bartholdy*, ed. Gerhard Schuhmacher, 277–304. Wege der Forschung, Bd. 494. Darmstadt: Wissenschaftliche Buchgesellschaft, 1982.

661. Horton, John. *Mendelssohn Chamber Music*. BBC Music Guides, 24. Seattle: University of Washington Press, 1972.

   Although the discussion of the repertoire is routine (focusing on the early piano quartets and the Sextet, the Octet, the two piano trios, and the string quartets), the opening chapters (on FMB and techniques of string playing and tradition and development in FMB's chamber music) will prove useful to many readers.

662. Kiddle, Ann M. "Mendelssohn's String Quartets: Analysis and Source Studies." Ph.D. diss., Oxford University, [forthcoming].

663. Klein, Hans-Günter "Korrekturen im Autograph von Mendelssohns Streichquartett Op. 80: Überlegungen zur Kompositionstechnik und Kompositionsvorgang." *Mendelssohn-Studien* 5 (1982): 113–22.

   Klein provides insightful observations regarding Mendelssohn's compositional process as it is evidenced in the first movement of his last string quartet. He includes a useful classification of the changes.

664. Kohlhase, Hans. "Studien zur Form in den Streichquartetten von Felix Mendelssohn Bartholdy." In *Zur Musikgeschichte des 19. Jahrhunderts,* ed. Constantin Floros, Hans Joachim Marx, and Peter Petersen, 75–104. Hamburger Jahrbuch für Musikwissenschaft, Bd. 2. Hamburg: Karl Dieter Wagner, 1977.

665. Krummacher, Friedhelm. *Mendelssohn—der Komponist: Studien zur Kammermusik für Streicher.* Munich: Wilhelm Fink, 1987.

   Adapted from the author's *Habilitation-Schrift* by the same title (University of Erlangen, 1972). A major study, drawing on unpublished manuscripts and correspondence and exploring the compositional issues involved in FMB's composition of chamber music with strings as these issues are revealed in manuscript revisions.

   Rev.: S. Großmann-Vendrey in *Österreichische Musik-Zeitung* 34

(1979): 233–34; D. Seaton in *Journal of the American Musicological Society* 32 (1979): 356–60; R. L. Todd in *Notes* 36 (1979/80): 95–96.

666. Krummacher, Friedhelm. "Zur Kompositionsart Mendelssohns: Thesen am Beispiel der Streichquartette." In Heinz-Klaus Metzger and Rainer Riehn, *Felix Mendelssohn Bartholdy,* 46–74. Musik-Konzepte, Band 14–15. Munich: edition text + kritik, 1980.

One of several important studies of Op. 80 (see also Cadenbach [no. 659] and Klein [no. 663]). This essay focuses on the ways in which FMB's revisions provide interpretive insights into the work.

667. Krummacher, Friedhelm, "Mendelssohn's Late Chamber Music: Some Autograph Sources Recovered." In *Mendelssohn and Schumann: Essays on Their Music and Its Context,* ed. Jon W. Finson and R. Larry Todd , 71–84. Durham, N.C.: Duke University Press, 1984.

The first major essay after the recovery of the autograph sources for the posthumously published chamber *opera* 80, 81, and 87 (now in the Biblioteca Jagiellońska, Kraków). It finds that while Op. 87 was clearly rejected because of the deficiencies in the musical material, Op. 80 was essentially complete and ready for publication. On Opus 80 see also Hans-Günter Klein's study of the compositional process (no. 663).

668. McDonald, J. A. "The Chamber Music of Felix Mendelssohn-Bartholdy." Ph.D. diss., Northwestern University, 1970. 501 p.

A careful examination, reviewing both well-known basics of the works' genesis and little-known facts concerning sources. It includes an edition of the early Piano Trio in C Minor (1820), and contains other important source-critical observations on works such as the Clarinet Sonata and the Viola Sonata. Includes a thematic catalog of FMB's chamber works, a listing of arrangements of FMB's chamber works, and an overview of the unpublished fugues for string quartet (see p. 254 of this book).

669. Todd, R. Larry. "The Chamber Music of Mendelssohn." In *Nineteenth-Century Chamber Music,* ed. Stephen E. Hefling, 170–207. New York: Schirmer Books, 1998.

A thoughtful and source-critical overview of a repertoire conspicuously lacking such an authoritative survey in English, despite many of the constituent works' enduring presence in the concert and scholarly canons. It discusses virtually all the chamber-music works, published and unpublished alike. Special attention is devoted to Opp. 1, 3, 12, 18, 20, 44, 49,

58, 66, and 80.

670. Ward Jones, Peter. "Mendelssohn's Opus 1: Bibliographical Problems of the C Minor Piano Quartet." In *Sundry Sorts of Music Books: Essays on the British Library Collections, Presented to O. W. Neighbour on His 70th Birthday*, ed. Chris Banks, Arthur Searle, and Malcolm Turne, 264–73. London: The British Library, 1993.

This article deals with the complicated publication history of Op. 1 and illuminates the extensive editorial problems posed by the work and its source-transmission history.

H. Music For Piano Alone

671. Chuang, Yue-Fun. "The Piano Preludes and Fugues by Felix Mendelssohn-Bartholdy: A Study of Their Unity and Formal Structure." Ph.D. diss., New York University, [in progress].

672. Dinglinger, Wolfgang. "Sieben Charakterstücke op. 7 von Felix Mendelssohn Bartholdy." *Mendelssohn-Studien* 10 (1997): 101–30.

The *Character Pieces* constituted one of FMB's early popular *opera*, but aside from the two fugues they have consistently eluded analytical discussion—one of many such problems in FMB reception history. This article explores the notion of the pieces as a cycle, as well as offering observations concerning stylistic gestures and the hermeneutic implications of the title.

673. Jost, Christa, trans. J. Bradford Robinson. "In Mutual Reflection: Historical, Biographical, and Structural Aspects of Mendelssohn's *Variations sérieuses*." In *Mendelssohn Studies*, ed. R. Larry Todd, 33–63. Cambridge: Cambridge University Press, 1992.

Op. 54 has generally garnered praise even from FMB's critics. This essay examines the ways in which the work reflects the occasion of its composition (an album that was to generate funds for the raising of Vienna's first Beethoven monument) and explores the ways in which the compositional process reveals FMB striving to bring the work more in line with that objective.

674. Jost, Christa. *Mendelssohns Lieder ohne Worte*. Frankfurter Beiträge zur Musikwissenschaft, ed. Lothar Hoffmann-Erbrecht, Bd. 14. Tutzing: Hans Schneider, 1988. ISBN 3795205158.

The definitive study of these works. It draws on published and unpublished music manuscripts and correspondence to explore the musical style, aesthetics, and reception history of the Songs without Words.

675. Jost, Christa. "Nach Italien der wortlosen Lieder wegen: Die Klaviermusik des reiselustigen Felix Mendelssohn Bartholdy." *Musik und Medizin* 8 (1982): 77–84.

676. Kahl, Willi. "Zu Mendelssohns Lieder ohne Worte." *Zeitschrift für Musikwissenschaft* 3 (1920–21): 459–69.

> Kahl asserts that FMB's first volume of *Lieder ohne Worte* (Op. 19[b]) were not truly generic innovations, but were inspired by Wilhelm Taubert's *An die Geliebte: Acht Minnelieder für das Pianoforte,* Op. 16. See also Jost (no. 675) Siebenkäs (no. 682).

677. Kahn, Johannes. "Ein unbekanntes 'Lied ohne Worte' von Felix Mendelssohn." *Die Musik* 16/11 (1924): 824–26.

> A commentary on a *Lied ohne Worte* in F Major [ca. 1841], with facsimile.

678. Reininghaus, Frieder. "Studie zur bürgerlichen Musiksprache: Mendelssohns 'Lieder ohne Worte' als historisches, ästhetisches und politisches Problem." *Die Musikforschung* 28 (1975): 34–51.

679. Risch, Claudia. "Felix Mendelssohns Lieder ohne worte." Lizenz-Arbeit der Philosophischen-Historischen Fakultät, University of Bern, 1982.

680. Schwarting, Heino. "Die 'Lieder ohne Worte' von Felix Mendelssohn Bartholdy: Untersuchungen und Betrachtungen über das erste Heft (Op. 19)." *Üben und Musizieren* 5 (1988): 426–31.

681. Smith, Robert Carrol. "Felix Mendelssohn's 'Six Preludes and Fugues,' Opus 35." D.M.A. diss., Indiana University, 1989.

682. Siebenkäs, Dieter. "Zur Vorgeschichte der Lieder ohne Worte von Mendelssohn." *Die Musikforschung* 15 (1962): 171–73.

> The article disputes Willi Kahl's suggestion (no. 676) that the Songs without Words were inspired by Taubert's *An die Geliebte*, Op. 16, and suggests that they were instead inspired by one of Taubert's songs texted Lieder: his unpublished setting of Wilhelm Müller's "Der Neugierige" (also set by Schubert in *Die schöne Müllerin*).

683. Tischler, Louise H. and Hans. "Mendelssohn's *Songs without Words.*" *The Musical Quarterly* 33 (1947): 1–16.

> The authors discuss the generic novelty of the *Lieder ohne Worte* and identify the presence of the style in other works, including Opp. 40, 49, 52,

and 66.

684. Tischler, Louise H. and Hans. "Mendelssohn's Style: The Songs without Words." *Music Review* 8 (1947): 256–73.

This article groups the *Lieder ohne Worte* into three categories according to texture and style: those modeled on solo Lieder; those modeled on duets; and those modeled on choral songs. It also traces the emergence of the style in a number of FMB's works prior to 1832, including Opp. 22, 101, 24, 12, and 28.

685. Todd, R. Larry. "From the Composer's Workshop: Two Little-Known Fugues by Mendelssohn." *The Musical Times* 131 (1990): 183–87.

Todd discusses two short piano fugues (in G minor and E-flat major) held in volume c. 8 of the M. Deneke Mendelssohn collection of the Bodleian Library, Oxford.

686. Todd, R. Larry. 'Gerade das Lied wie es dasteht': On Text and Meaning in Mendelssohn's *Lieder ohne Worte*." In *Musical Humanism and Its Legacy: Essays in Honor of Claude V. Palisca*, ed. Nancy Kovaleff Baker and Barbara Russano Hanning, 355–79. Stuyvesant, N.Y.: Pendragon, 1992.

The author discusses the aesthetics of musical and extramusical meaning in the *Lieder ohne Worte,* proceeding from FMB's well-known letter of 15 October 1842 and drawing on additional little-known correspondence to expand the insights provided by that letter. He also focuses on contemporary texted versions of some of the *Lieder ohne Worte* (from pp. 63, 19[b], 30, and 57).

687. Todd, R. Larry. "*Me voilà perruqué*: Mendelssohn's Six Preludes and Fugues Op. 35 Reconsidered." In *Mendelssohn Studies*, ed. R. Larry Todd, 162–99. Cambridge: Cambridge University Press, 1992.

An essential artice on an opus central to FMB's posthumous reception history as well as his contemporary prestige. Observations on the pervasiveness of fugal writing in FMB's oeuvre are followed by a detailed study of the compositional process for the opus as a whole (including the rejected material posthumously published in pp. 104[a] and 104[b]), explorations of thematic and tonal unity that create the gesture of a cycle for the entire opus, and a detailed analytical discussion of the Prelude and Fugue in E Minor, Op. 35, no. 1. Includes an extensive source-list for the works.

688. Todd, R. Larry. "Piano Music Reformed: The Case of Felix Mendelssohn Bartholdy." In *Nineteenth-Century Piano Music*, ed. R. Larry Todd,

178–220. New York: Schirmer Books, 1990.

Although FMB did not make a career of his pianism, most contemporaries described him as possessing technique and musicianship that rivaled those of the celebrated virtuosos of the day. This essay is an indispensable overview that deals with FMB's complete piano oeuvre (including the piano-duet repertoire), published and unpublished, and identifies significant influences on FMB's piano style. Divides the compositions into early (student) works (with special attention given to Opp. 6 and 7); *Lieder ohne Worte*; large forms in the mature works (focusing on Opp. 28, 35, 54, 82, and 83); and short forms in the mature works (focusing on Opp. 14, 15, 16, and 33, and the posthumous *opera* 104[a], 104[b], 117, and 118). It identifies as salient in this repertoire an attitude of reform, with an eye to creating "an antidote to what he regarded as the excesses and mediocrity of much contemporary piano music."

689. Todd, R. Larry. "A Sonata by Mendelssohn." *Piano Quarterly* 29 (1981): 30–41.

This essay includes commentary and the first edition of FMB's 1823 Sonata in B Minor.

690. Ward Jones, Peter. "Mendelssohn's First Composition." In *The Mendelssohns: Their Music in History*, ed. John Michael Cooper and Julie D. Prandi. Oxford: Oxford University Press, [forthcoming].

I. Organ Music

691. Beechey, Gwilyn. "Mendelssohn's Organ Music." *The Organ* 58 (1979/80): 67, 69–89.

692. Bötel, Freidhold. *Mendelssohns Bachrezeption und ihre Konsequenzen dargestellt an den Präludien und Fugen op. 37.* Beiträge zur Musikforschung, Bd. 14. Munich: Emil Katzbichler, 1984. 134 p. ISBN 3873972638.

Adapted from the author's dissertation (Heidelberg, 1982). Though Mendelssohn was brought up on organs made by Johann Joachim Wagner, a Schnittger pupil, he seems to have had sympathy for the then-modern, orchestral instrument built according to Vögler's principles. A letter to Schubring appears to suggest that Mendelssohn wanted a modern sound for these pieces. In addition to detailed analyses of Op. 37 (and of early versions of them where these have survived), the book also contains a list of all Bach organ works that Mendelssohn could have known, and a list of all of Mendelssohn's known organ works. A long analysis of "Schmücke dich, o liebe Seele," BWV 654, one of Mendelssohn's favorite Bach pieces, seeks to explain its fascination for and influence on him. [DM]

693. Busch, Hermann J. "Einige Beobachtungen zu den Orgelsonaten Mendelssohns." *Ars Organi* 36 (1988): 63–66.

   This article consists of suggestions for the registration of the Op. 65 sonatas, based on FMB's prefatory remarks and on nineteenth-century performance conventions.

694. Butler, Douglas Lamar. "The Organ Works of Felix Mendelssohn Bartholdy." D.M.A. diss., University of Oregon, 1973. 268 p.

   Butler discusses Mendelssohn's organ music in relation to: (1) organs and musical cultures encountered in Germany and Central Europe; (2) Mendelssohn's activities as conductor and performer; and (3) the relationship of Mendelssohn's organ sonatas to Baroque and Romantic "style procedures." Various movements of the sonatas are related to several stylistic categories: (1) English Baroque voluntary style; (2) chorale-based procedures; (3) fugue and fugal procedures; (4) the toccata (Baroque revival procedures); and (5) melodic ornamentation practice. Mendelssohn's organ works "fuse neo-Baroque counterpoint with uniquely graceful lyricism." [DM]

695. Butler, Douglas Lamar. "The Organ Works of Felix Mendelssohn Bartholdy." *The Diapason* 69, 70, and 71.

696. Edwards, Mark Douglas. "A Performer's Study of Three Organ Sonatas from the Eighteenth to the Twentieth Centuries: Bach, Mendelssohn, and Hindemith." D.M.A. diss., Southwestern Baptist Theological Seminary, 1993.

   In effect, a study of the versatility of the structural application of the term "sonata" in the context of the organ repertoire. Asserts that despite their generic designation the Op. 65 Sonatas are "essentially church compositions because of Mendelssohn's considerable use of the chorale."

697. Großmann-Vendrey, Susanna. "Stilprobleme in Mendelssohns Orgelsonaten op. 65." In *Das Problem Mendelssohn*, ed. Carl Dahlhaus, 185–94. Studien zur Musikgeschichte des 19. Jahrhunderts, Bd. 41. Regensburg: Gustav Bosse, 1974.

   This essay—by far one of the most substantial concerning this important opus in the nineteenth-century organ literature—proceeds from the disturbingly true assurtion that "the best known characteristic of

Mendelssohn's organ sonatas is the fact that they are hardly ever played," and attributes this situation to the works' considerable stylistic heterogeneity.

698. Hathaway, J. W. G. *An Analysis of Mendelssohn's Organ Works: A Study of Their Structural Features.* London: W. Reeves, 1898. 123 p. Rpt. New York: AMS Press, 1978. ISBN 0404129560. MT145.M5 H2 1978.

699. Henderson, A. M. "Mendelssohn's Unpublished Organ Works." *The Musical Times* 88 (1947): 347–48.

A description and discussion of the organ juvenilia of 1823, based on detailed notes from the the the author's 1900 trip to Berlin. Although Henderson strongly advocated publication of the works, they remained unpublished until Wm. A. Little's edition of 1991 (see Appendix B).

700. Moorehead, Douglas M. "Mendelssohn's Organ Sonatas: A Look at Number 3." *The AGO-RCCO Magazine* 9, no. 11 (1975): 28–33.

An overview of the Op. 65 sonatas followed by a look at issues of style, form, and performance practice in the A-major Sonata.

701. Na, Jin-Gyu. "Die langsamen Sätze in den Orgelsonaten von Mendelssohn bis Rheinberger." Ph.D. diss., University of Würzburg, [in progress].

702. Petrash, David Lloyd. "Felix Mendelssohn as Organ Composer: Unpublished and Little-Known Works." D.M.A. diss., North Texas State University, 1975. 25 p.

An early discussion of seven little-known works for organ: the Fugue in D Major (Jan. 1821), the Andante in D Major (May 1823), the Passacaglia in C Minor (May 1823), the Fantasia in G Minor (ca. 1827), the Fugue in E Minor (July 1839), the Fugue in F Minor (July 1839), and the Sonata in A Major (1839).

703. Raidt, Jürgen. "Die Rezeption der Orgelsonaten Felix Mendelssohn-Bartholdys im ausgehenden 19. Jahrhundert unter besonderer Berücksichtigung Frankreichs und Englands." Ph.D. diss., University of Bochum, [forthcoming].

704. Sabatier, François. "Les grandes oeuvres pour orgue de Mendelssohn." *L'Orgue: Cahiers et memoires* 24/2 (1980): 1–29. Trans. Eng. by J. Christopher O'Malley as "Mendelssohn's Organ Works." *American Organist* 16 (1982): 46–56.

A survey of the influences of J. S. Bach on FMB's Three Preludes and Fugues (Op. 37) and Six Sonatas (Op. 65), particularly in the predominance

of genuinely polyphonic textures. It includes a section detailing the specifications of the organs in the cathedrals at Bern and Munich; the Abbey of
Engelberg; the *Katharinenkirche* in Frankfurt am Main; the *Johanneskirche*
in Kronberg; Buckingham Palace; St. Peter's Cornhill, London; Christ
Church on Newgate Street, London; and Town Hall, Birmingham.

705. Todd, R. Larry. "New Light on Mendelssohn's *Freie Fantasie* (1840)." In
Literary and Musical Notes: A Festschrift for Wm. A. Little, ed. Geoffrey C.
Orth, 205–18. Bern: Peter Lang, 1995.

An important essay concerning FMB's activities as an organist and as
an activist in the Bach revival. Focuses on FMB's 1840 benefit organ
recital for the Leipzig Bach monument, devoting special attention to the
concluding "Freie Phantasie" on the chorale "O Haupt voll Blut und
Wunden." It focuses on the manuscript draft for this improvisation.

706. [Großmann-]Vendrey, Susanna "Die Orgelwerke von Felix Mendelssohn
Bartholdy." Ph.D. diss., University of Vienna, 1965.

Not available for examination.

707. Wilson, Roger B. "Collecting for Recording the Organ Works of
Mendelssohn: A Personal Odyssey." *The Diapason* 64/7 (1973): 3,15.

708. Zappalà, Pietro. "I Preludi dei 'Präludien und Fugen' op. 37 di Felix
Mendelssohn Bartholdy." In *La Critica del testo musicale: metodi e prob-
lemi della filologia musicale*, ed. Maria Caraci Vela, 287–318. Studi e testi
musicali: Nuova serie no. 4. Lucca: Libreria Musicale Italiana, [1995].
Trans. English John Michael Cooper as "Editorial Problems in
Mendelssohn's Op. 37 Organ Preludes." In *The Mendelssohns: Their Music
in History*, ed. John Michael Cooper and Julie D. Prandi. Oxford: Oxford
University Press, [forthcoming].

II. SACRED WORKS

A. Oratorios

709. Armstrong, Thomas. *Mendelssohn's Elijah*. London: Oxford University
Press, 1931. 38 p.

710. Bartelmus, Rüdiger. "Elia(s): Eine Prophetengestalt im Alten Testament
und ihre musikalisch-theologische Deutung durch Felix Mendelssohn
Bartholdy." *Musik und Kirche* 65 (1995): 182–97.

This essay examines the theological implications of the libretto
selected for Op. 70 and FMB's musical responses to those implications.

711. Edwards, F. G. "First Performances: I. Mendelssohn's *St. Paul.*" *The Musical Times* 32 (1891): 137–38.

712. Edwards, F. G. *The History of Mendelssohn's Oratorio "Elijah."* London: Novello, Ewer & Co., 1896. 141 p. Rpt. New York: AMS Press, 1976. ISBN 0404129013. ML410.M5 E2 1976.

Though dated in its particulars, this book is still an important and insightful resource. It devotes special attention to the development of the libretto, the circumstances and reception of the first performance, and the reworking that followed that tremendously successful event.

713. Ellison, Ross Wesley. "Mendelssohn's *Elijah*: Dramatic Climax of a Creative Career," *American Choral Review* 22 (1980): 3–9.

Adapted from the author's dissertation (no. 714). A basic article that situates FMB's last completed oratorio amid the events and other compositions of the last decade of the composer's life.

714. Ellison, Ross Wesley. "Overall Unity and Contrast in Mendelssohn's *Elijah.*" Ph.D. diss., University of North Carolina at Chapel Hill, 1978. 381 p.

715. Forchert, Arno. "Textanlage und Darstellungsprinzipien in Mendelssohns *Elias.*" In *Das Problem Mendelssohn*, ed. Carl Dahlhaus, 61–77. Regensburg: Gustav Bosse, 1974.

Forchert addresses recurrent themes in negative critiques of Elijah: the notion that the approach to the drama is inappropriate for the genre of the oratorio; the notion that there are too many generalizing arias and choruses that disrupt the drama; and Eric Werner's suggestion that the work suffers because the texts dealing with the *Elijah* plot are mixed with texts relating to much later developments in theological history.

716. Gottfried Wilhelm Fink, "Paulus." *Allgemeine Musikalische Zeitung* 34 (1837): cols. 497–506, 513–30.

717. Grove, George. "Mendelssohn's Oratorio 'St Paul.'" *The Musical Times* 50 (1909): 92–94.

This article focuses on the unpublished chorales, arias, and choruses, and suggests that their music is worthy of separate study and publication.

718. Jahn, Otto. "Über F. Mendelssohn Bartholdy's Oratorium Elias." *Allgemeine musikalische Zeitung* [Leipzig] 50 (1848): cols. 113–22, 137–43. Trans. English Susan Gillespie as "On F. Mendelssohn-

Bartholdy's Oratorio *Elijah*." In *Mendelssohn and His World*, ed. R. Larry Todd, 364–89. Princeton: Princeton University Press, 1991.

Jahn (1813–69) was an acquaintance of FMB, author of the first full-scale critical biography of Mozart (Leipzig: Breitkopf & Härtel, 1856–59), and author of a sizable study of *St. Paul* (no. 719). Despite its early date, this is in many ways a comprehensive article that reveals not only the esteem with which Op. 70 was viewed from its premiere, but also much about its textual and musical structure.

719. Jahn, Otto. *Über Felix Mendelssohn Bartholdys Oratorium "Paulus."* Kiel: n.p., 1842. Rpt. in his *Gesammelte Aufsätze über Musik*, 13–39. Leipzig: Breitkopf & Härtel, 1866.

A lengthy study of FMB's first oratorio, with running descriptive commentary on the music and plot of the work.

720. Kurzhals-Reuter, Arntrud. *Die Oratorien Felix Mendelssohn Bartholdys: Untersuchungen zur Quellenlage, Entstehung, Gestaltung und Überlieferung*. Mainzer Studien zur Musikwissenschaft, 12. Tutzing: Hans Schneider, 1978.

Adapted from the author's dissertation (University of Mainz, 1977). A landmark survey of the sources, plots, theological background, genesis, texts, and musical structure of Opp. 36, 70, and 95.

721. Meiser, Martin. "Das Paulusbild bei Mendelssohn und Mendelssohns christliche Selbsterfahrung." *Musik und Kirche* 62 (1992): 259–64.

New Testament scholars have formulated the scriptures' presentation of several discrete images of St. Paul: as theologian, missionary, Christian, martyr, and apostolic authority of the early church. This article examines the ways in which these images are reflected in FMB's treatment of his subject in Op. 36.

722. Mercer-Taylor, Peter. "Rethinking Mendelssohn's Historicism: A Lesson from *St. Paul*." *Journal of Musicology* 15 (1997): 208–29.

Adapted from the author's dissertation (no. 784). This study focuses on the chorales in Op. 36 and suggests that their increasingly complex settings reveal a culminating "self-reflexivity, or self-critique, in which the appropriateness of the chorale in this context is effectively raised as an issue within the musical discourse itself."

723. Mintz, Donald. "Mendelssohn's *Elijah* Reconsidered." *Studies in*

Romanticism 3 (1963): 1–9.

A careful review of the drama and structure of the dramatic scenes in Op. 70.

724. Staehelin, Martin. "Elias, Johann Sebastian Bach und der Neue Bund: Zur Arie 'Es ist genug' in Felix Mendelssohn Bartholdys Oratorium Elias." *Beiträge zur Geschichte des Oratoriums seit Händel: Festschrift für Günter Massenkeil*, ed. Rainer Cadenbach and Helmut Loos, 283–96. Bonn: Voggenreiter, 1986. Trans. English Susan Gillespie as "Elijah, Johann Sebastian Bach, and the New Covenant: On the Aria 'Es ist genug' in Felix Mendelssohn Bartholdy's Oratorio *Elijah*." In *Mendelssohn and His World*, ed. R. Larry Todd, 121–36. Princeton: Princeton University Press, 1991.

This essay is by far the most substantive study to explore the similarities between the aria "Es ist genug" in *Elijah* and "Es ist vollbracht" in J. S. Bach's *St. John Passion*.

725. Plank, Stephen. "Mendelssohn and Bach: Some New Light on an Old Partnership." *American Choral Review* 32, no. 1–2 (1990): 23–28.

An article on the similarities between "Es ist genug" (*Elijah*) and "Es ist vollbracht" from Bach's *St. John Passion*.

726. Reichwald, Siegwart. "The Musical Genesis of Felix Mendelssohn's *Paulus*." Ph.D. diss., Florida State University, 1998. 310 p.

727. Reimer, Erich. "Mendelssohns 'edler Gesang': Zur Kompositionsweise der Sologesänge im 'Paulus.'" *Archiv für Musikwissenschaft* 50 (1993): 44–70.

An important exploration of the mechanics and aesthetics of what Leon Botstein (no. 761) terms "the Mendelssohnian project." This article proceeds from Schumann's cautiously expressed reservation that the popularity of the music in *St. Paul* almost suggested that FMB may have consciously written some of the numbers with the intention of effectiveness for "das Volk." It examines the structure and musical language of the solo songs in exploring the aesthetic plausibility and ramifications of the music.

728. Reimer, Erich. "Regenwunder und Witwenszene: Zur Szenengestaltung in Mendelssohns 'Elias.'" *Die Musikforschung* 49 (1996): 152–71.

This study examines the dramatic structure of two scenes from *Elijah* from a textual and musical perspective to show that FMB's concern with the drama of the oratorio led him to introduce modifications in the Biblical texts, while also demonstrating a concern for fidelity to the texts' moral and ethical content.

729. Reimer, Erich. "Textanlage und Szenengestaltung in Mendelssohns Paulus." *Archiv für Musikwissenschaft* 46 (1989): 42–69. Abridged as "Zur Szenengestaltung in Mendelssohns *Paulus*" in *Blickpunkt FELIX Mendelssohn Bartholdy: Programmbuch Drei Tage für Felix vom 30.10 bis 1.11.1994*, ed. Bernd Heyder and Christoph Spering, 81–88. Cologne: Dohr, 1994.

> Reimer discusses the dramatic and musical structure of Op. 36, as well as its use of chorales.

730. Rothfahl, Wolfgang. "Zu den 'Chorälen' in Mendelssohns *Elias*." *Musik und Gottesdienst* 44 (1990): 247–51.

731. Schuhmacher, Gerhard. "Felix Mendelssohn Bartholdys Oratorien-Triptychon." *Musik und Kirche* 67 (1997): 376–81.

732. Werner, Jack. *Mendelssohn's "Elijah."* [London]: Chappell, 1965. 109 p. MT115.M53 W5.

733. Zywietz, Michael. *Adolf Bernhard Marx und das Oratorium in Berlin.* Schriften zur Musikwissenschaft aus Münster, No. 9. Hamburg; Wagner, 1996.

B. Chorale Cantatas

734. Griggs-Janower, D. "Mendelssohn's Chorale Cantatas: A Well-Kept Secret." *Choral Journal* 33/4 (1992): 31–33.

> There is little here in the way of new research (cf. the other items in this section), but it is an easily accessible overview.

735. Pritchard, Brian W. "Mendelssohn's Chorale Cantatas: An Appraisal." *The Musical Quarterly* 62 (1976): 1–24.

> The first published study of the chorale cantatas (although *Wer nur den lieben Gott läßt walten* is omitted) and a solid foundation for subsequent inquiries. It provides an overview of the glaring omissions from the so-called *Gesamtausgabe* (edited by FMB's friend Julius Rietz in the 1870s) before turning to focal repertoire. Pritchard devotes special attention to *O Haupt voll Blut und Wunden*. It is amply illustrated with facsimiles and music examples.

736. Schulze, Willi. "Mendelssohns Choralkantaten." In *Logos musicae: Festschrift für Albert Palm*, ed. Rüdiger Görner, 188–93. Wiesbaden: Franz Steiner, 1982.

737. Todd, R. Larry. "A Passion Cantata by Mendelssohn." *American Choral*

Review 25, no. 1 (1983): 2–17.

On the chorale cantata *O Haupt voll Blut und Wunden*. Todd argues (on the basis of FMB's correspondence) that the inspiration for work was a synthesis of J. S. Bach's *St. Matthew Passion* and a painting by Antonio del Castillo y Saavedra (1616–68).

738. Wüster, Ulrich. *Felix Mendelssohn Bartholdys Choralkantaten: Gestalt und Idee—Versuch einer historisch-kritischen Interpretation*. Bonner Schriften zur Musikwissenschaft, Bd. 1. Frankfurt am Main: Peter Lang, 1996. 497 p. ISBN 3631494599. ML410.M5 W97 1996.

Adapted from the author's dissertation by the same title (University of Bonn, 1993). An essential complement to Pietro Zappalà's book on the works (no. 740).

739. Zappalà, Pietro. *Le 'Choralkantaten' di Felix Mendelssohn-Bartholdy*. Collezioni di tesi Universitarie, Serie IV, 2. Venice: Fondazione Levi, 1991.

An expanded version of the author's dissertation (Università di Pavia, 1984). As a thorough and source-critical overview of major issues pertaining to an entire corpus of important but largely neglected works, a milestone in FMB research.

Rev.: J. M. Cooper in *Notes* 49 (1993): 1005–06; A. Polignano in *Rivista italiana di musicologia* 28 (1993): 395–98.

C. Psalm Settings

740. Brodbeck, David. "Some Notes on an Anthem by Mendelssohn." In *Mendelssohn and His World*, ed. R. Larry Todd, 43–64. Princeton: Princeton University Press, 1991.

A study of "Why, O Lord, Delay" (known in German as *Hymne: Lass, o Herr, mich Hülfe finden*), Op. 96.

741. Dinglinger, Wolfgang. "'. . . der letzte Schluß will mir nicht so recht werden': Anmerkungen zum 114. Psalm von Felix Mendelssohn Bartholdy." In *Professor Rudolph Stephan zum 3. April 1985 von seiner Schulern*, 77–80. Berlin: n.p., 1985 and Hedge de Le Motte-Haber, Christina Martin Schmidt, Wilhelm Seidel.

742. Dinglinger, Wolfgang. "Felix Mendelssohn Bartholdy: Der 95. Psalm op. 46: '. . . von dem nur ein Stück mir ans Herz gewachsen war.'" *Mendelssohn-Studien* 7 (1990): 269–86.

An important study of the compositional history of the last of the psalms for chorus and orchestra that FMB elected to publish. It focuses on textual and musical changes, and suggests that FMB may have been more comfortable setting scenic/dramatic psalm texts than he was with opera librettos because of his identification with the ethical and moral content of the psalms.

743. Dinglinger, Wolfgang. "Ein neues Lied: Der preußische Generalmusikdirektor und eine königliche Auftragskomposition." *Mendelssohn-Studien* 5 (1982): 99–111.

This article traces the composition of Mendelssohn's setting of Psalm 98 (Op. posth. 91) and situates the work in the liturgical reforms undertaken by Prussian King Friedrich Wilhelm IV in 1843.

744. Dinglinger, Wolfgang. *Studien zu den Psalmen mit Orchester von Felix Mendelssohn Bartholdy*. Berlin Musik Studien: Schriftenreihe zur Musikwissenschaft an den Berliner Hochschulen und Universituten, 1. Cologne: Studio, 1993. ISBN 3-86114-036-5.

A study of Psalms 115 (Op. 31), 42 (Op. 42), 95 (Op. 46), 114 (Op. 51), and 98 (Op. 91). Parts of the chapters on Psalms 95 and 98 were adapted from articles in the Berlin *Mendelssohn-Studien* in 1981 and 1989 (see nos. 742 and 743). Overlooked: Psalm 150 for chorus and orchestra, originally intended for Op. 36 (MN 28); sketches for Op. 42 in MN 19.

Rev.: K. Küster in *Die Musikforschung* 48 (1995): 86–87.

745. Robinson, Daniel Vehe. "An Analysis of the Psalms for Chorus and Orchestra by Felix Mendelssohn." D.M.A. diss., Stanford University, 1976. 125 p.

746. Rüdiger, Adolf. "Stimmliche Hilfen für die Einstudierung des Psalmes 43 für achtstimmigen gemischten Chor von Felix Mendelssohn Bartholdy." *Musica sacra* 108 (1988): 298–302.

747. Werner, Eric. "Felix Mendelssohn's Commissioned Composition for the Hamburg Temple: The 100th Psalm (1844)." *Musica Judaica: Journal of the American Society of Jewish Music* 7 (1984): 54–57.

748. Wolff, Hellmuth Christian. "Der zweite Psalm op. 78, 1 von Felix Mendelssohn Bartholdy." *Chormusik und Analyse: Beiträge zur Formanalyse und Interpretation mehrstimmiger Vokalmusik*, ed. Heinrich Poos, 1: 213–22. Mainz: Schott, 1983.

749. Zappalà, Pietro. "I salmi di Felix Mendelssohn Bartholdy." Ph.D. diss., Università di Pavia, 1992. 401 p.

D. Other Accompanied Sacred Choral Works

NB: See also Hatteberg (no. 617), above.

750. Brodbeck, David. "*Eine kleine Kirchenmusik*: A New Canon, A Revised Cadence, and an Obscure 'Coda' by Mendelssohn." *Journal of Musicology* 12 (1994): 179–205. Also abridged in *Bericht über den internationalen Kongreß der Gesellschaft für Musikforschung, Freiburg im Breisgau 1993*, ed. Hermann Danuser and Tobias Plebuch, 2: 346–50. Kassel: Bärenreiter, 1999.

> A deft journey through the densely tangled jungle of the works composed during FMB's service to Prussian King Friedrich Wilhelm IV in the winter of 1843–44, with emphasis on the psalm settings written during that winter and published posthumously. This essay concerns the *Jubilate Deo* published as the second part of the Te Deum in 1846, as well as *Magnificat and Nunc dimittis* (Op. 69, no. 2), the three psalms posthumously published as Op. 78, and the setting of Psalm 98 posthumously published as Op. 91. It explores the possibility of substantial editorial errors in the publication histories of these works.

751. Campbell, Robert Madison. "Mendelssohn's Te Deum in D." *American Choral Review* 28, no. 2 (1986): 3–16.

> Adapted from the author's dissertation (no. 752). Descriptive analysis of the work (which was first published in 1977), along with observations concerning evident stylistic influences.

752. Campbell, Robert Madison. "Mendelssohn's Te Deum in D: Influences and the Development of Style." D.M.A. diss., Stanford University, 1985. 172 p.

> This article summarizes Mendelssohn's early development, largely on the basis of Todd (no. 226). A close analysis of the piece in question, discussing the influences of Handel (*Dettingen* and *Utrecht Te Deums*) and Bach. There is a discussion of the bass realization in the Leipzig edition. Contains a list of publications of religious music by Mendelssohn recently pubished outside the bounds of the Leipzig edition. Nevertheless, the general impression is one of superficiality. [DM]

753. Linden, Albert van der. "Un Fragment inédit du 'Lauda Sion' de F. Mendelssohn." *Acta musicologica* 26 (1954): 48–64.

> The late masterpiece *Lauda Sion* was one of the earliest posthumous publications, and the edition by which the work has always been known is seriously flawed. (A critical edition is now available through Carus-Verlag; see Appendix B.) This essay examines one important movement that was

omitted from the edition.

754. Linden, Albert van der. "A propos du 'Lauda Sion' de Mendelssohn." *Revue Belge de musicologie* 17 (1963): 124–25.

An important early writing on FMB's late masterpiece.

755. Wüster, Ulrich. "'Aber dann ist es schon durch die innerste Wahrheit und durch den Gegenstand, den es vorstellt, Kirchenmusik . . .': Beobachtungen an Mendelssohns *Kirchen-Musik* op. 23." In *Felix Mendelssohn Bartholdy: Kongreß-Bericht Berlin 1994*, ed. Christian Martin Schmidt, 187–208. Wiesbaden: Breitkopf & Härtel, 1997.

An important examination of a collection in which the aesthetic merits rival the historical and theological interest. This study examines the implication of the stylistic and theological heterogeneity of the Op. 23 *Kirchenmusiken*. Like Todd, Wüster finds inspiration in a painting (in this case, *Mitten wir im Leben sind,* which may have been inspired by Titian's *Madonna del San Niccolo dei Frari*).

E. Other Unaccompanied Sacred Choral Works

Prefatory Note: See also Wüster (no. 755) on Op. 23.

756. Zappalà, Pietro. "Di alcuni motetti giovanili di Felix Mendelssohn Bartholdy." In *Ottocento e oltre: Scritti in onore di Raoul Meloncelli*, ed. Francesco Izzo and Johannes Streicher, 203–33. Rome: Editoriale Pantheon, 1993.

III. ARRANGEMENTS AND EDITIONS OF OTHER COMPOSERS' WORKS

757. Cooper, John Michael. "Felix Mendelssohn Bartholdy, Ferdinand David und Johann Sebastian Bach: Mendelssohns Bach-Auffassung im Spiegel der Wiederentdeckung der 'Chaconne.'" *Mendelssohn-Studien* 10 (1997): 157–79.

In 1840 Ferdinand David gave the first public performance of the "Chaconne" from Bach's Partita in D Minor for Unaccompanied Violin, BWV 1004—with an improvised piano accompaniment by FMB (published in 1847). This article examines the ways in which salient themes in the early phases of the Bach revival shaped FMB's and David's interpretation of the work, combining FMB's published edition of his heavily embellished rendition with FMB's piano accompaniment.

758. Feder, Georg. "Bachs Werke in ihren Bearbeitungen." Diss., Kiel, 1955. 378 p.

Feder discusses the 1829 performance of the *St. Matthew Passion* that Mendelssohn did not arrange in Zelter's fashion, and the several cuts Mendelssohn made in the work.

759. Feder, Georg. "Geschichte der Bearbeitungen von Bachs Chaconne." In *Bach-Interpretationen*, ed. Martin Geck, 168–89. Göttingen: Vandenhoeck und Ruprecht, 1969. Trans. English Egbert M. Ennulat as "History of the Arrangements of Bach's Chaconne." In *The Bach Chaconne for Solo Violin: A Collection of Views*, ed. Jon F. Eiche, 41–61. Athens, Georgia: American String Teachers Association, 1985.

An overview of the numerous arrangements of the D-minor "Chaconne" produced in the course of the nineteenth century. The work was first published in the context of the complete *Sonatas and Partitas* in 1802, but the first documented public performance occurred only in 1840, with Ferdinand David playing the violin and FMB improvising a piano accompaniment (published in 1847). This article provides useful insights in the strategies numerous composers (including major figures such as FMB, Schumann, and Brahms, as well as others such as Molique and Busoni) adopted in modernizing the work—and it provides compelling documentation of changing attitudes towards Bach's music over the course of the century.

760. Pruett, Jeffery Mark. "J. S. Bach's Chaconne in D Minor: An Examination of Three Arrangements for Pianoforte Solo." D.M.A. diss., The Louisiana State University, 1991.

See also the related studies by John Michael Cooper (no. 757) and Georg Feder (no. 759).

6. General Studies of the Music of Felix Mendelssohn Bartholdy

I.   General Surveys and Overviews
II. Mendelssohn and the Music of the Past
     (including Beethoven, Weber, and Schubert)
III. Secular Works
IV. Sacred Works
V.   Performance Practice
VI. Compositional Process

I.   GENERAL SURVEYS AND OVERVIEWS

761. Botstein, Leon. "The Aesthetics of Assimilation and Affirmation: Reconstructing the Career of Felix Mendelssohn." In *Mendelssohn and His World*, ed. R. Larry Todd, 5–42. Princeton: Princeton University Press, 1991.

   A sensitive and remarkably compact global perspective on the works, musical activities, and reception history of FMB. Suggests that while FMB and Wagner both harbored strong sentiments for German national identity in music, FMB has suffered in reception history because the communal and didactic aspects of his "project" were less consistent with the political and cultural climate of post-1848 Germany than were Wagner's individualistically and dramatically oriented ones.

762. Botstein, Leon. "Neoclassicism, Romanticism, and Emancipation: The Origins of Felix Mendelssohn's Aesthetic Outlook." In *The Mendelssohn Companion*, ed. Douglass Seaton. Westport, Connecticut: Greenwood, [forthcoming].

763. Brendel, Franz. "Robert Schumann mit Rücksicht auf Mendelssohn-Bartholdy und die Entwicklung der modernen Tonkunst überhaupt." *Neue Zeitschrift für Musik* 22 (1845): 113–15, 146–47, 149–50. Excerpts trans. English Susan Gillespie as "Robert Schumann with Reference to Felix Mendelssohn-Bartholdy and the Development of Modern Music in General." In *Mendelssohn and His World,*, ed. R. Larry Todd, 341–51. Princeton: Princeton University Press, 1991. Remainder of essay trans. English (with the same title) Jürgen Thym in *Schumann and His World,* ed. R. Larry Todd, 317–37. Princeton: Princeton University Press, 1994.

   A significant document not only as a general survey of FMB's works and an attempt to situate his music in the evolution-obsessed cultural climate of mid-nineteenth-century music, but also as a document of reception history. Brendel—who took over the editorship of Schumann's *Neue Zeitschrift für Musik* upon Schumann's retirement in 1845—was by training a historian more than a musician. His passionate concern about the historical development of German music produced several important articles that contributed decisively to the music-historical discourse in the second half of the century. Although his verdict that neither FMB nor Schumann would exert much lasting influence on the future of German music because they did not address what he considered the vital concern of the creation of a German national opera is no longer credible, his views on FMB's perceived academicism and Schumann's perceived lack of clear stylistic direction continue to resonate in the critical literature. The English translations by Susan Gillespie and Jürgen Thym are clear and responsible, and are extensively annotated by R. Larry Todd.

764. Bülow, Hans von. "Felix Mendelssohn." The foreword to the revised edition of the R*ondo capriccioso* (Munich: Joseph Aibl, 1880); rpt. in *Hans von Bülow: Briefe und Schriften*, ed. Marie von Bülow, 3: 403–06. Leipzig: Breitkopf & Härtel, 1896. Trans. English Susan Gillespie as "Felix Mendelssohn." In *Mendelssohn and His World,*, ed. R. Larry Todd, 390–94. Princeton: Princeton University Press, 1991.

   Written as a didactical introduction to a new edition of the *Introduction and Rondo capriccioso*, this essay also serves as a document of reception history and a review of FMB's musical aesthetics—and food for thought in performance-practice circles as well. It expresses reservations about the "untimely aging" of FMB's music, and attributes this danger not to any intrinsic weakness in the musical language, but to the current vogue of disdain for sentimentality (which, Bülow points out, had been recognized by Schiller as belonging to the Roman rather than Greek poets): "One plays into Mendelssohn things that are completely foreign to him;

and plays out of him the things that constitute his greatest virtue" (p. 392 of the English translation).

765. Dahlhaus, Carl. "Mendelssohn und die musikalische Gattungstradition." In *Das Problem Mendelssohn*, ed. Carl Dahlhaus, 55–60. Studien zur Musikgeschichte des 19. Jahrhunderts, Bd. 41. Regensburg: Gustav Bosse, 1974.

This article discusses the tension between two meanings of classical: paradigmatic (that is, representing a "point de perfection") on the one hand, and merely manifesting a certain sort of style on the other. Mendelssohn's "classicism" consists largely of his having accepted "Bach and Handel, Gluck and Mozart, Haydn and Beethoven" as the *classici auctores* on whose paradigmatic compositions ...[he] oriented himself," and in his acceptance of a traditional view of musical genres. Mendelssohn's classicism does not consist of a reliance on a traditional formal schema, for if such reliance were the essential aspect in a definition of classicism, the Chopin sonatas would merit the designation more than anything by Mendelssohn. [DM/JMC]

766. Dahlhaus, Carl. "Studien zur romantischen Musikästhetik." *Archiv für Musikwissenschaft* 42 (1985): 157–65.

FMB and the *Lieder ohne Worte* especially on p. 157–61. Discussion focuses on FMB's ideas concerning the referentiality (or lack thereof) of musical expression.

767. Engel, Hans. "Die Grenzen der romantischen Epoche und der Fall Mendelssohn." In *Festschrift Otto Erich Deutsch zum 80. Geburtstag*, ed. Walter Gerstenberg, 259–267. Kassel: Bärenreiter, 1963.

Engel surveys the use of the word "romantic" in England and Germany by Gerstenberg, Herder, Kant, Hagedorn, Goethe, Gleim, Uhland, and of course Tieck, Schlegel, the older Tieck, and E. T. A. Hoffmann. He emphasizes the difference between Romantic and Biedermeier tastes and argues half-heartedly against the perjorative use of the latter term—but then assigns FMB's music to that category and states (p. 271) that what differentiates between the two is "the degree of inner human power" of Romanticism, as opposed to the comfortableness (*Gemütlichkeit*) and lower stakes of Biedermeier art. [DM]

768. Friedrich, Gerda Bertram. "Die Fugenkomposition in Mendelssohns Instrumentalwerk." Bonn: [Privatdruck], 1969. 161 p.

Adapted from the author's dissertation by the same title (Bonn, 1969).

This study contains a list of all Mendelssohn's fugues, published and unpublished, taking single movements of multimovement works to be fugues if the entire movement is a fugue. It includes a discussion of the early, unpublished fugues includes the little-known string-quartet fugues of 1821 but omits those found in the string symphonies. It suggests that, in general, the late-Baroque style that underlies Mendelssohn's fugues is modified by the introduction of classical sonata elements, romantic song elements, and elements of virtuosity. [DM/JMC]

769. Garratt, John A. "Mendelssohn's Babel: Romanticism and the Poetics of Translation." *Music and Letters* 80 (1999): 23–49.

Perhaps one of the most important overviews of FMB's historicist aesthetics. This article suggests that most of the historicizing gestures in FMB's works represent the act of translation as it is understood in literary scholarship: a relaying of ideas from one mode of communication to another, with emphasis on the problems involved in knowing and understanding the audiences who would receive each. Thus, FMB's use of chorales (especially in the Piano Fugue in E Minor, Op. 35, no .1) and other archaic musical styles (as in the "Reformation" Symphony) are acts not of pseudo- or hyper-religious piety (Rosen) or vapid reactionary musical taste, but attempts to engage listeners in a complicated process of communication and a dialectically synthesized understanding of musical styles past and present.

770. Geck, Martin. "Religiöse Musik 'im Geist der gebildeten Gesellschaft': Mendelssohn und sein *Elias.*" In *Von Beethoven bis Mahler: Die Musik des deutschen Idealismus*, 256–79. Stuttgart: J. B. Metzler, 1993. ISBN 3476009300. Rpt in *Von Beethoven bis Mahler: Leben und Werk der grossen Komponisten des 19. Jahrunderts,* 256–79. Reinbek bei Hamburg: Rowohlt-Taschenbuch-Verlag, 2000. ISBN 349960891X.

Coupled with a section titled "Franz Liszt—Streiter für Fortschritt" in the context of a chapter titled "Im Dienst der Volksbildung: Franz Liszt und Felix Mendelssohn Bartholdy," this is a thoughtful and in many ways provocative attempt to grasp the ways in which the lives and works of the two seemingly irreconcilable composers reflected a common sense of mission vis-à-vis their public. Geck explains the development of FMB's approach to this mission by examining the differences between *St. Paul* and *Elijah*, and likens FMB's musical style and historicism in his later years to the aesthetics of the "Nazarene" painters, especially Wilhelm von Schadow. Contains an "excursion" titled "Essay. Gruß" on FMB's Heine setting "Leise zieht durch mein Gemüth," Op. 19[a], no. 5.

771. Giani, Maurizio. "Felix Mendelssohn-Bartholdy: Un romantico per il nos-
tro tempo." *Musica/Realtà* 20 (1999): 79–91.

Giani argues that FMB's aesthetics of musical style, function, and
expression were far ahead of those of the middle and later nineteenth century, and remarkably close to those of the later twentieth century.

772. Grey, Thomas S. "*Tableaux vivants*: Landscape, History Painting, and the
Visual Imagination in Mendelsohnn's Orchestral Music." *Nineteenth-
Century Music* 21 (1997): 38–76.

An important study, generously illustrated, of the ways in which
FMB's carefully cultivated visual imagination (see p. 133–34 of this book)
was "translated" into his musical imagination in certain orchestral works.
Grey also examines ways in which visual artists managed to convey or sug-
gest narrative progress in paintings and drawings, and explores the ways in
which these ideas relate to techniques observed in FMB's music.
Discussed: the *Hebrides* Overture (Op. 26) and the "Italian" and "Scottish"
Symphonies.

773. Jessop, Craig Don. "An Analytical Survey of the Unaccompanied Choral
Works for Mixed Voices by Felix Mendelssohn-Bartholdy." D.M.A. diss.,
Stanford University, 1981. 111 p.

A general work that entails style criticism and considerations of performance practice. Discussion includes: various of the choral songs designated "to be sung outdoors" ("*im Freien zu singen*"); the motets Opp. 23
and 39, and the motets Op. posth. 78.

774. Johns, Susanne. *Das szenische Liederspiel zwischen 1800 und 1830: Ein
Beitrag zur Berliner Theatergeschichte*. Quellen und Studien zur
Musikgeschichte von der Antike bis in die Gegenwart, 20. Bern: Peter
Lang, 1988. 2 vols. ISBN 3631404352. ML1729.8.B5 J63 1988.

Adapted from the author's dissertation (University of Tübingen,
1988). See especially p. 269–95. A discussion of the history of the "staged
song-play" from Johann Friedrich Reichardt in the late eighteenth century
up through the so-called *Amusiertheater* of the nineteenth century, focusing on its role in society.

775. Jordahl, Robert Arnold. "A Study of the Use of the Chorale in the Work of
Mendelssohn, Brahms and Reger." Ph.D. diss., Eastman School of Music,
University of Rochester, 1965. 452 p.

According to Jordahl, Reger, Brahms, and Mendelssohn are the only nineteenth-century composers seriously interested in the chorale. This dissertation investigates uses of earlier techniques and their reconciliation with "nineteenth century stylistic exigencies." Mendelssohn is found to have attempted to reconcile past practices with the "stylistic principles of classicism." The chorales used by all three composers are indexed. [DM]

776. Klinkhammer, Rudolf. *Die langsame Einleitung in der Instrumentalmusik der Klassik und Romantik: Ein Sonderproblem in der Entwicklung der Sonatenform*. Kölner Beiträge zur Musikforschung, Bd. 65. Regensburg: Gustav Bosse, 1971. 206 p. ISBN 3764925744. ML448 .K66.

Chapter V ("Die langsame Einleitung in der Romantik") discusses the change to song-like structures as well as the presentation of material from the slow introduction into the main body of the movement by various means such as motivic connection. Also discussed: the use of the slow introduction as a unifying factor of the entire cyclical sonata form by extending its influence beyond the first movement. There is a useful summary of Mendelssohn's procedures in his slow introductions. [DM]

777. Koch, Armin. "Die Bedeutung des Chorals im Werk Felix Mendelssohn Bartholdys." Ph.D. diss., University of Würzburg, [in progress].

778. Konold, Wulf. "Funktion der Stilisierung: Vorläufige Bemerkungen zum Stilbegriff bei Mendelssohn." In *Felix Mendelssohn Bartholdy*, ed. Heinz-Klaus Metzger and Rainer Riehn, 3–7. Musik-Konzepte, Band 14/15. Munich: edition text + kritik, 1980.

An insightful if also largely conjectural essay suggesting that the stylistic attributes in FMB's music that have engendered much debate are the product of a delicate balancing of musical styles of the past with those of the early nineteenth century. The point of departure is Schumann's oft-quoted dictum that FMB was "the Mozart of the nineteenth century, the most brilliant musician who most clearly penetrates the contradictions of the present, and the first to resolve them." Konold suggests that FMB strove to achieve something like Hegel's "universal poesis" [*Universalpoesie*] in the context of the civil freedoms of early nineteenth-century society through a synthesis of formal and generic conventions of the past with those of the present.

779. Kramer, Lawrence. *Classical Music and Postmodern Knowledge*. Berkeley: University of California Press, 1995. 297 p. ISBN 0520088204. ML3845 .K813 1995.

An important contribution to the English-language literature on the sociology of nineteenth-century musical styles, with FMB situated squarely in the center of the genre- and topic-based discourse among poets, composers, and audiences. Chapter 5 ("*Felix culpa*: Mendelssohn, Goethe, and the Social Force of Musical Expression") focuses on FMB's importance in cultivating society's image of Goethe as poet and social force; despite the titular similarities this essay is neither derived from, nor a source for, Kramer's essay (no. 780) in the Cambridge University Press *Mendelssohn Studies* (no. 16). Chapter 6 ("The Lied as Cultural Practice: Tutelage, Gender, and Desire in Mendelssohn's Goethe Songs") explores the ways in which the composer's musical style in these settings may reflect his personal relationship with the poet.

780. Kramer, Lawrence. "*Felix culpa:* Goethe and the Image of Mendelssohn." In *Mendelssohn Studies*, ed. R. Larry Todd, 64–79. Cambridge: Cambridge University Press, 1992.

This essay proceeds from the assertion that "the critical reception of Mendelssohn has been both made and marred by the association of art with irrationalism" (p. 65) and the resulting suggestion that FMB's music is somehow timid or unemotional in comparison with that of more emotionalist composers such as Beethoven and Brahms. It points out that Goethe's similarly classicist mode of expression has never been accused of being "confoundedly genteel" (Shaw) and suggests that FMB's works dealing expressly with Goethian subjects are not self-restrained or formalist, but "explicit assertions of exuberance, heterodoxy, and passion" (p. 65). The article focuses on the *Calm Sea and Prosperous Voyage* Overture as a case study.

781. Krummacher, Friedhelm. "Klassizismus als musikgeschichtliches Problem." In *International Musicological Society: Report of the Eleventh Congress Copenhagen 1972*, ed. Henrik Glahn, Søren Sørensen, and Peter Ryom, II: 518–26. Copenhagen: Hansen, 1974.

Asserts that the basic problem with Mendelssohn's "classicistic" sonata movements is "the maintenance of the formal housing when other sorts of material are involved." If *Klassizismus* lies not in purely epigonal work but in a confrontation with the classical, then the concept, stated radically, threatens to dissolve because the confrontation necessarily leads to something new. [DM]

782. Marshall, Linda Duckett. "An Introduction to the Romantic Fugue: Selected German Composers, 1835–1857." D.M.A. diss., Indiana University, 1983. 187 p.

783. Meloncelli, Raoul. "Felix Mendelssohn-Bartholdy, proposta per una nuova prospettiva critica." In *Scritti in onore di Luigi Ronga*, 331–44. Milan:

Riccardo Ricciardi Editore, 1973.

An important contribution from a leading voice in Italian Mendelssohn scholarship. Meloncelli draws heavily on Alfred Einstein's remarks on FMB but argues for a substantially different conclusion: in effect, that FMB's posthumous reception has suffered not because he conformed to conventions and traditions, but because his music does not lend itself to such conformities.

784. Mercer-Taylor, Peter. "Mendelssohn and the Musical Discourse of the German Restoration." Ph.D. diss., University of California at Berkeley, 1995. 343 p.

Along with John A. Garratt's essay on "Mendelssohn's Babel" (no. 769), potentially one of the most far-reaching contributions to the revisionist view of FMB's life and works. The author explores the notion of a "metastyle"—"a [musical] language which takes the issue of style itself as its subject matter" (p. 62)—with regard to FMB's works and his activities in the cultural context of the *Vormärz*. Focuses on major works in the large public-oriented genres: *St. Paul*, the G-minor Piano Concerto, the *Capriccio brillant*, the D-minor ("Reformation") Symphony; and the A-major ("Italian") Symphony; also considers the problematical A-minor ("Scottish") Symphony and its relationship to "the music of German memory." (See also no. 593).

785. Mintz, Donald. "Mendelssohn and Romanticsm." *Studies in Romanticism* 3 (1964): 217–24.

This essay asserts the notion that the function of music as a means of communication is unique to the Romantic period, and that Romantic music therefore must be approached with this criterion in mind. (See also the studies by Thomas Schmidt-Beste [no. 790] and John A. Garratt [no. 769]). Mintz draws on FMB's well-known 1842 letter to Marc-André Souchay to explore FMB's views on the matter, and applies them to the *Hebrides* Overture, the A-major String Quartet (Op. 13), and the D-major String Quartet (Op. 44, no. 1).

786. Newman, William S. *The Sonata since Beethoven: The Third and Final Volume of a History of the Sonata Idea*. Chapel Hill: University of North Carolina Press, 1969. ML1156 .N4S63. 2nd edn., New York: W. W. Norton, 1972. ISBN 0393006247. ML1156.N4 S63 1972. 3rd edn., New York: W. W. Norton, 1983. 870 p. ISBN 0393952908. ML1156 .N44 1983. Section on FMB Trans. German Gerhard Schuhmacher as "Mendelssohns Sonaten." In *Felix Mendelssohn Bartholdy*, ed. Gerhard Schuhmacher,

201–18. Wege der Forschung, 494. Darmstadt: Wissenschaftliche Buchgesellschaft, 1982.

A survey of the structural organization of FMB's sonatas and principal features of his sonata-form movements, in the context of the most important statistical overview of numerous composers' approaches to the sonata idea.

787. Pachnicke, Peter. "Fragen eines Außenseiters nach der Modernität des Felix Mendelssohn Bartholdy." In *Felix Mendelssohn—Mitwelt und Nachwelt: Bericht zum 1. Leipziger Mendelssohn-Kolloquium am 8. und 9. Juni 1993,* ed. Leon Botstein, 71–78. Wiesbaden: Breitkopf & Härtel, 1996.

788. Rosen, Charles. "Mendelssohn and the Invention of Religious Kitsch," in *The Romantic Generation,* 569–98. Cambridge, Mass.: Harvard University Press, 1995. 723 p. ISBN 0674779339.

Those who take offense at the title will be no less offended by the essay: this is an unrelenting rehearsal of the condescension and critical platitudes by which FMB has been conventionally dismissed since Brendel, Wagner, and Liszt portrayed him as a failed prodigy and unsuccessful heir to the Beethovenian legacy. The opening section ("Mastering Beethoven") offers some thought-provoking musical comparisons between Beethoven's works and the E-major Piano Sonata (Op. 6), the Seven Character Pieces (Op. 7), and the A-major and E-flat-major String Quartets (pp. 13 and 12). The title derives from the concluding section of the essay, which attributes a "pseudo-religious" or "hyper-religious" character to the Piano Fugue in E Minor (Op. 35, no. 1) and the last movement of the Piano Trio in C Minor (Op. 66)—acknowledging the value of the former and dismissing the latter.

789. Rummenhöller, Peter. "Die 'vierstimmige Choralgeschiklichkeit': Bemerkungen zur Harmonik Mendelssohns." *Musica* 39 (1985): 18–25.

This article explores the role of four-part chorale-like textures in Romantic musical style and suggests that such gestures serve a dual function in FMB's music. On the one hand, they constitute the grammatical foundation of his music theory; on the other, they represent the synthesis of two seemingly disparate aspects of his style: Romantic emotionalism and academicist historicism, or "feeling" and "patina."

790. Schmidt[-Beste], Thomas Christian. *Die ästhetischen Grundlagen der Instrumentalmusik Felix Mendelssohn Bartholdys.* Stuttgart: M & P Verlag für Wissenschaft und Forschung, 1996.

Adapted from the author's dissertation (University of Heidelberg,

1995), this is a vitally important exploration of FMB's aesthetic outlook. Except for the unfortunate paucity of references to FMB's concertos, it treats virtually every realm of his instrumental compositions. It begins with an overview of his aesthetic upbringing, then moves to an exploration of the aesthetics of his creative process. Chapter 4 focuses on FMB's understanding of music as an act of quasi-linguistic communication, but also includes an important section on FMB and the public. The final chapter explores ways in which FMB's aesthetics permit referentiality (in either a programmatic or structural/procedural sense), focusing on the concert overtures (especially Opp. 21 and 32), the "Italian," "Scottish," and "Reformation" Symphonies, the *Lieder ohne Worte*, and the Piano Trio in C Minor (Op. 66).

791. Schönfelder, Gerd. "Zur Frage des Realismus bei Mendelssohn." *Beiträge zur Musikwissenschaft* 14 (1972): 169–83. Rpt. in *Felix Mendelssohn Bartholdy*, ed. Gerhard Schuhmacher, 354–75. Wege der Forschung, Bd. 494. Darmstadt: Wissenschaftliche Buchgesellschaft, 1982.

This essay concerns the ways in which FMB's works may be viewed as manifestations of conflict: namely, the disparity between the classicizing ideal that played an important role in his upbringing and education and the reality of the present in which and for which he worked and wrote. Focuses on the String Quartet in E-flat Major, Op. 12, and Beethoven's quartet in the same key (Op. 74). It contains frequent recourse to comments and quotations from Robert Schumann.

792. Schuhmacher, Gerhard. "Wenn Komponisten erwachsen werden: Zum Beispiel Mozart und Mendelssohn Bartholdy." *Neue Zeitschrift für Musik* 144/6 (1983): 4–8.

793. Siegmund-Schultze,Walther. "Zur Wort/Ton-Problematik in Mendelssohns Lied- und Kantatenschaffen." In *Das musikalische Erbe in der sozialistischen Gesellschaft: Ausgewählte Studien zu Problemen der Interpretation und Wirkung* 23/6 (1974): 20–28.

794. Silber Ballan, Judith. "Marxian Programmatic Music: A Stage in Mendelssohn's Musical Development." In *Mendelssohn Studies*, ed. R. Larry Todd, 149–61. Cambridge: Cambridge University Press, 1992.

An attempt to assess the extent of Adolph Bernhard Marx's influence on FMB in early and middle-period works such as the *Midsummer Night's Dream* Overture, the "Reformation" Symphony, and the *Calm Sea and Prosperous Voyage* Overture. The article asserts that such explicitly programmatic works become less prominent in FMB's oeuvre after about 1833 because of the increasingly distant friendship between the two. (No mention is made of the *Fair Melusine* Overture, composed in 1833–36.)

795. Silbermann, Alphons. "Kunst, aus vielfältigem Zwiespalt geboren: Über Felix Mendelssohn Bartholdy." In *Blickpunkt FELIX Mendelssohn Bartholdy: Programmbuch Drei Tage für Felix vom 30.10 bis 1.11.1994,* ed. Bernd Heyder and Christoph Spering, 11–16. Cologne: Dohr, 1994.

796. Spies, Claudio. "Samplings." In *Mendelssohn and His World,*, ed. R. Larry Todd, 100–20. Princeton: Princeton University Press, 1991.

   This essay contemplates several moments in FMB's works that this author (and many others) find exceptionally beautiful, explaining such moments in terms of specific compositional techniques. Mentioned: the Intermezzo from the Incidental Music to *Midsummer Night's Dream* (Op. 61); the *Fair Melusine* Overture, Op. 32; the A-major ("Italian") Symphony Op. posth. 90; the *Hebrides* Overture, Op. 26; and the 1822 string sinfonia in D major.

797. Steinberg, Michael P. "Schumann's Homelessness." In *Schumann and His World*, ed. R. Larry Todd, 47–79. Princeton: Princeton University Press, 1994.

   Pages 55–65 ("Mendelssohn; or, Subjectivity"), examine Mendelssohn's relationship to Schumann from a cultural historian's perspective. Much of the material is taken directly from the essays by Steinberg (no. 368) and Michael Marissen (no. 834) in the Winter 1993 issue of *The Musical Quarterly* (no. 11).

798. Stephan, Rudolf. "Über Mendelssohns Kontrapunkt: Vorläufige Bemerkungen." In *Das Problem Mendelssohn*, ed. Carl Dahlhaus, 201–07. Studien zur Musikgeschichte des 19. Jahrhunderts, Bd. 41. Regensburg: Gustav Bosse, 1974.

   The author discusses the sources of FMB's interest in and practice of counterpoint, including Palestrina, J. S. Bach, Handel, Mozart, and Beethoven; also draws on remarks by contemporary theorists (especially Moritz Hauptmann). He devotes considerable attention to the issues posed by contrasts in rhythm and melodic structure within individual themes. FMB compositions considered: the String Quartet in A Major, Op. 13; "Frage," Op. 9, no. 1; *Aus tiefer Noth*, Op. 23, no. 1; and the *Capriccio* for String Quartet, Op. posth. 81, no. 3.

799. Todd, R. Larry. "On Stylistic Commonalities in the Music of Felix Mendelssohn and Fanny Hensel." In *The Mendelssohns: Their Music in*

History, ed. John Michael Cooper and Julie D. Prandi. Oxford: Oxford University Press, [forthcoming].

800. Trame, Richard H. "The Male Chorus, Medium of Art and Entertainment: Its History and Literature." In *Choral Essays: A Tribute to Roger Wagner,* ed. William Belan, 19–29. San Carlos: Thomas House, 1993.

801. Vitercik, Greg. *The Early Works of Felix Mendelssohn: A Study in the Romantic Sonata Style.* Musicology: A Book Series, 12. Philadelphia: Gordon and Breach, 1992. ISBN 2881245366. ML410.M5 V6 1992 .

Adapted from the author's Ph.D. dissertation of the same title (State University of New York, 1985). This study discusses the early string *sinfonie*, as well as the C-minor Symphony (Op. 11), the A-major String Quintet (Op. 18), the Octet for Strings (Op. 20), the *Midsummer Night's Dream* Overture (Op. 21), the *Hebrides* Overture (Op. 26), the *Calm Sea and Prosperous Voyage* Overture (Op. 27), the *Lobgesang* (Op. 52), and the "Scottish" Symphony (Op. 56). Vitercik proposes to set aside the misguided criticisms of Liszt, Wagner, and many subsequent authors but never quite questions their central assumption: that after about 1836 FMB entered into a compositional decline that compromised the greatness of the later works.

Rev.: D. Seaton in *Notes* 50 (1993): 574–76.

802. Vitercik, Greg. "Mendelssohn the Progressive." *Journal of Musicological Research* 8 (1989): 333–74.

Like Schoenberg's celebrated study of Brahms (1947), this essay challenges an enduring myth about FMB: the notion that he was a "supremely gifted, but supremely unadventurous prodigy afflicted with a fatal facility." The article suggests that FMB achieved a functionally coherent balance between form and idea in the context of a highly individualized approach to sonata form. It focuses on the third movement of the Octet for Strings and the second movement of the String Quintet in A Major, Op. 18.

803. Werner, Eric. "Instrumental Music Outside the Pale of Classicism and Romanticism." In *Instrumental Music: A Conference at Isham Memorial Library, May 4, 1957*, ed. David G. Hughes, 57–65. Isham Library Papers, 1. Cambridge, Mass.: Harvard University Press, 1959.

A wide-ranging paper (with discussion following) touching briefly (and sometimes confusingly) on many important background topics and issues.

804. Werner, Jack. "The Mendelssohnian Cadence." *The Musical Times* 97 (1956): 17–19.

   The author discerns in much of FMB's music a distinctive cadence (consisting of an extension of the tonic minor triad, usually at the conclusion of a movement or piece) and traces the origins of this cadence to Jewish liturgical music. FMB compositions considered: Opp. 28, 30, 38, 53, 54, and 70, as well as Opp. posth. 90 and 102.

II. MENDELSSOHN AND THE MUSIC OF THE PAST (INCLUDING BEETHOVEN, WEBER, AND SCHUBERT)

805. Bässler, Hans. ". . . die Verbindung alten Sinns mit neuen Mitteln? Die Auseinandersetzung mit der Geschichte in der romantischen Musik am Beispiel Felix Mendelssohn." *Musik und Bildung* 20 (1988): 570–77.

806. Sterndale Bennett, R. "Mendelssohn as Editor of Handel." *Monthly Musical Record* 86 (1956): 83–94. Trans. German Gerhard Schuhmacher as "Mendelssohn als Herausgeber Händelscher Werke." In *Felix Mendelssohn Bartholdy*, ed. Gerhard Schuhmacher, 44–63. Wege der Forschung, Bd. 494. Darmstadt: Wissenschaftliche Buchgesellschaft, 1982.

   This article considers the correspondence between FMB and William Sterndale Bennett, focusing on the authors' discussion of the edition-history of *Samson*.

807. Bockholdt, Rudolf. "Zum vierstimmigen Choralsatz J. S. Bachs." In *The International Musicological Society: Report of the Eleventh Congress Copenhagen 1972*, ed. Henrik Glahn, Søren Sørensen, and Peter Ryom, II: 277–287. Copenhagen: Wilhelm Hansen, 1974.

   FMB's setting of "Allein Gott in der Höh sei Ehr" (from *St. Paul*) is used as a foil in a discussion of Bach's chorale style. Mendelssohn's chorales are based in the "relation of chords to foreign tones" as opposed to Bach's "genuinely polyphonic" chorales.

808. Bowen, José Antonio. "The Conductor and the Score: A History of the Relationship Between Interpreter and Text in the Generation of Mendelssohn, Berlioz, and Wagner." Ph.D. diss., Stanford University, 1994. 3 vols.

   This study considers theories of how conductors were to interpret orchestral scores in the mid-nineteenth century, especially the ways in which the older understanding of a musical artwork as a unique, contextually defined temporal moment was transformed into a view of the artwork as a stable text. It presents valuable information on Berlioz, Wagner, Hegel, and Schumann, among others.

809. Bowen, José A. "Mendelssohn, Berlioz, and Wagner as Conductors: The Origins of the Ideal of 'Fidelity to the Composer.'" *Performance Practice Review* 6 (1993): 77–88.

Adapted from the author's dissertation (Stanford University, 1994), this article attributes to FMB and Berlioz an attitude that saw the conductor's task as "essentially re-creative," while Wagner "was the first to regard it as a creative or interpretive act" (p. 77). The section discussing FMB focuses on his edition of Handel's *Israel in Egypt* (published by the English Handel Society in 1846).

810. Chrysander, Friedrich. "Mendelssohns Orgelbegleitung zu *Israel in Ägypten.*" *Jahrbücher für musikalische Wissenschaft* 2 (1867): 249–67.

Because FMB's editions of Handel (as well as his ideas on how to approach Handel's music) still exert considerable influence, this essay remains a central source for those who use or consult FMB's editions. Corrects FMB's understanding of the sources for *Israel* and critiques his approach to continuo realization.

811. Dadelsen, Georg von. "Alter Stil und alte Techniken in der Musik des 19. Jahrhunderts." Ph.D. diss., Freie Universität Berlin, 1951. 138 p.

This study includes an excellent discussion of individualism and its changing relation to tradition. Dadelsen confines the designation "romantic" to those composers "whose works of art grew from a passionate abandonment to an ideal fantasy-world in which common reality appears to be overcome." FMB finds that because two starting points are the baroque contrapuntal techniques learned under Zelter and the anti-dialectical lyric piano piece of Ludwig Berger, FMB was never able to unify these disparate elements in his instrumental music. There is a long discussion of Mendelssohn's keyboard fugues in the light of the Bach fugues that they resemble or from which they may be said to derive. Invariably, the Mendelssohn subjects—to say nothing of the entire pieces—are found inferior by comparision and lacking on their own. [DM/JMC]

812. Deutsch, Otto Erich. "The Discovery of Schubert's Great C-major Symphony: A Story in Fifteen Letters." *The Musical Quarterly* 38 (1952): 528–32.

FMB played a vital role in the revival of Schubert's "Great" C-Major Symphony in 1839. This article is an epistolary chronicle detailing the work's rediscovery, related in letters between FMB, Robert Schumann, Clara Schumann, Ignaz Moscheles, Breitkopf & Härtel, the composer's brother at the Philharmonic Society of London, Ernst Adolf Becker, Ferdinand Schubert, and Josef Doppler (Ferdinand Schubert's agent). See also Krause (no. 827).

813. Doflein, Erich. "Historismus in der Musik." In *Die Ausbreitung des Historismus Über die Musik*, ed. Walter Wiora, 9–39. Studien zur Musikgeschichte des 19. Jahrhunderts, Bd. 14. Regensburg: Gustav Bosse, 1969.

Historicism is defined (or perhaps one might better say "exemplified") as follows: "Works and masters [of the past] were named not as examples but as unique phenomena of art whereby their place as historical figures was documented." An attempt is made to distinguish among "Historismus," "Historizismus," and "Historizitat," an attempt that perhaps reflects as much an obsession with definition as an effort to keep conceptual matters clear. There is considerable discussion of the drastic social as well as musical effects of historicism, e.g., the changes in repertoire and in the function of the performing musician. Mendelssohn is discussed as an example of the new attitude, and a section of the paper is devoted to *St. Paul*, which is compared not to the original *St. Matthew Passion*, but to the cut version of the work conducted by Mendelssohn in 1829. Particular attention is also given to Mendelssohn's "historical concerts" in the Gewandhaus. Spohr is also extensively discussed. [DM/JMC]

814. Downs, Philip George. "The Development of the Great Repertory in the Nineteenth Century." Ph.D. diss., University of Toronto, 1964. 2 vols.

Downs discusses the social and philosophical reasons for the development of "the great repertory"; i.e., the standard repertory, linking it partly to the freeing of music from mimetic theory and specific social purposes. Programs of concert series in London, Vienna, and Paris were subjected to computer analyses that were "interpreted in a variety of ways." [DM]

815. Fabiano, Andrea, with Cristina Rosetto, Gianni Ruffin, and Luca Zoppelli. "Cronaca di una riscoperta." In *Ritorno a Bach: Dramma e ritualità delle passioni,* ed. Elena Povellato, 185–96. Venice: Marsilio Editori, 1986.

816. Federhofer, Hellmut. "Zur Generalbaßpraxis im 19. Jahrhundert." *Musik und Kirche* 60 (1990): 1–10.

817. Fellerer, Karl Gustav. "Mendelssohns Orgelstimmen zu Händelschen

Werken." *Händel-Jahrbuch* 4 (1931): 79–97.

Fellerer perceives in FMB's organ parts to Handel's works a flawed understanding of the *Generalbaß*, a misunderstanding of the appropriate forces for realizing the *continuo* part, and—largely because of the reinterpretation of individual movements—a romanticized introduction of stylistically inappropriate elements into Handel's music. It focuses on his organ parts (most of them in manuscript) to the *Dettingen Te Deum, Messiah, Israel in Egypt*, and *Solomon*.

818. Forchert, Arno. "Von Bach zu Mendelssohn." In *Bachtage Berlin: Vorträge 1970 bis 1981*, ed. Günther Wagner, 211–23. Neuhausen-Stuttgart: Hänssler, 1985.

819. Forner, Johannes. "Mendelssohn und die Bachpflege in Leipzig." *Arbeitsberichte zur Geschichte der Stadt Leipzig* 10/2 (1972): 85–98.

820. Geck, Martin. *Die Wiederentdeckung der Matthäuspassion im 19. Jahrhundert: Die zeitgenössischen Dokumente und ihre ideengeschichtliche Deutung.* Studien zur Muikgeschichte des 19. Jahrhunderts, Bd. 9. Regensburg: Gustav Bosse, 1967. 181 p. ML410.B13 G24.

A study of Mendelssohn's performance of 1829 with, as the subtitle says, documents and a cultural-historical interpretation. At the time of writing, Mendelssohn's conducting score was still in private possession, although it was available to Geck. (It is now in the Bodleian Library, Oxford.) Geck concludes that despite cuts and some changes in instrumentation, Mendelssohn's performance was essentially "werktreu." [DM/JMC]

821. Godwin, Jocelyn. "Early Mendelssohn and Late Beethoven." *Music and Letters* 55 (1974): 272–85.

Godwin inventories and describes some instances in which Beethoven's late style evidently influenced FMB's early works and suggests (somewhat predictably, given the date of the study) that if FMB's studies "had led him further, say to an understanding of Beethoven's fugues, or of why Beethoven could so often dispense with song-like themes, his music as a whole might interest us more." (Such remarks, of course, are less statements about FMB's music than they are about "us.") The article does propose, however, that the clarity of FMB's allusions to Beethoven's late works might have helped to lead Biedermeier audiences "gently" back to that difficult repertoire.

822. Großmann-Vendrey, Susanna. *Felix Mendelssohn Bartholdy und die Musik*

der Vergangenheit. Studien zur Musikgeschichte des 19. Jahrhunderts, Bd. 17. Regensburg: Gustav Bosse, 1969. 254 p. ML410.M5 G8.

An essential tool for any scholar who needs to investigate FMB's activities involving earlier musicians. This book includes extensive discussions of programs from concerts and music festivals, references to FMB's own works, and extensive quotations from contemporary reviews.

Rev.: F. Krummacher in *Die Musikforschung* 25 (1972): 394–96; E. Werner, "Mendelssohniana," in *Die Musikforschung* 28 (1975): 29–31; response by Großmann-Vendrey in *Die Musikforschung* 28 (1975): 444.

823. Großmann-Vendrey, Susanna. "Mendelssohn und die Vergangenheit." In *Die Ausbreitung der Historismus über die Musik*, ed. Walter Wiora, 73–84. Studien zur Musikgeschichte des 19. Jahrhunderts, Bd. 14. Regensburg: Gustav Bosse, 1969.

An essential complement to the author's volume on FMB and the music of the past (no. 822). This article explores the cultural considerations that produced FMB's historicist interests, identifying Enlightenment ideas concerning ethics, morals, and human critical and rational faculties along with Goethe's views on historical progress as foremost among these considerations.

824. Hohenemser, Richard. *Welche Einflüße hatte die Wiederbelebung der älteren Musik im 19. Jahrhundert auf die deutschen Komponisten?* Leipzig: Breitkopf & Härtel, 1900. 135 p.

Hohenemser begins with an overview of the awakening of interest in old music and proceeds to detail the influence of this music on nineteenth-century composers ranging from Beethoven to Ett, and from Eiblinger to Liszt and the Caecelians. (There is also a discussion of the motet composers of the second half of the eighteenth century.) So far as Mendelssohn is concerned, careful distinctions are drawn between the influence on him of the "old Italians" and of Bach. This article remains very useful and interesting. [DM]

825. Kinsky, Georg. "Was Mendelssohn Indebted to Weber? An Attempted Solution to an Old Controversy." *The Musical Quarterly* 19 (1933): 178–86.

A discussion of the significance or coincidence of similar passages in the "Mermaids' Song" from Weber's *Oberon* and the concluding melody of FMB's *Midsummer Night's Dream* Overture.

826. Konold, Wulf. "Mendelssohn und der späte Beethoven." In *Münchener Beethoven-Studien*, ed. Johannes Fischer, 183–91. Munich: Katzbichler, 1992.

   A valuable overview of FMB's activities as performer and promoter of Beethoven's late works, as well as his compositional attempts to deal with that phenomenon. The article focuses on the relationship between Beethoven's String Quartet in A Minor, Op. 132, and FMB's early quartet in A major (Op. 13).

827. Krause, Peter. "Unbekannte Dokumente zur Uraufführung von Franz Schuberts großer C-Dur-Sinfonie durch Felix Mendelssohn Bartholdy." *Beiträge zur Musikwissenschaft* 29 (1987): 240–50.

   A supplement to Deutsch's important study of the rediscovery of the C-Major Symphony (no. 812). The author emphasizes Robert Schumann's enthusiasm, but most of the article is devoted to the (at the time) newly-recovered autograph score for the Symphony and the ways in which it was used and studied for the premiere.

828. Krummacher, Friedhelm. "Bach, Berlin und Mendelssohn: Über Mendelssohns kompositorische Bach-Rezeption." In *Jahrbuch des Staatlichen Instituts für Musikforschung Preußischer Kulturbesitz,* ed. Günther Wagner, 44–78. Stuttgart: J. B. Metzler, 1993.

829. Krummacher, Friedhelm. "Synthese des Disparaten: Zu Beethoven späten Quartetten und ihrer frühen Rezeption." *Archiv für Musikwissenschaft* 37 (1980): 99–134.

   A thoughtful study (especially p. 106–21) of the reception history of Beethoven's late quartets, proceeding from the important observation that because those works' popularity and consensually granted greatness have increased substantially in the last few decades, one cannot assume that nineteenth-century composers responded to them in the same fashion that they might have if the works had been more familiar and accepted. The author considers the late quartets' scholarly and critical reception history as reflected in the writings of Dahlhaus, Eggebrecht, Marx, Ratz, Riemann, Rochlitz, and Schenker, and examines signs of their influence in FMB's String Quartet in A Major, Op. 13.

830. Lange, Wilgard. "Händel-Rezeption bei Felix Mendelssohn Bartholdy." Ph.D. diss., Universität Halle, 1980. 267 p.

831. Lange, Wilgard. "Mendelssohns Händel-Bearbeitungen." In *Georg Friedrich Händel im Verständnis des 19. Jahrhunderts: Bericht über die*

wissenschaftlichen Konferenz zu den 32. Händelfestspielen der DDR am 13. Und 14. Juni 1983 in Halle (Saale), ed. Walther Siegmund-Schultze, 70–77. Musikwissenschaftliche Beiträge, 11. Halle: Abt[eilung] Wissenschaftspublizistik der Martin-Luther-Universität Halle-Wittenberg, 1984.

832. Levis, William Henry. "A Comparison of the Orchestration of the Subordinate Themes in the First Movements of the Symphonies of Beethoven, Schubert, Mendelssohn, and Schumann." D.M.A. diss., University of Missouri at Kansas City, 1973. 244 p.

833. Lockwood, Lewis. "Mendelssohn's Mozart: A New Acquisition." *Princeton University Library Chronicle* 34 (1972): 62–68.

   Lockwood describes a matched set of bound volumes of the works of Mozart brought out by Breitkopf & Härtel under the title *Oeuvres Complettes*; six of the seven volumes were owned by FMB, and were donated to Princeton University's Firestone Library by one of his descendants. The article provides important information for exploring the oft-reiterated comparisons of the two composers (see especially R. Larry Todd's essay on "Mozart according to Mendelssohn" [no. 844]).

834. Marissen, Michael. "Religious Aims in Mendelssohn's 1829 Berlin-Singakademie Performances of Bach's St. Matthew Passion." *The Musical Quarterly* 77 (1993): 718–26.

   The author identifies religious and other issues that evidently influenced FMB's decisions in presenting the *St. Matthew Passion* to the public in his 1829 performances. Most importantly, the cuts seem to have eradicated all texts that "risk being perceived as anti-Jewish."

835. Meloncelli, Raoul. "Palestrina e Mendelssohn." In *Atti del II Convegno internazionale di studi palestriniani: "Palestrina e la sua presenza nella musica e nella cultura europea dal suo tempo ad oggi."* In *Anno europeo della musica, 3–5 maggio 1986*, ed. Lino Bianchi and Giancarlo Rostirolla, 439–60. Palestrina: Fondazione Pierluigi da Palestrina, 1991.

   A careful examination of the oft-overlooked but nevertheless important influence of Palestrina and the "Palestrina style" on FMB. Focuses on FMB's *Te Deum* (1826), *Tu es Petrus*, Op. posth. 111 (1827), two of the motets from Op. 23, the Op. 39 motets, and his setting of Psalm 115 (*Non nobis Domine*). Identifies Handel as one means by which FMB studied and became conversant in the "stile antico."

836. Niemöller, Klaus Wolfgang. "Die Händelüberlieferung im historischen

Notenarchiv des Musikvereins Düsseldorf: Zur Händelpflege des 19. Jahrhunderts im Umkreis von Mendelssohn und Schumann." In *Georg Friedrich Händel—ein Lebensinhalt: Gedenkschrift für Bernd Baselt* (1934–1993), ed. Klaus Hortschansky and Konstanze Musketa, 207–25. Schriften des Händel-Hauses in Halle, 11. Kassel: Bärenreiter, 1995.

Given the prominence of FMB and Düsseldorf in the nineteenth-century Handel Renaissance, an important documentary study. It examines the scores for oratorios, anthems, and the *Dettingen Te Deum* held in the archives of the Düsseldorf Musikverein, and offers observations as to the insights they provide on nineteenth-century views and interpretations of Handel's works.

837. Pape, Matthias. *Mendelssohns Leipziger Orgelkonzerte 1840: Ein Beitrag zur Bach-Pflege im 19. Jahrhundert*. Wiesbaden: Breitkopf & Härtel, 1988. 51 p. ISBN 3765102466. ML410.M5 P3 1988.

A thorough documentation of the organ recital FMB gave in the Leipzig Thomaskirche in 1840 to raise funds for the city's first monument to J. S. Bach. This book includes specifications on the organ, details on the program, and reviews. See also R. Larry Todd's essay "New Light on Mendelssohn's *Freie Fantasie* (1840)" (no. 705).

Rev.: R. L.Todd in *The Musical Times* 130 (1989): 374; G. Schuhmacher in *Musik und Kirche* 62 (1992): 282.

838. Rudloff, Helmuth. "The Influence of Johann Sebastian Bach on the Organ Works of Felix Mendelssohn." In *Organy i muzyka Oranowe III*, ed. J. Krassowski. Gdansk: PWSM, 1980.

839. Schulze, Hans-Joachim. "Bach—Leipzig—Mendelssohn." In *Felix Mendelssohn—Mitwelt und Nachwelt: Bericht zum 1. Leipziger Mendelssohn-Kolloquium am 8. und 9. Juni 1993*, ed. Leon Botstein, 79–83. Wiesbaden: Breitkopf & Härtel, 1996.

840. Spering, Christoph. "Affekt und Emotion: Bemerkungen zu Felix Mendelssohns Einrichtung der Matthäuspassion von Johann Sebastian Bach." In *Blickpunkt FELIX Mendelssohn Bartholdy: Programmbuch Drei Tage für Felix vom 30.10 bis 1.11.1994*, ed. Bernd Heyder and Christoph Spering, 61–67. Cologne: Dohr, 1994.

841. Stanley, Glenn. "Mozarts *Messias* and Mendelssohns *Israel in Ägypten*: Zur Frühgeschichte der Aufführungspraxis historischer Musik." In *Kongreßbericht zum VII. Internationalen Gewandhaus-Symposium: Wolfgang Amadeus Mozart—Forschung und Praxis im Dienst von Leben, Werk, Interpretation und Rezeption anläßlich der Gewandhaus-Festtage in*

Leipzig vom 3. bis 6. Oktober 1991, ed. Renate Herklotz, Renate Schaaf, and Karl-Heinz Köhler, 94–100. Dokumente der Gewandhausgeschichte, 9. Leipzig: Gewandhaus, 1993.

842. Steinberg, Michael [P.]. "Das Mendelssohn-Bach-Verhältnis als ästhetischer Diskurs der Moderne." In *Felix Mendelssohn—Mitwelt und Nachwelt: Bericht zum 1. Leipziger Mendelssohn-Kolloquium am 8. und 9. Juni 1993*, ed. Leon Botstein, 84–88. Wiesbaden: Breitkopf & Härtel, 1996.

843. Thistlethwaite, N. "Bach, Mendelssohn, and the English Organist, 1810–1845." *British Institute of Organ Studies* 7 (1983): 34–36.

844. Todd, R. Larry. "Mozart According to Mendelssohn: A Contribution to *Rezeptionsgeschichte*." In *Perspectives on Mozart Performance*, ed. R. Larry Todd and Peter Williams, 158–203. Cambridge Studies in Performance Practice, 1. Cambridge: Cambridge University Press, 1991.

This essay examines the role of Mozart's works in FMB's activities and compositions, and argues that FMB's efforts in performing Mozart "served to strengthen and confirm Mozart's canonization." It includes an overview of FMB's performances of Mozart's works, and examines several instances in which Mozart provided a compositional point of departure for FMB. References to *Die beiden Pädagogen* (1821), the Sinfonia VIII for String Orchestra (1822), and the D-minor *Kyrie* (1825).

845. Uszkoreit, H. G. "Händel und Mendelssohn." In *Händel-Ehrung der Deutschen Demokratischen Republik: Konferenzbericht Halle, 11–19 April 1959*, ed. Walther Siegmund-Schulze, 215–18. Leipzig: Deutscher Verlag für Musik, 1961.

A summary with emphasis on Mendelssohn as an interpreter of Handel.

846. Wehnert, Martin. "Mendelssohns Traditionsbewußtsein und dessen Widerschein im Werk." *Deutsches Jahrbuch der Musikwissenschaft* 16 (1971): 5–45.

An important essay that uses FMB's correspondence and contemporary writings as a springboard to suggest that it is simplistic to consider all his musical references to the past as historicist. Instead, such gestures reflect a self-conscious awareness of tradition, a belief in the ethical importance of such respect, and an attempt to construct a dialogue between tradition and modernity. Considers the *Hebrides* Overture and the Piano Fugue in E Minor, Op. 35, no. 1.

847. Wolff, Christoph. "Bachs und Mendelssohns Matthäus-Passion." In *Bach*

und Brahms: Almanach/Sommerakademie J. S. Bach, ed. pp. 94–103. Stuttgart: n.p. 1983.

848. Wright, Barbara David. "Johann Sebastian Bach's *Matthäus-Passion*: a Performance History, 1829–1854." Ph.D. diss., University of Michigan, 1983. 458 p.

III. SECULAR WORKS

849. Bélance-Zank, Isabelle. "The Three-hand Texture: Origins and Use." *Journal of the American Liszt Society* 38 (1995): 99–121.

This article examines the usage and aesthetic implications of the so-called "three-hand texture" in works by a variety of composers, including FMB (Op. 35, no. 1, and Op. 40) as well as Fanny Hensel, Beethoven, Weber, Liszt, Debussy, Ravel, and Prokofiev.

850. Braun, Werner. "Romantische Klavierchoräle." *Geistliche Musik: Studien zu ihrer Geschichte und Funktion im 18. und 19. Jahrhundert,* 119–42. Hamburger Jahrbuch für Musikwissenschaft, ed. Constantin Floros, Hans Joachim Marx, and Peter Petersen, Bd. 8. Laaber: Laaber: 1985.

Braun considers chorale and pseudo-chorales by four composers: FMB (the fugue from Op. 35, no. 1), Robert Schumann (nos. 4 and 42 from the *Album for the Young*, Op. 68), Chopin (Op. 15, no. 3 and Op. 37, no. 1), and Liszt (Psalm 37 from the *Geneva Psalter*). Examines the ways in which the composers' confessional perspective (Catholic or Protestant) influenced the musical character and function of the chorale gestures.

851. Coeuroy, André, and Claude Rostand. *Les Chefs-d'oeuvre de la musique de chambre*. Paris: Éditions Le Bon Plaisir, Plon, 1952. 262 p. MT140 .C633.

Opp. 49, 12, 13, 44, 80, 81, 18, 87, 20 are briefly discussed in a somewhat patronizing tone. The sections in question, p. 169–173, are signed A. C.

852. Draheim, Joachim. *Vertonungen antiker Texte vom Barock bis zur Gegenwart (mit einer Bibliographie der Vertonungen für den Zeitraum von 1700 bis 1978)*. Heuremata: Studien zur Literatur, Sprachen und Kultur der Antike, 7. Amsterdam: B. R. Grüner BV, 1981. 289 p. ML79 .D7 1981.

Adapted from the author's dissertation of the same title (Heidelberg, 1978), this article is useful for material on FMB's *Antigone* and *Oedipus at Colonos*.

853. Fagius, Hans. "The Organ Works of Mendelssohn and Schumann and Their Link to the Classical Tradition." In *Proceedings of the Göteborg International Organ Academy 1994,* ed. Hans Davidsson and Sverker Jullander, 325–51. Skrifter fran Musikvetenskapliga avdelningen, No. 39. Göteborg: Göteborgs Universitariat, 1995.

Not available for examination.

854. Fellerer, Karl Gustav. "Mendelssohn in der Klaviermusik seiner Zeit." In *Das Problem Mendelssohn,* ed. Carl Dahlhaus, 195–200. Studien zur Musikgeschichte des 19. Jahrhunderts, Bd. 41. Regensburg: Gustav Bosse, 1974.

Fellerer surveys the characteristics of FMB's piano works and discusses likely influences for the lyricism of his style (especially Berger, Moscheles, Schubert, and Taubert).

855. Filosa, Albert James. "The Early Symphonies and Chamber Music of Felix Mendelssohn Bartholdy." Ph.D. diss., Yale University, 1970. 221 p.

A useful study that focuses first on FMB's background and musical training (so far as was known about these before R. Larry Todd's book on the subject [no. 226]) before turning to the early string *sinfonie* and chamber works (many of which are still unpublished).

856. Flashar, Hellmut. "F. Mendelssohn-Bartholdys Vertonung antiker Dramen." In *Berlin und die Antike: Architektur, Kunstgewerbe, Malerei, Skulptur, Theater und Wissenschaft vom 16. Jahrhundert bis heute— Aufsätze,* ed. Willmuth Arenhövel and Christa Schreiber, 351–61. Berlin: Wasmuth, 1979. Rpt. in *Hellmut Flashar: Ausgewählte kleine Schriften,* ed. Manfred Kraus, 563–79. Berlin: Akademie-Verlag, 1989.

857. Gebhardt, Thomas. "'Es gibt Schlimmeres als Serpente': Ein nahezu vergessenes Instrument in Mendelssohns Orchester." In *Blickpunkt FELIX Mendelssohn Bartholdy: Programmbuch Drei Tage für Felix vom 30.10 bis 1.11.1994,* ed. Bernd Heyder and Christoph Spering, 89–96. Cologne: Dohr, 1994.

858. Glusman, Elfriede. "Taubert and Mendelssohn: Opposing Attitudes towards Poetry and Music." *The Musical Quarterly* 57 (1971): 628–35. Trans. German Gerhard Schuhmacher as "Taubert und Mendelssohn: Gegensätzliche Haltungen zu Dichtung und Musik." In *Felix Mendelssohn Bartholdy,* ed. Gerhard Schuhmacher, 628–35. Wege der Forschung, Bd. 494. Darmstadt: Wissenschaftliche Buchgesellschaft, 1982.

This study focuses on possible relationships (suggested by Willi Kahl and others) between Taubert's *Minnelieder: An die Geliebte*, Op. 16, and FMB's *Lieder ohne Worte*. It concludes that the *Lieder ohne Worte* "exist in a purely musical sphere."

859. Holt, Marilyn Barnes. "Developmental Procedures in the Sonata Form Movements of the Symphonies of Beethoven, Schubert, Mendelssohn, and Schumann." Ph.D. diss., Case Western Reserve University, 1973. 359 p.

860. Kaiser, Antje. "Aus dem Sinngehalt der Dichtung: Die Bühnenmusiken von Beethoven und Mendelssohn Bartholdy." *Musik und Gesellschaft* 36 (1986): 166–76.

861. Klauwell, Otto. *Geschichte der Programmusik von ihren Anfängen bis zur Gegenwart.* Leipzig: Breitkopf & Härtel, 1910. 426 p. Rpt. Wiesbaden: Martin Sänding, [1968]. ML3300 .K67 1968.

Mendelssohn is mentioned only briefly as remaining in the camp of those who organized pieces according to purely musical principles. He is said to have blended the poetry of romanticism with Classical purity of form. [DM]

862. Köhler, Karl-Heinz. "Das Jugendwerk Felix Mendelssohns: Die vergessene Kindheitsentwicklung eines Genies." *Deutsches Jahrbuch für Musikwissenschaft* 7 (1962): 18–35. Rpt. in Gerhard Schuhmacher, ed., *Felix Mendelssohn Bartholdy*, 11–36. Wege der Forschung, Bd. 494. Darmstadt: Wissenschaftliche Buchgesellschaft, 1982.

Along with R. Larry Todd's book on FMB's musical education (no. 226), this study is a crucial source of information for those interested in FMB's early musical development. Provides an overview of the early volumes of bound manuscripts and the source problems presented by these early works, as well as a closer study of selected compositions, including Lieder, choral songs, the early operas and operettas, sacred works, and the early concertos and string *sinfonie*. It divides the early development into several phases: 1819-early 1821; late March to December 1821; 1822; and 1823–25.

863. Kohlhase, Hans. "Brahms und Mendelssohn: Strukturelle Parallelen in der Kammermusik für Streicher." In *Brahms und seine Zeit: Synposion 1983,* ed. Constantin Floros, Hans Joachim Marx, and Peter Petersen, 59–85. Hamburger Jahrbuch für Musikwissenschaft, Bd. 7. Laaber: Laaber, 1984.

864. Konold, Wulf. "Die Widersprüche der Zeit versöhnt." In *Blickpunkt FELIX Mendelssohn Bartholdy: Programmbuch Drei Tage für Felix vom 30.10 bis 1.11.1994*, ed. Bernd Heyder and Christoph Spering, 17–25. Cologne: Dohr, 1994.

865. Lambour, Christian. "'Wenn es Ihnen vielleicht gefällig wäre, Herr Mendelssohn?': Felix Mendelssohn Bartholdy als Pianist." In *Studia Organologica: Festschrift für John Henry van der Meer zu seinem fünfundsechzigsten Geburtstag,* ed. Freidemann Hellwig, 311–19. Wissenschaftliche Beibände zum Anzeiger des Germanischen Nationalmuseums, ed. Gerhard Bott, Bd. 6. Tutzing: Hans Schneider, 1987.

866. Levis, William Henry. "A Comparison of the Orchestration of the Subordinate Themes in the First Movements of the Symphonies of Beethoven, Schubert, Mendelssohn, and Schumann." D.M.A. diss., University of Missouri at Kansas City, 1973. 229 p.

867. Lindeman, Stephen David. "Formal Novelty and Tradition in the Early Romantic Piano Concerto." Ph.D. diss., Rutgers University, 1995. 505 p.

　　At the core of this study is the conflict between form, content, and pianistic virtuosity. It begins with a survey of the emergence of this conflict in the works of Mozart and Beethoven, and then turns to the ways in which a number of composers dealt with the generic issues presented by solo-piano writing: Dussek, Field, Moscheles, Ries, Spohr, and Schubert are presented as the prelude to the lengthier and more detailed chapters on Weber, FMB, J. B. Cramer, Valentin Alkan, Clara Wieck, Robert Schumann, and Franz Liszt.

868. Mandt, H. "Die Entwicklung des Romantischen in der Instrumentalmusik Felix Mendelssohn Bartholdys." Diss., University of Cologne, 1927.

869. Metzner, Günter. *Heine in der Musik: Bibliographie der Heine-Vertonungen.* Tutzing: Hans Schneider, 1990. 12 vols. ML134.5.H43 M47 1989.

　　FMB in Vol. 5, p. 449–83.

870. Michaels, Jost. "Die Verbindung von Flöte und Klarinette in den Werken von Weber und Mendelssohn, Teil 1: Ein Beitrag zu der Entwicklung romantischer Klangvorstellungen und ihrer orchestralen Verwirklichung." *Das Orchester* 40 (1992): 874–82, 1036–42.

871. Niecks, Frederick. *Programme Music in the Last Four Centuries: A Contribution to the History of Musical Expression.* London: Novello, 1907. 548 p. Rpt. New York: Haskell House, 1969. ISBN 0838303110. ML3300 .N4 1969.

　　In the history of scholarship on this subject, a work that would be dated were it not for the extent, clarity, and eloquence with which it documents the importance of extramusical elements in the fame achieved by FMB's instrumental works—thus refuting the cliché that he was an advocate of absolute music. For opponents of programmatic music, Niecks asserts, FMB represents "an extremely inconvenient fact."

872. Niemöller, Klaus Wolfgang. "Poesie und Klang in der deutschen Romantik: Franz Schubert—Felix Mendelssohn Bartholdy—Robert Schumann." In *Die Welt der Symphonie*, ed. Ursula von Rauchhaupt, 145–64. Braunschweig-Westermann, 1972.

873. Pelker, Bärbel. *Die deutsche Konzertouvertüre* (1825–1865): *Werkkatalog und Rezeptionsdokumente*. Europäische Hochschulschriften, Reihe XXXVI: Musikwissenschaft, Bd. 99. Frankfurt am Main: Peter Lang, 1993. 2 vols. ISBN 3631431473. ML128.O5 P45 1993.

A vital documentary/statistical history of a genre in whose history FMB plays a central role. Volume I includes a brief prose overview of the history of the genre's development to 1870 and the first part (A-M) of the "Werkkatalog"; Volume II concludes the "Werkkatalog" and provides the bibliography and list of libraries. Included by FMB are Opp. 21, 26, 27, 32, and 101. The entries for individual works include a transcription of the title page of the first German edition; an overview of the scoring; the date of publication (by month whenever possible) for the parts, score, and available arrangements; an inventory of publication catalogs that advertise the work; the location of known autograph manuscripts and contemporary manuscript copies; information on the dates of composition and the première; contemporary periodical references to the work or performances of it; and other, later references.

874. Porter, Cecilia Hopkins. *The Rhine as Musical Metaphor: Cultural Identity in German Romantic Music*. Boston: Northeastern University Press, 1996. 322 p. ISBN 1555532845. ML1629.4 .P67 1996.

Adapted from the author's Ph.D. dissertation ("The Rhenish Manifesto: 'The Free German Rhine' as an Expression of German National Consciousness in the German Lied" [University of Maryland, 1975]).

875. Rapoport, Erez. "The Smoothing Over of Formal Junctures as a Stylistic Element in Mendelssohn's Instrumental Music." Ph.D. diss., City University of New York, [forthcoming].

876. Reininghaus, Frieder. "Zwischen Historismus und Poesie: Über die Notwendigkeit umfassender Musikanalyse und ihre Erprobung an Klavierkammermusik von Felix Mendelssohn Bartholdy und Robert Schumann." *Zeitschrift für Musiktheorie* 14 (1973): 22–29; 5 (1974): 34–44.

A thoughtful essay proceeding from the disparities between the contemporary and posthumous reception histories of FMB and Schumann. It suggests that for modern scholars the best protection against falling prey to the politicized vicissitudes of these reception histories is careful analysis.

877. Riehn, Rainer. "Das Eigene und das Fremde: Religion und Gesellschaft im Komponieren Mendelssohns." In *Felix Mendelssohn Bartholdy*, ed. Heinz-Klaus Metzger and Rainer Riehn, 123–46. Musik-Konzepte, Bd. 14/15. Munich: edition text + kritik, 1980.

The biographical organization of this essay serves as a foil for a study of (a) issues that confronted Jews in nineteenth-century Germany; and (b) ways in which these issues intersected with the role of Protestantism in FMB's professional and private life. Works cited to illustrate the points include the *Hebrides* Overture and *Elijah*.

878. Steinbeck, Susanne. *Die Ouvertüre in der Zeit von Beethoven bis Wagner: Probleme und Lösungen*. Freiburger Schriften zur Musikwissenschaft, ed. Hans Heinrich Eggebrecht, Bd. 3. Munich: Katzbichler, 1973. 170 p. ML1261 .S8.

An important survey that identifies the conflict produced by changing ideas concerning the meaning and function of the overture as the mechanism by which the genre, at the time of Liszt, had grown to connote an extramusical program almost of necessity. FMB, of course, played a critical role in this transformation of meaning because of his four programmatic concert overtures (Opp. 21, 26, 27, and 32).

879. Thäle, Johanne Dorothea. "Die Klaviersonate bei Mendelssohn Bartholdy, Chopin, Schumann und Liszt: Ein Beitrag zur Geschichte der Klaviersonate des 19. Jahrhunderts." Diss., University of Halle, 1973. 2 vols.

880. Thomas, Matthias. *Das Instrumentalwerk Felix Mendelssohn-Bartholdys: Eine systematisch-theoretische Untersuchung unter besonderer Berücksichtigung der zeitgenössischen Musiktheorie*. Göttinger Musikwissenschaftlichen Arbeiten, 4. Kassel: Bärenreiter-Antiquariat in Komm, 1972. 267 p. ML410.M5 T48.

Adapted from the author's dissertation: "Satztechnik und Form in den Instrumentalwerken Felix Mendelssohn-Bartholdys, unter besonderer Berücksichtigung der zeitgenössischen Theorie" (Göttingen, 1972).

881. Todd, R. Larry. "A Mendelssohn Miscellany." *Music and Letters* 71 (1990): 52–64.

This article focuses on a volume of miscellaneous manuscripts held in the Bodleian Library, Oxford. Devotes special attention to the early piano compositions.

882. Wilcke, G. *Tonalität und Modulation im Streichquartett Mendelssohns und Schumanns*. Leipzig: 1933, 87p. C. Herseburger.

> Not available for examination. Adapted from the author's dissertation (University of Rostock, 1923).

IV. SACRED WORKS

883. Chambers, Robert Ben. "The Shorter Choral Works with Sacred Text by Felix Mendelssohn." D.M.A. diss., Southwestern Baptist Theological Seminary, 1984. 168 p.

884. Clostermann, Annemarie. *Felix Mendelssohn Bartholdys kirchenmusikalisches Schaffen: Neue Untersuchungen zu Geschichte, Form und Inhalt.* Mainz: B. Schott's Söhne, 1989. 229 p. ISBN 3795717981. ML410.M5 C6 1989.

> Adapted from the author's dissertation ("Das kirchenmusikalische Schaffen Felix Mendelssohn Bartholdys" [Ph.D., University of Cologne, 1985]). A useful basic introduction to all the published sacred works, with substantial remarks on the theological issues involved.

> *Rev.*: J. M Cooper in *Notes* 48 (1992): 1260–61; G. Schuhmacher in *Musik und Kirche* 67 (1997): 394–95.

885. Ehemann, Wilhelm. "Das Motettenwerk von Schütz, Mendelssohn, Distler und die Restauration." In *Voce et Tuba: Gesammelte Reden und Aufsätze 1934–1974*, ed. Dietrich Berke, Christiane Bernsdorff-Engelbrecht, and Helmut Kornemann, 316–43. Kassel: Bärenreiter, 1976.

886. Feder, Georg. "Zwischen Kirche und Konzertsaal: Zu Mendelssohns geistlicher Musik." In *Religiöser Musik in nicht-liturgischen Werken von Beethoven bis Reger*, ed. Günter Massenkeil, Klaus Wolfgang Niemöller, and Walter Wiora, 97–117. Studien zur Musikgeschichte des 19. Jahrhunderts, Bd. 51. Regensburg: Gustav Bosse, 1978.

887. Fellinger, Imogen. "Bemerkungen zu einer Theorie des Oratoriums im 19. Jahrhundert." In *Gesellschaft für Musikforschung: Bericht über den Internationalen Musikwissenschaftlichen Kongreß, Berlin 1974*, ed. Hans Hellmut Kühn and Peter Nitsche, 381–83. Kassel: Bärenreiter, 1980.

888. Greeson, Brantley Dees. "A Survey of Selected Sacred Choral

Compositions by Felix Mendelssohn." Ph.D. diss., University of Southern Mississippi, 1974. 184 p.

889. Holcomb, Stephen Norris. "A Conductor's Study of Selected Sacred Choral Works for Mixed Voices by Franz Schubert and Felix Mendelssohn Bartholdy." D.M.A. diss., Southwestern Baptist Theological Seminary, 1993. 245 p.

Discusses especially the *Hymne*, Op. 96, and Op. 69 motets.

890. Hutchings, Arthur. *Church Music in the Nineteenth Century*. London: Jenkins, 1967. 166 p. ML3131 .H88 1967. Rpt. Westport, Conn.: Greenwood, 1977. ISBN 0837196957. ML3131 .H88 1977.

"The bad [church] music of the nineteenth century is less often inappropriately secular than falsely sacred." FMB was "certainly not the parent of the nineteenth century brand of 'churchliness' in music; that unctuous harmonium style can be traced back to the conventionally religious Vienna of the Congress pageant, fast making money to pay for the war and Napoléon and fast bleeding its visitors. The unctuous style we hear every Christmas is found in church music by Schubert and the Chevalier Neukomm, both known in private letters to be agnostic." Mendelssohn's Anglican canticles are too long for the "cathedral daily repertory," and were intended "chiefly for choral festivals." Hutchings includes what he calls "the church-like psalms" in his discussion of church music. "Not to know these is to have an incomplete conception of his [Mendelssohn's] stature." The article is unsystematic and cranky but has some interesting moments and insights. [DM]

891. Kappner, Gerhard. "Die gottesdienstliche Musik von Felix Mendelssohn Bartholdy." *Musica sacra* 112/1 (1992): 7–10.

892. Kellenberger, Edgar. "Felix Mendelssohns geistliche Musik als 'judenchristliches Zeugnis'?" *Musik und Gottesdienst* 46 (1992): 166–76.

893. Kellenberger, Edgar. "Felix Mendelssohn als Librettist eines Moses-Oratoriums: Erstedition mit Kommentar." *Musik und Kirche* 63 (1993): 126–39.

894. Krummacher, Friedhelm. "Kunstreligion und religiöse Musik: Zur ästhetischen Problematik geistlicher Musik im 19. Jahrhundert." *Die Musikforschung* 32 (1979): 365–93.

This essay probes the dichotomy between "art-religion" and "religious music," devoting special attention to Hegel (who evidently coined the term *Kunstreligion*) and Wagner (whose essay on the subject ranks among his more important writings). Krummacher considers works by

Beethoven, Liszt, and Brahms, as well as FMB's Opp. 23, no. 1, 65, 69, no. 1, and 70.

895. Mansfield, O. A. *Organ Parts of Mendelssohn's Oratorios and Other Choral Works Analytically Considered.* London: William Reeves, 1907. 80 p. MT115.M53 M3.

896. Mies, Paul. "Über die Kirchenmusik und über neu entdeckte Werke bei Felix Mendelssohn Bartholdy." *Musica sacra* 83 (1963): 212–17, 246–50.

897. Oechsle, Siegfried. *Symphonik nach Beethoven: Studien zu Schubert, Schumann, Mendelsohn und Gade.* Kieler Schriften zur Musikwissenschaft, Bd. 40. Kassel: Bärenreiter, 1992. 404 p. ISBN 376181058X. ML1255 .O32 1992 .

Adapted from the author's dissertation: "Symphonik auf neuer Basis: Schubert, Schumann, Mendelssohn und Gade" (Kiel, 1989).

898. Parkinson, Del R. "Selected Works for Piano and Orchestra in One Movement, 1821–1853." Ph.D. diss., Indiana University, 1974. 133 p.

899. Schuhmacher, Gerhard. "Gesicherte und ungesicherte Kirchenliedvorlagen als Themen Mendelssohns." *Jahrbuch für Hymnologie und Liturgik* 28 (1984): 146–54.

900. Sposato, Jeffrey S. "Mendelssohn's Theological Evolution: A Study of Textual Choice and Change in the Composer's Sacred Works." Ph.D. diss., Brandeis University, [in progress].

901. Stanley, Glenn. "Bach's *Erbe*: The Chorale in the German Oratorio of the Early Nineteenth Century." *Nineteenth-Century Music* 11 (1987): 121–49.

This article discusses *St. Paul*, Op. 36.

902. Stanley, Glenn. "The Oratorio in Protestant Germany: 1812–1848." Ph.D. diss., Columbia University, 1988. 356 p.

903. Wehner, Ralf. *Studien zum geistlichen Chorschaffen des jungen Felix Mendelssohn Bartholdy.* Musik und Musikanschauung im 19. Jahrhundert: Studien und Quellen, Bd. 4. Cologne: Studio, 1991. 283 p. ISBN 3895640247. ML410.M5 W33 1996.

Adapted from the author's dissertation (University of Leipzig, 1991), this is an authoritative study of a musically rewarding and unfortunately neglected repertoire. It includes introductory observations on the state of recent FMB scholarship, followed by a chapter on FMB's compositional process as evidenced in the autographs for the early works (focusing on the five-voice vocal fugue *Die Himmel erzählen* and the versions of the *Jube dom'ne*). The next chapter treats FMB's chorale settings (focusing on the chorale motet *Jesus meine Zuversicht* and the early chorale cantatas *Christe, du Lamm Gottes, Jesu meine Freude*, and *Wer nur den lieben Gott läßt walten*). This is followed by an extended investigation of FMB's work on polyphony, focusing on smaller works (the *Gloria, Magnificat,* and *Te Deum* of 1822) and larger ones (the full-scale motets for chorus and orchestra, *Tu es Petrus* and *Hora est*). The remaining chapters deal with works for double-choir; the various stylistic influences in the 1825 *Kyrie* in D Minor; and the work that FMB at one point described as his best: the posthumously published *Tu es Petrus.* In addition to plentiful music examples, the book also includes extensive bibliographic references, a full-scale classified bibliography, and an appendix of music deleted from the *Te Deum* and the *Kyrie.*

904. Werner, Eric. "Mendelssohns Kirchenmusik und ihre Stellung im 19. Jahrhundert." In *Bericht über den Internatonalen Musikwissenschaftlichen Kongress Kassel 1962*, ed. Georg Reichert and Martin Just, 207–10. Kassel: Bärenreiter, 1963.

Werner agrees with Hermann Kretschmar's remark that FMB's greatest historical significance lies in his contribution to the realm of sacred music, and proposes to augment Rudolf Werner's landmark study of that repertoire (no. 905) by a more developed understanding of Romanticism as well as a more thorough understanding of liturgical history. This article surveys the genres represented in the sacred works and explores the dilemma posed for FMB by the changes in liturgical function that affected music.

905. Werner, Rudolf. *Felix Mendelssohn Bartholdy als Kirchenmusiker.* Veröffentlichungen der Deutschen Musikgesellschaft Ortsgruppe Frankfurt, 2. Frankfurt am Main: n.p., 1930. 190 p. ML410.M5 W4.

Adapted from the author's dissertation of the same title (University of Frankfurt am Main, 1929). One of the first full-length surveys to draw extensively on manuscript sources, this is still an essential resource for work on FMB's sacred music.

906. Zywietz, Michael. *Adolf Bernhard Marx und das Oratorium in Berlin.* Schriften zur Musikwissenschaft aus Münster, No. 9. Eisenach: K. D. Wagner, 1996. 380 p. ISBN 3889790747. ML410.M3828 Z98 1996.

Adapted from the author's Ph.D. dissertation by the same title (University of Münster, 1995).

## V.	PERFORMANCE PRACTICE

907.	Erdmann, Hans, and Hans Rentzow. "Mendelssohns Oratorien-Praxis: Ein bisher unbekannter Brief des Meisters vom Jahre 1840." *Musica* 6 (1952): 352–55.

> The first edition of a letter dated 22 March 1840 in which FMB discusses practical issues for a Schwerin performance of *St. Paul* and Haydn's *Creation*. It contains detailed information concerning the number and placement of the musicians.

908.	Gleich, Clemens von. "Originale Tempo-Angaben bei Mendelssohn." In *Festschrift Rudolf Elvers zum 60. Geburtstag*, ed. Ernst Herttrich and Hans Schneider, 213–22. Tutzing: Hans Schneider, 1985.

> Notes those of Mendelssohn's first editions that have metronome markings. Metronome markings in the Piano Quartet, Op. 3. no. 1, cannot be maintained when the triplets begin. No one conducts the *Midsummer Night's Dream* Overture up to indicated tempo. The Cello Sonta Op. 45, no. 1 poses problems like those of Op. 3. The explanation according to the theories of W. R. Talsma is that before 1850 the metronome markings referred not to a single tick of the metronome but to a cycle of the pendulum, that is to two ticks of the metronome. Of course in a ternary meter, this leads to the necessity of working out a two against three count, but everyone is used to that. Most people today will perceive this halving of the apparent metronome markings as leading to tempos that are too slow but it is better to adjust upward from these than to drag. [DM]

909.	Heyder, Bernd. "Die erste 'Paulus'-Aufführung im Spiegel zeitgenössischer Dokumente." In *Blickpunkt FELIX Mendelssohn Bartholdy: Programmbuch Drei Tage für Felix vom 30.10 bis 1.11.1994*, ed. Bernd Heyder and Christoph Spering, 69–80. Cologne: Dohr, 1994.

910.	Golightly, John Wesley. "The Piano Between 1800 and 1850: The Instrument for Which the Composers Wrote." D.M.A. diss., Ohio State University, 1980. 118 p.

> This article includes studies of Stein/Streicher, Graf, Härtel, Walter, Clementi, Broadwood, Érard, Pape, Petzold, and Pleyel instruments. It also contains a section about the "piano ideas" of a number of composers, including Mendelssohn. At first Mendelssohn was content to play on the pianos that came to hand, but after about 1832 he preferred Érard instruments in particular and the English action in general. He had been brought up on a Broadwood and it was to a Broadwood that he returned at the end of his life.

911. Meier, Ernst. "Mendelssohn und die Orgel seiner Zeit." *Musik und Gottesdienst* 37 (1983): 149–55.

912. Murray, Thomas. "Performance Style for Mendelssohn." *Diapason* 67, no. 9 (1976): 6–7, 18.

> Murray surveys FMB's activities as a performing organist, the specifications of the instruments he knew, and contemporary reports on his playing and interpretation.

913. Parkins, Robert. "Mendelssohn and the Érard Piano." *The Piano Quarterly* 32/5 (1984): 53–58.

> Because of FMB's position as a virtuoso pianist and a widely recognized composer of music for the piano, it is important to understand the nature of the sounds he wrote for in his music and produced in his playing. This essay includes descriptions of his playing and describes the sounds and effects of the instruments for which he wrote.

914. Ricks, Robert. "Are Our Audiences 'Skeered to Clap'? A Brief Survey of Applause Practices." *Journal of the Conductor's Guild* 16 (1995): 66–75.

915. Tenhaef, Peter. "Mendelssohn—der romantische Klassizismus." In *Studien zur Vortragsbezeichnung in der Musik des 19. Jahrhunderts*, 201–11. Kassel: Bärenreiter, 1983.

> Adapted from the author's disertation of the same title

916. Weiss, Hermann F. "Unbekannte Zeugnisse zu den Leipziger Aufführungen von Felix Mendelssohn Bartholdys Bühnenmusik zur *Antigone* in den Jahren 1841 und 1842." *Die Musikforschung* 51 (1998): 50–57.

VI. COMPOSITIONAL PROCESS

Prefatory Note: One of several laudable features of FMB scholarship since World War II is that many studies consider and evaluate primary sources and issues of revision in the composer's compositional process. To list all these studies here would require removing them from other parts of this book where most readers will look for and/or find them more easily. The studies listed below are only sources whose primary focus is the *process* of compositional development (as opposed to, for example, a study of an individual work whose genesis is chronicled within the study).

917. Brodbeck, David. "'Eine kleine Kirchenmusik': A New Canon, A Revised Cadence, and an Obscure 'Coda' by Mendelssohn." *Journal of Musicology 12 (1994): 179-205*. Also (abridged) in *Musik als Text: Bericht über den Internationalen Kongreß der Gesellschaft für Musikforschung, Freiburg im Breisgau 1993*, ed. Hermann Danuser and Tobias Plebuch, 346-51. Kassel: Bärenreiter, 1998.

   A careful examination of the complex compositional and publication histories of Opp. 69, 78, and 91, and establishes that the version published by Breitkopf & Härtel entails some significant misrepresentations of FMB's last thoughts on the works (the edition published by Ewer & Co. in London in 1847 fares better).

918. Eppstein, Hans. "Nochmals: Zur Entstehungsgeschichte von Mendelssohns 'Lied ohne Worte' op. 62, 3." *Die Musikforschung* 42 (1989): 149.

919. Eppstein, Hans. "Zur Entstehungsgeschichte von Mendelssohns 'Lied ohne Worte' op. 62, 3." *Die Musikforschung* 26 (1973): 486–90.

920. Gerlach, Reinhold. "Mendelssohns Kompositionsweise: Vergleich zwischen Skizzen und Letztfassung des Violinkonzerts op. 64." *Archiv für Musikwissenschaft* 28 (1971): 119–33.

   An important contribution to FMB sketch scholarship that surveys the evolution of the main theme of the first movement of the Violin Concerto (Op. 64) as it is documented in sketches held in Volume 19 of the former *Mendelssohn Nachlaß*. See also the earlier study by Worbs (no. 938) and Gerlach's follow-up study (no. 921).

921. Gerlach, Reinhold. "Mendelssohns Kompositionsweise (II): Weitere Vergleiche zwischen den Skizzen und der Letztfassung des Violinkonzerts op. 64." In *Das Problem Mendelssohn*, ed. Carl Dahlhaus, 149–67. Studien zur Musikgeschichte des 19. Jahrhunderts, Bd. 41. Regensburg: Gustav Bosse, 1974. Rpt. in Gerhard Schuhmacher, *Felix Mendelssohn Bartholdy*. Wege der Forschung, 494. Darmstadt: Wissenschaftliche Buchgesellschaft, 1982.

   A sequel to Gerlach's study in *Archiv für Musikwissenschaft* (no. 921), this essay takes a broader view of the compositional goals evident in FMB's revisions of the Violin Concerto.

922. Gülke, Peter. "Unkomponierte Musik bei Mendelssohn?" In *Felix Mendelssohn—Mitwelt und Nachwelt: Bericht zum 1. Leipziger Mendelssohn-Kolloquium am 8. und 9. Juni 1993*, ed. Leon Botstein, 123–26. Wiesbaden: Breitkopf & Härtel, 1996.

923. Jost, Christa. "Neue Materialen zu Mendelssohns Lied ohne Worte in e-moll op. 62 Nr. 3." In *Bericht über den Internationalen Musikwissenschaftlichen Kongress, Bayreuth 1981*, ed. Christoph-Hellmut Mahling and Sigrid Wiesmann, 407–09. Kassel: Bärenreiter, 1981.

924. Klein, Hans-Günter. "Korrekturen im Autograph von Mendelssohns Op. 80: Überlegungen zur Kompositionstechnik und zum Kompositionsvorgang." *Mendelssohn-Studien* 5 (1982): 113–22.

    A detailed and thoughtful survey of the revisions and compositional goals evident in the recently discovered autograph for the F-minor String Quartet. It is useful as a model for how severely misguided many notions of FMB's compositional process are, and for formulating a new assessment of the processes by which his musical ideas developed.

925. Krummacher, Friedhelm. "Über Autographe Mendelssohns und seine Kompositionsweise." In *Gesellschaft für Musikforschung: Bericht über den internationalen musikwissenschaftlichen Kongreß Bonn 1970*, ed. Carl Dahlhaus, Hans Joachim Marx, Magda Marx-Weber, and Günther Massenkeil, 482–85. Kassel: Bärenreiter, 1971.

    This essay provides general observations on FMB's compositonal process as evidenced by the manuscripts for the chamber music. It discusses the reasons for the relative paucity of sketches (as opposed to full-scale drafts or working full scores); differentiates between different varieties of extended scores (fair copies [*Reinschriften*] or composing scores [*Arbeitsmss.*]); identfies the principal kinds of variants that occur (tonal, harmonic, melodic, and structural); and discusses the applications of studies of FMB's compositional processes. An essential introduction to the subject. [DM]

926. Krummacher, Friedhelm. "Zur Kompositionsart Mendelssohns: Thesen am Beispiel der Streichquartette." In *Das Problem Mendelssohn*, ed. Carl Dahlhaus, 169–84. Studien zur Musikgeschichte des 19. Jahrhunderts, 41. Regensburg: Gustav Bosse, 1974. Expanded in *Felix Mendelssohn Bartholdy*, ed. Heinz-Klaus Metzger and Rainer Riehn, 46–74. Musik-Konzepte, Bd. 14/15. Munich: edition text + kritik, 1980.

    This article examines the compositional issues evident in the autograph for FMB's important string quartets. Emphasis is placed on the nature of motivic potential and the evident reasoning behind FMB's concentrated efforts to formulate lyrical rather than sharply chiseled motives.

927. Mintz, Donald [Manturean]. "*Melusine*: A Mendelssohn Draft." *The*

Musical Quarterly 43 (1957): 480–99. Trans. German Gerhard Schuhmacher as *"Melusine*: Ein Entwurf Mendelssohns." In *Felix Mendelssohn Bartholdy*, ed. Gerhard Schuhmacher, 177–200. Wege der Forschung, 494. Darmstadt: Wissenschaftliche Buchgesellschaft, 1982.

928. Mintz, Donald Manturean. "The Sketches and Drafts of Three of Felix Mendelssohn's Major Works." Ph.D. diss., Cornell University, 1960. 2 vols.

A landmark in FMB scholarship, devoted to an exploration of FMB's compositional style as documented by his revisions in three major works: the D-minor Piano Trio, Op. 49; *Elijah*, Op. 70; and the A-major ("Italian") Symphony, Op. posth. 90. Mintz proceeds from a conviction that FMB was a bona fide Romantic rather than some kind of quasi-reactionary composer, and discovers in the revisions evidence of FMB's participation in fundamentally Romantic issues. The assumed chronology concerning the "Italian" Symphony has now been called into question, but many of the volume's observations continue to generate momentum in nineteenth-century scholarship.

929. Schuhmacher, Gerhard. "Zwischen Autograph und Erstveröffentlichung: Zu Mendelssohns Kompositionsweise, dargestellt an den Streichquartetten op. 44." *Beiträge zur Musikwissenschaft* 15 (1973): 253–61. Rpt. in *Felix Mendelssohn Bartholdy*, ed. Gerhard Schuhmacher, 263–76. Wege der Forschung, Bd. 494. Darmstadt: Wissenschaftliche Buchgesellschaft, 1982.

The author probes the changes in the autographs for the String Quartet in E Minor, Op. 44, no. 2, with an eye to the process by which FMB moved from the general idea of the composition to the final form, focusing largely on structural revisions.

930. Seaton, Douglass. "A Draft for the Exposition of the First Movement of Mendelssohn's 'Scotch' Symphony." *Journal of the American Musicological Society* 30 (1977): 129–35.

Seaton compares the draft version of the passage with the final version. While some significant basic structural decisions were evidently made early on, others—such as the matter of how to begin the exposition and the length of the main thematic areas, were the result of concentrated work and produced the pronounced overall unity observed in the final version from its première (see Schumann's early review in the *Neue Zeitschrift für Musik* 39/18 (15 May 1843): 155–56; also Longyear's essay on Op. 56 [592]).

931. Seaton, Stuart Douglass. "A Study of a Collection of Mendelssohn's Sketches and Other Autograph Material: Deutsche Staatsbibliothek Mus. Ms. Autogr. 19." Ph.D. diss., Columbia University, 1977. 250 p.

A vital study in FMB scholarship, not least of all because of its systematic classification of the documents that were produced in FMB's distinctive compositional process. The volume around which the study centers is a posthumously assembled miscellany of sketches and drafts written in the mid- and later 1830s. Special attention is devoted to the materials pertaining to Opp. 42, 52, and 56, but other works represented include Opp. 35, 36, 40, 42, 44, 55, 60, 61, 62, and 64, as well as Opp. posth. 74, 92, and 102.

932. Thomas, Mathias. *Das Instrumentalwerk Felix Mendelssohn Bartholdys: Eine systematisch-theoretische Untersuchung unter besonderer Berücksichtigung zeitgenössischer Musiktheorie.* Göttinger musikwissenschaftliche Arbeiten, Bd. 4. Kassel: Bärenreiter, 1972. 267 p.

Adapted from the author's dissertation ("Satztechnik und Form in den Instrumentalwerken Felix Mendelssohn-Bartholdys, unter besonderer Berücksichtigung der zeitgenössischen Theorie" [University of Göttingen, 1971]). One of surprisingly few large-scale studies of the role of texture and form in FMB's orchestral works. Thomas devotes considerable attention to all the concert overtures and symphonies, and explores the roles of, and scorings associated with, specific textures that tend to occur at certain points in FMB's instrumental works.

933. Thomas, Mathias. "Zur Kompositionsweise in Mendelssohns Ouvertüren." In *Das Problem Mendelssohn*, ed. Carl Dahlhaus, 129–48. Studien zur Musikgeschichte des 19. Jahrhunderts, Bd. 41. Regensburg: Gustav Bosse, 1974.

Adapted from the author's dissertation, this is a compact study of the role of orchestral color and texture in the conception of FMB's concert overtures (Opp. 21, 26, 26, 27, 32, and 95).

934. Todd, Ralph Larry. "The Instrumental Music of Felix Mendelssohn-Bartholdy: Selected Studies Based on Primary Sources." Ph.D. diss., Yale University, 1979. 544 p.

A seminal document in FMB scholarly reception history. Part I is a thorough study of FMB's compositional education, focusing on a composition workbook used during ca. 1819–21; this workbook includes several autonomous compositions, but functions primarily as a record of FMB's instruction in counterpoint under Zelter (see no. 226). Part II is a study of five selected genres represented in FMB's instrumental works, including *Lieder ohne Worte*, string octet and string quintet, concerto, and concert overture. All chapters explore the influence of Zelter's teaching on FMB's composition, and all deal extensively with unpublished primary sources representing various stages of the compositional process.

935. Todd, R. Larry. "The Unfinished Mendelssohn." In *Mendelssohn and His World*, ed. R. Larry Todd, 158–84. Princeton: Princeton University Press, 1991.

An overview of the substantial quantity of compositions that FMB left unfinished, and a careful investigation of some reasons why they may have been set aside. This article focuses on an incomplete draft for the exposition of a piano sonata in G major.

936. Todd, R. Larry, and Robert Parkins. "Mendelssohn's Fugue in F Minor: A Discarded Movement of the First Organ Sonata." *Organ Yearbook* 14 (1983): 61–77.

The late 1830s and early 1840s witnessed FMB's composition of a number of pieces for organ that were rejected, but this article demonstrates that some important ideas from one discarded piece, a fugue in F minor, were retained in the first and third movements of the F-minor Organ Sonata.

937. Wilson [Kimber], Marian. "Mendelssohn's Works for Solo Piano and Orchestra: Sources and Composition." Ph.D. diss., Florida State University, 1993. 497 p.

An essential document for anyone exploring the composition, performance history, publication history, and reception history of FMB's works for solo piano and orchestra; focuses on the early Concerto in A Minor, the *Capriccio brillant* (Op. 22), the G-minor Concerto (Op. 25), the *Rondo brillant* (Op. 29), the D-minor Concerto (Op. 40), and the *Serenade and Allegro giojoso* (Op. 43). For each work there is a discussion of the historical background, the form, and the compositional process. This book includes extensive recourse to sketches, drafts, and other unpublished materials, as well as significant early editions.

938. Worbs, Hans Christoph. "Die Entwürfe zu Mendelssohns Violinkonzert e-moll." *Die Musikforschung* 12 (1959): 79–81.

The first major study of the compositional process revealed in the sketches for the Violin Concerto, Op. 64. It focuses on the successive improvements of the main theme and the second theme of the first movement.

Appendix A.
A Bibiliographic Introduction to
Research Concerning Fanny Hensel

I.   Life-and-Works Studies
II. Editions of Letters
III. Family Relationships and Reception History
IV. Studies of Music Manuscripts and Papers
V.   Studies of Hensel's Music

I.   LIFE-AND-WORKS STUDIES

939. Blozan, Claudio. "'Un richiamo di sogni': Fanny Mendelssohn Hensel tra idillio ed emancipazione artistica (1833–1843)." *Nuova rivista musicale italiana* 27 (1993): 563–94.

940. Cai, Camilla. "Fanny Mendelssohn Hensel as Composer and Pianist." *The Piano Quarterly* 35 (1987): 46–50.

941. Elvers, Rudolf, ed. *Fanny Hensel, geboren Mendelssohn Bartholdy, 14. November 1805–14, Mai 1847: Dokumente ihres Lebens. Katalog zur Ausstellung Berlin 1972.* Staatsbibliothek Preußischer Kulturbesitz, Ausstellungskataloge, 2. Berlin-Daheim: Staatsbibliothek Preußrscher Kulterbestiz, 1972.

942. Hirtler, Eva. "'Kräht ja doch kein Hahn danach'? Komponistinnen verschiedener Jahrhunderte im Musikunterricht." *Musik und Bildung* 28, no. 1 (1996): 24–29.

943. Huber, Annegret. "'Dies ist nun gestern, Sonntag Vormittag, . . . vom Stapel gelaufen': Sonntagsmusik im Hause Mendelssohn Bartholdy." *Musica* 49 (1995): 118–19.

944. Labell, Christa. "Komponistinnen des 19. Jahrhunderts: Clara Schumann,

Louisa Adolpa Le Beau, Johanna Kinkel, Fanny Hensel." Magisterarbeit Universität Bremen, 1983.

945. Reich, Nancy B. "The Power of Class: Fanny Hensel." In *Mendelssohn and His World*, ed. R. Larry Todd, 86–99. Princeton: Princeton University Press, 1991.

946. Rothenberg, Sarah. "'Thus Far, But No Farther': Fanny Mendelssohn-Hensel's Unfinished Journey." *Musical Quarterly* 77 (1993): 689–708.

947. Streicher, Johannes. "Per Fanny Mendelssohn-Hensel: Minima italica e altre divagazioni." In *Ottocento e oltre: Scritti in onore di Raoul Meloncelli*, ed. Francesco Izzo and Johannes Streicher, 235–66. Rome: Editoriale Pantheon, 1993.

948. Tillard, Françoise. *Fanny Mendelssohn*. Paris: Éditions Belfond, 1992. 389 p. ISBN 2714429432. Trans. English Camille Naish as *Fanny Mendelssohn*. Portland, Ore.: Amadeus, 1996. 399 p. ISBN 0931340969. ML410.H482. Trans. German Ralf Stamm as *Die verkannte Schwester: Die späte Entdeckung der Komponistin Fanny Mendelssohn Bartholdy*. Munich: Kindler, 1992. 400 p. ISBN 3463402459 ML410.H482.

A seminal contribution, if also one extensively derived from Sebastian Hensel's family memoir (no. 352). Although the perspectives drawn from Austen's England and late-nineteenth-century France may be a bit inappropriate for Hensel's mid-nineteenth-century German context, the book contributes much in the way of synthesizing and updating information and ideas otherwise available primarily through older sources that are now difficult to obtain.

949. Whalen, Meg Freeman. "Fanny Mendelssohn Hensel's Sunday Musicales." *Journal of the Conductor's Guild* 14, no. 1 (1993): 8–19.

II.　EDITIONS OF LETTERS

950. Alexander, Boyd. "Some Unpublished Letters of Abraham Mendelssohn and Fanny Hensel." *Mendelssohn-Studien* 3 (1979): 9–50.

951. Citron, Marcia J., ed. and trans. *The Letters of Fanny Hensel to Felix Mendelssohn*. [Stuyvesant, N.Y.]: Pendragon, 1987. 687 p. ISBN 0918728525.

An essential tool for research concerning both FH and FMB. Letters are given in English and German and extensively annotated. Includes a useful prose introduction on the relationship between the siblings and the letters included. (Unfortunately, this comprises only about half of FH's surviving letters to FMB.)

952. Elvers, Rudolf. "Durchgerutscht: Einige Bemerkungen zur Ausgabe des Briefwechsels zwischen Fanny Hensel und Felix Mendelssohn Bartholdy." *Mendelssohn-Studien* 11 (1999): 131–44.

953. Elvers, Rudolf. "Fanny Hensels Briefe aus München 1839." In *Ars Iocundissima: Festschrift für Kurt Dorfmüller zum 60. Geburtstag*, ed. Horst Leuchtmann and Robert Münster, 65–81. Tutzing: Hans Schneider, 1984.

954. Hellwig-Unruh, Renate. "'Ein Dilettant ist schon ein schreckliches Geschöpf, ein weiblicher Autor ein noch schrecklicheres . . .': Sechs Briefe von Fanny Hensel an Franz Hauser (1794–1870)." *Mendelssohn-Studien* 10 (1997): 215–26.

955. Koch, Paul-August. *Fanny Hensel geb. Mendelssohn (1805–1847)— Komponistin. Eine Zusammenstellung der Werke, Literatur und Schallplatten*. Frankfurt am Main: Zimmermann, 1993.

956. Köhler, Karl-Heinz. "Mendelssohn(-Bartholdy), Fanny (Cäcilie)." Article in *The New Grove Dictionary of Music and Musicians*, ed. Stanley Sadie, 12: 134. London: Macmillan, 1980.

957. Krautwurst, Franz. "Fanny Mendelssohn Hensel." Article in *Die Musik in Geschichte und Gegenwart*, ed. Friedrich Blume, 16: col. 658–62. Kassel: Bärenreiter, 1979.

958. Lambour, Christian and Phyllis Benjamin, eds. "Quellen zur Biographie von Fanny Hensel, geb. Mendelssohn Bartholdy." *Mendelssohn-Studien* 6 (1986): 49–105; 7 (1990): 171–217.

An important documentary study of FH's familial relationships—the first of a series of studies documenting her life planned for the *Mendelssohn-Studien*. This article comprises four parts. Part I includes annotated critical editions of letters written to FH by her aunt Henriette Mendelssohn and her uncle Jacob Salomon Bartholdy. Part II comprises a series of critically edited and annotated letters to FH from FMB, on the occasion of her wedding in October 1829. Part III (pp. 171–78) gives an 1822 letter from Lea and Fanny Mendelssohn Bartholdy to Henriette Mendelssohn; while Part IV (pp .178–217) constitutes Phyllis Benjamin's study of a diary-album for Fanny (no. 964).

III. FAMILY RELATIONSHIPS AND RECEPTION HISTORY

959. Citron, Marcia J. "Felix Mendelssohn's Influence on Fanny Hensel as a Professional Composer." *Current Musicology* 37/38 (1984): 9–17.

960. Citron, Marcia J. "Fanny Mendelssohn Hensel: Musician in Her Brother's Shadow." In *The Female Autograph*, 12–13 (1984): 171–80.

961. Lowenthal-Hensel, Cécile. "Mutter und Sohn: Fanny und Sebastian Hensel," in *Die Mendelssohns in Berlin: Eine Familie und ihre Stadt*, ed. Rudolf Elvers and Hans-Günter Klein (Berlin, 1983), 58–73.

IV. STUDIES OF MUSIC MANUSCRIPTS AND PAPERS

962. Benjamin, Phyllis. "A Diary-Album for Fanny Mendelssohn Bartholdy." *Mendelssohn-Studien* 7 (1990): 179–217.

   Part IV of Christian Lambour's series of studies of biographical documents (no. 960). The album in question, given to FH on Christmas Eve of 1828, contains drawings and a number of musical sketches.

963. Elvers, Rudolf. "Verzeichnis der Musik-Autographen von Fanny Hensel im Mendelssohn-Archiv zu Berlin." *Mendelssohn-Studien* 1 (1972): 169–74.

964. Elvers, Rudolf. "Weitere Quellen zu den Werken von Fanny Hensel." *Mendelssohn-Studien* 2 (1975): 215–20.

965. Klein, Hans-Günter. "Autographe und Abschriften von Werken Fanny Hensels im Mendelssohn-Archiv zu Berlin: Verzeichnis der Abschriften und der Neuerwerbungen 1976–1990." *Mendelssohn-Studien* 7 (1990): 343–45.

966. Klein, Hans-Günter. "'...dieses allerliebste Buch': Fanny Hensels Noten-Album." *Mendelssohn Studien* 8 (1993): 141–58.

   Includes numerous facsimiles.

967. Klein, Hans-Günter. *Die Kompositionen Fanny Hensels in Autographen und Abschriften aus dem Besitz der Staatsbibliothek zu Berlin, Preussischer Kulturbesitz: Katalog*. Musikbibliographische Arbeiten, 13. Tutzing: Hans Schneider, 1995. 146 p. ISBN 3795208203.

968. Klein, Hans-Günter. "Quellen zu Werken Fanny Hensels in der Musikabteilung der Staatsbibliothek zu Berlin." *Mendelssohn-Studien* 8 (1993): 159–60.

V. STUDIES OF HENSEL'S MUSIC

969. Brickman, Scott Thomas. "Analysis and Interpretation of Fanny Hensel's *Italien, Notturno*, and Piano Trio (First Movement)." Ph.D. diss., Brandeis University, 1996. 102 p.

970. Cai, Camilla. "Virtuoso Texture in the Piano Music of Fanny Hensel." In *The Mendelssohns: Their Music in History*, ed. John Michael Cooper and Julie D. Prandi. Oxford: Oxford University Press, [forthcoming].

971. Citron, Marcia J. "The Lieder of Fanny Mendelssohn Hensel." *The Musical Quarterly* 69 (1983): 570–94.

972. Gundlach, Willi. "Die Chorlieder von Fanny Hensel: Eine späte Liebe?" *Mendelssohn-Studien* 11 (1999): 105–30.

973. Hellwig-Unruh, Renate. "Die Cholerakantate von Fanny Hensel." *Musica Germany* 50 (1996): 121–23.

974. Huber, Annegret. "Fanny Hensel-Mendelssohn: Liedhaftes Komponieren—ohne Worte und mit Worten." Ph.D. diss., University of Vienna, [in progress].

975. Huber, Annegret. "In welcher Form soll man Fanny Hensels 'Choleramusik' aufführen?' *Mendelssohn-Studien* 10 (1997): 227–46.

976. Lehmann, Richard William. "The Cantatas and Oratorio of Fanny Mendelssohn Hensel." Ph.D. diss., University of Wisconsin at Madison, [in progress].

977. Thym, Jürgen. "Crosscurrents in Song: Five Distinctive Voices." In *German Lieder in the Nineteenth Century,* ed. Rufus Hallmark, 153–85. New York: Schirmer Books, 1996.

978. Toews, John E. "Memory and Gender in the Remaking of Fanny Mendelssohn's Musical Identity: The Chorale in *Das Jahr*." *The Musical Quarterly* 77 (1993): 727–48.

979. Vana, Marilee Ann. "Fanny Mendelssohn Hensel's *Festspiel*, Ma Ms. 37: a Modern Edition and Conductor's Analysis for Performance." D.M.A. diss., University of North Carolina at Greensborough, 1996.

Appendix B.
Principal Editions, Facsimiles, and Publications of Mendelssohn's Works

The following inventory is intended (a) to organize Mendelssohn's works in a fashion consistent with his own understanding of their groupings; (b) to distinguish clearly between those compositions he published and those he elected to suppress or failed to publish; (c) to facilitate a more accurate understanding of the works' chronology than is possible from previous work-lists (largely because of the misleading serial and opus numbers assigned to the early posthumous publications); and (d) to identify the principal early editions, critical editions, and facsimile editions of the works as of this writing. The chronological organization differs from that of previous FMB work-lists in that each work is placed according to its completion—or, in the case of the unpublished and posthumously published works, the latest rather than earliest surviving manuscript. For the unpublished and posthumously published compositions, the entries provide the earliest and latest dates that can be assigned on the basis of their manuscript sources and other documents.

This list is distilled from material in my more extensive "Prologomenon" to an FMB catalog (no. 457) included in Douglass Seaton's *The Mendelssohn Companion* (no. 14). Readers who wish to see a complete inventory of known surviving manuscript sources (as of this writing) may consult that item. Not included in this list are Mendelssohn's composition exercises (thoroughly inventoried by R. Larry Todd in *Mendelssohn's Musical Education* [no. 226]) and the untexted canons.

The following information is provided in the entries:

1. Title (as the work is generally known in the English-speaking world, with other common designations given in brackets).

2. Scoring.

3. Dates that may be assigned on the basis of the known autographs and other facts (dates surmised on the basis of evidence other than a specific date on

a surviving or reported manuscript are enclosed in brackets).

4. Publication information (city, publisher, and date) for significant editions. Although complete publication histories are not always possible in an inventory of the present size and score, I have generally included:

    a) the first German, English, and (in certain relevant cases) French editions, leading up to the work's publication ;

    (b) the work's location in the so-called *Gesamtausgabe* edited by Julius Rietz (R) and/or the more recent *Leipziger Ausgabe* (L); and

    (c) any important subsequent editions.

    Except where otherwise indicated, "edn." refers to the simultaneous publication of score and/or parts and/or piano(-vocal) scores, as relevant. Excerpts and arrangements published separately during Mendelssohn's lifetime (e.g., the many arrangements and editions of the "war march of the priests" from *Athalia*) are identified only when they preceded publication of the complete work.

5. Principal facsimiles or facsimile editions.

Abbreviations

Bibliographic abbreviations and abbreviations concerning instruments and instrumentation conform to those used in the *New Grove*. Except where otherwise indicated, the sources listed are scores. Types of sources are identified by the following abbreviations:

R: *Felix Mendelssohn Bartholdy, Werke*, ed. Julius Rietz (Leipzig: Breitkopf & Härtel, 1874–77)

L: *Leipziger Ausgabe der Werke Felix Mendelssohn Bartholdys*, ed. Internationale Felix-Mendelssohn-Gesellschaft (Leipzig: 1960-)

FS: full score

PS: piano score or piano-vocal score

inc: denotes a work whose source begins at the beginning but breaks off before the end

Index to the List

I. SECULAR WORKS

A. Stage Works

1. Published by Mendelssohn

Die Hochzeit des Camacho, **Op. 10** (opera in two acts). Date: 10 August 1825–[1827]. Libretto: F. Voigts, after Cervantes, *Don Quixote.* Edn: Berlin: Laue, [1828 (PS, arr. by FMB)]; R xv (FS).

Incidental Music to Sophocles's *Antigone,* **Op. 55** (ch, orch). Date: 4 February 1842–[1843]. Edn: London: Ewer, [1843]; Leipzig: Kistner, [1843], [1844] (PS, complete), [1851] (FS); R xv.

Incidental Music to Shakespeare's *A Midsummer Night's Dream,* **Op. 61** (solo vv, ch, orch). Date: [1843]–1844. Edn: Leipzig: Breitkopf & Härtel, [1844] (PS 4 hnds by FMB and PS—both excerpts only; words in German); London: Ewer, [1844] (PS 4 hnds by FMB; words in English) and [1845] (complete PS without texts); Leipzig: Breitkopf & Härtel, [1848] (FS); R xv. To be combined with the programmatic concert overture, Op. 21, composed in 1826–27 and published in 1833 (see p. 230, below).

2. Unpublished and Posthumously Published Stage Works

Quel bonheur pour mon coeur (dramatic scene for S and T, orch). Date: [1820]. Text: ?. Edn: Unpublished.

Ich, J. Mendelssohn (Lustspiel in 3 scenes). Date: 1820. Text: ?. Edn: Unpublished.

Die Soldatenliebschaft (comic opera in 1 act). Date: 30 November 1820. Libretto: J.L. Casper. Edn: Unpublished

Die beiden Pädagogen (Singspiel in 1 act). Date: [ca. March 1821].

Libretto: J.L. Casper, after Scribe, *Les deux précepteurs*. Edn: L v.

Die wandernden Komödianten (comic opera in 1 act). Date: 30 November–9 December 1821. Libretto: J.L. Casper. Edn: Unpublished.

Die beiden Neffen, oder der Onkel aus Boston (comic opera in 3 acts). Date: 6 November 1823. Libretto: J.L. Casper. Edn: Unpublished

[Die Heimkehr] aus der Fremde [Son and Stranger], Op. posth. 89 (Liederspiel in 1 act). Date: 12–31 December 1829. Libretto: Karl Klingemann. Edn: Leipzig: Breitkopf & Härtel [1851] and London: Ewer, [1851] (PS by FMB, with English text by Henry F. Chorley); R xv.

Incidental Music to Caldéron de la Barca's *The Steadfast Prince [Der standhafte Prinz]*. Date: 18 March 1833. Edn: Unpublished.

Incidental Music to Victor Hugo's *Ruy Blas*, Op. posth. 95. Date: 14 February–8 March 1839. Edn: Leipzig: Kistner [1851](PS 4 hands and FS—overture only), [1853] (PS—Lied, Op. 77, no. 3); London: Ewer, [1851] (PS 4 hands—overture only); R xviii.

Incidental Music to Sophocles' *Oedipus at Colonos*, Op. posth. 93. Date: 25 February 1845–2 August 1846. Edn: Leipzig: Breitkopf & Härtel, [1851] (PS and vocal parts), [1852] (FS and orch parts for overture); London: Ewer, [1851] (PS and vocal parts, words by W. Bartholomew); R xv.

Incidental Music to Racine's *Athalia*, Op. posth. 74. Date: May 1843–12 November 1845. Edn: London: Ewer, [1848] (PS); Leipzig: Breitkopf & Härtel, [1848/49] (PS, PS 4 hands, parts for overture, and FS); R xv.

Die Lorelei, **Op. posth. 98** (opera in 3 acts; inc.). Date: [ca. 1847]. Libretto: E. Geibel. Edn: Leipzig: Breitkopf & Härtel [1852] (PS, PS without words, PS 4 hands without words); London: Ewer, [1852] (PS and PS 4 hands—finale to Act I only; English texts by W. Bartholomew), [1868] (PS and PS 4 hands—"Ave Maria" and "Winzer-Chor" only, published individually); Leipzig: Rieter-Biederman (PS and PS 4 hands—"Ave Maria" and "Winzer-Chor" only, published individually); R xv.

B. Orchestral Works (Symphonies, Overtures, and Concertos)

1. Published by Mendelssohn

Symphony No. 1 in C minor, Op. 11 (orch). Date: [1824]–1829. Edn:

London: Cramer, Addison, & Beale, [1830] (PS 4 hnds with vn, vc ad lib); Berlin: Schlesinger, [1834] (parts and PS 4 hnds, and PS of Allegro only), [1847/48] (FS); R i.

Overture to *A Midsummer Night's Dream*, Op. 21 [*Ein Sommernachtstraum*] (orch). Date: 6 August 1826–10 July [1832]. Edn: London: Cramer, Addison, & Beale, [1832](PS 4 hnds by FMB and parts); Leipzig: Breitkopf & Härtel, [1832] (PS 4 hnds by FMB and parts), [1833/34] (PS),[1835] (FS); R ii.

Remarks: Often performed with Op. 61 incidental music (see p. 228, above).

Capriccio brillant, **Op. 22** (pf, orch). Date: 18 September 1831–18 May 1832. Edn: Leipzig: Breitkopf & Härtel, and London: Mori & Lavenue, [1832] (parts and PS serving as pf solo arrangement), [1843] (PS 4 hands), [1862] (FS); R viii.

Piano Concerto No. 1 in G Minor, Op. 25 (pf, orch). Date: [1830–31]. Edn: London: Mori & Lavenue, [1832], and Leipzig: Breitkopf & Härtel, [1833] (parts); *idem*, [1862] (FS); R viii.

The Hebrides **Overture, Op. 26** *[Die Hebriden]* (orch). Date: 7–11 August 1829–20 June 1832. Edn: Leipzig: Breitkopf & Härtel, [1833] (PS 4 hands by FMB), [1834] (parts and PS), [1835] (FS); London: Mori & Lavenue; R ii.

Calm Sea and Prosperous Voyage **Overture** *[Meeresstille und glückliche Fahrt]*, **Op. 27**. Date: [1828–35]. Edn: Leipzig: Breitkopf & Härtel, and London: Mori & Lavenue [1835] (PS, PS 4 hands, parts, and score); R ii.

Rondo brillant **in E-flat major, Op. 29** (pf, orch). Date: 29 January–14 March 1834. Edn: London: Mori & Lavenue, [1834] (parts); Leipzig: Breitkopf & Härtel, [1834/35] (parts), [1835] (PS 4 hands), [1865] (FS); R viii.

The Fair Melusine **Overture** *[Ouvertüre zum Mährchen der schönen Melusine]* **Op. 32** (orch). Date: 14 November 1833–21 January 1836. Edn: Leipzig, Breitkopf & Härtel, [1836]; R ii.

Piano Concerto No. 2 in D minor, Op. 40 (pf, orch). Date: 26 July–5 August 1837. Edn: London: Novello, and Leipzig: Breitkopf & Härtel [1838] (pf and string parts), [1862] (FS); R viii.

Serenade and Allegro giojoso, **Op. 43** (pf, orch). Date: 1 April 1838. Edn: London: Novello, and Bonn: Simrock [1839] (orch parts and pf part serving as pf solo arr.); [1860] (FS); R viii.

Overture in C Major for Wind Instruments, Op. 24 (wind insts/winds and perc). Date: 27 June 1826–Christmas 1838. Edn: London: Cramer, Addison & Beale, and Bonn: Simrock, [1839] (parts, PS, and PS 4 hands by C. Czerny), [1852] (FS); R vii.

[Symphony No. 2]. See *Lobgesang, eine Symphonie-Kantate nach Worten der heiligen Schrift*, Op. 52, under "Accompanied Secular Choral," below (p. 233).

Symphony No. 3 in A Minor, Op. 56 ("Scottish"). Date: 30 July 1829–20 January 1842. Edn: London: Ewer, [1842], Leipzig: Breitkopf & Härtel, [1842] (PS 4 hnds, arr. by FMB), [1843] (score and parts); R i.

Violin Concerto in E Minor, Op. 64 (vn, orch). Date: 16 September 1844–[1845]. Edn: Leipzig: Breitkopf & Härtel, [1845] (parts and PS with vn), [1851] (PS 4 hands), [1862] (score); R iv.

2.   Unpublished and Posthumously Published Orchestral Works

[Concerto Movement] ("Rezitativo—allegro") in D Minor (pf/str). Date: 7 March–12 April 1820. Edn: Unpublished.

Sinfonia No. 1 in C Major (str). Date: [Before 5 September 1821]. Edn: L i.

Sinfonia No. 2 in D Major (str). Date: [Before 5 September 1821]. Edn: L i.

Sinfonia No. 3 in E Minor (str). Date: [Before 5 September 1821]. Edn: L i.

Sinfonia No. 4 in C Minor (str). Date: 5 September 1821. Edn: L i.

Sinfonia No. 5 in B-flat Major (str). Date: 15 September 1821. Edn: L i.

Sinfonia No. 6 in E-flat Major (str). Date: [?autumn 1821]. Edn: L I.

Sinfonia No. 7 in D Minor (str). Date: [?1821–22]. Edn: L i.

Sinfonia No. 8 in D Major (str/orch). Date: 6–30 November 1822. Edn: L i.

Violin Concerto in D Minor (vn, str). Date: 1822. Edn: Yehudi Menuhin (New York: Peters, 1952) (PS); L ii (FS).

Piano Concerto in A Minor (pf, str). Date: [1822]. Edn: L ii.

Sinfonia No. 9 in C Major (str). Date: 12 March–26 December 1823. Edn: L i.

Double Concerto in D Minor (pf, vn, str). Date: 6 May 1823. Edn: L ii.

Sinfonia No. 10 in B Minor (str). Date: 13 May 1823–18 May 1823. Edn: L i.

Sinfonia No. 11 in F Minor (str). Date: 14 June–12 July 1823. Edn: L i.

Sinfonia No. 12 in G Minor (str). Date: 27 August–17 September 1823. Edn: L i.

Concerto in E Major for Two Pianos (2 pf, orch). Date: 17 October 1823. Edn: L ii.

Sinfonia No. 13 in C Minor (1 movement only) (str). Date: 29 December [1823]. Edn: L i.

Concerto in A-flat for Two Pianos (2 pf, orch). Date: 5 September–12 November 1824. Edn: L ii

Symphony "No. 5" in D Minor, Op. posth. 107 ("Reformation") (orch). Date: 12 May 1830–11 November 1832. Edn: Bonn: Simrock, and London: Novello, Ewer & Co., [1868] (parts, PS, PS 4 hands, FS); R i.

Concert Piece in F, Op. posth. 113 (cl, bassett-hn, orch). Date: 6 January 1833. Edn: Christian Rudolf Riedel (Wiesbaden: Breitkopf & Härtel, 1989). See also posthumously published chamber music (p.255).

Overture in C Major, Op. posth. 101 ("Trumpet") (orch). Date: 4 March 1826–10 April 1833. Edn: Leipzig: Breitkopf & Härtel, [1867] (PS, PS 4 hands, FS); R i.

Symphony "No. 4" in A Major, Op. posth. 90 ("Italian") (orch). Date: 13 March 1833–[June 1834]. Edn: Leipzig: Breitkopf & Härtel, and London: Ewer, [1851] (parts, PS, PS 4 hands, FS); R i. Facsimile Edn: Ed. John Michael Cooper and Hans-Günter Klein (Wiesbaden: Ludwig-Reichert-Verlag, 1997).

Fantasie und Variationen über [Carl Maria von Weber's] *Preziosa* (2 pf, orch). Date: May 1833. Edn: Unpublished.

[Three Marches for Harmonie Musik in E-flat] (ww). Date: [?ca. 1833–34]. Edn: Roger Garrett, (Ft. Lauderdale, Fla.: Bauerbach, 1999).

Trauermarsch, Op. posth. 103 (orch). Date: [ca. 8 May 1836]. Edn: Leipzig: Rieter-Biedermann, [1868] (parts, PS, PS 4 hands, FS); R vii.

[Symphony in B-flat] (orch) (inc.). Date: [ca. 1838–39]. Edn: Unpublished.

Ruy Blas **Overture**, Op. posth. 95 (orch). Date: 8 March 1831. Edn: Leipzig: Kistner, [1851].

Marsch [in D] componirt zur Feyer der Anwesenheit des Malers Cornelius in Dresden, April 1841, Op. posth. 108 (orch). Date: [1841]. Edn: Leipzig: Rieter-Biedermann, [1868] (parts, PS, PS 4 hands, FS); R iii.

Piano Concerto in E Minor (pf, orch) (inc.). Date: [ca.1842–44]). Edn: Unpublished.

Symphony in C Major (orch). Date: [ca. 1844–45]. Edn: Unpublished.

Not dated:

[Orchestral movement in G minor/C major] (orch). Edn: Unpublished.

C. **Accompanied Secular Choral Works**

1.   Published by Mendelssohn

Lobgesang: Eine Symphonie-Cantate nach Worten der heiligen Schrift, **Op. 52** *[Hymn of Praise]*. Date: July–27 November 1840. Edn: Leipzig: Breitkopf & Härtel, and London: Novello, [1841] (parts, PS, FS); R xiv; Douglass Seaton, ed. (Stuttgart: Carus, 1989); ed. Wulf Konold (Wiesbaden: Breitkopf & Härtel, 1998).

Die erste Walpurgisnacht, **Op. 60**. Date: 15 July 1831–15 July 1843. Text: Goethe. Edn: Leipzig: Kistner, and London: Ewer, [1844] (parts, PS, FS); R xv.

(Festgesang) An die Künstler **Op. 68** (male vv, brass). Date: 19 April 1846. Text: Schiller. Edn: Bonn: Simrock, and London: Ewer, [1846] (parts, PS, FS); R xv.

2.   Unpublished and Posthumously Published Accompanied Secular Choral Works

In rührend feierlichen Tönen (wedding cantata) (SATB solos, ch, pf). Date: 13 June 1820 [*recte* 1821]. Text: ?. Edn: Unpublished.

Große Festmusik zum Dürerfest (solo vv, ch, orch). Date: before 18 April 1828. Text: Levetzow. Edn: Hatteberg (no 618).

Begrüßung ("Humboldt Cantata") (solo vv, ch, orch). Date: 12 September 1828. Edn: Unpublished.

Festgesang (**"Möge das Siegeszeichen"**) (ch, pf). Date: 30 March 1838. Edn: Christoph Hellmundt (Leipzig: Breitkopf & Härtel, [1997]).

Festgesang ("Gutenberg" Cantata) (male ch, orch). Date: before 25 June 1840. Edn: Leipzig: Breitkopf & Härtel, [1840] (PS); London: Ewer & Co., [1844] (version for mixed chorus—PS); R xv.

Gott segne Sachsenland ("Lied zur Feier der Enthüllung der Statue Friedrich August von Sachsen") (double male ch, brass). Date: 2 June 1843. Edn: Reinhard Kapp, in *Richard Wagner: Sämtliche Werke, Bd. 16: Chorwerke mit einer Dokumentation zum Thema Wagner und der Chor und zu den Chorwerken Wagners* (Mainz: Schott, 1993), 219–23.

D. Concert Arias (All Unpublished or Posthumously Published)

Che vuoi mio cor? (A FS, str). Text: ?. Date: [?1823]. Edn: Berlin, [n.p.], [1880] (PS by A. Matthias, German text in Berlin edn. by W. Osterwald) and Milan: F. Lucia.

Ch'io t'abbandono (bar, pf). Text: Metastasio. Date: 5 September 1825. Edn: Unpublished.

Tutto è silenzio (S, orch) (inc.). Text: ?. Date: 23 February 1829. Edn: Unpublished.

Infelice!/Ah, ritorna, età dell' oro (S, orch). Text: Metastasio. Date: 3 April 1834. Edn: Unpublished.

Infelice!/Ah, ritorna, età felice [Unglückseel'ge!/Kehret wieder, gold'ne Tage], Op. posth. 94 (S, orch). Text: Metastasio. Date: 15 January 1843. Edn: Leipzig: Breitkopf & Härtel [1851 (words in Italian and German)] (parts, PS, FS); London: Ewer, [1851 (words in Italian and English)] (parts, PS, FS).

On Lena's Gloomy Heath (bar, orch). Text: Ossian [J. Macpherson]. Date: [ca. 1846]. Edn: Unpublished.

Not dated:

O lasst mich einen Augenblick noch hier (B, orch) (inc.). Text: Goethe. Edn: Unpublished.

E. Choral Songs

1. Published by Mendelssohn

NB: Songs are identified first by text incipit, then by title(s).

Six Songs for Four-Part Mixed Chorus, to Be Sung Outdoors [Sechs vierstimmige Lieder . . . im Freien zu Singen], [vol. 1], Op. 41

(SATB). Edn: Leipzig: Breitkopf & Härtel, [1838], and London: Ewer, [1844 (PS with English texts)]; R xvi.

No. 1. Ihr Vögel in den Zweigen schwank ("Im Walde"). Text: Platen. Date: January 1838.

No. 2. Entflieh 'mit mir. Text: Heine. Date: [22 January 1834]–22 May 1835.

No. 3. Es fiel ein Reif. Text: Heine. Date: [22 January 1834]–22 May 1835.

No. 4. Auf ihrem Grab. Text: Heine. Date: [22 January 1834]–22 May 1835.

No. 5. Der Schnee zerrinnt ("Mailied"). Text: Hölty. Date: 23 November 1837.

No. 6. Und frische Nahrung ("Auf dem See"). Text: Goethe. Date: 6 April 1839.

Six Songs for Four-Part Mixed Chorus, to Be Sung Outdoors [Sechs vierstimmige Lieder . . . im Freien zu Singen], Vol. 2, Op. 48 (SATB). Edn: Leipzig: Breitkopf & Härtel, [1840], and London: Ewer [1844 (PS with English texts)]; R xvi.

No. 1. O sanfter süsser Hauch ("Frühlingsahnung," "Am ersten Frühlingstag"). Text: Uhland. Date: 5 July 1839.

No. 2. Liebliche Blume ("Die Primel"). Text: Lenau. Date: [1839]

No. 3. Süsser, goldner Frühlingstag ("Frühlingsfeier"). Text: Uhland. Date: 28 December 1839.

No. 4. Wie lieblicher Klang ("Lerchengesang," "Canon"). Text: ?. Date: 15–19 June 1839. Facsimile: In Schneider (no. 84).

No. 5. O wunderbares tiefes Schweigen ("Morgengebet"). Text: Eichendorff. Date: 18 November 1839.

No. 6. Holder Lenz, du bist dahin ("Herbstlied," "Herbstklage"). Text: Lenau. Date: 26 December 1839.

Lieblich mündet der Becher Wein ("Ersatz für Unbestand") (male vv). Text: Rückert. Date: 22 November 1839. Edn: In *Deutscher Musenalmanach* (Leipzig: Kistner, [1839]) and independently by Leipzig: Kistner, [1840] R xvii.

Six Songs for Four-part Male Chorus [Sechs Lieder für vierstimmigen Männerchor], Op. 50 (4 male vv). Edn: Leipzig: Kistner, [1840], and London: Ewer, [1844 (words in English by W. Bartholomew) R xvii.

No. 1. Setze mir nicht, du Grobian ("Türkisches Schenkenlied," "Türkisches Trinklied"). Text: Goethe. Date: [1838].

No. 2. Wer hat dich, du schöner Wald ("Der Jäger Abschied," "Der deutsche Wald"). Text: Eichendorff. Date: 6 January 1840.

No. 3. Wie Feld und Au' so blinkend im Thau ("Sommerlied"). Text: Goethe. Date: [1837].

No. 4. Am fernen Horizonte ("Wasserfahrt"). Text: Heine. Date: [ca. February 1837].

No. 5. Was quälte dir dein armes Herz? Liebesschmerz. ("Liebe und Wein," "Vin à tout prix"). Text: ?. Date: 7 December 1839.

No. 6. Vom Grund bis zu den Gipfeln ("Wanderlied"). Text: Eichendorff. Date: 6 January 1840.

Six Songs for Four-Part Mixed Chorus, to Be Sung Outdoors [Sechs vierstimmige Lieder . . . im Freien zu Singen], Vol. 3, Op. 59 (SATB). Edn: Leipzig: Breitkopf & Härtel, [1843], and London: Ewer, [1843 (words in English by W. Bartholomew)]; R xvi.

No. 1. Im Grün erwacht der frische Muth ("Im Grünen"). Text: Chézy. Date: 23 November 1837 [ca. March 1843].

No. 2. Tage der Wonne, kommt ihr so bald ("Frühzeitiger Frühling"). Text: Goethe. Date: 17 June 1843.

No. 3. O Thäler weit, o Höhen ("Abschied vom Wald"). Text: Eichendorff. Date: 3–4 March 1843.

No. 4. Die Nachtigall, sie war entfernt ("Die Nachtigall," "Canon"). Text: Goethe. Date: 19 June 1843–12 July 1845. Facsimile of 12.07.45 in Ernst Wolff (no. 98), facing p. 168.

No. 5. Wann im letzten Abendstrahl ("Ruhethal"). Text: Uhland. Date: 4 March 1843.

No. 6. Durch schwankende Wipfel ("Jagdlied," "Vorüber"). Text: Eichendorff. Date: 5 March 1843.

2. Unpublished and Posthumously Published Choral Songs

Einst ins Schlaraffenland zogen (4 male vv). Date: [1820]. Edn: Unpublished.

Lieb und Hoffnung (4 male vv). Date: [1820]. Edn: Unpublished.

Kein bess're Lust in dieser Zeit ("Jägerlied") (4 male vv). Date: 20 April 1822. Text: Uhland. Edn: Unpublished.

Seht, Freunde, die Gläser ("Lob des Weins") (solo male vv, male ch). Date: [1822]. Edn: Unpublished.

Wenn der Abendwind durch die Wipfel zieht (SAT). Date: 23 August 1828. Edn: Unpublished.

Lasset heut am edlen Ort (SATB). Date: 25 December 1828. Text: Goethe. Edn: Unpublished. Facsimile: *Festlied zu Zelters siebzig-sten Geburtstag am 11. Dezember 1828* (Leipzig: Bibliographisches Institut, [1928])

Der weise Diogenes (canon, 4 male vv). Date: 11 February 1833. Text: R. Reinick. Edn: Unpublished. Facsimile: In supplement to *Die Musik* 8/2 (1908–9).

Seht doch diese Fiedlerbänden ("Musikantenprügelei") (4 male vv). Date: 23 April 1833. Text: R. Reinick. Edn: In Kopfermann (no. 641).

Worauf kommt es überall an ("Dreistigkeit") (4 male vv). Date: 23 February 1837. Edn: Unpublished.

Trunken müssen wir alle sein ("Lob der Trunkenheit") (4 male vv). Date: [1838]. Text: Goethe. Edn: Unpublished.

Wozu der Vöglein Chöre belauschen ("Lied aus Ruy Blas"). See *Incidental Music to Victor Hugo's Ruy Blas*, Op. 95, above, and Op. 77, below.

Schlummernd an des Vaters Brust ("Nachtgesang") (4 male vv). Date: 15 January 1842. Edn: In *Repertorium für deutschen Männergesang* 2 (Leipzig: Kahnt, [1856]); R xvii.

Auf, Freunde, laßt das Jahr uns singen ("Die Stiftungsfeier," "Lied für die Stiftungsfeier der Gesellschaft der Freunde der Musik in Berlin") (SATB). Date: 15 January 1842. Edn: In *Repertorium für deutschen Männergesang* 3 (Leipzig: Kahnt, [1859]); R xvii.

Wohl perle im Glase der purpurne Wein ("Die Frauen und die Sänger") (SATB). Date: 25 January 1846. Text: Schiller. Edn: Unpublished. Facsimile in Schneider, (no. 84).

Six Songs for Four-part Male Chorus [Sechs Lieder für vierstimmigen Männerchor], Vol. 2, Op. posth. 75 (4 male vv). Edn: Leipzig: Kistner, [1849], and London: Ewer, [1849 (words in English)]; R xvii.

No. 1. Wem Gott will rechte Gunst erweisen ("Der frohe

Wandersmann"). Date: 8 February–24 November 1844. Text: Eichendorff.

No. 2. Schlafe, Liebchen, weil's auf Erden ("Abendständchen," "Ständchen"). Date: 14 November 1839. Text: Eichendorff.

No. 3. So lang man nüchtern ist ("Trinklied," "Trinklied aus dem Divan"). Date: [ca. February 1837]. Text: Goethe.

No. 4. So rückt denn in die Runde ("Abschiedstafel"). Date: 12 February ?1838–November 1844. Text: Eichendorff.

Four Songs for Four-part Male Chorus [Vier Lieder für vierstimmigen Männerchor], Vol. 3, Op. posth. 76 (4 male vv). Edn: London: Ewer, [1849 (words in English)], and Leipzig: Breitkopf & Härtel, [1850]; R xvii.

No. 1. Gaben mir Rath und gute Lehren ("Das Lied vom braven Mann"). Date: [1837]. Text: Heine.

No. 2. Wo solch' ein Feuer noch gedeiht ("Rheinweinlied"). Date: 9 February 1844. Text: Herwegh.

No. 3. Was uns einst als deutsche Brüder ("Lied für die Deutschen in Lyon"). Date: 8 October 1846. Text: Stoltze.

No. 4. Nun zu guter Letzt ("Comitat"). Date: 14 September 1847. Text: von Fallersleben.

Six Songs for Four-part Mixed Chorus [Sechs vierstimmige Lieder], vol. 4, Op. posth. 88 (SATB). Edn: London: Ewer, [1850/51 (words in English by W. Bartholomew)], and Leipzig: Breitkopf & Härtel, [1850/51]; R xvi.

No. 1. Mit der Freude zieht der Schmerz ("Neujahrslied"). Date: 8 August 1844–1 October 1845. Text: Hebbel.

No. 2. Ich hab' ein Liebchen ("Der Glückliche"). Date: 20 June 1843. Text: Eichendorff.

No. 3. O Winter, schlimmer Winter ("Hirtenlied"). Date: 14–19 June 1839. Facs: in Schneider (no. 84) [See also Op. 57, no. 2.]

No. 4. Kommt, lasst uns geh'n spazieren ("Die Waldvöglein"). Date: 19 June 1843. Text: Schütz.

No. 5. Durch tiefe Nacht ein Brausen zieht ("Deutschland"). Text: Geibel.

No. 6.   Durch Feld und Buchenhallen ("Der wandernde Musikant"). Date: 10 March 1840–ca. March 1843. Text: Eichendorff.

Four Songs for Four-part Mixed Chorus [Vier vierstimmige Lieder], Vol. 5, Op. posth. 100 (SATB). Edn: Leipzig: Breitkopf & Härtel, [1852], and London: Ewer, [1852 (words in English)]; R xvi.

No. 1.   Die Bäume grünen überall ("Andenken"). Date: 8 August 1844–1 October 1845. Text: Hoffmann von Fallersleben.

No. 2.   Saatengrün, Veilchenduft ("Lob des Frühlings"). Date: 20 June 1843. Text: Uhland.

No. 3.   Berg und Thal will ich durchstreifen ("Frühlingslied"). Date: [?1843–44]. Text: ?.

No. 4.   O Wald, du kühlender Bronnen ("Im Wald," "Waldlust"). Date: 14–19 June 1839. Text: ?.

Four Songs for Four-part Male Chorus [Vier Lieder für vierstimmigen Männerchor], Op. posth. 120 (4 male vv). Edn: Leipzig: Breitkopf & Härtel, 1874; R xvii.

No. 1.   Auf, ihr Herrn und Damen schön ("Jagdlied," "Jagdgesang"). Date: 27 November 1837.

No. 2.   Seid gegrüßet, traute Brüder ("Morgengruß des thüringischen Sängerbundes"). Date: 20 February 1847. Text: ?.

No. 3.   Süsse Düfte, milde Lüfte ("Im Süden"). Date: 24 November 1837. Text: ?.

No. 4.   Im Nebelgeriesel, im tiefen Schnee ("Zigeunerlied"). Text: Goethe.

Sahst du ihn herniederschweben, Op. posth. 116 (mixed vv). Date: 8 July 1845. Text: F. Aulenbach. Edn: Leipzig: J. Rieter-Biedermann, [1869]; R xiv; Wm. A. Little (1995).

Not dated:

In Frankfurt auf der Zeile, da steht ein junger Mann (2 male vv). Edn: Unpublished.

F.   **Songs and Vocal Duets**

1. Published by Mendelssohn

NB: Songs are identified first by text incipit, then by title(s).

Twelve Songs [Zwölf Gesänge], Op. 8. Edn: Berlin: Schlesinger, [1828], and London: Ewer, [1845 (nos. 1–11 only—words in English and German; English texts by W. Bartholomew)]; R xix.

1. Holder klingt der Vogelsang ("Minnelied"). Text: Hölty.

4. Es ist ein Schnitter, der heisst Tod ("Erntelied"). Text: from *Des Knaben Wunderhorn*. Date: 24 January 1824.

5. Lass dich nur nichts nicht dauern ("Pilgerspruch"). Text: P. Flemming. Also published with English text in *Apollo's Gift, or the Musical Souvenir* (London: S. Chappell, 1829).

6. Jetzt kommt der Frühling ("Frühlingslied, in schwäbischer Mundart"). Text: Robert. Date: 2 April 1824. Also published as "Maid of the Valley" (English text by W.E. Attfield) in *The Musical Gem: A Souvenir for 1834* (London: Mori & Lavenu, [1833]).

7. Man soll hören süsses Singen ("Maienlied"). Text: Jakob von der Warte.

8. Die Schwalbe flügt ("Andres Maienlied," "Hexenlied"). Text: Hölty.

9. Das Tagewerk ist abgethan ("Abendlied"). Text: J.H. Voss.

10. Einmal aus seinen Blicken ("Romanze, aus dem Spanischen"). Text: F. Voigts?

11. Willkommen im Grünen ("Im Grünen"). Text: J.H. Voss.

Composed by Fanny Mendelssohn and published in Op. 8:

2. Was ist's, das mir den Athem hemmet ("Das Heimweh"). Text: F. Robert.

3. Schöner und schöner schmückt sich der Plan ("Italien"). Text: F. Grillparzer.

12. Duet: An des lust'gen Brunnens Rand ("Suleika und Hatem"). Text: Goethe (Marianne von Willmer?). Edn: R xviii, xix.

Twelve Songs [Zwölf Lieder], Op. 9. Edn: Berlin: Schlesinger, [1830], and London: Ewer, [1845 (words in English and German; English texts by W. Bartholomew)]; R xix.

1. Ist es wahr? ("Frage"). Text: "H. Voss." Also published with the title "Is it true?" (text by Walter Thornton) in *The Musical Gem: A Souvenir for 1834* (London: Mori & Lavenu, [1833]).

2. Kennst du nicht das Gluthverlangen ("Geständnis," "Frage"). Text: ? Date: 3 December 1831.

3. Sie trug einen Falken auf ihrer Hand ("Wartend: Romanze"). Text: Droysen. Date: 3 April 1829.

4. Ihr frühlingstrunknen Blumen ("Im Frühling"). Text: Droysen. Date: 27 January 1830–6 December 1845.

5. Ach, wie schnell die Tage fliehen ("Im Herbst"). Text: K. Klingemann. Date: 6 August 1830–21 November 1843.

6. Wie so gelinde der Fluth bewegt ("Scheidend," "Auf der Fahrt"). Text: "H. Voss." Date:13 January 1830–August 1830.

   Remarks: The opening measures are alluded to in the *Calm Sea and Prosperous Voyage* Overture, Op. 27 (see p. 230, above).

8. Die linden Lüfte sind erwacht ("Frühlingsglaube"). Text: Uhland. Date: 19 January 1830–27 January 1830.

9. In weite Ferne will ich träumen ("Ferne"). Text: Droysen.

11. Herr, zu dir will ich mich retten ("Entsagung"). Text: Droysen. Date: 30 May 1832.

Composed by Fanny Mendelssohn and published in Op. 9:

7. Fern und ferner schallt der Reigen ("Sehnsucht"). Text: Droysen.

10. Und wüssten's die Blumen ("Verlust"). Text: Heine.

12. Im stillen Klostergarten ("Die Nonne"). Text: Uhland.

Far from the moveless dark bright eye ("Charlotte und Werther"). Edn: As "Charlotte to Werter," with text by W. F. Collard, in *Apollo's Gift, or the Musical Souvenir for 1831* (London: S. Chappell, [1830]). Date: 1829.

   Remarks: The music of this song was reused for "Es freut sich Alles weit und breit" ("Seemans Scheidelied,") text by Hoffmann von Fallersleben, published in 1850. Mendelssohn had nothing to do with this retexting, however, or with the others published by Hoffmann von Fallersleben in the 1850s.

Leg in den Sarg mir mein grünes Gewand ("Todeslied der Bojaren") (male vv, pf). Edn: In K. Immermann, *Alexis* (Düsseldorf: Schaub, 1832); R xix. Date: [before 12 December 1831]–3 October 1841.

Trala, a frischer Bua bin i (TT). Edn: In K. Immermann, *Andreas Hofer* (Düsseldorf: Schaub, 1834). Date: 9 December 1833)

Six Songs [Sechs Gesänge], Op. 19[a] (S, pf). Edn: Leipzig: Breitkopf & Härtel, [1833], and London: Ewer [1845 (words in English and German; English texts by William Bartholomew)]; R xix.

1. In dem Walde süße Töne ("Frühlingslied"). Text: Ulrich von Lichtenstein. Date: 21 February–24 February 1830.

2. Als ich das erste Veilchen erblickt ("Das erste Veilchen," "Der ersten Liebe Verlust," "Der erste Verlust"). Text: E. Ebert. Date: 24 September 1831–4 July 1832.

3. Mein Sohn, wo willst du hin so spät? ("Winterlied, aus dem Schwedischen," "Volkslied"). Text: folksong.

4. In dem Mondenschein im Walde ("Neue Liebe"). Text: Heine.

5. Leise zieht durch mein Gemüth ("Gruß," "Frühlingslied"). Text: Heine. Date: 19 September 1832–22 December 1836.

6. Bringet des treusten Herzens Grüsse ("Reiselied," "In die Ferne"). Text: Ebert. Date: 16 October 1830–January 1831.

Two Eichendorff Lieder. Edn: Supplement to *Neue Zeitschrift für Musik 8* (1838), and Elberfeld: Arnold, [1850/51]; R xix.

1. Und wo noch kein Wandrer gegangen ("Das Waldschloß," "Die Waldfrauen"). Text: Eichendorff. Date: 7 August 1835.

2. Wenn die Sonne lieblich schiene ("Pagenlied," "Auf der Reise," "Der wandernde Musikant," "Der Zitherspieler"). Text: Eichendorff. Date: 25 December 1832–1 October 1835.

Six Songs [Sechs Gesänge], Op. 34 (S, pf) Edn: Leipzig: Breitkopf & Härtel, [1837], and London: Ewer, [1845/46 (words in English and German; English texts by W. Bartholomew)]; R xix.

1. Leucht heller als die Sonne ("Minnelied," "Mailied"). Text: from *Des Knaben Wunderhorn*. Date: 11 May 1834–22 December 1836. Facsimile: In Wolff, (no. 98), facing p. 129.

2. Auf Flügeln des Gesanges ("Abendlied"). Text: Heine. Date: [ca. August–December 1835] 1 October 1835. Facsimile in Wolff (no. 98), facing p. 92.

3. Es brechen im schallenden Reigen ("Frühlingslied"). Text: K. Klingemann.

4. Ach, um deine feuchten Schwingen ("Suleika"). Text: Goethe (i.e., Marianne von Willemer).

   Remarks: See also under unpublished songs, below (p. 250).

5. Ringsum erschallt in Wald und Flur ("Sonntags," "Sonntagslied"). Text: K. Klingemann. Date: 28 December 1834–31 January 1836. Facsimile in Ernst Wolff, *Felix Mendelssohn Bartholdy* (no 98), facing p. 127).

6. Der Herbstwind rüttelt die Bäume ("Reiselied"). Text: Heine.

Two Byron Romances (S, pf). Edn: in *Album Musical auf das Jahr 1837* (Leipzig: Breitkopf & Härtel, 1836), and independently (Leipzig: Breitkopf & Härtel, [1837]); R xix.

1. There Be None of Beauty's Daughters ("Keiner von der Erde Schönen"). Date: 3 August 1833.

2. Sun of the Sleepless ("Schlafloser Augen," "Erinnerung"). Date: 31 December 1834–[ca. 1835].

Six Songs [Sechs Lieder], Op. 47 (S, pf). Edn: Leipzig: Breitkopf & Härtel, [1839], and London: Ewer, [1846 (words in English and German; English texts by W. Bartholomew)]; R xix.

1. Wie der Quell so lieblich klinget ("Minnelied," "Im Walde"). Text: L. Tieck. Date: 15 August 1838–Christmas 1845.

2. Über die Berge steigt schon die Sonne ("Morgengruß"). Text: Heine. Date: Christmas 1845.

3. Durch den Wald, den dunklen ("Frühlingslied"). Text: Lenau. Date: 17 April 1839–Christmas 1845.

4. Es ist bestimmt in Gottes Rath ("Volkslied"). Text: E. von Feuchtersleben. Date: 18 April 1839.

5. Sie wandelt im Blumengarten ("Der Blumenstrauß"). Text: Klingemann. Date: 5 May 1832–Christmas 1845.

6. Schlummre und träume ("Bei der Wiege," "Wiegenlied"). Text: Klingemann. Date: 15 August 1833–[?ca. April 1839]. Facsimile: In Moscheles (no. 313).

Wozu der Vöglein Chöre belauschen ("Lied aus *Ruy Blas*") (2 vv, pf). Text: Hugo. Edn: In A. Schmidt, ed., *Orpheus: musikalisches Taschenbuch auf das Jahr 1840* (Leipzig and Vienna: F. Riedl, 1839). See *Incidental music to Victor Hugo's Ruy Blas,* above, and Op. posth. 77, no. 3, below.

[Drei zweistimmige Volkslieder] (2 vv, pf). Edn: R xviii; first published individually, and then together by Schlesinger in [1857].

1. Wie kann ich froh und lustig sein. Text: P. Kaufmann. Edn: In *Album neuer Original-Compositionen für Gesang und Piano* (Berlin: Schlesinger, [1837]). Date: 3 September 1837.

2. Wenn ich auf dem Lager liege ("Abendlied"). Text: Heine. Edn: In *Album neuer Original-Compositionen für Gesang und Piano* (Berlin: Schlesinger, [1838]). Date: 3 September 1837–19

January 1840.

3. Ich stand gelehnet an den Mast ("Wasserfahrt"). Text: Heine. Edn: In *Album neuer Original-Compositionen für Gesang und Piano* (Berlin: Schlesinger, [1838/39]).

By Celia's Arbour All the Night [An Celias Baum in stiller Nacht] ("The Garland," "Der Blumenkranz") (S, pf). Text: T. Moore. Edn: London: Ewer, and Braunschweig: Spehr, [1841]; R xix. Date: 24 May 1829–6 February 1841.

Six Songs [Sechs Lieder], Op. 57 (S, pf). Edn: Leipzig: Breitkopf & Härtel, [1842/43], London: Wessel & Stapleton, [?1843 (words in English and German; English texts by W. Bartholomew)], and Paris: Grus [1843 (with French texts by L. Delâtre)]; R xix.

1. Es ist in den Wald gesungen ("Altdeutsches Lied"). Text: Heinrich Schreiber. Date: 26 July 1839–Christmas 1845.

2. O Winter, schlimmer Winter ("Hirtenlied," "Des Hirten Winterlied"). Text: Uhland. Date: 20 April 1839 –18 November 1840.

3. Was bedeutet die Bewegung? ("Suleika"). Text: Goethe (i.e., Marianne von Willemer). Date: [1839]–Christmas 1845.

4. Von allen schönen Kindern auf der Welt ("O Jugend, o schöne Rosenzeit," "Rheinisches Volkslied"). Text: Zuccalmaglio. Date: 9 January 1841–Christmas 1845. Facsimile: Sabine Zahn, *Das Niederrheinische Musikfest* 1818–1958: eine Dokumentation (Cologne: n.p., 1984).

5. Wenn durch die Piazzetta die Abendluft weht ("Venetianisches Gondellied," "Rendez-vous"). Text: after Thomas Moore. Date: 17 October 1842–Christmas 1845.

6. Laue Luft kommt blau geflossen ("Wanderlied," "Frische Fahrt"). Text: Eichendorff. Date: 29 April 1841–19 May 1843.

Six Duets [Sechs zweistimmige Lieder], Op. 63 (SS, pf). Edn: Leipzig: Kistner, [1844], and London: Ewer, [1844 (words in English and German)]; R xviii.

1. Ich wollt' meine Lieb'. Text: Heine. Date: 22 December 1836.

2. Wie war so schön doch Wald und Feld ("Abschiedslied der Zugvögel," "Herbstlied"). Text: Hoffmann von Fallersleben. Date: 20 May 1844).

3. Wohin ich geh' und schaue ("Gruß"). Text: Eichendorff. Date:

[ca. December 1836]–26 March 1844.

4. Ach, wie so bald verhallet der Reigen ("Herbstlied"). Text: Klingemann. Date: [1844].

   Remarks: The manuscript version of this Lied bears a different text ("Ach, wie so schnell bist du entschwunden"), possibly not by Klingemann. The piece also exists as a *Lied ohne Worte* 16 October 1836; see unpublished piano solo, below.

5. O säh ich auf der Heide dort ("Volkslied"). Text: after R. Burns. Date: 17 October 1842–Christmas 1845.

6. Maiglöckchen läutet in dem Thal ("Maiglöckchen und die Blümelein"). Text: Hoffmann von Fallersleben. Date: 23 January 1844–[ca. December 1836].

Six Songs [Sechs Lieder], Op. 71 (S, pf). Edn: Leipzig: Breitkopf & Härtel, [1847], and London: Ewer, [1847 (words in English and German)]; R xix.

1. Werde heiter, mein Gemüthe ("Tröstung"). Text: Hoffmann von Fallersleben. Date: 22 December 1845–20 January 1847. Facsimile: In Dahlgren (no. 275) after p. 52.

2. Der Frühling naht mit Brausen ("Frühlingslied," "Frühling"). Text: Klingemann. Date: Christmas 1845–21 March 1846.

3. Diese Rose pflück' ich hier ("An die Entfernte"). Text: Lenau. Date: 22 Sep. 1847.

4. Auf dem Teich, dem regungslosen ("Schilflied," "Die Nacht"). Text: Lenau. Date: 3 November 1842–24 March 1845.

5. Ich wandere fort ins ferne Land ("Auf der Wanderschaft"). Text: Lenau. Date: Christmas 1845–27 July 1847.

6. Vergangen ist der lichte Tag ("Nachtlied"). Text: Eichendorff. Date: Christmas 1845–1 October 1847.

2. Unpublished and Posthumously Published Songs and Vocal Duets

Ihr Töne schwingt euch ("Lied zum Geburtstag meines guten Vaters") (S, pf). Date: 11 December 1819). Facsimile: In Wolff, *Mendelssohn* (no. 98) facing p. 13.

Ave Maria (S, pf). Text: after W. Scott. Date: [1820]. Edn: Unpublished.

Pauvre Jeanette (S, pf). Date: [1820]. Edn: In Todd (no. 226), 148.

Raste Krieger, Krieg ist aus (S, pf). Text: after W. Scott. Date: [1820].

Edn: In Leven, "Mendelssohn als Lyriker" (no. 650).

Da ging ich hin ("Die Nachtigall") (S, pf). Date: [ca. 1821]. Edn: Unpublished.

Nacht ist um mich her ("Der Verlassene") (S, pf). Date: 24 September 1821. Edn: In Leven, "Lyriker" (no. 650).

Ein Tag sagt es dem andern (S, A, "cembalo"). Date: [ca. 1822]. Edn: Unpublished.

Von allen deinen zarten Gaben (S, pf). Edn: In Leven, "Lyriker" (no. 650). Date: 18 September 1822.

Schlummre sanft und milde ("Wiegenlied") (S, pf). Edn: In Leven, "Lyriker" (no. 650). Date: 18 September 1822.

Sanft weh'n im Hauch der Abendluft (S, pf). Text: Matthison. Date: 28 December 1822. Edn: Unpublished.

Rieselt hernieder ("Der Wasserfall") (S, pf). Text: Klingemann. Date: [ca. 1823]. Edn: In Leven, "Lyriker" (no 650).

Er ist zerbrochen ("Faunenklage") (S, pf). Date: 8 June 1823. Edn: Unpublished.

Sicheln schallen (S, pf). Text: Hölty. Date: [ca. June 1823]. Edn: Unpublished.

Tanzt dem schönen Mai entgegen (S, pf). Text: ?. Date: [ca. June 1823]. Edn: Unpublished.

Am Seegestad (S, pf). Text: Matthison. Date: 26 September 1823. Edn: Unpublished.

Durch Fichten (S, pf). Text: Matthison. Date: [ca. September 1823]. Edn: Unpublished.

Ich denke dein (S, pf). Text: Matthisson. Date: 1 October [?1823]. Edn: Unpublished.

Rausche leise, grünes Dach (S, pf). Text: A. von Schlippenbach. Date: [?December 1824]. Edn: Unpublished.

Mitleidsworte, Trostesgründe, neue Dornen diesem Herzen ("Glosse") (S, pf). Text: F. Robert. Date: 1 (or 7?) June 1825. Edn: Unpublished.

Es rauscht der Wald (S, pf). Date: [ca. 1827]. Edn: Unpublished.

[Four Songs] (S, pf). Text: ?. Date: 1 May 1830. Edn: Unpublished.

    1.   Sanft entschwanden mir ("Der Tag")

    2.   Immer fort ("Reiterlied")

3. Leb wohl mein Lieb' ("Abschied")

4. Ich danke Gott ("Der Bettler")

Es freut sich Alles weit und breit ("Seemans Scheidelied"). See "Far from the moveless dark bright eye" ("Charlotte und Werther"), above (p. 241).

Weiter, rastlos, atemlos vorüber ("An Marie") (S, pf). Text: ?. Date: [ca. 1830]—frag. Edn: Carl Reinecke (Munich: Aibl, [1882]).

Remarks: Published with "Erwartung," "An ihrem Grabe," and "Warum ich weine." Edn. gives text in German and French.

Ich reit' ins finstre Land hinein ("Reiselied") (S, pf; inc.). Text: Uhland. Date: 1830. Edn: Unpublished.

Auf, schicke dich recht feierlich ("Weihnachtslied"). Text: C.F. Gellert. Date: 19–20 December 1832. Edn: In Hans Gerber, *Albert Baur: Ein Lebensbild aus der Zeit deutsches musikalischen, religiösen und politischen Aufbruchs im 19. Jahrhundert* (Freiburg im Breisgau: Waldkircher, 1971).

Warum sind denn die Rosen so blaß? (S, pf). Text: Heine. Date: ?May 1834. Edn: Unpublished.

Ich weiß mir'n Mädchen ("Mailied," "Andres Mailied," "Hüt' du dich") (S, pf). Text: from *Des Knaben Wunderhorn*. Date: 14 May 1834. Edn: Unpublished.

Was will die einsame Thräne? ("Erinnerung") (S, pf). Text: Heine. Date: [ca. 17 April 1837]. Edn: Unpublished.

Zarter Blumen leicht Gewinde ("Lied der Freundin," "Die Freundin") (S, pf). Text: Goethe (i.e., Marianne von Willemer). Date: 13 July 1837. Facsimile: Ed. Max Schneider (Düsseldorf: Goethe-Museum and Internationale Felix-Mendelssohn-Gesellschaft, 1960). Edn: Unpublished.

Mein Liebchen, wir sassen beisammen ("Im Kahn," "Auf dem Wasser," "Wasserfahrt") (S, pf). Text: Heine. Date: 12 December 1837–January 1846. Facsimile: in Moscheles, (no. 313). 148.

So schlaf in Ruh'. Text: Hoffmann von Fallersleben. Date: 22 March 1838. Edn: Unpublished.

O könnt' ich zu dir fliegen. Date: 15 August 1838. Edn: Unpublished.

Nun mußt du mich auch recht verstehn ("Auf Wiedersehn") (S, pf). Text:? Date: 25 January 1840. Edn: Unpublished.

An den Rhein, zieh nicht an den Rhein ("Warnung vor dem Rhein")

(S, pf). Text: C. Simrock. Date: [ca. 25 February 1840]. Edn: Bonn: Simrock, [1849]; R xix.

Ich hör ein Vöglein ("Im Frühling") (S, pf). Text: A. Böttger. Date: 20 April 1841–8 July 1841. Edn: in A. Böttger, *Gedichte*, 2nd edn. (Leipzig: Klemm, 1846).

Mein Vater ist ein Appenzeller (S, pf). Text: Folksong. Date: 29 September 1842. Edn: Unpublished.

Der Geissbub bin ich auch noch da (S, pf). Text: Swiss folksong. Date: 29 September 1842. Edn: Unpublished.

Und über dich wohl stimmt (S, pf). Date: 9 July 1844. Edn: Unpublished.

Three Duets [Drei zweistimmige Lieder], Op. posth. 77 (2 vv, pf). Edn: Leipzig: Kistner, [1848/49], and London: Ewer, [1849 (words in English and German)]; R xviii.

1. Das ist der Tag des Herrn ("Sonntagsmorgen," "Sonntagslied," "Morgenlied"). Text: Uhland. Date: 3 December 1836–7 March 1840.

2. Ein Leben war's im Aehrenfeld ("Das Aehrenfeld"). Text: Hoffmann von Fallersleben. Date: 18 January 1847.

3. Wozu der Vöglein Chöre belauschen ("Lied aus Ruy Blas"). See Incidental Music to Victor Hugo's *Ruy Blas*, p. 229, above; see also under song title in Songs and Vocal Duets Published by Mendelssohn.

Three Songs [3 Gesänge], Op. posth. 84 (low v, pf). Edn: Leipzig: Breitkopf & Härtel, [1850/51], and London: Ewer, [1850 (words in English and German)]; R xix.

1. Da lieg' ich unter den Bäumen ("Verschwunden"). Text: Klingemann. Date: 5 December 1831–12 October 1844.

2. Im Walde rauschen dürre Blätter ("Herbstlied"). Text: Klingemann. Date: 26 February 1839.

3. Mit Lust thät ich ausreiten ("Jagdlied"). Text: from *Des Knaben Wunderhorn*. Date: 25 May 1834.

Six Songs [Sechs Gesänge], Op. posth. 86 (v, pf). Edn: London: Ewer, [1850 (words English and German)], and Leipzig: Breitkopf & Härtel, [1850/51]; R xix.

1. Es lauschte das Laub. Text: Klingemann. Date: [ca. 1826].

2. Erwacht in neuer Stärke ("Morgenlied"). Text: J.H. Voss. Date:

3 December 1836–12 May 1846.

3. Ein Blick von deinen Augen ("Die Liebende schreibt"). Text: Goethe. Date: 10 August 1831–25 November 1831.

4. Allnächtlich im Traume seh' ich dich. Text: Heine. Date: [ca. 1837].

5. Mein Herz ist wie die dunkle Nacht ("Der Mond"). Text: Geibel. Date: Christmas 1845–21 March 1846.

6. Der trübe Winter ist vorbei ("Altdeutsches Frühlingslied"). Text: F. von Spee. Date: 7 October 1847.

Six Songs [Sechs Gesänge], Op. posth. 99 (S, pf). Edn: Leipzig: Breitkopf & Härtel, [1852], and London: Ewer, [1852 (words in English and German)]; R xix.

1. Ach, wer bringt die schönen Tage ("Erster Verlust"). Text: Goethe. Date: 9 August 1841.

2. Die Sterne schau'n. Text: A. von Schlippenbach. Date: Unknown.

3. Wisst ihr wo ich gerne weil' ("Lieblingsplätzchen"). Text: F. Robert. Date: [ca. June 1830].

4. Ein Schifflein ziehet leise ("Das Schifflein"). Text: Uhland. Date: 6 June 1841.

5. Wenn sich zwei Herzen scheiden ("Fahrwohl"). Text: Geibel. Date: 22 December 1845–Christmas 1845.

6. Es weiß und rät es doch keiner. Text: Eichendorff. Date: [September 1842].

Not dated:

Bist auf ewig du gegangen ("Erwartung") (S, pf). Edn: Carl Reinecke (Munich: Aibl, [1882]).

Remarks: Published with "An Marie," "An ihrem Grabe," and "Warum ich weine." Edn. gives text in German and French.

Der Eichwald brauset ("Des Mädchens Klage") (S, pf). Text: Schiller. Edn: London: Ewer, and Leipzig: Schuberth, [1866]; R xix. Facsimile in *Emil Naumanns Illustrierte Musikgeschichte* [6th edn., n.d.], before page 537).

Catina belina ("Canzonetta Veneziana") (S, pf). Date: Unknown. Possibly not by Mendelssohn. Edn: Unpublished.

Ein Mädchen wohnt (S, pf). Date: Unknown. Possibly not by

Mendelssohn. Edn: Unpublished.

Ich flocht ein Kränzlein schöner Lieder ("Lieben und Schweigen") (S, pf). Text: Konstantin von Tischendorf. Edn: In *Die musikalische Welt* (1872).

Ich soll bei Tage und bei Nacht (S, pf). Date: Unknown. Possibly not by Mendelssohn. Edn: Unpublished.

Ja, wär's nicht aber Frühlingszeit (v, pf). Date: Unknown. Possibly not by Mendelssohn. Edn: Unpublished.

Meine Ruh ist hin ("Gretchen") (v, pf). Text: Goethe. Edn: Unpublished.

Vier trübe Monden sind entflohn ("An ihrem Grabe") (v, pf). Edn: Carl Reinecke (Munich: Aibl, [1882]).

Remarks: Published with "An Marie," "Erwartung," and "Warum ich weine." Edn. gives text in German and French.

Weinend seh ich in die Nacht ("Warum ich weine!") (S, pf). Edn: Carl Reinecke (Munich: Aibl, [1882]).

Remarks: Published with "An Marie," "Erwartung," and "An ihrem Grabe." Edn. gives text in German and French.

Wie die Blumen (S, pf). Text: Unknown. Possibly not by Mendelssohn. Edn: Unpublished.

Ach um deine feuchten Schwingen ("Suleika"). Edn: Unpublished.

Remarks: Auctioned in 1959, this song is described in the Sotheby's catalog as "[a]n entirely different setting from Op. 34, no. 4.–Unpublished."

Es weh'n die Wolken über Meer ("Abschied") (S, pf). Edn: Unpublished.

G. Chamber Music

1. Published by Mendelssohn

Piano Quartet No. 1 in C Minor, Op. 1 (vn, va, vc, pf). Date: 20 September–18 October 1822. Edn: Paris: Maurice Schlesinger [1823] (parts); and [1839] (arr. pf 4 hands by F. Mockwitz), [1856] (parts and FS); R ix.

Piano Quartet No. 2 in F Minor, Op. 2 (vn, va, vc, pf). Date: 9 November–3 December 1823. Edn: Berlin: Schlesinger, [1824] (parts), [1843] (PS 4 hands by F. Mockwitz), and [1856] (parts and

FS); R ix.

Remarks: Third mvt. published as "Intermezzo," arr. for fl and pf by John Thompson, in *The Harmonicon* 8 (1830): 236–40.

Violin Sonata in F Minor, Op. 4. Date: 3 June 1823. Edn: Berlin: Laue, [1824] (parts); Leipzig: Hofmeister, [1833] (parts—new edn.), [1850] (parts and FS); London: Ewer, [1850] (parts and FS); R ix.

Piano Quartet No. 3 in B Minor, Op. 3 (vn, va, vc, pf). Date: 7 October 1824–18 January 1825. Edu: Berlin: Laue, [1825] (parts); Paris: Richault [1827] (parts; "nouvelle édition avec changemens and corrections par l'Auteur"); Leipzig: Hofmeister, [1833] (parts–new edn.), [1861] (parts and FS); R ix.

String Quartet No. 1 in E-flat Major, Op. 12 (2 vn, va, vc). Date: 14 September 1829. Edn: Paris: Richault, [1830] (parts); Leipzig: Hofmeister, [1830] (parts), [1836] (PS 4 hands) [1841] (FS); Berlin: Schlesinger, [1839] (PS 4 hands); R vi.

String Quartet No. 2 in A Major, Op. 13 (2 vn, va, vc). Date: 26/27 October 1827–2 January 1832. Edn: Leipzig: Breitkopf & Härtel, and Paris: Richault, [1830] (parts and PS 4 hands by FMB); Leipzig: Breitkopf & Härtel, and London: Ewer, [1843] (FS and new edn. of PS 4 hands); R vi; L iii.

Variations concertantes in D Major for Cello and Piano, Op. 17 (vc, pf). Date: 30 January 1829. Edn: London: Cramer, Addison, & Beale, [1830], and Vienna: Mechetti, [1830/31]; R ix.

The Evening Bell. See under "Unpublished, Posthumously Published" (p. 254, below).

String Quintet No. 1 in A Major, Op. 18 (2 vn, 2 va, vcl). Date: 31 March 1826–23 February 1832. Edn: Bonn: Simrock, and Paris: Richault, [1833] (parts); Bonn: Simrock, [1838] (PS 4 hands), [1849] (FS); R v.

Octet for Strings, Op. 20 (4 vn, 2 va, 2 vc). Date: 15 October 1825. Facsimile: Ed. Jon Newsom (Washington, D.C.: Library of Congress, 1976). Edn: Leipzig: Breitkopf & Härtel, [1833] (parts and PS 4 hnds), [1848] (FS); R v.

Cello Sonata no. 1 in Bb major, Op. 45 (vc, pf). Date: 13 October 1838. Edn: Leipzig: Kistner, and London: Novello, [1839]; R ix.

Three String Quartets, Op. 44 (2 vn, va, vc). Edn. (all published separately): Leipzig: Breitkopf & Härtel, [1839] (parts), [1839/40] (PS 4 hands by F. Mockwitz, rev. by FMB), [1840] (FS); R vi; L iii.

No. 1 in D major. Date: 24 July 1838.

No. 2 in E minor. Date: 18 June 1837.

No. 3 in Eb major. Date: 6 February 1838.

Piano Trio No. 1 in D Minor, Op. 49 (vn, vc, pf). Date: 18 July 1839–?23 September 1839 Edn: Leipzig: Breitkopf & Härtel, and London: Ewer, [1840] (parts and FS); R ix.

Cello Sonata No. 2 in D Major, Op. 58 (vc, pf). Date: [ca. June 1843]. Edn: Leipzig: Kistner, and London: Ewer, [1843]; R ix.

Piano Trio No. 2 in C Minor, Op. 66 (vn, vc, pf). Edn: Leipzig: Breitkopf & Härtel, London: Ewer, and Paris: Schlesinger, [1846] (parts and FS); R ix. Date: 30 April 1845.

2.   Unpublished and Posthumously Published Chamber Music

Trio in C Minor (vn, va, pf). Date: 9 May 1820. Edn: In J. A. McDonald, "The Chamber Music of Felix Mendelssohn-Bartholdy" (no. 668)

Fuga, Largo in D Minor (vn, pf). Date: [ca. 12 May 1820]. Edn: In R. Larry Todd, *Education* (no. 226).

Andante and Fugue in D Minor (vn, pf). Date: [ca. July 1820]. Edn: Unpublished.

Violin Sonata in F Major (vn, pf). Date: [1820]. Edn: Renate Unger (Leipzig: Deutscher Verlag für Musik, 1977).

Prelude ("Andante") and Fugue in D Minor, G Minor (vn, pf). Date: [ca. 1820]. Edn: In R. Larry Todd, *Education* (no.226).

Theme and Variations in C Major (vn, pf). Date: [ca. 1820]. Edn: In Todd, *Education* (no. 226).

Andante in G Minor (vn, pf). Date: [ca. 1820]. Edn: In Todd, *Education* (no. 226).

Fugue in G Minor (vn, pf). Date: [ca. December 1820]. Edn: In Todd, *Education* (no. 226).

Remarks: Exists in a version for organ, as well; see p. 267, below.

Piece in G Minor/major (vn, pf). Date: [ca. 1820]. Edn: In Todd, *Education* (no. 226).

Prelude in D Major (vn, pf). Date: [ca. 1820]. Edn: In Todd, *Education* (no. 226).

Fugue in D Major (vn, pf). Date: [ca. 1820]. Edn: In Todd, *Education*. (no. 226)

Fugue in D Minor (vn, pf). Date: [ca. 1820]. Edn: In Todd, *Education*. (no. 226)

Fugue in D Major (vn, pf). Date: [ca. 1820]. Edn: In Todd, *Education* (no. 226).

Fugue in D Minor (vn, pf). Date: [ca. December 1820]. Edn: In Todd, *Education* (no. 226).

> *Remarks*: Exists also in a version for organ, dated 3 December; see p. 263, below.

Andante in D Minor (vn, pf). Date: [ca. 1820]. Edn: In Todd, *Education* (no. 226).

Fugue in D Minor (vn, pf). Date: [ca. 1820]. Edn: In Todd, *Education* (no. 226).

Allegro in C Major (vn, pf). Date: [ca. 1820]. Edn: In Todd, *Education* (no. 226).

Fugue in C Major (vn, pf). Date: [ca. 1820]. Edn: In Todd, *Education* (no. 226).

Fugue in D Minor (vn, pf). Date: [ca. 1820–21]. Edn: In Todd, *Education* (no. 226).

> *Remarks*: Exists also in a version for organ, dated 6 January; see p. 267, below.

Fugue in A Minor (vn, pf). Date: [ca. 1820–21]. Edn: In Todd, *Education* (no. 226).

Fugue in C Major (vn, pf). Date: [ca. 1820–21]. Edn: In Todd, *Education* (no. 226).

Fugue in C Major (vn, pf). Date: 17 January 1820 [?recte 1821]. Edn: In Todd, *Education* (no. 226).

Fugue in C Minor (vn, pf). Date: [ca. 1820–21]. Edn: In Todd, *Education* (no. 226).

Fugue in C Major (vn, pf). Date: 20 January 1820 [?recte 1821]. Edn: In Todd, *Education* (no. 226).

Fugue in C Minor (vn, pf). Edn: In Todd, *Education* (no. 226). MS: GB-Ob MDM c.43 (A; 24 January 1820 [?recte 1821]).

> *Remarks*: The source includes a sketch for this fugue and a second complete version dated 28 [January 1821].

Minuet in G Major (vn, pf). Date: [ca. 1820–21]. Edn: Unpublished.

Violin Sonata in D Minor (vn, pf). Date: [1821]. Edn: Unpublished.

[Twelve Fugues] (str qt). Date: 24 March 1821–ca. 4 May 1821. Edn: Unpublished.

Piano Quartet in D Minor (vn, va, vc, pf). Date: [1822]. Edn: In McDonald, "The Chamber Music" (no. 668).

String Quartet in E-flat Major (2 vn, va, vc). Date: 25 March 1823. Facsimile: Berlin: Hermann Erler, 1879, and London: Neumeyer, [1880]. Edn: Unpublished.

Violin Sonata in D Minor (vn, pf). Date: [ca. June 1823]. Edn: Unpublished.

Viola Sonata in C Minor (va, pf). Date: 23 November 1823–14 February 1824. Edn: Leipzig: Peters, 1966; New York: Belwin Mills, [n.d.].

Clarinet Sonata in E-flat Major (cl, pf). Date: 17 April [1824]. Edn: Eric Simon and Felix Guenther (New York: Sprague-Coleman, 1941); Gerhard Allroggen (Wiesebaden: Breitkopf & Härtel, 1987).

Sextet in D Major, Op. posth. 110 (vn, 2 va, vc, cb, pf). Date: 10 May 1824. Edn: Leipzig: Kistner, [1868] (parts and FS), [1869] (PS 4 hands); R ix.

Fugue in E-flat Major for String Quartet, Op. posth. 81, no. 4. Date: 1 November 1827 Edn: Leipzig: Breitkopf & Härtel, [1850] (parts), [1851] (FS); R vi.

Remarks: published with Op. 81, nos. 1–3 under the title *Andante, Scherzo, Capriccio u. Fuge.*

The Evening Bell (hp, pf). Date: November 1829. Edn: London: Chappell, 1876 (parts and pf arrangement).

Remarks: The erroneous statement, given in the *New Grove* work-list and elsewhere, that this work was first published in a volume titled *Musical Haunts in London* stems from a misunderstanding. George Grove made the association of the two titles in his original *Dictionary,* but in fact *Musical Haunts in London* is the title of an 1895 book by F.G. Edwards in which the compositional history of *The Evening Bell* is related. I thank Mr. Peter Ward Jones for sharing this information.

Concert Piece in F Major, Op. posth. 113 (cl, basset-hn, pf). Date: 30 December 1832. Edn: Offenbach: André, [1869] (PS and parts); R vii. See also posthumously published orchestral works, above. (p. 232)

Concert Piece in D Minor, Op. posth. 114 (cl, bassett-hn, pf). Date: 19

January 1833. Edn: Offenbach: André, [1869] (PS and parts); R vii.

Piano Trio in A Major (vn, vc, pf). Date: [?ca. 1834]. Edn: Unpublished.

String Quartet Movement in F Major (2 vn, va, vc). Date: [?ca. 1834].

Assai tranquillo in B Minor (vc, pf). Date: 25 July 1835. Facsimile: In Reinhold Sietz, "Das Stammbuch von Julius Rietz," *Studien zur Musikgeschichte des Rheinlandes* 52 (1962): 219–20.

Violin Sonata in F Major (vn, pf). Date: 15 June 1838. Edn: Yehudi Menuhin (Leipzig: Peters, 1953).

Capriccio **in E Minor for String Quartet, Op. posth. 81, no. 3.** Date: 5 July 1843. Edn: Leipzig: Breitkopf & Härtel, [1850] (parts), [1851] (FS); R vi.

> *Remarks*: published with Op. 81, nos. 1–2 and 4 under the title *Andante, Scherzo, Capriccio u. Fuge.*

String Quintet in B-flat Major, Op. posth. 87 (Date: 8 July 1845. Edn: Leipzig: Breitkopf & Härtel, and London: Ewer, [1850] (parts), [1850/51] (FS); R v.

Lied ohne Worte **in D Major, Op. posth. 109** (vc, pf). Date: [ca. October 1845]. Edn: Leipzig: Senff, and London: Novello, Ewer & Co., [1868]; R ix.

Andante **in E Major for String Quartet, Op. posth. 81, no. 1** (2 vn, va, vc). Date: [ca. August 1847]. Edn: Leipzig: Breitkopf & Härtel, [1850] (parts), [1851] (FS); R vi.

> *Remarks*: published with Op. 81, nos. 2–4 under the title *Andante, Scherzo, Capriccio u. Fuge.*

Scherzo **in A Minor for String Quartet, Op. posth. 81, no. 2** (2 vn, va, vc). Date: [ca. August 1847]. Edn: Leipzig: Breitkopf & Härtel, [1850] (parts), [1851] (FS); R vi.

> *Remarks*: published with Op. 81, nos. 1 and 3–4 under the title *Andante, Scherzo, Capriccio u. Fuge.*

String Quartet in F minor, Op. posth. 80. Date: September 1847. Edn: Leipzig: Breitkopf & Härtel, and London: Ewer, [1850] (parts and PS 4 hands), [1851] (FS); R vi.

Not dated:

Allegro (bn, pf). Edn: Unpulished.

Duet in D Minor (2 vn). Edn: Unpublished.

Theme in A Major for Variation (str qt). Edn: Unpublished.

Allegretto in E Major (vc, fl, cl, 2 hn). Edn: Unpublished.

Remarks: Instrumentation of "Frühlingslied," Op. 8, no. 6.

H. Music for Piano Alone

1. Published by Mendelssohn

Capriccio in F-sharp Minor, Op. 5 (pf). Date: 23 July 1825. Edn: Berlin: Schlesinger, [1825], London: Clementi, Collard, & Collard, [?1828], Leipzig: Hofmeister, and London: Ewer, [1843]; R xi.

Sonata in E Major, Op. 6 (pf). Date: 22 March 1826. Edn: Berlin: Laue, [1826]; R xi.

Fugue in E Minor (pf). Date: 16 June 1827. Edn: *Notre temps* 7 (Mainz: Schott, 1842); R xi.

Seven Character-Pieces [*Sieben Characterstücke*], Op. 7 (pf). Edn: Berlin, Laue, [1827], and Leipzig: Hofmeister, [1833] (new edn.); R xi.

No. 1 in E minor. Date: 6 June 1826–18 October 1828.

No. 2 in B minor. Date: 17 July 1824.

No. 3 in D major.

No. 4 in A major. Date: 4 June 1826.

No. 5 in A major.

No. 6 in E minor.

No. 7 in E major.

Scherzo in B Minor (pf). Date: 12 June 1829. Edu.: *Berliner allgemeine musikalische Zeitung 6* (1829), and in *Album du pianiste* [no. 1] (Berlin: Schlesinger, [1838]); R xi.

Introduction and Rondo capriccioso, Op. 14 (pf). Date: 19 September 1831. Edn: London: Cramer, Addison & Beale, [1830/31], and Vienna: Mechetti, and Paris: Richault, [1831]; R xi.

Fantasia on "The Last Rose of Summer," Op. 15 (pf). Date: ?1827. Edn: London: Cramer, Addison, & Beale, [1830/31], and Vienna: Mechetti, [1831]; R xi.

Trois fantaisies ou caprices, Op. 16 (pf). Edn: London: Cramer, Addison, & Beale, and Vienna: Mechetti, [1831] (published individually); R xi.

No. 1 in A minor. Date: 4 September 1829 .

No. 2 in E minor. Date: 13 November 1829–22 February 1835.

No. 3 in E major (originally titled "Am Bach"). Date: 4–5 September 1829.

Two Musical Sketches [*Zwei Clavierstücke*]. Edn: In *The Musical Gem: A Souvenir for 1834* (London: Mori & Lavenue, [1833]), and independently (Leipzig: Senff, [1859/60]); R xi.

No. 1 in B-flat major.

No. 2 in G minor.

Songs without Words, Vol. 1, Op. 19[b] (pf). Date: 20 July 1832. Edn: London: Novello ("Original Melodies for the Pianoforte"), [1832], and Bonn: Simrock, [1833]; R xi; Rudolf Elvers and Ernst Herttrich (Munich: Henle, [1981].).

No. 1 in E major. Date: August/September 1831–19 April 1832.

No. 2 in A minor. Date: 11 December 1830.

No. 3 in A major ("Jägerlied").

No. 4 in A major. Date: 14 September 1829.

No. 5 in F-sharp minor.

No. 6 in G minor ("Venetianisches Gondellied," "Auf einer Gondel") Date: 16 October 1830–1 June 1831.

Fantasia in F-sharp Minor ("Sonate Écossaisse"), Op. 28 (pf). Date: 29 January 1833. Edn: Bonn: Simrock, [1834]; R xi.

Songs without Words, Vol. 2, Op. 30 (pf). Edn: Bonn: Simrock, and London: Novello, [1835]; R xi; Rudolf Elvers and Ernst Herttrich (Munich: Henle, [1981]. Facsimile: In Schneider (no. 84).

No. 1 in E-flat major.

No. 2 in B-flat minor. Date: 26 June 1830–30 September 1830.

No. 3 in E major.

No. 4 in B minor. Date: 4 January 1833–30 January 1834.

No. 5 in D major. Date: 12 December 1833.

No. 6 in F-sharp minor ("Venetianisches Gondellied").

Three Caprices, Op. 33 (pf). Edn: Leipzig: Breitkopf & Härtel, and London: Mori & Lavenue, [1836]; R xi.

No. 1 in A minor. Date: 9 April 1834.

No. 2 in E major. Date: 12 September 1835.

No. 3 in B-flat minor. Date: 25 July 1833.

Scherzo a capriccio in **F-sharp Minor** (pf). Date: 29 October 1835. Edn: In *L'album des pianistes* (Paris: Schlesinger, 1836), and independently by Bonn: Simrock, and London: Cramer, Addison & Beale, [1836]; R xi.

Six Preludes and Fugues, Op. 35 (pf). Edn: Leipzig: Breitkopf & Härtel, and London: Mori & Lavenue, [1837]; R xi.

No. 1 in E minor. Date: 16 June 1827–21 November 1831.

No. 2 in D major. Date: 11 January 1835–6 December 1836.

Remarks: See also "Fughetta in D major" under unpublished and posthumously published organ works, below)

No. 3 in B minor. Date: 21 September 1832–8 December 1836.

No. 4 in A-flat major. Date: 6 January 1835–7 October 1836.

No. 5 in F minor. Date: 3 December 1834–19 November 1836.

No. 6 in B-flat major. Date: 27 November 1836–3 January 1837.

Songs without Words, Vol. 3, Op. 38 (pf). Edn: Bonn: Simrock, and London: Novello, [1837]; R xi; Rudolf Elvers and Ernst Herttrich (Munich: Henle, [1981].

No. 1 in E-flat major.

No. 2 in C minor. Date: 29 March 1836. Facsimile: In Jost, (no. 675), 142.

No. 3 in E major. Date: 2 January 1835.

No. 4 in A major.

No. 5 in A minor. Date: 5 April 1837.

No. 6 in A-flat major ("Duetto"). Date: 27 June 1836.

Gondellied ("Barcarole") in A Major (pf). Date: 5 February 1837. Edn: Published as supplement to *Neue Zeitschrift für Musik* 14 (1841), and independently by London: Ewer, [1841]; R xi.

Andante cantabile and Presto agitato in B Major (pf). Date: 25 January 1833–22 June 1838. Edn: In *Musikalisches Album auf das Jahr 1839* (Leipzig: Breitkopf & Härtel, [1838]), and independently by Leipzig: Breitkopf & Härtel, [1838/39]; R xi.

Etude in F Minor (pf). Date: 13 March 1836 Edn: I. Moscheles and F.J. Fétis, *Méthode des méthodes de piano* (Paris, [ca. 1840]), and independently by Berlin: Schlesinger, [1841/42].

Songs without Words, Vol. 4, Op. 53 (pf). Edn: Bonn: Simrock, and London: Ewer, [1841]; R xi; Rudolf Elvers and Ernst Herttrich

(Munich: Henle, [1981]).

No. 1 in A-flat major. Date: 28 February 1839.

No. 2 in E-flat major. Date: 24 February 1835. Facsimile: In Jost, (no. 675), 52.

No. 3 in G minor ("Gondellied"). Date: 14 March 1839. Facsimile: In Jost, (no. 675), 160.

No. 4 in F major ("Abendlied"). Date: 1 May 1841.

No. 5 in A minor ("Volkslied"). Date: 30 April 1841.

No. 6 in A major. Date: 1 May 1841.

Prelude and Fugue in E Minor (pf). Date: 13 July 1841. Edn: Prelude published with fugue of 16 June 1827 (see p. 257, above) in *Notre temps* 7 (Mainz: Schott, 1842), and independently by London: Ewer, [1842]; R xi.

Variations sérieuses **in D Minor, Op. 54** (pf). Date: 4 June 1841 Edn: in *Album-Beethoven* (Vienna: Mechetti, [1841]), and indendently by London: Ewer, [1841], and Vienna: Mechetti, [1842]; R xi.

Songs without Words, Vol. 5, Op. 62 (pf). Date: 31 January 1844–9 June 1844. Edn: Bonn: Simrock, and London: Ewer, [1844]; R xi; Rudolf Elvers and Ernst Herttrich (Munich: Henle, [1981], Robin Langley (Kassel: Bärenreiter, 1982) [version for pf 4 hands].

No. 1 in G major. Date: 6–12 January 1844.

No. 2 in B-flat major. Date: 29 July –13 September 1843.

No. 3 in E minor ("Trauermarsch"). Date: 19 January–13 September 1843. Facsimile: in Jost (no. 674), 178.

No. 4 in G major.

No. 5 in A minor ("Venetianisches Gondellied"). Date: 24 January 1841–11 October 1842. Facsimile in Wehner (no. 521), 55, 56.

No. 6 in A major ("Frühlingslied"). Date: 1 June 1842–12 November 1843.

Songs without Words, Vol. 6, Op. 67 (pf). Edn: Bonn: Simrock, and London: Ewer, [1845]; R xi; Rudolf Elvers and Ernst Herttrich (Munich: Henle, [1981]).

No. 1 in E-flat major. Date: 29 July 1843–13 January 1845.

No. 2 in F-sharp minor. Date: 3–25 May 1845.

No. 3 in B-flat major. Date: 25 May–23 November 1845.

No. 4 in C major ("Spinnerlied"). Date: 5–25 May 1845.

No. 5 in B minor. Date: 5 January–24 December 1844.

No. 6 in E major. Date: 24 December 1844–13 January 1845.

Six Pieces for the Piano-forte, Composed as a Christmas Present for His Young Friends by Felix Mendelssohn Bartholdy [Christmas Pieces, *Kinderstücke*], Op. 72 (pf). Edn: London: Ewer, [1847], and Leipzig: Breitkopf and Härtel, [1848]; R xi.

No. 1 in G major. Date: 24 June 1842.

No. 2 in E-flat major.

No. 3 in G major. Date: 21 June 1842.

No. 4 in D major.

No. 5 in G minor.

No. 6 in F major.

2.   Unpublished   and   Posthumously   Published   Works   for Piano Alone

Sonata in D Major (2 pf). Date: [ca. October 1819].

Remarks: Peter Ward Jones has recently shown that this is probably Mendelssohn's earliest surviving composition.

[Allegro] in G Minor (2 pf). Date: 21 February [1820].

Lento—Vivace in G Minor (pf 4 hands). Date: 1820.

[Four Little Pieces] (pf). Date: [ca. 1820]. Edn: In Todd, *Education*.

No. 1 in G major.

No. 2 in G minor (canon).

No. 3 in G major.

No. 4 in G minor (canon).

Theme and Variations in D Major (pf). Date: [ca. 1820]. Edn: In Todd, *Education*.

[Six Little Pieces] (pf). Date: [1820]. Edn: Unpublished.

No. 1. Allegro in C major.

No. 2. [Allegro] in G minor.

No. 3. Andante in A major.

No. 4. Allegro molto in B minor.

[No.] 5. [Piece in E minor].

No. 6. [Piece in A minor].

Andante in F Major (pf). Date: [1820]. Edn: Unpublished.

Piece in D Major/D Minor (No Tempo—Adagio) (pf). Date: 11 May 1820. Edn: Unpublished.

Sonata in A Minor (pf). Date: 12 May 1820. Edn: Unpublished.

Largo in D Minor (pf). Date: [1820]. Edn: Unpublished.

[Piece in F Minor] (pf). Date: [1820]. Edn: Unpublished.

Recitativo (Allegro) in E Minor (pf). Date: [1820]. Edn: Unpublished.

[Piece in E Minor] (pf). Date: [1820]. Edn: Unpublished.

Largo-allegro in C Minor (pf). Date: [1820]. Edn: Unpublished.

Andante in C Major (pf). Date: [1820]. Edn: Unpublished.

Adagio in D Major (pf). Date: [1820]. Edn: Unpublished.

Presto in C Minor (pf). Date: 1 July 1820. Edn: Unpublished.

Sonata in E Minor (pf). Date: 13 July 1820. Edn: Unpublished.

Sonata in F Minor (pf). Date: [1820]. Edn: Unpublished.

Sonata in F Major (pf; inc.). Date: [1820]. Edn: Unpublished.

Andante and Presto in C Major (pf 4 hands). Date: [1820]. Edn: Unpublished.

Etude in D Minor (pf). Date: 28 [?December 1820]. Edn: Unpublished.

Etude in A Minor (pf). Date: 28 December 1820. Edn: Unpublished.

Allegro in A Minor (pf). Date: 5 January 1821. Edn: Unpublished.

Etude in C Major (pf). Date: 30 March [1821]. Edn: Unpublished.

Sonata in G Minor, Op. posth. 105 (pf). Date: 18 August 1821. Edn: London: Novello, Ewer & Co., and Leipzig: Rieter-Biedermann, [1868]; R xi.

Largo-Allegro di molto in C Minor/Major (pf). Date: [1821].

Sonatina in E Major (pf). Date: 13 December 1821. Facsimile: In Klein (no. 967) between p. 152 and 153.

[Three Fugues] (pf). Date: [1822]. Edn: Unpublished.

No. 1 in D minor.

No. 2 in D minor.

No. 3 in B minor.

Fantasia in C Minor (pf). Date: [ca. 1823]. Edn: Unpublished.

Allegro in D Minor (pf). Date: 19 February 1823. Edn: Unpublished.

Sonata in B-flat Minor (pf). Date: 27 November 1823. Edn: R. Larry Todd (New York: Peters, 1981).

Capriccio **in E-flat Major** (pf). Date: [ca. 1823–24]. Edn: Unpublished.

Fantasia in D Minor (pf 4 hands). Date: 15 March 1824. Edn: Unpublished.

Prestissimo in F Minor (pf). Date: 19 August 1824. Edn: Unpublished.

Fugue in G Minor (pf). Date: 11 September 1824. Edn: Unpublished.

Vivace in C Minor (pf). Date: 29 January 1825. Edn: Unpublished.

Fugue in C-sharp Minor (pf). Date: 5 January 1826. Edn: Unpublished.

Andante **and Canon in D Major** (pf). Date: [ca. January 1826].

Fugue in E-flat Major (pf). Date:11 September 1826. Edn: Unpublished.

Perpetuum mobile in C Major, Op. 119 (pf). Date: 24 November 1826–[ca. June 1829]. Edn: Leipzig: Kistner, [1873], and London: Novello, Ewer & Co., [1874]; R xi.

Fugue in E Minor (pf). Date: 16 January 1827. Edn: Unpublished.

Sonata in B-flat Major, Op. posth. 106 (pf). Date: 31 May 1827. Edn: London: Novello, Ewer & Co., and Leipzig: Rieter-Biedermann, [1868]; R xi.

Lied [ohne Worte] **in E-flat Major** (pf). Date: 14 November 1828. Facsimile: In Klein (no. 967), between p. 152 and 153.

Scherzo **in B Minor** (pf). Date: 12 June 1829. Edn: Unpublished.

Andante **Con Moto in A Major** (pf). Date: 21 May–3 June 1830. Edn: J. Draheim, 1984.

Lied [ohne Worte] **in A Major** (pf). Date: 13 June 1830. Facsimile: In Jost (no. 674), 31. Edn: Unpublished.

Con moto **in A Major** (pf). Date: 3 November 1831. Edn: Unpublished.

Presto agitato **in B Minor** (pf). Date: 25 March 1833. Edn: Unpublished.

Lied [ohne Worte] **in F-sharp Minor** (pf). Date:16 October 1836. Facsimile: in Jost, (no 675), 128. Edn: Unpublished.

Remarks: Published in texted form as vocal duet, Op. 63, no. 4.

Prelude in F Minor (pf). Date: 13 November 1836. Edn: Unpublished.

Con moto **in B-flat Minor** (pf). Date: [?ca. 1836–37]. Edn: Unpublished.

[Allegretto] **in A Major** (pf). Date: 22 April 1837. Edn: Leopold Hirschberg, in *Jede Woche Musik* [Berlin], 19 October 1927.

Facsimile: In Petitpierre (no. 70) 122–23; and Ward Jones, (no. 232), 20.

Capriccio in E Major, Op. posth. 118 (pf). Date: 11 July 1[837]. Edn: Breitkopf & Härtel, 1872.

Allegro in E Minor ("Albumblatt: Lied ohne Worte"), Op. posth. 117 (pf). Date: [ca. 1836]. Edn: London: Ewer, and Leipzig: Leede, [1859]; first ascribed opus no. 117 in London: Novello, [1870], and Leipzig: Kistner, [1872].

Sonata in G Major (pf; inc.). Date: [ca. 1839–41]. Facsimile: In Todd, "Unfinished" (no. 935), 158–84. Edn: Unpublished.

Allegro brillant in A Major, Op. posth. 92 (pf duet). Date: 23 March 1841. Edn: Leipzig: Breitkopf & Härtel, and London: Ewer, [1851]; R x.

Lied ohne Worte in F-sharp Minor (pf). Date: 5 April 1839. Edn: Unpublished.

Lied ohne Worte in F Major (pf). Date: [ca. 1841]. Facsimile: in *Die Musik* 16/11 (August 1924]). Edn: Unpublished.

Variations in E-flat Major, Op. posth. 82 (pf). Date: 25 July 1841. Edn: Leipzig: Breitkopf & Härtel, and London: Ewer, [1850]; R xi.

Variations in B-flat Major, Op. posth. 83 (pf). Date: [ca. 1842]. Edn: Breitkopf & Härtel, [1850]; R xi.

Andante and Variations in B-flat Major, Op. posth. 83a (pf 4 hands). Date: [ca. June 1842]–10 February 1844. Edn: Breitkopf & Härtel, and London: Ewer, [1850].

Remarks: Originally part of Op. 72.

Sostenuto in F Major (pf). Date: [ca. June 1842]. Edn: Unpublished.

Remarks: Originally part of Op. 72.

Lied [ohne Worte] in D Major (pf; inc.). Date: [ca. 19 Jan 1843]. Edn: Unpublished.

Lied [ohne Worte] in D Major (pf). Date: 18 March 1843]. Edn: Unpublished.

[Piece in B-flat Major] (pf; inc.). Date: 5 January 1843. Edn: Unpublished.

Lied ohne Worte in D minor ("Allegro marcato alla marcia," "Reiterlied") (pf). Date: 12 December 1844–4 April 1846. Edn: Ernst Walker (London: Novello, 1947); Rudolf Elvers and Ernst Herttrich (Munich: Henle, [1981]).

Presto in F-sharp Minor (pf). Date: 29 October 1845. Edn: Unpublished.

Piece in F Major ("Auf fröhliches Wiedersehn") (pf). Date: 4 April 1847. Edn: Unpublished.

Lieder ohne Worte, **Vol. 7, Op. posth. 85** (pf). Edn: London: Ewer, [1850], and Bonn: Simrock, [1850/51]; R xi; Rudolf Elvers and Ernst Herttrich (Munich: Henle, [1981]).

No. 1 in F major. Date: 24 December 1844–4 April 1846.

No. 2 in A minor. Date: 9 June 1834–4 April 1846). Facsimile: In Jost, (no. 676), p. 151.

No. 3 in E-flat major. Date: [ca. August 1835] 2 September 1846.

No. 4 in D major. Date: 3 May 1845–4 April 1846.

No. 5 in A major. Date: 7 May 1845.

No. 6 in Bb major. Date: 1 May 1841.

Lieder ohne Worte, **vol. 8, Op. posth. 102** (pf). Edn: London: Novello, Ewer, & Co., [1867], and Bonn: Simrock, [1868]; R xi; Rudolf Elvers and Ernst Herttrich (Munich: Henle, [1981]).

No. 1 in E minor. Date: 1 June 1842.

No. 2 in D major. Date: 11 May 1845–4 April 1846.

No. 3 in C major ("Kinderstück"). Date: 12 December 1845.

No. 4 in G minor. Date: 4 February 1841.

No. 5 in A major ("Kinderstück"). Date: 12 December 1845.

No. 6 in C major. Date: 5 July 1842.

Three Preludes, Op. posth. 104[a] (pf). Edn: London: Novello, Ewer & Co., and Leipzig: Senff, [1868], R xi.

No. 1 in B-flat major. Date: 9 December 1836.

No. 2 in B minor. Date: 12 October 1836.

No. 3 in D major. Date: 27 November 1836.

Three Studies, Op. 104[b] (pf). Edn: Leipzig: Senff, [1868]; R xi.

No. 1 in B-flat minor. Date: 9 June 1836.

No. 2 F major. Date: 21 April 1834.

No. 3 in A minor.

Not dated:

Allegro vivace in F minor (pf; inc.). Edn: Unpublished.

Andante in G minor (pf 4 hds). Edn: Unpublished.

Sonata in A major (pf). Edn: Unpublished. Possibly not by Mendelssohn.

Lied [ohne Worte] **in E-flat Major** (pf). Edn: Unpublished.

I. ORGAN MUSIC

1. Published by Mendelssohn

Three Preludes and Fugues, Op. 37. Edn: London: Novello, [1837], and Leipzig: Breitkopf & Härtel, [1837/38]; R xii; Wm. A. Little, ed., *Felix Mendelssohn Bartholdy: Complete Organ Works*, vol. 1 (London: Novello, 1990).

> No. 1 in C minor. Date: 30 July 1834–8 September 1840.

> No. 2 in G major. Date: 1 December 1836–8 September 1840.

> No. 3 in D minor. Date: 29 March 1833–8 September 1840.

Fughetta **in A Major**. Date: [ca. 1840]. Edn: Carl Geißler, *Neues vollständiges Museum für die Orgel* 8 (1840–41); Little, *Complete Organ Works*, vol.1.

> *Remarks:* Sharply cut version of Op. 7 no. 5; arrangement may have been prepared by Carl Geißler, a friend of Mendelssohn and editor of the *Museum*.

Six Sonatas, Op. 65. Edn: London: Coventry & Hollier, Leipzig: Breitkopf & Härtel, [1845]; R xii; Little, *Complete Organ Works*, vols. 2–4.

> No. 1 in F minor/F major. Date: 18 August 1844–[?Spring 1845].

> No. 2 in C minor/C major. Date: 14 July 1839–[?Spring 1845)].

> No. 3 in A major. Date: 9 August 1844–[?Spring 1845].

> No. 4 in B-flat major. Date: 2 January 1845–[?Spring 1845].

> No. 5 in D major. Date: 9 September 1844–[?Spring 1845].

> No. 6 in D minor/D major. Date: 27 January 1845–[?Spring 1845].

2.   Unpublished and Posthumously Published Organ Works

Prelude in D Minor. Date: 28 November 1820. Edn: Little, *Complete Organ Works*, vol. 5.

Fugue in D Minor. Date: 3 December 1820. Edn: Little, *Complete*

Organ Works, vol. 5.

Fugue in G Minor. Date: December 1820. Edn: Little, *Complete Organ Works*, vol. 5.

Remarks: Also for vn, pf; see p. 253.

[Toccata] in D Minor (inc.). Date: [late 1820–early 1821]. Edn: Little, *Complete Organ Works*, vol. 5.

Fugue in D Minor. Date: 6 January 1821. Edn: Little, *Complete Organ Works*, vol. 5.

Remarks: Also for vn, pf; see p. 253.

Andante **in D Major**. Date: 9 May 1823. Edn: Little, *Complete Organ Works*, vol. 5.

[Passacaglia] in C Minor. Date: 10 May 1823. Edn: Little, *Complete Organ Works*, vol. 5.

Wie groß ist des Allmächt'gen Güte (chorale and variations). Date: 30 July–2 August 1823. Edn: Little, *Complete Organ Works*, vol. 5.

Postlude in D Major. Date: 8 March 1831. Edn: Little, *Complete Organ Works*, vol. 5.

Remarks: In a later version in C as Op. 65 no. 2, third movement; see above.

[Piece in E Major] (inc.). Date: [ca. 1823]. Edn: Unpublished.

Fuga pro organo pleno in D Minor. Date: 29 March 1833–cf. Op. 37, no. 3, above). Edn: Little, *Complete Organ Works*, vol. 5.

Andante con moto in G Minor. Date: 11 July [1833]. Edn: Little, *Complete Organ Works*, vol. 5.

Fantasie and Fugue in G Minor. Date: [ca. mid–1823]. Edn: Little, *Complete Organ Works*, vol. 5.

[Organ Piece in G Minor for Vincent Novello's Album]. Date: 11 July 1833. Edn: Unpublished.

Fughetta in D Major. Date: [?July 1834]. Edn: Little, *Complete Organ Works*, vol. 1.

Remarks: Organ version of piano fugue, Op. 35 no. 2.

Two Fugues for Organ Duet. Date: 11 January 1835. Edn: Little, *Complete Organ Works*, vol.

No. 1 in C minor. Arrangement of Op. 37 no. 1, fugue.

No. 2 in D major. Arrangement of Op. 35 no. 2, fugue.

Fugue in E Minor. Date: 13 July 1839. Edn: Little, *Complete Organ Works*, vol. 1.

Fugue in F Minor. Date: 18 July 1839–[ca. 1844]. Edn: Little, *Complete Organ Works*, vol. 1.

Fantasia [On "O Haupt voll Blut und Wunden"]. Date: [?ca. August 1840]. Edn: in R. Larry Todd, Appendix to *Felix Mendelssohn Bartholdy, O Haupt voll Blut und Wunden* (Madison, Wisconsin: A–R, 1981).

Prelude in C Minor. Date: 9 July 1841. Edn: Little, *Complete Organ Works*, vol. 1. Facsimile in *Exeter Hall* 1 (1868).

***Andante* in F Major**. Date: 21 July 1844. Edn: Little, *Complete Organ Works*, vol. 2.

***Allegretto* in D Minor**. Date: 22 July 1844. Edn: Little, *Complete Organ Works*, vol. 2.

Remarks: A version of Op. 65 no. 5, movement 2, in D minor rather than the B minor of the final version.

***Andante* and Variations in D Major**. Date: 23 July 1844. Edn: London: Novello, Ewer, & Co., 1898; Little, *Complete Organ Works*, vol. 2.

Remarks: The 1898 Novello/Ewer edition was coupled with the Allegro in B-flat (see below, p. 269).

Allegro, Chorale, and Fugue in D Major. Date: 25 July 1844. Edn: Little, *Complete Organ Works*, vol. 2.

***Con Moto Maestoso* in A Major**. Date: 9 August 1844. Edn: Little, *Complete Organ Works*, vol. 2.

Remarks: Cf. Op. 65 no. 3, movement 1.

***Andante* and *Con moto* in A Major**. Date: 17 August 1844. Edn: Little, *Complete Organ Works*, vol. 2.

Remarks: Cf. Op. 65 no. 3, movement 2.

***Allegro* in D Major**. Date: 9 September 1844. Edn: Little, *Complete Organ Works*, vol. 2.

Remarks: Cf. Op. 65 no. 5, movement 3.

***Andante* in B Minor**. Date: 9 September 1844. Edn: Little, *Complete Organ Works*, vol. 2.

Remarks: Cf. Op. 65 no. 5, movement 2.

Chorale in A-flat Major. Date: 10 September 1844. Edn: Little, *Complete Organ Works*, vol. 2.

Adagio in A-flat Major. Date: 19 December 1844. Edn: Little, *Complete Organ Works*, vol. 2.

Remarks: Cf. Op. 65 no. 1, movement 2.

Grave and *Andante con moto* in C Minor. Date: 21 December 1844. Edn: Little, *Complete Organ Works*, vol. 3.

Remarks: Cf. Op. 65 no. 2, movements 1 and 2.

Allegro moderato e grave in F Minor. Date: 28 December 1844. Edn: Little, *Complete Organ Works*, vol. 3.

Allegro in B-flat Major. Date: 31 December [1844]. Edn: London: Novello, Ewer, & Co., 1898; Little, *Complete Organ Works*, vol. 2.

Remarks: The 1898 Ewer editon was coupled with the Andante and Variations in D major (see above, p. 268).

Chorale in D Major. Date: [ca. December 1844]. Edn: Little, *Complete Organ Works*, vol. 2.

Remarks: Cf. Op. 65 no. 5, movement 1.

Allegro con brio in B-flat Major. Date: 2 January 1845. Edn: Little, *Complete Organ Works*, vol. 3.

Remarks: Cf. Op. 65 no. 4, movement 1.

Andante Alla Marcia in B-flat Major. Date: 2 January 1845. Edn: Little, *Complete Organ Works*, vol. 3.

Remarks: Cf. Op. 65 no. 4, movement 2.

Chorale [and Variations] in D Minor. Date: 26 January 1845. Edn: Little, *Complete Organ Works*, vol. 3.

Remarks: Cf. Op. 65 no. 6, movement 1.

Finale (Andante Sostenuto) in D Major. Date: 2 January 1845. Edn: Little, *Complete Organ Works*, vol. 3.

Remarks: Cf. Op. 65 no. 6.

Fugue in D Minor. Date: 27 January [1845]. Edn: Little, *Complete Organ Works*, vol. 3.

Remarks: Cf. Op. 65 no. 6.

Moderato in C Major. Date: [?ca. January 1845]). Edn: Little, *Complete Organ Works*, vol. 3.

Remarks: Cf. Op. 65 no. 2, movement 3.

Allegro moderato maestoso in C Major. Date: [ca. 1845]. Edn: Little, *Complete Organ Works*, vol. 3.

Fugue in B-flat Major. Date: 2 April 1845. Edn: Little, *Complete Organ Works*, vol. 3.

   Remarks: Cf. Op. 65 no. 4, movement 4.

Allegro assai **in C Major**. Date: [ca. January 1845]. Edn: Little, *Complete Organ Works*, vol. 3.

II. SACRED WORKS

A. Oratorios

1. Published by Mendelssohn

St. Paul [Paulus], **Op. 36** (solo vv, ch, orch). Date: 1833–36. Edn: London: Novello, [1836 (PS by FMB; overture for pf 4 hnds; words in English by W. Ball); Bonn: Simrock, [1836 (choral parts and PS by FMB; overture for pf 4 hnds)], [1837] (score, orchestra parts, and PS 4 hands of overture only); R xiii; ed. R. Larry Todd (Stuttgart: Carus, 1997).

Elijah [Elias], **Op. 70** (solo vv, ch, orch). Date: 15 August 1844–47. Edn: Bonn: Simrock, and London: Ewer, [1847] (PS, choral parts, and solo parts), [1848] (orchestral parts and FS); R xiii; ed. Paul Horn (Stuttgart: Carus, 1978 [No. 28 only]); ed. R. Larry Todd (Stuttgart: Carus, 1994).

2. Posthumously Published Oratorio

[Christus], **Op. posth. 97** (solo vv, ch, orch). Date: [?ca. 1847]. Edn: Leipzig: Breitkopf & Härtel, [1852] (PS, PS without words, and FS); London: Ewer, [1852] (PS, with English text by W. Bartholomew), [1860] (score); R xiii; R. Larry Todd (Stuttgart: Carus, 1994).

   Remarks: The title of this incomplete oratorio stems exclusively from the composer's friend Ignaz Moscheles.

B. Chorale Cantatas (All Posthumously Publsihed)

Christe, du Lamm Gottes (ch, str). Date: Christmas 1827–11 November 1829. Edn: Oswald Bill (Neuhausen-Stuttgart: Hänssler, 1977).

Jesu, meine Freude (ch, str). Date: 22 January 1828. Facsimile: ed. O. Jonas (Chicago: Newberry Library, 1966). Edn: Brian W. Pritchard (Hilversum: Harmonia, 1972); Günter Graulich (Stuttgart: Carus,

1979).

Wer nur den lieben Gott läßt walten (S, ch, str). Date: [ca. April–July 1829]. Edn: Oswald Bill (Kassel: Bärenreiter, 1976); Thomas C. Schmidt (Stuttgart: Carus, 1996).

O Haupt voll Blut und Wunden (Bar, ch, orch). Date: 12–14 September 1830. Edn: Martin Lutz (PS) (Wiesbaden: Breitkopf & Härtel, 1973); Oswald Bill (Stuttgart: Carus, 1980); R. Larry Todd (Madison: A-R, 1981).

Vom Himmel hoch, da komm' ich her (S, Bar, ch, orch). Date: 28 January 1831. Edn: Karen Lehmann (Stuttgart: Carus, 1984).

Wir glauben all' an einen Gott (ch, orch). Date: [ca. March 1831]. Edn: Günter Graulich (Stuttgart: Carus, 1980).

Ach Gott, vom Himmel sieh darein (bar, ch, orch). Date: January–5 April 1832. Edn: Brian W. Pritchard (Hilversum: Harmonia, 1972); Günter Graulich (Stuttgart: Carus, 1980).

C. Psalm Settings

1. Published by Mendelssohn

Non nobis Domine [Nicht unserm Namen, Herr] **(Psalm 115), Op. 31** (S, ch, orch). Date: 15 November 1830–19 May 1835. Edn: Bonn: Simrock, London: Hedgley, [?1845] (PS, with English text by W. Bartholomew), R xiv; R. Larry Todd (Stuttgart: Carus, 1994).

Wie der Hirsch schreit **(Psalm 42), Op. 42** (S, ch, orch). Date: 22 December 1837. Edn: Leipzig: Breitkopf & Härtel, [1838] (choral parts and PS by FMB), [1839] (FS and orchestral parts); London: Novello, [1838] (PS by FMB; words in English); R xiv; Günter Graulich (Stuttgart: Carus, 1980).

Defend me, Lord **(Psalm 31) (ch)**. Date: 27 February 1839. Edn: The *National Psalmodist* (London: Coventry & Hollier, 1839); ed. Barbara Mohn (Stuttgart: Carus, 1996).

Da Israel aus Aegypten zog **(Psalm 114), Op. 51** (8 vv, orch). Date: 9 August 1839–23 September 1840. Edn: Leipzig: Breitkopf & Härtel, [1840/41] (parts and PS [by FMB]), London: Novello, [1841] (PS by FMB; words in English), [1841] (score); R xiv; Oswald Bill (Stuttgart: Carus, 1982).

Kommt, laßt uns anbeten **(Psalm 95), Op. 46** (T, ch, orch). Date: 6 April 1838–3 July 1841. Edn: Leipzig: Kistner, [1842] (FS, PS, and parts);

London: Novello, [1842] (PS with words in English); R xiv; R. Larry Todd (Stuttgart: Carus, 1990).

2. Unpublished and Posthumously Published Psalm Settings

Gott du bist unsre Zuversicht **(Psalm 46)** (5 vv). Date: [ca. June 1821]. Edn: Zappalá (Stuttgart: Carus, 1997).

Die Himmel erzählen **(Psalm 19)** (2S,A,T,B). Date: 16 June 1820 [?recte 1821]. Edn: (Stuttgart: Carus, 1997).

Ich weiche nicht von deinen Rechten **(Psalm 119: 102)** (4 vv). Date: [?1823]. Edn: Zappalà (no. 756), 203–33; Stuttgart: Carus, 1997.

Deine Rede präge ich meinem Herzen **(Psalm 119:11)** (4 vv). Date: [?1823]. Edn: Zappalà (no. 756), 203–33; Stuttgart: Carus, 1997.

Jauchzet Gott alle Lande **(Psalm 66: 1, 2, 20)** (SSA solos, SSA double choir, bc). Date: 8 March 1822. Edn: Zappalà (Stuttgart: Carus, 1997).

Lord hear the voice **(Psalm 5)** (4 male vv). Date: 26 February 1839. Edn: ed. Barbara Mohn (Stuttgart: Carus, 1996).

[Seven Psalm Melodies and Harmonizations] (ch). Date: 3 November 1843. Edn: ed. Barbara Mohn (Stuttgart: Carus, 1996).

Dem Herrn der Erdkreis (Psalm 24).

Warum toben die Heiden (Psalm 2).

Gott als ein König gewaltlich regirt (Psalm 93).

Nun singt ein neues Lied dem Herrn (Psalm 98).

Ihr Völker auf der Erde (Psalm 100).

Auf dich setz' ich Herr mein Vertrauen (Psalm 31).

Wer in des allerhöchsten (Psalm 91).

Why, O Lord, Delay [Hymne: Lass, o Herr, mich Hülfe finden] **(Psalm 13), Op. posth. 96** (A, ch, org or orch). Date: 12 December 1840–16 January 1843. Edn: organ version: movements 1–3 only (without opening number) as *Anthem for a Mezzo Soprano, with Chorus* (London: Cramer, Addison, & Beale, [1841]) and as *Drei geistliche Lieder* (Bonn: Simrock, [1841]); the added movement 4 was published as a supplement, London: Cramer et. al, [1843]. Orchestral version: posthumously published as *Hymne*, Op. 96 (Bonn: Simrock, [1852]; PS London: Novello, [1852]); Günter Graulich (Stuttgart: Carus, 1978), David Brodbeck (Stuttgart: Carus, 1996).

Singet dem Herrn ein neues Lied (Psalm 98), Op. posth. 91 (dbl ch, orch, org). Date: 27 December 1843. Edn: Leipzig: Kistner, [1851] (parts, PS, FS), London: Ewer, [1851 (PS with English words by W. Bartholomew)]; R xiv; R. Larry Todd (Stuttgart: Carus, 1990).

Jauchzet dem Herrn alle Welt **(Psalm 100)** (SATB). Date: 1 January 1844. Edn: Musica sacra 8 (Berlin: Bote & Bock, 1863); R xiv.

Three Psalms, Op. posth. 78 (8 vv). Edn: Leipzig: Breitkopf & Härtel, and London: Ewer, [1849] (published individually); R xiv; David Brodbeck (Stuttgart: Carus, [1998]).

> Warum toben die Heiden (Psalm 2) (solo vv, ch). Date: [ca. 15 December 1843]. Edn: Stuttgart: Carus, 1967.

> Richte mich Gott (Psalm 43) (8 vv). Date: 3 January 1844. Edn: Stuttgart: Carus, 1990.

> Mein Gott, mein Gott, warum hast du mich verlassen (Psalm 22) (solo vv, ch). Date: [1844]. Edn: Carus: Stuttgart, 1968.

Denn er hat seinen Engeln befohlen (Psalm 91) (dbl ch). Date: 15 August 1844. Edn: Berlin: H. Moser, in *Volksliederbuch für gemischten Chor* (Leipzig: C. F. Peters, 1915), 122–27; ed. Thomas Schmidt-Beste, Stuttgart: Carus, 1997.

> *Remarks*: Reused (orchestrated) in *Elijah*, Op. 70. According to Rudolf Werner, the piece was published shortly after it was presented to the Berlin *Domchor*; this edition, however, dates from 1915.

D. Other Accompanied Sacred Choral Works

1. Published by Mendelssohn

Three Sacred Pieces, Op. 23 [*Kirchen-Musik*] (ch, org/orch). Edn: Bonn: Simrock, [1832] (parts and vocal score with figured basso continuo), and Bonn: Simrock, [1838] (FS for No. 2, parts only for nos. 1 and 3); R xiv.

> No. 1. Aus tiefer Noth (T, ch, org). Date: 18–19 October 1830. Edn: Günter Graulich (Stuttgart: Carus, 1979).

> No. 2. Ave Maria (T, dbl ch, org/orch). Date: 30 September 1830–17 November 1831 [arr. 8 vv]. Edn: Günter Graulich (Stuttgart: Carus, 1977).

> No. 3. Mitten wir im Leben sind (2S, 2A, 2T, 2B).

Three Motets [*Drei Motetten*]**, Op. 39** (female ch, org or pf). Edn: Bonn: Simrock, and London: Novello, [1838] (motets published individually); R xiv; Günter Graulich (Stuttgart: Carus, 1977).

1. *Hear My Prayer, O Lord* [Veni, Domine] (SSA, org). Date: 31 December 1830.

2. *O Praise the Lord* [Laudate pueri] (SSA, org). Date: 14 August 1837.

3. *O Lord, Thou Hast Searched Me Out* [Surrexit Pastor] (SSAA, org). Date: 30 December 1830.

Te Deum, **Morning Service ("We praise thee O God")** (A major) (SSATB solos, chor, org). Date: 16 July 1843. Edn: London: Ewer, [1846]; R xiv.

Verleih' uns Frieden (ch, orch). Date: 10 February 1831. Edn: Leipzig: Breitkopf & Härtel, [1839] (FS and PS; words in German and Latin); London: Novello, [1839] (PS, with title "Da pacem Domine: motett/Grant us thy peace: prayer"; words in English and German); R xiv. Facsimile: In supplement to *Allgemeine musikalische Zeitung* 51 (1839).

Lord Have Mercy upon Us (ch, org). Date: 24 March 1833. Edn: London: Ewer, [1842], and *Album für Gesang* (Leipzig: Bösenberg, 1842); Günter Graulich (Stuttgart: Carus, 1992).

Remarks: As Peter Ward Jones kindly pointed out in a personal communication, the title "For the Evening Service," which appeared in the first edition in the *Album für Gesang* for 1842, is a misnomer for the chorus "Lord Have Mercy upon Us," and may have resulted from a lack of familiarity with the English liturgy. More appropriate is the title of the first Ewer edition (ca. 1842): "Responses to the Commandments."

Hear My Prayer [Hör mein Bitten] (S, ch, org or orch). Text: W. Bartholomew (paraphrase of Ps. 55). Date: 25 January 1844–February 1847. Edn: Berlin: Bote & Bock, [1845] (version with org acc, and arrangement for S and pf); London: Ewer, [1845] (version with org acc); London: Novello, Ewer & Co., [1880] (version with orch); R xiv; R. Larry Todd (Stuttgart: Carus, 1985).

Three Motets [Drei Motetten], Op. 69 (SATB, org). Edn: (London: Ewer, [1847], and) Leipzig: Breitkopf & Härtel, 1848.

Jubilate Deo (O be joyful in the Lord). Date: 5 April 1847. Edn: London: Ewer, [1847] (without opus no., as second part of the *Te Deum*, which had already been published independently in 1846; see p. 274, above).

Magnificat and *Nunc dimittis* published together as Magnificat and

Nunc dimittis, Op. 69 (London: Ewer, [1847]):

Evening Service [*Magnificat*] (My soul doth magnify the Lord). Date: 12 June 1847.

Benedictus [i.e., *Nunc dimittis*] (Lord now lettest thou thy people). Date: 13 June 1847. Edn: Günter Graulich (Stuttgart: Carus, 1976).

2.   Unpublished And Posthumously Published Other Accompanied Sacred Works

Gloria in E-flat Major (2SATB, ch, orch). Date: [ca. March 1822]. Edn: Hatteberg (no. 617).

Magnificat in D Major (SATB, ch, orch). Date; 19 March–31 May 1822. Edn: Pietro Zappalà (Stuttgart: Carus, 1997).

Jesu, meine Zuversicht (motet) (2SATB, ch, pf). Date: 9 June 1824. Edn: Günther Graulich (Stuttgart: Carus, 1991).

Salve regina (S, str). Date: 9 April [?1824]). Edn: Rudolf Werner (no. 905); Günter Graulich (Stuttgart: Carus, 1980).

Kyrie in D Minor (ch, orch). Date: 6 May 1825. Edn: Ralph Leavis (Oxford: Oxford University Press, 1964) (PS); R. Larry Todd (Stuttgart: Carus, 1986).

Te Deum in D Major (2S 2A 2T 2B, dbl ch, bc). Date: 5 December 1826. Edn: L vi/1 (1966; rev. edn. 1988); Werner Burkhardt (Stuttgart: Carus-Verlag, 1976).

Salvum fac populum tuum (soloists, ch, orch). Date: 18 July [?1827 or 1828]. Edn: Unpublished.

Tu es Petrus, Op. posth. 111 (ch, orch). Date: 14 November 1827–18 November 1829. Edn: Bonn: Simrock, and London: Novello, Ewer, & Co., [1868] (PS); R xiv; Brian W. Pritchard (Hilversum: Harmonia, 1976); John Michael Cooper (Stuttgart: Carus, 1996).

Was mein Gott will (ch). Date: 29 April 1827. Edn: Unpublished.

Ave maris stella (S, orch). Date: 5 July 1828. Edn: Hans Ryschawy (Stuttgart: Carus, 1993).

Hora est (bar, 16 vv, org). Date: 14 November 1828–6 December 1828. Edn: M. Hützel (Stuttgart: Carus, 1981).

O beata et benedicta [Zum Feste der Dreieinigkeit] (motet) (2S, A, org). Date: 30 December 1830. Edn: Paul Horn (Stuttgart: Carus, 1978).

Responsorium and Hymnus [Vespergesang], Op. 121 (T, male ch, vcl, org). Date: 5 February 1833. Edn: Leipzig: Leuckart, [1873]; R xiv; Günter Graulich (Stuttgart: Carus, 1979).

[Pieces for *St. Paul* **(Op. 36)]** (solo vv, ch, orch).

No. 2 Chorale, "Ach bleib mit deiner Gnade" (4 vv, orch). Date: [ca. 1834–35]. Edn: Unpublished.

No. 3 Recit., "Die Menge der Gläubigen" (S, str). Date: [ca. 1834–35]. Edn: Unpublished.

No. 13 Chorus, "Herr Gott, dess' die Rache ist, erscheine" (B, male vv, orch). Date: [ca. 1834–35]. Edn: Unpublished.

Lobt ihn mit Pfeifen" (SATB solos, ch, orch). Date; [ca. 1834–35]. Edn: Unpublished.

Recitative and Women's Chorus, "Danket dem Gott/Danket dem Herrn, dem freundlichen Gott" (T, female vv, orch). Date: [ca. 1834–35]. Edn: Unpublished.

No. 32 Chorus: "Danket den Göttern" (female vv, orch). Date: [ca. 1834–35]. Edn: Unpublished.

Duet, "Gelobet sey Gott" (T B, orch). Date: [ca. 1834–35]. Edn: Unpublished.

Chorale, "O treuer Heiland Jesu Christ" (ch, orch colla parte). Date: [ca. 1834–35]. Edn: Unpublished.

Recit. "Paulus sandte hin" (STB, orch). Date: [ca. 1834–35]. Edn: Unpublished.

No. 28 Recit. and chorale, "Mit unser Macht ist nichts getan" (B, ch, orch) (inc.). Date: [ca. 1834–35]. Edn: Unpublished.

No. 16 Arioso, "Doch der Herr, er leitet die Irrenden recht," Op. posth. 112, no. 1 (S, pf). Date: [ca. 1835]. Edn: as *Zwei geistliche Lieder,* no. 1 (Bonn: Simrock, [1868]); R xiv; Günter Graulich (Stuttgart: Carus, 1978).

Aria, "Der du die Menschen lässest sterben," Op. posth. 112, no. 2 (S, pf). Edn: as *Zwei geistliche Lieder,* no. 2 (Bonn: Simrock, [1868]); R xiv; Günter Graulich (Stuttgart: Carus, 1978).

No. 42 Chorale, "Erhebe dich, o meine Seel." Date: [ca. 1835–36]. Edn: Unpublished.

No. 43 Chorus, "Des Herrn Will gescheh." date: [ca. 1835–36]. Edn: Unpublished.

Remarks: The relationship of these numbers to the final version of the oratorio, as well as a thorough exploration of them in intrinsically musical terms, remains to be investigated. With the exception of the arioso "Doch der Herr" and the aria "Der du die Menschen lässest sterben," which were published by Simrock in 1868, the numbers remain unpublished. The aria "Ich habe den Heiden," later replaced by the duet "Denn also hat uns der Herr geboten," is extant only in fragmentary form (the last page of what was evidently an autograph fair copy is given on page ten of D-B MN 19); the other numbers are transmitted in complete or virtually complete form in D-B MN 28. A performance of the latter group was given in Chemnitz in October 1995, but they remain unpublished.

Herr Gott, dich loben wir ("Lied zur Feier des tausendjährigen Bestehens von Deutschland") (solo vv, dbl ch, orch, org). Date: 16 January 1843. Edn: R. Larry Todd (Stuttgart: Carus, 1997).

[Three chorale harmonizations] (ch, ww, br). Date: December 1843.

1. Allein Gott in der Höh'. Edn: Günter Graulich (Stuttgart: Carus, 1985).

2. Vom Himmel hoch da komm ich her. Edn: Unpublished.

3. Wachet auf. Edn: Unpublished.

Lauda Sion, Op. posth. 73 (solo vv, ch, orch). Date: 10 February 1846. Edn: London: Ewer, [1848] (PS; words in English and Latin), and Mainz: Schott, [1849] (PS and FS; two printings: one with words in Latin and German, the other with words in Latin, German, and English); R xiv; R. Larry Todd (Stuttgart: Carus, 1996).

Er wird öffnen die Augen der Blinden (ch, orch). Date: [1846]. Edn: Unpublished.

Remarks: Intended for Elijah.

E. Other Unaccompanied Sacred Choral Works (All Unpublished or Posthumously Published)

In secula seculorum amen (vocal fugue) (4 vv). Date: [?1821]. Edn: Unpublished.

Ich will den Herrn nach seiner Gerechtigkeit preisen (motet) (4 vv). Date: [1821]. Edn: Unpublished.

Tag für Tag sei Gott gepriesen (motet) (5 vv). Date: [1821]. Edn: Unpublished.

Jube dom'ne (SATB, dbl ch). Date: 23–25 October–4 November 1822.

Edn: Günter Graulich (Stuttgart: Carus, 1980); Ralf Wehner (Leipzig: Deutscher Verlag für Musik, 1993).

Kyrie in C Minor (SAATB, dbl ch). Date; 12 November 1823. Edn: Günther Graulich (Stuttgart: Carus-Verlag, 1980–based on MS in D-F); Ralf Wehner (Leipzig: Deutscher Verlag für Musik, 1993).

[Two Sacred Pieces] (ch).

   1. *[Wie groß ist des Allmächt'gen Güte].* Date: [July 1823]. Edn: Unpublished.

      Remarks: No text; see also unpublished and posthumously published organ works, above.

   2. *Allein Gott in der Höh' sey Ehr.* Date: 10 September 1824 (two versions). Edn: Unpublished.

Two sacred choruses, Op. posth. 115 (male ch). Date: [ca. 1833–34]. Edn: Leipzig: Rieter-Biedermann, [1868] (PS), [1869] (score); R xiv; Günter Graulich (Stuttgart: Carus, 1980).

   1. *Beati mortui*

   2. *Pueriti autem.*

Und ob du mich züchtigest (canon, 5 vv). Date: 24 December 1835. Edn: Unpublished.

Pater peccavi, **Canone a 3** (3 vv). Date: 7 August 1841. Edn: Unpublished.

Venez et chantez ("Cantique pour l'Eglise wallone de Francfort") (4 vv). Date: [1846]. Edn: Barbara Mohn (Stuttgart: Carus, 1996).

Die deutsche Liturgie (8vv). Date: 28 October 1846. Edn. (nos. 1–3 only): *Musica sacra* 7 (Berlin: Bote & Bock, 1855); R xiv; Judith Silber Ballan (Stuttgart: Carus, 1997).

   Kyrie. Edn: Günter Graulich (Stuttgart: Carus, 1975).

   Heilig. Edn: Günter Graulich (Stuttgart: Carus, 1975).

   Ehre sei Gott in der Höhe. Edn: Günter Graulich (Stuttgart, 1975).

   [Unpublished:]

   Responses

   Amens

   Ehre sei dem Vater (dbl ch). Date: 17 January 1844–5 March 1845.

Six Anthems, Op. posth. 79 [Sechs Sprüche] (dbl ch). Edn: Leipzig: Breitkopf & Härtel, [1849 (score and choral parts)], and London:

Ewer, [1849 (score with piano reduction; words in English)]; R xiv/C.

Rejoice, o ye people [Frohlocket ihr Völker] ("Weihnachten"). Date: 15 December 1843.

Thou, Lord, our refuge hast been [Herr Gott du bist unsre Zuflucht] ("Am Neujahrstage"). Date: 25 December 1843.

Above all praises [Erhaben o Herr über alles Lob] ("Am Himmelfahrtstage"). Date: 9 October 1846.

Lord, on our offences [Herr gedenke nicht unsrer Uebelthaten] ("In der Passionszeit"). Date: 14 February 1844.

Let our hearts be joyful [Lasset uns frohlocken] ("Im Advent"). Date: 5 October 1846.

For our offenses [Um unsrer Sünden willen] ("Am Charfreitag"). Date: 18 February 1844.

"Gott fürchten ist die Weisheit" (canon for 4 vv). Date: 24 January 1847. Edn: Unpublished.

III. ARRANGEMENTS, TRANSCRIPTIONS, AND EDITIONS OF OTHER COMPOSERS' WORKS

Bayerischer Walzer aus Bamberg (pf). Date: [ca. 1830]. Edn: Unpublished.

Sechs Schottische National-Lieder, gesungen von Mad. Alfred Shaw in den Concerten zu Leipzig (S, pf). Date: [ca. 1839]. Edn: Leipzig: Kistner, 1839, repr. with commentary by Rudolf Elvers, Leipzig: Deutscher Verlag für Musik, 1977.

J. S. BACH:

Partita No. 3 in E Major for Unaccompanied Violin, BWV 1006, Preludio. Date: [ca. 1841]. Edn: Unpublished.

Partita No. 2 in D Minor for Unaccompanied Violin, BWV 1004, Chaconne. Date: [ca. 1840–47]. Edn: London: Ewer, 1847 (vn, pf).

Orchestral Suite No. 3 in D Major, BWV 1068 (orch). Date: [ca. 1838]. Edn: Leipzig: B. Senff, and London: Ewer, [1866?] (edition of BWV 1068 by Ferdinand David, "die Clarinetten und die drei Trompeten arrangirt von Felix Mendelssohn Bartholdy").

Gottes Zeit ist die allerbeste Zeit, BWV 106. Date: [ca. 1833–34?]. Edn:

Unpublished.

St. Matthew Passion [Matthäuspassion], BWV 244. Date: [1829] Edn: Unpublished.

LUDWIG VAN BEETHOVEN:

Piano Sonata in A-flat, Op. 26, third movement ("Marcia funebre") (arr. orch). Date: Unknown. Edn: Unpublished.

LUIGI CHERUBINI:

Overture to *Les deux journées [Der Wasserträger]* (orch). Date: 9 January 1837. Edn: Unpublished.

DOMENICO CIMAROSA:

Terzetto ("Le faccio un inchino") from *Il matrimonio segreto* (orch). Date: [ca. 1846]. Edn: Unpublished.

Remarks: Orchestrated for the Leipzig Gewandhaus Orchestra; performed in second "Historisches Konzert" of 1846–47 season (see Dörffel [no. 116]).

GEORGE FRIDERIC HANDEL:

Dettingen Te Deum. Date: 1820s. Edn: Unpublished.

Messiah (organ part). Date: early 1840s. Edn: Unpublished.

Israel in Egypt. Date: September 1833–7 Nov. 1836.

Solomon (organ part). Date: Unknown. Edn: Unpublished.

IGNAZ MOSCHELES:

Septet in D major, Op. 88 (vn, va, cl/vn, hn/va, vc, db, pf). Date: August 1833.

WOLFGANG AMADEUS MOZART:

Concerto in E-flat Major for Two Pianos, K. 265, cadenza. Date: 1 June 1832. Edn: Unpublished.

Symphony No. 41 in C Major, K. 551 ("Jupiter"), first movement (pf). Date: [ca. 1821]. Edn: Unpublished

Name Index

Compositions Index

In the interest of providing a more useful tool to the reader, the index of compositions includes only those works mentioned or discussed in the body of the text. Mention of these and other works not indicated in the text proper can also be found in the list of editions, publications, and families (see Appendix B). Numbers in italics refer to page numbers refer to entries within this book.

Subject Index

NB: Numbers in italics refer to page numbers; all other numbers refer to entries within this book.

COMPOSER RESOURCE MANUALS

GUY A. MARCO, *General Editor*

1. Heinrich Schütz (1981)
   by Allen B. Skei

2. Josquin Des Prez (1985)
   by Sydney Robinson Charles

3. Sergei Vasil'evich Rachmaninoff
   (1985)
   by Robert Palmieri

4. Manuel de Falla (1986)
   by Gilbert Chase and
   Andrew Budwig

5. Adolphe Adam and Léo Delibes
   (1987)
   by William E. Studwell

6. Carl Nielsen (1987)
   by Mina F. Miller

7. William Byrd (1987)
   by Richard Turbet

8. Christoph Willibald Gluck (1987)
   by Patricia Howard

9. Girolamo Frescobaldi (1988)
   by Frederick Hammond

10. Stephen Collins Foster (1988)
    by Calvin Elliker

11. Antonio Vivaldi (1988)
    by Michael Talbot

13. Johannes Ockeghem and Jacob
    Obrecht (1988)
    by Martin Picker

14. Ernest Bloch (1988)
    by David Z. Kushner

15. Hugo Wolf (1988)
    by David Ossenkop

16. Wolfgang Amadeus Mozart (1989)
    by Baird Hastings

17. Nikolai Andreevich Rimsky-
    Korsakov (1989)
    by Gerald R. Seaman

18. Henry Purcell (1989)
    by Franklin B. Zimmerman

19. G. F. Handel (1988)
    by Mary Ann Parker-Hale

20. Jean-Philippe Rameau (1989)
    by Donald Foster

21. Ralph Vaughan Williams (1990)
    by Neil Butterworth

22. Hector Berlioz (1989)
    by Jeffrey A. Langford and Jane
    Denker Graves

23. Claudio Monteverdi (1989)
    by K. Gary Adams and Dyke Kiel